CAREER-VOCATIONAL EDUCATION FOR HANDICAPPED YOUTH

Sidney R. Miller
Patrick J. Schloss

Southern Illinois University
Carbondale, Illinois

AN ASPEN PUBLICATION®
Aspen Systems Corporation
Rockville, Maryland
London
1982

118178

Library of Congress Cataloging in Publication Data

Miller, Sidney R.
Career-vocational education for handicapped youth.

Includes bibliographies and index.
1. Handicapped children—Vocational education.
2. Career education.   I. Schloss, Patrick J.   II. Title.

LC4019.7.M54   371.9   82-1772
ISBN: 0-89443-685-6   AACR2

Library of Congress Catalog Card Number: 82-1772
ISBN: 0-89443-685-6

Printed in the United States of America

1 2 3 4 5

To Emerson and Lois Janssen, who have provided models for other parents concerned for their adolescents' vocational development, and to Dr. Marianne Frostig, whose tenacity, creativity, and commitment have advanced the quality of services to the handicapped.

In Memoriam

To R. Curtis Whitesel, Editorial Director of the Rehabilitation and Special Education Divisions of Aspen Systems. His insistence on quality, content, and style greatly contributed to the authors' efforts. Curt's influence on this work and the work of others is a fitting memorial to his personal and professional integrity.

Table of Contents

Foreword

During the past few summers, I have directed university studies for vocational and career education, special education, and general education personnel who had accepted responsibility for secondary level special needs students. Although most were experienced teachers, none had experience or special training in serving the mildly handicapped adolescent. My goals with these educators were those of (1) informing them about the social, psychological, educational, and career-vocational characteristics of adolescents with special needs; and (2) providing them with skills in developing, implementing, and evaluating secondary level career and vocational education programs.

I have been quite frustrated in these teacher-training endeavors by the relative absence of books and related materials that adequately address the multiple and complex problems of providing an appropriate career-related education for mildly handicapped adolescents in the school setting. Although a number of professional books have appeared on the market within the last five years, each has major deficiencies. Most approach the topic either as special or as vocational educators and fail to provide an adequate integration of the concepts and practices of these two professional areas. While most available texts do devote major attention to programs, such practical issues as integrating academic instruction and behavior management are neglected and treated superficially. Finally, although psychological and social needs of the handicapped adolescent are discussed, these characteristics seldom are clearly linked to the instructional programs and materials described.

With this general discontent over available teacher education and resource materials with a career education orientation, I was elated when I reviewed the book manuscript by Professors Miller and Schloss. The book not only avoided the deficiencies that I had found in available texts; it also provided a number of other positive features. It addressed issues of human development, including motivation, values development, and adolescent sexuality and translated these into meaningful program implications and practices. It described a wealth of practical classroom instructional/intervention strategies that were based on concepts and data from the current professional and research literature. Of special significance is the authors' representation of concepts, attitudes, and practices appropriate to serving the mildly handicapped adolescent rather than, as I detected in other available books, to serving elementary handicapped or severely handicapped adult populations.

I was also impressed by the practical discussion of the critical interrelationships among the handicapped adolescent, the school, outside support agencies, and the employer. The authors emphatically recognize that if a useful career-oriented educational program is to be successful for the handicapped adolescent, the program must extend beyond the classroom, not only in concept, but in practice.

To further emphasize this commitment to translating concepts into practice, Miller and Schloss describe in useful detail exemplary programs for secondary-aged handicapped youth. In fact, this feature of concept-to-practice can be observed throughout the text and reflects the wealth of classroom teaching experiences of both authors. This practical orientation should be appealing to both inservice and preservice educators.

In sum, I look forward to next summer. I now have a text that, not only will make my teaching much easier, but also will provide the students with conceptually sound, empirically based, and practically oriented information.

William I. Gardner, Ph.D.
Professor
Department of Studies in
Behavioral Disabilities
University of Wisconsin

Acknowledgments

A special note of appreciation is expressed to Professor David A. Sabatino and Professor William I. Gardner for contributing to this volume and shaping many of the views it contains. Additionally, we wish to thank our wives, Dr. Pamela Miller and Mrs. Cindy Schloss who, beyond the traditional moral support, lent their professional writing and editing skills. Mrs. Barbara Davis deserves special appreciation for putting up with our poor handwriting and numerous editorial changes as she prepared this manuscript. The teaching staff at McKinley School for Behavior Disordered Students was of special help in assisting the authors to develop the descriptors for the classification system (detailed in Chapter 3). Additionally, thanks also go to our graduate students, Dr. Cecilia Jones, Ms. Donna Phillips, Mr. John Sachs, Mr. Edward Wiggins, and Mrs. Denise Sedlak, for their assistance in reviewing the manuscript and collecting references. Finally, the authors would like to thank Johann Gutenberg for making the printing of books possible.

Prologue

David A. Sabatino, Ph.D.
Southern Illinois University

GENESIS OF A DESIRE

The Prologue fits between the Foreword to the text, an opinionated abstract, and Chapter One. It is therefore not a synopsis, nor is it a part of the textual content. It is a set of preparatory statements that should entice the reader to indeed read the pages to follow. Since the authors are my very good friends and colleagues, if not my most avid critics, I shall attempt to slay two mockingbirds with the same stone—you, as the reader, and they, as the writers, both of whom have committed or are about to commit unreasonable acts in the name of education.

They, the writers, have, in the pages to follow, asked you to learn new skills for the sake of applying them with youths. Those skills should greatly aid you in managing the academic, vocational, social, and personal development of youths in this nation's secondary schools.

But, then, you are motivated to learn these skills, and probably just as motivated to apply them. That speaks well for you as a dedicated professional, anxious to see improvements in the lives of the youths you will soon serve—and, I hasten to add, most definitely influence.

Yes, the text you read is a worthy investment of your time and will increase your pool of professional talents. The question of your professional competency is, however, not the issue. The real issue may be one of the opportunity to practice these skills in a reasonable manner in the organization where you are employed. Certainly, there is nothing new written here. The principles, program and service applications, and intervention delivery strategies are tried and tested. What is here is a very good organization of what could be accomplished, if indeed it can be accomplished.

The question worthy of our attention is directed to the policies that permit, if not promote, secondary school programming. The intent of this introduction, then, is to examine the secondary schools as an organization and to review a few of the selected surface-level reasons for the academic and social failure of today's youths. The term "surface-level" refers to the obvious, known symptoms that result in at least four tragic student responses to noxious academic and social pressures. They are

1. truancy
2. drop-out/stop-out
3. disruptive, norm-violating behaviors
4. delinquency

The intent of the authors goes beyond all the obvious professional skill development and hopefully will create within you a desire to see policies written that will alter current practices in the secondary schools. That desire must be strong, for you will wage an uphill battle against tradition, self-preservation, a maintenance attitude that seeks the status quo, and a philosophy that what is taught is more important than how it is learned.

There is a new sound emanating from the pages of this text—the soft whisper of recognition. There is an acknowledgment that a group of secondary students is currently in trouble and historically have not been well received by the schools. There is a view that some of these students may be mildly handicapped. There is a note of urgency that the secondary schools may be the last major front upon which education or reeducation can occur before patterns of life become fixed. There is the disappointment that all is not right and that chronic disabilities associated with handicapping conditions are not "cured" in the elementary schools—that, indeed, the discrepancy between actual and expected grade level achievement grows each year that a mildly handicapped student with an academic underachievement deficit attends school. There is the reality that placing a youth into a low (tract) section of a regular class, or into attendance in a specialized program, promotes social rejection—that social rule learning and the capability to display a range of appropriate social behaviors have been stunted by inadvertent reinforcement with labels of "bad" and a full array of socially disapproving terminologies and educational techniques.

Five years ago, a text addressing the academic, career, and behavioral management of adolescent youths would not have been salable. It would have been without a user audience. Today, the interest in secondary handicapped youths has expanded greatly. That audience (you as a member) can become a cohort of concerned educators, offering the professional leadership in policy making. The social-political organization known as the schools must seek alternatives that are sensitive to secondary mildly handicapped youths who are failing academically and socially. In so doing, we will no longer sound as the mockingbird but rather have a distinctive note of direction for those to whom we are advocates.

A mature profession does not simply respond to the needs of society but claims a role in determining what society should need and how social institutions as well as individual professional careers can be shaped to the services of an emerging social order . . . the responsible professional person becomes the architect of social change. (Hobbs, 1965, p. 16)

Let's examine a few selected facts that may have considerable bearing on the social and organizational pressures found in the secondary schools.

View Number 1

More elementary students receive services. It is the year of our Lord, 1981. According to 1979-80 data from the National Center for Educational Statistics (NCES) nearly 98 percent of all *known* handicapped elementary school-aged children receive specialized services, whereas, only 92 percent of all *known* secondary school-aged children receive services.

Why Does That Difference Exist?

First, we must be careful to acknowledge that the key word in View Number 1 is "known" number of handicapped. The transition of mildly handicapped children from the early elementary to secondary schools often lacks consistency in planning, policy, and philosophy, generating a confusing service motive.

The word "current" will be used to denote what has occurred since PL 94-142 became law in November 1975. It is agreed that signing into law The Education for All Handicapped Children Act was a milestone in special education. However, unlike the position taken by the Council of Exceptional Children, the passage of PL 94-142 into law was not the end to a quiet revolution, but the continuation of an evolution in the social conscience of the American people that, at anytime, could backfire or be interrupted.

A new tip to an old iceberg is represented in the very language of PL 94-142. It is apparent that The Education for All Handicapped Children Act does not say—handicapped children and youths. Historically, the focal point of specialized educational services has been the elementary school-aged child, that is, before 1975 and PL 94-142. The law specifies that all unserved and underserved populations of handicapped be provided an appropriate education. Thus, the law focuses on the sharp contrast between the current service delivery levels in the secondary schools as opposed to those provided before 1975. In 1973-74, NCES reported that 95 percent of the students at the elementary level were receiving special education services, while only 58 percent of the handicapped in the secondary schools were being served. In fact, the service level has jumped from nearly 60 percent to greater than 90 percent of the known handicapped in six short years.

There is growing evidence to suggest that as early as the beginning of the middle-school experience, mildly handicapped children encounter attitudes prejudicial to their school attendance (Lilly, S., 1970). There seems to be an attitude that "cute little handicapped children who can be controlled" should be provided an appropriate educational opportunity, but it appears that a federal mandate is required to obtain service for secondary youth. Physically larger, more overtly aggressive, abusive, norm-violating adolescents, who are chronically disruptive and less easily controlled, intimidate many secondary educators. The result has been a serious lessening of educational programs for handicapped adolescents, impairing the very possibility if not the will to provide appropriate educational services (Keogh & Levitt, 1976).

View Number 2

Educators differ concerning service provision. Some secondary educators maintain that the responsibility for educating troublesome adolescents should be left with the juvenile institutions, courts, drug centers, private schools, or other private and public agencies (Morgan, 1979). Once the student leaves the protective walls of the self-contained elementary classroom and encounters the emphasis on departmentalized academics on the secondary level, the social and personal development of the youth is no longer viewed as the responsibility of the school (Krathwohl, 1965). Specifically, some middle- and secondary-school educators believe that special education for handicapped students is unwarranted, because handicapping conditions are often associated with depressed parental standing in the community and a child-family attitude that no one cares (Iano, Ayers, Heller, McGettigan, & Walker, 1974). Another prevailing attitude of secondary school educators is one of self-determination that is translated as the capability to learn without intervention (Shotel, Iano, & McGettigan, 1972) and that short-term remediation is acceptable, but that long-term special education, in the form of flexible curricula and intensive teaching approaches, should not be a part of the regular curriculum flow (Rucker & Vincenzo, 1970).

Among the school problems that permeate the literature are truancy, suspension, dropping out, and disruptive, alienated, violent, and vandalistic behaviors. It is well documented that the traditional school programs have failed to meet the educational needs of youths in transitional settings. Glasser (1978) cautions, however, that "blaming school problems on bad homes or bad communities is a sad rationalization that too many educators embrace" (p. 71). Special education, correctional education, and alternative education programs assume a complementary role with mental health and social services in combining socialization experiences, direct education, and opportunities to identify and pursue occupational and vocational objectives. But, alas, to what extent does interagency cooperation exist? Are agencies willing to assume a coordinated primary/secondary treatment role? Denial of the problem is not a treatment form, nor is it necessarily a good thing that PL 94-142 had to be levied to force all of us to respond to the handicapped. The key to unlocking the door seemingly involves three factors: (1) *teacher-principal attitude,* or the very atmosphere of acceptance represented by the building; (2) *level of information* about educational interventions, or what constitutes a reasonable set of instructional objectives given a handicap; and (3) increased interagency relationships or the communication between child study team members' community and those agencies that serve youths and families. Let the 1980s begin an ideological renaissance in the secondary schools with an *attitude* that willingly includes the education of all handicapped youths as potentially meaningful and contributing members of society.

View Number 3

There is a perceived difference between special and the other educations. One critical difference between regular or vocational education and special education is the manner by which educators define a curriculum. Regular and vocational educational curricula are defined by the subject matter being taught, e.g., mathematics, reading, science, building trades, or metals. Special education is defined, not as a curriculum, but as either a place or population, e.g., self-contained classes for the mentally retarded, Braille for the visually handicapped, auditory training for the aurally handicapped, and resource rooms for the learning-disabled. There has been a fear that a specialized service approach, which does not have an identifiable curriculum, will be dependent upon the adaptability of other curricula. Therefore, the responsibility for curricula adaptability will fall to the regular educator. That is precisely what has been proposed in PL 94-142.

Consequently, the responsibility for the mildly handicapped student falls into a void. Regular or vocational educators insist that handicapped students are the responsibility of special educators. Special educators insist that the responsibility is with regular and/or vocational education and that they should work in a supportive capacity. What results is an attitude of rejection by all educators towards special education students, influencing negatively the ensuing relationship or level of teacher-pupil interaction. Mainstreaming in the secondary schools has become an excuse to do little, when, as a concept, it is most appropriately viewed as a mutual (shared) responsibility for mildly handicapped youth.

Equally true, however, special educators have carried the popularity of mainstreaming as a requirement for all handicapped children and youths too far. It is simply an armchair philosophy (Lilly, M.S., 1977) advanced by academic special educators that suggests that a total dependence on self-contained special classes is unnecessary or unwarranted. A range of alternative programs and schools is needed. Many secondary, mildly handicapped students with severe academic achievement deficits need a full-day, self-contained special class, in many cases, for their entire educational career. The idea that a special education curriculum is placement (classroom environment sensitive), and that certain instruction is better achieved in some settings than others, is highly appropriate; in fact, it is effective education. Sapon-Shevin (1978) has taken just such a stance noting that mainstreaming can be viewed as a technical problem. She advances the argument that a technical response is within our current capabilities to deliver, provided that we do not become saturated by the controversial dichotomy of what is "regular" and what is "special" education. The result of this dichotomy is an educational program that causes further isolation and results in a superficial integration of the handicapped into educational programs as a merely symbolic gesture of the times.

In reality, special and regular education need, in combination with vocational education, every conceivable type of academic environment. Attitudinally, there cannot exist two or three different educational programs. A special education that advocates for the handicapped and a regular education that becomes an adversary simply defeat the hoped-for results of an integrated curriculum for the handicapped. Role relationships as practiced must change; an era of opening a multitude of career options for secondary school and handicapped students should begin.

View Number 4

Most special education programs in the secondary schools are not differentiated in type from their elementary counterparts. *Functionality* is critical to students in the secondary schools. What is necessary are functional curricula that address student concerns that are generally related to their "careers." To that end, career education, or the preparation of the person for all aspects of life, is important. How many mildly handicapped students will experience a course in consumer education? How many will have the opportunity to retrieve materials from a career information center, on their reading level, or to receive prevocational planning, or for that matter, how many can obtain admission to vocational classes? What is the percentage of handicapped youths who will be able to enter a work study experience as part of their pregraduation experiences? There are still high schools that fail to provide any program option to the traditional special regular program open for handicapped students.

There is a critical absence of commercially usable career information materials available to teachers. At best, a few high interest, low-reading-level materials exist. In even shorter supply are packages of activities for any objectives a teacher may want to use that integrate academic, vocational, social, and personal development-enabling steps.

In particular, high school teachers need materials that attempt to delineate a unique or unusual learning style and that can be used to accommodate:

1. a preferred perceptual mode for learning—visual/auditory
2. a preferred use of distinctive feature learning in contrast to perceptual memory learning
3. a communication deficit in the reception or expression of motor speech, or in the facility and ease of using a primary or secondary language symbol system
4. academic achievement and motivational deficits

Most secondary learning and behaviorally disordered youth are earmarked by unique social and academic learning styles, wherein the student is unsuccessful in mastery of the classroom environment, adaptation to a curriculum, and the compensatory social and academic learning expected.

Many of the special educators now working in secondary schools have been, in fact, elementary special educators, or at best prepared professionally to work as elementary special educators. That is one reason most continue to use the remedial model of teaching basic skills or tutoring to supplant an academic program in which youths are failing. Coordination with vocational education, liaison, and brokerage functions among regular educators provides an environment in which the student can learn skills necessary for successful vocational entry into community living and for personal career fulfillment.

View Number 5

The secondary schools continue to emphasize an academic focus to the exclusion of social development. The nature of learning and behavioral deficits is such that high school-aged youths' comparison of self with others frequently leaves them with a sense of inferiority unless such inadequacies can be compensated or offset by success in other areas.

Simply, persons who fail to achieve something expected of self and expected of others begin to question themselves and develop a greater incidence of off-task academic behaviors, some of which are socially acceptable and some of which are unacceptable in most controlled environments. There is little question that of all handicapping conditions known, the problem of emotional disturbance, manifesting itself as emotional instability, becomes clearly evident during the early secondary school period (Clarizio & McCoy, 1976). The preparation period for adolescents characterized by exaggerated attempts at defining appropriate independent behaviors (Mussen, Conger, & Kagan, 1969) becomes apparent in the search for values (McCandless, 1970) during adolescence. The search of adolescents to define themselves in relationship to peer acceptance, while maintaining their personal identity against the requirements of society, takes place between the ages of 13 and 18.

Secondary educators who operate in the classroom without providing a framework for human interactions to be displayed, reviewed, sorted, and learned deny the student-teacher relationship. This results in one-sided manipulation (Wagner, 1972). Evaluation of the conditions or context for learning is an indispensable and necessary partner to evaluation of a child's academic growth.

This is an enormous task when one considers the proposition that a high positive relationship exists between the level of performance children exhibit and the character and type of school environment in which they function. The three factors that contribute heavily to the process of creating a wholesome environment are: (1) teacher influence (the extent of contingent use of teacher attention to produce desirable change in student behavior), (2) peer influence (the extent to which peers affect self-confidence and assurance by acceptance or anxiety and self-doubt through nonacceptance), and (3) curriculum influence (the extent that it contributes to social and educational growth). The latter suggests that the type of curriculum, instructional methods, and the teaching materials become a major component of the classroom environment and must be considered in any evaluation of the conditions and context for learning.

Wilde and Sommers (1978) agree that the focus must shift from eliminating to preventing behavior problems when teaching disruptive adolescents. Four suggestions are offered for formulating a consistent approach to a structured program: (1) furnish students with a rationale for the subject matter to be presented; (2) build a positive classroom structure by informing students of goals and objectives for them as individuals; (3) structure the classroom in such a way that students know they will, to some extent, choose their own goals; and (4) provide students some options in class discipline, allowing them input in rule formation.

View Number 6

A change in attitude must accompany all other changes. It is clearly not my intent to demean secondary school educators and their responsible roles with normally achieving (academically and socially) youth. The authors note that, since the 1960s, we have known that the problematic student in the secondary school experiences repeated trouble in society upon graduation from high school, i.e., alcoholism, repeated need for community mental health services, high divorce rate, incarceration, etc. The main criticism should be directed toward the public schools' traditional fear and therefore denial of intervention for seriously behaviorally disordered youths. One of the principle failures is that of the evolution of specialized education in the regular classroom requiring daily contact between regular and special educators. Regular or vocational classroom teachers are simply on their own in providing intervention—a nonworkable solution to a very old problem.

Although no "master plan" can be suggested for managing difficult students, there are certain developments that could provide workable interventions for emotionally disturbed adolescents. The first is to alter the traditional view of a curriculum to include social-personal domains along with academic-vocational domains. Disruptive secondary students may not be "seriously impaired" in the same sense as the smaller elementary students or those with childhood schizophrenia. Middle-school children seemingly send out an urgent plea for help by increasing their rates of inappropriate behaviors. Two of the major manifestations are tardiness and truancy. The attitude of many secondary school educators is, let someone trained or equipped to handle the problem do it. But, truancy should not be handled by attendance officers, the courts, or school social workers acting without cooperative planning with the teacher. Truancy is, in the mind of the student, only a step toward dropping out—one solution to the problem of social and academic failure.

It is all too true that any number of problems confront the educator attempting to work with troubled youths or youths in trouble. They range from limited teaching materials to disruptive pupil interaction, frequently misunderstood by the principal and colleagues as the absence of classroom control procedures. All of these problems are compounded by many family, community, and even school policy variables, far beyond the control of the educator.

Probably the most critical factor is a change in administrative attitude. Dedicated secondary school educators have historically (before PL 94-142) provided their talents, professional skills, and personal patience to the handicapped. External pressures to provide for the handicapped in the secondary schools have increased tremendously in the past few years. Internal pressures from the school (organizational pressures) have also been strongly felt by special educators, stemming from many sources. Regular educators are frequently caught between the pressures to prepare the able youth for postsecondary programs, and the now mandated law. It is simply not easy, and probably not a particularly comforting assurance to be a secondary school educator responsible for a traditionally, none too popular, mildly handicapped youth.

View Number 7

Handicapped children do not outgrow their chronic disabilities or their need for service. Some educators reason that if opportunity is provided to adjust handicapping conditions in the elementary school, then those youths who don't appear to be different physically or mentally should "outgrow" their disability, and consequently the need for service. The development of programs for mildly handicapped secondary students is viewed as a relatively low educational priority (Scranton & Downs, 1975). Such a view is widely held by secondary teachers who treat school and academic learning as a privilege, not a right. Many secondary classes are taught with an "I present it, you learn it, or else" attitude by the teacher, which is well-supported by the principal. Evidence for these generalities may be drawn from the fact that 85 percent of the referrals for service to school psychologists are from the elementary school (Hohenshil, 1975).

We are not saying that adolescents with handicaps are all sweet, kind, loving students who have been misguided by the system. Youths who have repeatedly experienced academic and social failure are frequently bitter, angry, and even aggressive towards others. They may manipulate adults, especially school officials, if they have a sense of rejection emanating from the system. This thought is offered as a consideration, a hypothesis, that may explain some portion of the frustration felt by these youths. Adolescents are aware of the complex nature of modern society. Their fears range from insecurities, experienced from past failure, to prejudicial attitudes they have felt as peers and adults. Most youths are extremely frightened by the unknown, and by the uncertainty associated with adult living.

What are the avenues open for youths academically? Can they go to college? What doors are open vocationally? Do they possess enough basic skills to enter job training? If so, what areas of work will be opened? All these questions surround the issue of school failure and the view of self that students incorporate based on these experiences.

Handicapped youths do not outgrow their disabilities. The disabilities, in fact, tend to grow more complex as the entire scope of their feelings for self becomes intensified, compounded by negative experiences from the past. A case in point is that a few years ago, it was assumed that learning-disabled children no longer had perceptual impairments after the age of 12. One of the reasons was that perceptual tests no longer seemed able to ascertain perceptual impairments. Therefore, it was felt that secondary programming was unnecessary. Nothing could be further from the truth.

View Number 8

Secondary youths, especially those with learning and behavior deficits, may need lifelong support. Balow and Bloomquist (1965) reported on a sample of 32 males studied at the University of Minnesota Psycho-Educational Clinic during the 1948 to 1953 period. Ten to fifteen years later, the men were 20 to 26 years of age. Selection of the sample was based on sex, age, clinical diagnostic classification, intelligence, and amount of retardation in reading. Balow and Bloomquist note:

> that reading trouble had hindered them in academic work and that their own efforts had been the important element in improving their reading skills. . . . Many appeared to have a negative and slightly defeatist

attitude about life in general. Only three of the thirty-two are married.
(p. 48)

They did attain average adult reading proficiency (approximately tenth-grade level), graduate from high school, reveal mild behavioral disorders, and were employed in a wide range of occupations, with a disproportionate number in semiskilled and unskilled jobs.

Carter (1964) found that students who entered high school, having obtained grade-level reading proficiency, tended to continue their education, whereas a group one or more years retarded in reading at the time of high school entry did not continue their formal education, evidenced poorer high school adjustment, and obtained significantly poorer employment as evidenced in earning power.

Preston and Yarington (1967) reported an eight-year follow-up of 50 children enrolled in the University of Pennsylvania Reading Clinic. The children ranged in age from 6 to 17 years when first seen. Forty-six of the clients had received remedial instruction; four had not. Their intelligence quotients (IQs) ranged from 53 to 126. Preston and Yarington reported that retarded readers generally take a longer time to complete their formal school experience. Obviously, the delay is caused by failures. As one would expect, the disabled readers did appear to represent a higher percentage of dropouts from high school, and their corresponding rate of unemployment was much higher.

Hardy (1968) followed 35 males into adult life some years after their remedial experience. The length of remediation was 3 to 50 months, with over one-half having received remedial help for at least 10 months or more. The reading skill of Hardy's subjects had improved from the point of referral, but 60 percent still were 20 months or more below grade level. Forty percent were retarded 20 or more months at point of referral, while 23 percent were retarded that same amount at exit point as they were when dismissed from remediation. A negative relationship existed between reading skill development, number of grades repeated, and chronological age. Hardy concluded that if the programs requiring reading were custom tailored and vocational programs offered, the severely disabled readers were able to make adequate progress.

There seems to be some evidence that if remediation and family support, including belief in the child and his or her future, are sustained, a more positive outcome is evident. At least, special and regular educators do *not* have any data suggesting that remediation is either nonessential or that the adult lives of severe reading-disabled children are predetermined losses. On the contrary, persistent remediation and planned entry into each step or stage of adult activity seem to bear positive results. The emotional lift of knowing that working with severe learning-disabled youth can be viewed as a most worthwhile investment is certainly worth the tedious, expensive, frequently heartrending short-term effects of such efforts.

View Number 9

The "basic overriding need is, of course, to close the gap that sees half of the nation's handicapped children not receiving an education appropriate to their needs" (National Advisory Committee on the Handicapped, 1976, p. 51118). Clearly, the issue is that 92 percent of the nation's *known* handicapped are receiving services. With an estimate of all handicapped set at 12 percent and a service delivery at an actual 10 percent (handicapped total for the elementary of its population), what is the actual percentage of youths served in the secondary schools? According to 1978-79 NCES data, it was 5.9 percent or roughly one-half of the total number of handicapped served in the elementary schools.

The outstanding problem remains the issue of what happens to underserved secondary students. If youths succeed in school, their chances are greater for success in society (Lambert & Bower, 1961). School attendance is a critical variable. Evidence indicates that secondary students who have records of non-attendance are properly considered as having identifiable problems. For example, Burke and Simons (1965) reported that 76 percent of nonattenders were reading below grade level, 73 percent had been retained in a grade two or more years, and only 59 percent tested within the normal IQ range. The majority experienced failure in at least one grade. While not all of these youths can be considered as learning-disabled or emotionally disturbed, the lack of secondary school interventions for those having such problems will result in about 59 percent being unsuccessful in their achievement (Barone, 1977). Data supporting Barone's conclusion were drawn from a five-year follow-up study by the U.S. Department of Labor, whose data yielded the following conclusions:

1. A total of 525,000 (21 percent) will be either fully employed or enrolled in college.
2. A total of 1 million (40 percent) will be underemployed and at the poverty level.
3. A total of 200,000 (8 percent) will be in their home community and idle much of the time.
4. A total of 650,000 (26 percent) will be unemployed and on welfare.
5. A total of 75,000 (3 percent) will be totally dependent and institutionalized. (Barone, 1977, p. 6)

View Number 10

The real issue goes beyond the quantity of service to be delivered to those yet unserved, to the quality of services and programs provided to those who do receive services. It is evident that the quality of life for most people is directly related to the positive influence of the secondary school program. The speculation that learning deficits are one of the major contributors to school-related adjustment problems grows from evidence taken from school records of troubled adolescents. Morgan (1979), in a very recent national study of the incidence of handicapped children in juvenile delinquent facilities across the United States, found that 44 percent of the incarcerated adolescents sampled evidenced long histories of pronounced academic underachievement.

Burke and Simons (1965) examined the various reasons for truancy. They found that 76 percent of the youths who were chronically truant were reading far below grade level, 59 percent had normal IQs, and the most frequent reason given for being truant was a lack of interest in school (47 percent). However, a review of school records indicated that 92 percent had histories of chronic disruptive behavior in school. The remaining profile was characterized by inadequate school adjustment and repeated grade failure. Seventy-three percent had failed at least two different times. From the 90 percent of the truant group who went on to drop out of school altogether, 95 percent had long court histories.

Douglas (1969), in a conclusive study on dropouts, characterized them as follows:

1. an academic record of poor school achievement (rarely do they exceed fourth-grade reading skill)
2. family background of low economic and definitive cultural status that differentiates them (currently the highest percentage of dropouts are youths with Hispanic cultural-linguistic characteristics)
3. poor school achievement despite continued "social" promotion
4. record of absenteeism
5. lack of membership in organized school activities
6. poor verbal abilities in relationship to nonverbal abilities
7. records of chronic disruptive behavior in school
8. peer group identified from among a similar group
9. attitude toward school ranging from distrust to disdain

In response to the latter point, as stated earlier, it must be remembered that many youths are stopped from going to secondary school. In fact, some researchers believe that as many students are stopped as voluntarily drop out of school (Empey & Erickson, 1966). French (1969) found that in a group with measured IQs in excess of 110, 20 percent disliked school and 18 percent were asked to leave. That phenomenon of stopping youth, in one way or another, from attending secondary school was reported in a 1915 classic study on truancy by Hiatt. In 1973, Washington studied 56 high school students from the Midwest fairly intently. His data indicated that financial worries, need for jobs, low grades, and trouble at home were the most common problems.

A number of disciplines are now interested in the relationship between delinquency (formal adjudication by the courts) and learning disabilities. There is nothing very new about the assumed relationship. It was first reported as early as 1926, when Percival noted that 99 percent of those failing in first grade were locked into a failure mode the remainder of their school careers, which ultimately terminated in antischool behavior. Years later, Roman (1957) observed what she called the reading-related triad. Reading failure begets truancy, and truancy begets delinquency.

What are the causes or, better yet, what are the theoretical contributors to that multiplicity of symptoms associated with educational disabilities in adolescents? The truth is, they are numerous. They vary from youth to youth, depending upon the type and amount of intervention during earlier years; parental, school, and self-expectancies during adolescence; and the emotional support base and personal reinforcement during a crisis.

From the perspective of the student, once school success is impaired, a self-fulfilling prophecy may be placed into motion. The theme of that self-fulfilling prophecy is that academic achievement is difficult to obtain; therefore, the child focuses on attention-getting behaviors, or resorts to withdrawn behaviors. Thus, the theory of an aggressive-passive withdrawn behavioral continuum upon which youths distribute themselves seemingly has merit.

Gruhn and Krause (1968) compared 73 handicapped high school-aged students with a nonhandicapped group. They found that the handicapped students saw themselves as different, becoming extremely rigid in view of self, and reported a noticeably reduced level of aspiration. Mulligan (1969) reported on a study demonstrating that 60 percent of a group of poor, almost nonreaders yielded high frequency outputs of antisocial behaviors. Yamamoto, Lembright, and Corrigan (1966) related self-concept to social-personal adjustment with various populations of children and youths. They noted that, in general, youths with lower self-concept scores were frustrated, unhappy, and often hostile. Coppersmith (1967) determined that age was not a factor, but that from preschool to college age social acceptability related positively to emotional adjustment and negatively to anxiety. Thus, early poor school achievement sets into motion what may be hypothesized to be lowered self-concept, lowered expectancy of performance, a fear of failure based on previous failure, and aggressive or withdrawn behavior occurring in greater frequency.

Those youths experiencing academic difficulties literally give up on themselves in school, and sometimes they express their hostility caused by failure toward the school—the so-called alienated youth syndrome. Many of these youths begin expressing norm-violating behaviors through increased truancy, drop out or are stopped out by the schools, become highly aggressive, join gangs, and display violent-vandalistic behaviors. The incidence of learning-disabled youths in a population of adjudicated children runs quite high in lower socioeconomic communities.

CONCLUSION

It is the opinion, if not the motivation, of the authors of this text that a new era is dawning—one where policies that are youth centered will open the doors to promoting the resources, facilities, alternative programming, and personnel necessary for secondary youths in trouble—or is it troubled secondary youths?

This text conveys the skills necessary for you to represent that handful of talented people capable of altering the lives of secondary students. To that end, may I suggest, that, if you are interested, we should begin to develop those policies locally within states, among all agencies serving these youths—and federally. To accomplish both of those objectives—read on.

REFERENCES

Balow, B., & Bloomquist, M. Young adults ten to fifteen years after severe reading disability. *Elementary School Journal,* 1965, *66,* 44-48.

Barone, S. Career education and the handicapped. In R. D. Bhaerman (Ed.), *Career education and basic academic achievement: A descriptive analysis of the research.* Washington, D.C.: U.S. Office of Education, May 1977.

Burke, N. S., & Simons, A. Factors which precipitate dropouts and delinquency. *Federal Probation,* 1965, *29,* 28-32.

Carter, R. P. *A descriptive analysis of the adult adjustment of persons once identified as disabled readers.* Unpublished doctoral dissertation, Indiana University, 1964.

Clarizio, H. F., & McCoy, G. F. *Behavior disorders in children* (2nd ed.). New York: Thomas Y. Crowell Co., 1976.

Coppersmith, S. *The antecedents of self-esteem.* San Francisco: Freeman, 1967.

Douglas, H. R. An effective junior high school program for reducing the number of dropouts. *Contemporary Education,* 1969, *41,* 34-37.

Empey, L. T., & Erickson, M. L. Hidden delinquency and social status. *Social Force,* 1966, *44,* 546-554.

Frauenheim, J. G. Academic achievement characteristics of adult males who were diagnosed as dyslexic in childhood. *Journal of Learning Disabilities,* 1978, *11,* 476-483.

French, J. Characteristics of high ability dropouts. *NASSP Bulletin,* 1969, *53,* 67-79.

Glasser, W. Reaction to Bruce L. Dants: Parents' anxiety adds to fear. *School Counsel,* 1978, *26,* 90-91.

Gruhn, H., & Krause, S. On the social behavior of physically handicapped children and teenagers. *Probleme und Ergebnisseder Psychologic,* 1968, *23,* 73-86.

Hardy, M. I. *Clinical follow-up study of disabled readers.* Unpublished doctoral dissertation, University of Toronto, 1968.

Hobbs, N. How the Re-ed plan developed. In N. J. Long, W. C. Morse, & R. C. Newman (Eds.), *Conflict in the classroom.* Belmont, Calif.: Wadsworth Publishing Co., 1965.

Hohenshil, T. H. Call for reduction: A vocational educator views school psychological services. *Journal of School Psychology,* 1975, *13,* 58-62.

Iano, R. P., Ayers, D., Heller, H. B., McGettigan, J. F., & Walker, V. S. Sociometric status of retarded children in an integrative program. *Exceptional Children*, 1974, *40*, 267-271.

Keogh, B. K., & Levitt, M. L. Special education in the mainstream: A confrontation of limitations. *Focus on Exceptional Children*, 1976, *8*, 1-11.

Krathwohl, D. R. Stating objectives appropriately for program, for curriculum, and for instructional materials development. *Journal of Teacher Education*, 1965, *12*, 83-92.

Lambert, N. M., & Bower, E. M. *Bower's two-step process for identifying emotionally handicapped pupils*. Princeton, N.J.: Educational Testing Service, 1961.

Lilly, M. S. Merger of categories: Are we finally ready? *Journal of Learning Disabilities*, 1977, *10*, 115-121.

Lilly, S. Special education: A teapot in a tempest. *Exceptional Children*, 1970, *37*, 43-49.

McCandless, B. R. *Adolescents—Behavior and development*. Hinsdale, Ill.: The Dryden Press, 1970.

Morgan, D. I. Prevalence and types of handicapping conditions found in juvenile correctional institutions: A national survey. *Journal of Special Education*, 1979, *13*(3), 283-295.

Mulligan, W. A study of dyslexia and delinquency. *Academic Therapy Quarterly*, 1969, *4*(3), 177-187.

Mussen, P. H., Conger, J. J., & Kagan, J. *Child development and personality*. New York: Harper & Row, 1969.

National Advisory Committee on the Handicapped. Study report. Washington, D.C.: U.S. Government Printing Office, 1976.

Preston, R. C., & Yarington, D. J. Status of fifty retarded readers eight years after reading clinic diagnosis. *Journal of Reading*, 1967, *11*, 122-129.

Roman, M. *Reaching delinquents through reading*. Springfield, Ill.: Thesaurus, 1957.

Rucker, C. N., & Vincenzo, F. M. Maintaining social acceptance gains made by mentally retarded children. *Exceptional Children*, 1970, *36*, 679-680.

Sapon-Shevin, M. Another look at mainstreaming: Exceptionality, normality, and the nature of difference. *Phi Delta Kappan*, 1978, *60*, 119-121.

Scranton, T. R., & Downs, M. C. Elementary and secondary learning disabilities programs in the U.S.: A survey. *Journal of Learning Disabilities*, 1975, *8*, 394-399.

Shotel, J. R., Iano, R. P., & McGettigan, J. F. Teacher attitudes associated with the integration of handicapped children. *Exceptional Children*, 1972, *38*, 677-683.

Wagner, H. Attitudes of and toward disadvantaged students. *Adolescence*, 1972, *7*, 435-446.

Wilde, J. W., & Sommers, P. Teaching disruptive adolescents: A game worth winning. *Phi Delta Kappan*, 1978, *59*, 342-343.

Yamamoto, K., Lembright, M. L., & Corrigan, A. M. Intelligence, creative thinking, and sociometric choice among fifth grade children. *Journal of Experimental Education*, 1966, *34*(3), 83-89.

Chapter 1

Career Education

Prior to the 1950s in American education, mildly handicapped secondary-aged youths were perceived as slow in the academic classroom, yet having the intellect, sensory-motor, and social skills to achieve in such areas as carpentry, plumbing, auto-mechanics, and other occupational areas. During the first half of the twentieth century, such occupations were frequently highly prized by the community in which the youths resided and by the nation-at-large (Miller, Ewing, & Phelps, 1980). By the end of the 1950s, the nation's perceptions of the mildly handicapped and the types of occupations that were valued by society had changed.

The Russian launching of the space satellite, Sputnik, altered the nation's educational and occupational priorities in the late 1950s. The federal government saw its political survival resting on reaching the moon before the Russians and encouraged a change in focus from a general craft- and labor-oriented society to a society in which all students were directed toward further education in colleges and universities. The student with educational handicaps was often labeled mentally retarded or emotionally disturbed in an educational system that provided a strict academic focus that frequently had little to do with the student's capacity to learn.

When services were provided to handicapped youths, the training commenced at the end of their educational preparation (McCandless, 1970; Rice, 1975) rather than at the onset of adolescence. Also, the latitude of career choices given to those youths became more heavily regulated by their standing on five basic factors: (1) socioeconomic background, (2) parental attitudes, (3) school achievement, (4) peer values, and (5) intelligence (Rice, 1975; Shaw & McKay, 1972). Handicapped youths, regularly seen in conflict with community values, have tended to be rated low on three or more of these factors (Heggen & Irvine, 1967).

Beginning in the late 1960s under the U.S. Commissioner of Education, Sidney Marland, the federal government, in concert with some institutions of higher education, began to look to the concept of Career Education as a strategy for

1

diversifying the nation's education goals. The emphasis on science in public school curricula and on college training as the only path for the high school graduate was producing manpower shortages in day-to-day service areas such as small appliance repair, sales, and building maintenance. Simultaneously, the U.S. Congress was passing legislation designed to encourage state and local educational agencies to develop new instructional patterns. The state and local school districts' response was faint, and dollars appropriated to encourage new educational curriculum patterns and training programs frequently were unspent (Miller, Ewing, & Phelps, 1980).

Despite the initial coolness of state and local response, the U.S. Office of Education continued to press the concept of Career Education. The concept was intended to interface with the educational needs of the total population. The operational intent was to enable individuals to select career patterns that allowed them to pursue their interests while simultaneously integrating those interests with potential vocational goals as well as academic and recreational needs. Career Education was thus conceived as an omnipresent process that catered to the individual needs of each student.

Despite the existence of this conceptual framework, state and local school education officials continued to prepare high school graduates primarily for the halls of academia. Only as the nation moved into the 1970s, and educators and local legislators began to recognize that their communities suffered from an overabundance of teachers and engineers, and an underabundance of tool and die makers and other craft-related personnel, did the career education movement gain momentum and acceptability.

The momentum was accelerated in the area of the handicapped by the litigation and legislation that required schools to provide appropriate education for students either incapable, unprepared, or uninterested in higher education. As a result, students previously encouraged to drop out of school or who dropped out because the curriculum yielded them no benefits, found themselves with educational opportunities that more closely reflected their needs and interests (Sabatino, 1979). Further, the courts and the U.S. Congress expanded the handicapped population that must be served by special education. Prior to the passage of The Education for All Handicapped Children Act, PL 94-142, the schools provided special education services to students in the elementary schools. PL 94-142 expanded the age range to 3 to 21 years of age and mandated junior and senior high schools to develop appropriate programs for handicapped adolescents. This factor, combined with the increased financial commitment of the federal government during the late 1970s and early 1980s, produced momentum in the development of training programs for future school personnel, delivery of service programs for the handicapped population, and the collection of demographic data on the secondary-aged handicapped population.

CAREER EDUCATION PROCESS

Career Education's conceptual advantage over other delivery of service models is that it seeks to incorporate several aspects of a student's educational program, including academics, vocational training, and recreation. As a result, it enables both the educator and the student to integrate a number of program aspects in identified goals and to develop a more diversified program (Figure 1-1) that reflects the following essential educational ingredients:

Student

The student is in the center of this nuclear structure. All aspects of the student's dreams, potential, and needs are brought together to ensure an appropriate program design to accommodate the belief that individuals should be productive, harmonious, and creative members of the community.

Academic Needs

Academics are the foundation from which individuals build other aspects of their aspirations. Thus, reading, language arts, mathematics, health and society, and social studies constitute the basic core of the academic component.

Vocational Goals

Regardless of academic achievement, individuals are expected to be investigating, exploring, and experiencing occupational areas. The areas could range from physician to mechanic, and from banker to meat packer. Selection of an interest area is not intended to preclude other occupational interests as the student's needs and skill levels change.

Life Experiences

Experiences in school, the community, and other milieus are believed to influence a student's values and goals. Career Education is perceived as employing these experiences in the development of a program suited to a student's future pursuits.

Recreational Needs

This area focuses primarily on physical endeavors such as team sports, individual sports, and intellectual games, in which the sound body is an integral part of educational activities.

Figure 1-1 Career Education Program

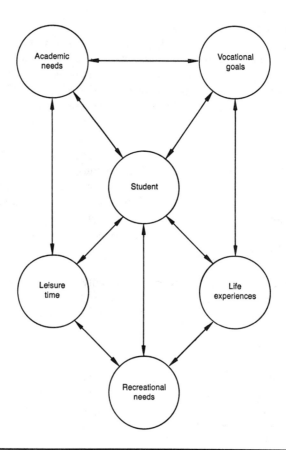

Leisure Time

A final component of the nuclear structure is the preparation of students to use their time in activities that contribute to the enjoyment of life and to good mental health and community conviviality. This area has grown in importance as the nation's labor force has experienced increased idle time. Social scientists have become aware that individuals are frequently unprepared to cope with the additional time and opportunities it provides.

Unlike other program models, the Career Education model (Figure 1-2) allows the solely academically oriented students to pursue their goals and students who are uncertain of their life-direction to explore their options.

Figure 1-2 Career Education Model

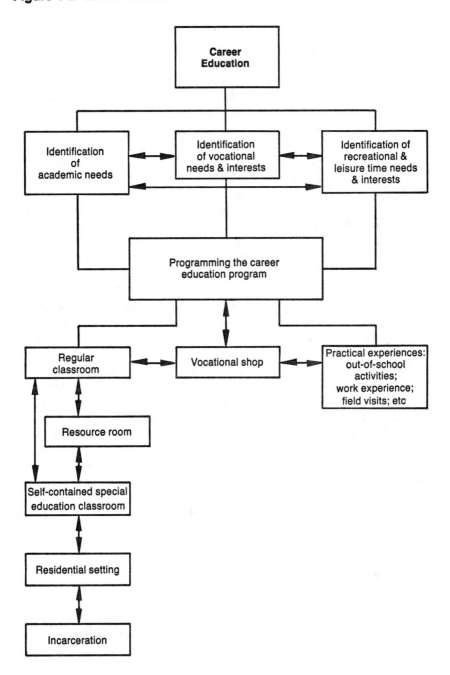

BARRIERS TO IMPLEMENTATION

As educators in the late 1960s sought to develop appropriate programs for adolescents, three distinct difficulties became obvious. The first difficulty dealt with the inadequacy of information related to program efficacy. The literature searches ended with the finding that numerous programs have been proposed but few have been formally evaluated in terms of strengths and weaknesses. Most of the literature simply reviews programs, the procedure used to implement them, and perceived outcomes. The outcomes are not supported by formal data-based evaluations.

The second difficulty is the physiological, biological, and cognitive development of the adolescent. As has been noted by numerous researchers (Ausubel, 1957; Bruner, 1966; Erikson, 1968; & Piaget, 1969), adolescents experience significant physical, biological, and cognitive changes, beginning around 12 to 13 years of age. The adolescent's problems, magnified by poor school performance difficulties, frequently result in student conflict with authority and community norms. Adolescents generally enter a period of role experimentation (Erikson, 1968) and develop the ability to think abstractly (Flavell, 1963; Piaget, 1969) without the assistance of sensory data. During this period, adolescents begin defining their role in society (Erikson, 1968; Evans & Potter, 1970; McCandless, 1970) and seek to determine the career path they want to explore and eventually follow. It is not a period in which human and management procedures can whimsically be determined.

The third difficulty is that only an estimated one-fourth to one-third of all special education programs in the United States are directed at the adolescent student, and fewer than 10 percent are specifically designed for handicapped youth in the schools (Subcommittee on Elementary, Secondary and Vocational Education, 1977). The committee observed that less than 20 percent of the youths leaving schools would be fully employed or seek additional education. Of the remaining students, 40 percent would be underemployed, and 20 percent would be unemployed. The number of programs has increased during the late 1970s and early 1980s, but the money, time, and personnel involved in serving the problem adolescent are still far less than that provided for children in the preprimary and primary grades.

COOPERATIVE ARRANGEMENTS

Handicapped youths often have trouble comprehending and coping with community and societal demands, and the success of any secondary program is dependent on seven educational components:

1. indepth preplanning of programs and facilities
2. adequate use of equipment and facilities
3. appropriate training of teachers
4. concern for practical application of the academic and vocational training
5. counseling from various state agencies
6. use of community facilities
7. use of community leaders

Despite mandates by the Congress and the Department of Education, the cooperation among and between agencies at the federal, state, and local levels has been disjointed, poorly coordinated, and reluctant. Among the organizations with whom programs should seek to establish contact and from whom they legally can seek assistance are state-wide Departments of Employment, Vocational Rehabilitation, Education, and Welfare, along with the courts. The large number of programs without outside agency assistance is perplexing considering the demonstrated need to have a coordinated and integrated program with community groups (Scurlock, West, Keith & Viaille, 1964).

Existing work experiences have been incorporated into the secondary school curriculum often with the cooperation of the state rehabilitation agency, employment service, and sheltered workshops. These work study programs have had the benefit of involving agencies in the vocational rehabilitation of handicapped students prior to graduation. The agencies have been reluctant to involve themselves in the cases and programs of other agencies, fearing such cooperation will weaken their autonomy as independent agencies with their own personnel and budget.

Communication problems, in many cases, have existed between the secondary schools and rehabilitation agencies, resulting in sporadic services. State employment services generally have not sought a working relationship with secondary special education programs and many believe it is not within their priority structure to provide jobs to handicapped youths. Generally, heads of families, members of minority groups, and women are seen as the appropriate political population to assist in identifying jobs.

POPULATION VARIABLES

Studies have shown that youths introduced to vocational training at an early age tend to accommodate to the training more readily than youths who enter the programs at a later age. James (1966) reported, however, that older youths tend to be more realistic in career outlook. It was also reported that students from higher socioeconomic backgrounds foresaw a greater number of job possibilities. Conversely, youths from lower socioeconomic neighborhoods tended to underestimate themselves and their career opportunities, and thus, limit their potential in obtaining positions that might be closely allied with their training and interests. James also noted that those who had outside experience tended to do better than those who remained in restricted environments. Gorelick (1966), in contrast, found that youths with realistic expectations were no more successful in obtaining jobs than those with unrealistic vocational expectations. Thus, data are inclusive as to when to provide training and whom to train during the school years. What is acknowledged is that the schools must provide such training to the handicapped student.

Parnicky and Kahn (1963), reporting on 437 youths, said the most accurate criterion for measuring the future success of youth was the youth's performance in the field. Deno, Henye, Krantz, and Barklind (1965) reported that out of 483 youths involved in a vocational program, those with high IQs remained in school and were the most successful in obtaining appropriate employment. Those who had trouble in retaining a position were more often nonwhite, left school early, tended to be in conflict with societal codes, had multiple handicaps, and represented the lower quartile of the socioeconomic scale.

Cegelka (1976) found fewer females in career/vocational programs and that those in such programs were trained for low-paying jobs not covered by federal wage regulations. These findings were previously cited by Gillespie and Fink (1974). They noted that females received training in housekeeping, while males received preparation in carpentry, construction, and auto repairs.

Currently, the data provided to vocational counselors, educators, and correctional officers are scant. The designing of programs with integrated curricula dealing with educational and vocational needs must turn again to theoretical postulates to generate a data base upon which future programs can be built. Without question, these programs must reflect the needs of male and female students whose socioeconomic and educational backgrounds are diverse and sometimes at variance with dominant cultural expectations.

PERSONNEL NEEDS

While the demand for improved and increased integrated programs grows, and the thirst of administrators for more appropriately trained teachers mushrooms, there has been a documented lack of direction from state governments in improving the level of preparation among educators and counselors needed to work with the handicapped individuals (Miller, Sabatino, & Larsen, 1980). Simultaneously, there is a need to upgrade the quality of programs for these youths. A study by Miller, Lotsof, and Miller (1976) of program needs indicates that the public schools are requiring more people with specialized training in behavior management, curriculum instruction, and diagnosis for secondary youths. In other studies (Miller, Sabatino, & Larsen, 1980) the majority of regular classroom teachers, vocational shop teachers, and special educators knew little about the needs of the handicapped youth, the types of programs needed, how to integrate the various discrete components of the high school curriculum, the types of instructional strategies to be used, and the procedures for ensuring the handicapped adolescent a free and appropriate education.

Since 1977, the Office of Special Education has encouraged universities and colleges to initiate career-vocational teacher-training programs. At this juncture, nearly 300 colleges and universities have initiated such training programs. Only 9 of the 50 states have differentiated certification in which secondary training is separate from elementary handicapped training. The effort to differentiate certification has been stalled in many states because of pressure by state departments not to increase the number of certificates and because of special education administrators who prefer maximum flexibility in utilizing their personnel, be it an elementary or secondary population. The need for highly qualified personnel in secondary education becomes more acute when the student is a handicapped youth with a history of academic failure, social conflict, and school failure, and whose crisis of identity, self-worth, and identifying of potential self as a contributing member of society is being questioned by adult authority, peers, and self. The content and process that the teachers of the secondary handicapped youth utilize frequently vary significantly from the content and management procedures used by the elementary school teacher. In fact, one of the common problems cited in the literature (Brolin & D'Alonzo, 1979; Phelps & Lutz, 1977) is the need to acquaint personnel with instructional options that differ significantly from the general instructional remedial model practiced in the schools.

INTEGRATED CONTENT AND PROCESS

The dichotomies between and among programs, services, personnel, and goals in career-vocational education have produced doubts among public officials over the efficacy of the concept and the educability of the chronic disruptive youth. Too frequently career-vocational programs have featured a separation of the academic from the vocational program, though operationally they are dependent and ultimately rise or fall according to the efficacy of each other. The imperative, then, is to build an integrated career-vocational education program that includes the components of academic and vocational assessment, career exploration, programming and instruction, job coaching, and program evaluation.

The belief has been perpetuated among educators that there are differences between the interest and efforts of those who teach the basic academic areas and those who teach in the vocational areas. Yet, the U.S. Congress, in passing recent vocational legislation, noted that meaningful work experience and training should be combined with formal education, enabling students to acquire knowledge skills and appropriate attitudes. Sloan (1975) broadens the concept from simply academic and vocational preparation to include basic life management, personal-social development, and career-vocational placement producing a prototype of the integrated curriculum. An analysis of any configuration of Career Education demonstrates that a student's success is dependent on not only academic and vocational competency, but also the ability to manage finances, attend to health needs, utilize leisure time, and interact successfully with coworkers and members of the general community. The task analysis of these components cannot be instructionally separated, and a student whose career goal is carpentry cannot ignore measurement, blueprint interpretation, and interaction with other workers on the job.

Herr (1972), noting the integrated nature of the instructional process and content, called for a systems approach to the treatment of handicapped youth. It is necessary, then, to look at the total program in terms of student need. The program, as expressed in Figure 1-3, should first consider the student's interests, needs, levels of performance, and motivation through a process of formal and informal testing and interviewing.

Figure 1-3 Total Program

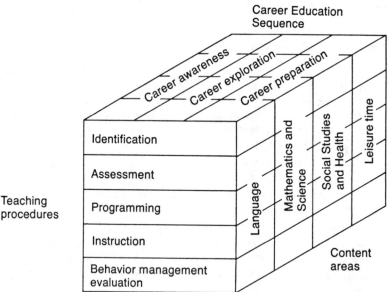

TEACHING PROCEDURES

Identification

The majority of handicapped youths have been identified prior to their entry into the secondary school environment. The identification probably occurred at the elementary-school level. However, some youths' school-related problems do not surface until adolescence. The problems could range from mild academic disabilities to more severe behavior disorders. When such students exhibit handicaps, it becomes the responsibility of the classroom or shop teacher to refer the student to school personnel to identify the specific learning impediment(s) and develop programmatic solutions.

Assessment

The formal and informal testing of handicapped youths should involve measurements of academic, career-vocational, and social behavior and competencies. The academic tests must include the measurement of reading, writing, social studies, and mathematics skills. In addition, career-vocational measures should be used. These measures often assess not only career preparation aptitude, but also self-concept and the student's level. Formal and informal tests, along with interviews for assessing the student's ability to communicate orally and interact with other individuals, should provide the career education personnel with adequate information related to the educational process.

The interpretation of test results and observational data has tended to focus on the overt, provocative performance of the youth. The resulting treatment of the student placed heavy emphasis on conduct management, with a secondary emphasis on the basic academic skills. The treatment efficacy of such models has not been sustained. This lack of payoff, along with the well-cited dubious efficacy of most purely vocational programs for the handicapped, clearly demonstrates that the overall look at youths has been inadequate. Handicapped youths, like society, cannot be viewed in component parts to the exclusion of other parts. The assessment must be based on student needs, interests, and how the test and observational data interface, and not solely on vocational and psychological information. It must encompass the total of the youth's interests, academic and career-vocational skills, social aptitude, and leisure time needs. These competencies must be assessed in a manner that provides a wide number of personnel with operational information. Too frequently the results of testing are couched in language not easily understood. The resulting data reports must communicate the youth's educational needs both clearly and completely.

Programming

Unlike testing and assessment, which take into consideration the individual's needs, interests, and goals, the programming efforts must interface the student's competencies in a variety of areas. To achieve this interface effectively, the instructors must possess, or have at their disposal, a wide variety of instructional materials and aids. The program configuration includes:

- Self-contained classroom (full time): the student spends the entire day in the classroom receiving the prescribed instruction.

- Resource room (part time): the student spends a minimal amount of time in the resource room, receiving assistance and support at a level which enables him or her to function successfully in the regular classroom.

- Peer tutoring and support: the peer provides assistance to the student in areas of skill development, socialization, and career direction, while the youth participates in an ongoing program.

- Academic/vocational preparation: the student spends one-half the time in academic areas and one-half the time in shop and industrial arts training.

- Work study: the student attends regular classes for a short period in the morning and then works during the afternoon at a monitored site for a regulated amount of time.

- Vocational study: the student receives instruction in academic areas, while also attending a vocational training center where preparation in specific career-vocational preparation is emphasized.

The above program configuration (described in detail in Chapter 10) should be carefully interfaced with the student's identified needs, interests, and competencies.

Instruction

The demand for increased and improved programs for handicapped youths has also resulted in more and improved instructional materials and procedures. While there has been an over-reliance on materials for the elementary students in the past, there is now emerging a core of instructional materials, tactics, curriculum guides, and program outlines that appear to meet the needs and interests of adolescents. It is essential that these materials be used in providing instructional assistance for the adolescents who require programs and materials that deviate from the traditional themes, formats, and performance levels. The glaring weakness of instruction has been the dichotomy between the programs and materials, and between methods and student learning. Among the types of materials and methods now surfacing are:

- programmed instructional materials for slower learning youths
- high interest, low-vocabulary reading materials
- career-oriented materials for handicapped adolescents concerned with vocational development
- reading material emphasizing retention and development of basic academic skills (e.g., vocabulary, comprehension, and retention)

This list includes just a few of the many factors that must be taken into consideration in selecting and using materials. One of the variables found by many secondary school teachers to be a reliable motivator with the handicapped youth is the use of a wide variety of instructional materials that deviate in content, format, and theme. For example, use of audiovisual equipment and guest lecturers may heighten the interest of disruptive youth. A secondary concept is that the material should interface with the student's competency level.

For example, Sabatino (1974) recommends a vocational curriculum which de-emphasizes the use of standard textbooks and emphasizes an instructional approach with preprogrammed high interest, low-vocabulary material. This material would be specifically geared to the reading and interest level of the students and would interface with the student's career-vocational goals and needs. While there has been some attempt at developing this material, the review of the literature reveals significant gaps in its availability (Sachs & Miller, 1980). When such material is not available in the educational milieu, it can often be obtained through regional media and materials centers.

Behavior Management

The management of classroom behavior as it relates to either the class or individual students is an essential component of the education process, since disruptive or self-disruptive behavior is an obvious impediment to learning.

A program of instructional approaches and materials without appropriate behavioral management tactics is ultimately doomed when it involves youths who have experienced years of school frustration. The theories of Skinner (1968), Bandura (1969), and Lazarus (1971) as well as instructional programs based on these theories (Clarizio & McCoy, 1976; Hewett, 1968; Kunzelman, 1970; Peter, 1965; Sabatino & Schloss, 1981; Smith, 1970) acknowledge the necessity of moving from the level of concrete reinforcement to more abstract social reinforcers. Too frequently educators have reinforced the completion of a task (ratio measure) and have not supported the length of time the student will work at a task (interval measure). Nor, have they measured the intensity of the student's involvement in an activity.

In working with an adolescent, baseline behavior (the point at which the student is operating in a specified area) must be pinpointed. Once this has been determined, the teacher and student can develop meaningful and realistic goals and objectives as they relate to reading, mathematics, social studies, science, and vocational development. This can be accomplished through the use of such management tools as performance contract, peer pressure, and traditional operant conditioning.

Performance contracting, a popular management tool, is the form of an agreement between a teacher and a student. In the agreement, the student acknowledges that for a specified quantity of performance he or she will receive a reward (e.g., money, tokens, food, and/or free time). If the student is unable, or not ready, to work in consultation with the teacher, the teacher alone must establish the goals and objectives. In addition, once realistic objectives are established, contingencies for completion of the specific quantity at a specified level of quality are determined.

When the teacher has reached the point of being able to work in concert with the student, the teacher must consult the student about objectives and contingencies. It is a designated purpose of performance contracting that the agreement be a joint and not a unilateral decision. Once every two to three weeks an evaluation of the goals, objectives, methods, and materials is necessary to determine whether the program is achieving the stated objectives. Often student and teacher, once the goals and objectives have been pinpointed, neglect to determine whether the original conclusions were appropriate, relevant, and effective. Evaluation and reevaluation are essential components of any program.

Evaluation

School personnel are frequently guilty of establishing programs in the fall and then waiting until spring to scrutinize their usefulness and effectiveness in teaching the student. The gap between the program initiation and evaluation is great. By the time the educator knows the effectiveness of the program, it is often too late to redirect or reorganize it to meet the student's needs. Evaluation, thus, must be part of the ongoing educational experience and should occur every two to three weeks. This continuous evaluation process can be best conducted through the use of informal teacher-made criterion reference tests, observation, and checklists of accomplishments. The student's and program's efficacy can be viewed by measuring the performance of the student against delineated objectives formulated for the evaluation period. If the student's progress is reflective of the objectives, then learning is occurring. Should there be a lag, then the educator must reassess, reprogram, and/or develop new instructional goals, objectives, materials, and strategies for a student.

CAREER EDUCATION SEQUENCE

Career Awareness

Many students are unaware of the large number of career-vocational opportunities that can be identified and pursued. Some handicapped youths have a restricted view of their career-vocational opportunities, and thus foredoom their ultimate success. Most of these same students are unfamiliar with the thousands of listings of career opportunities found in the major Sunday newspapers or in the Department of Employment listings. These students need to be informed about these opportunities through reading various types of materials published by governmental and private agencies, by discussing their career-vocational interests with a counselor, by talking with recruitment officers, and by viewing films and searching computer files, both of which are designed to inform youth of job opportunities. These same individuals also may be unable to perceive the overlapping knowledge and skills that they possess that are applicable to a wide variety of career-vocational opportunities. Similarly, these same individuals are also unable to perceive the overlapping knowledge and skills that a wide variety of career-educational opportunities require, such as radio and television repairs, computer maintenance, automobile and truck mechanics, and small aircraft repair. A well-designed career awareness program may facilitate the student's recognition of many career-vocational opportunities.

Career Exploration

Once students have identified fields of interest, a program can then be established that enables them to explore the skills and competencies demanded by the potential career. This exploration can occur at a job station within the school, at a local business or agency that employs individuals with similar training, through discussions with professional individuals with career guidance training, and through practice in the selected career areas. Frequently, individuals select a career goal without exploring the essential skills required for its successful performance, and without knowing the advantages and disadvantages of the potential career. As a result, a high number of trained individuals become disenchanted with their chosen career either prior to formal entrance into the field or shortly after gaining employment. One method of minimizing this development is through the early and frequent exposure of the youths to high-preference career-vocational activities.

Career Prerequisites

To develop effective career-vocational education programs counselors, teachers, and youths should first consult reference material that outlines the nature of the career and its prerequisite skills. These career reference outlines are found in the *Dictionary of Occupational Titles Supplement* (U.S. Department of Labor, 1968) and the *Supplement of the Occupational Outlook Handbook* (U.S. Department of Labor, 1974-75). Such material generally describes the career but does not specifically describe vocations as they exist in the local community where the disruptive youth resides. Information concerning local opportunities is generally best found in the local newspaper's job classified section, the state's department of employment, private job placement agencies, and school placement services.

Career Preparation

Once a decision has been made as to which of the careers explored is most preferable, and it has been determined that the selection is appropriate to the student's interests and skills or potential skills, training begins. This preparation includes not only the technical competency specifically associated with the career, but also the underlying academic and informational levels associated with effective career performance that must be provided through directed instruction. In the past, the lack of joint academic and career-vocational preparation has led to the failure of participating youths. Counselors and teachers should use the career choice as the guideline for academic and vocational training and experience. The primary aim of career preparation is to prepare youths to assume a responsible career position in the community, and it is not to legislate them into undesired conditions. The schools must correct the experiences and instruction provided to the handicapped youth.

ACADEMIC AREAS

In the aerospace industry, many engineers believe the fusing of materials is more lasting than the bonding process. In Career Education, many educators believe the fusion process in integrating the instructional process is more lasting than teaching individual subjects without clearly demonstrating their interdependence. If the student is taught and expected to carry out an integrated curriculum program, then the likelihood of success is enhanced. This integrated process obviously requires the overt or tacit concurrence of the instructor. For illustrative purposes the following will deal with the curriculum areas separately, but instructionally they should be integrated.

Language

Communication, whether sent via words, pictures, audio media, or some combination of the three, has been demonstrated to be essential for career success and growth. A shipping clerk must be able to read and interpret invoices, and a mechanic must be able to read blueprints. But reading is only one portion of language competency that is essential for success and growth. Writing and oral speech, whether terse and to the point or long and detailed, are prerequisites to success for the lawyers, philosophers, and physicians, as well as fast food waiters. In planning programs for handicapped youths, educators must take the language variables into consideration in charting an educational program. Educators can no longer assume that because students are not seeking a college degree they do not need basic language competencies.

Mathematics and Science

Whether one be an aerospace engineer or automotive mechanic, an understanding of mathematics and science is necessary. The mechanic needs mathematics to measure and compute the size of a gasket, and science to comprehend the function of the combustion engine, just as the engineer needs these two skills and competencies to design an electrical system or appreciate a new development in electromagnetic energy production. Mathematics and science are essential to the man or woman determined to contribute to his or her own and to the community's growth and welfare.

Social Studies and Health

Without the recognition of how a chosen career interfaces with society's needs and directions, and how good health contributes to improved job attendance and effectiveness, the individual is at a severe disadvantage. One of the major difficulties contributing to a youth's inability to maintain prolonged employment is the lack of position-stability awareness in an ever-changing job market. Often, youths will select a career that within a short time is no longer considered critical by the community and is soon phased out. Such experiences often provoke frustration and anger in the youths, and contribute to renewed conflicts with society. A recognition of the job market's ebb and flow can assist the youths to read the changes and to adjust their career directions.

Health, whether mental or physical, has a less tangible, though equally significant, influence on career retention and growth. Whether appreciated or not, the youth's appearance, attendance, and rapidity of performance often determine the duration of employment in a particular position. Regular attendance and work effectiveness can be as important a factor as knowledge. If handicapped youths are to succeed, they must recognize such influences and learn how to deal with them on the job.

COPING WITH THE OUTSIDE WORLD

Successful programs prepare the youth for the world of work, home, family, and community. Achievement of this requires the school to provide a structure that readies the youth to move beyond the existing range of opportunities and that results in better preparation for the adult world. The following range of experiences is recommended:

Observing

Observation provides an awareness of academic needs and career availability in the community. Youths can achieve this through undertaking a wide variety of experiences in the field, viewing tapes and listening to records, and communicating with peers.

Comparing

Youths can spend time at specified commercial establishments developing improved awareness concerning the skills and competencies required in identified career paths and comparing their readiness for such a position with the actual demands of the position.

Working with Support

At this level, actual experience at a learning center in work situations or simulated work situations is provided. Similar experiences can be made available to youths at training stations in the community, such as retail stores, industries, or special workshops. The academics are generally directly related to the work experiences, but when appropriate, may have a global direction.

Working in the Community

This is the final educational step in the career-vocational program for the student. During this period, youths are expected to function in a legitimate work environment without daily support from the school. The school's primary responsibility is periodic monitoring of student success and performance gains. To administer such experiences successfully, teachers, psychologists, psychometrists, counselors, work coordinators, shop instructors, and administrative personnel must be trained and prepared to work in unison. Programs for the handicapped youth have been fragmented and have concentrated on the psychological, and not the educational, aspects of the career-vocational preparation process (Gadlin, 1966; Miller, 1978; Sabatino, 1974). There is a growing recognition of this as demonstrated by the new programs now being designed by universities, state departments of education, and local school districts (Miller, 1980).

COMPREHENSIVE SERVICES

The services provided by high schools, until lately, have been directed primarily at the college bound youth. These same services, which could have benefited the handicapped youth, were either denied or rendered at such a superficial level as to be of little practical use. Under emerging mandates of federal and state laws, secondary schools are going to be under closer scrutiny to provide the following:

1. assessment services
2. counseling
3. programming
4. academic instruction
5. career-vocation awareness, exploration, and preparation
6. community experience
7. program evaluation and reprogramming

A wide range of personnel is essential for serving the secondary-aged handicapped student; these personnel include: teachers, psychologists, psychometrists, career counselors, work school coordinators, shop teachers, administrators, and special educators all working in traditional and specialized environments to provide essential experiences required in career skill attainment and postschool success. When high schools are unable to provide such services, they can be obtained from the state vocational/technical educational agency, regional career-vocational centers, cooperative program agreements among high schools, and special agreements with either state institutions or private organizations. Among the state and private agencies that can be used are the State Employment Agency, State Department of Commerce and Industry, the Chamber of Commerce, the State Department of Education, the Salvation Army, Goodwill Industries, and the Jewish, Catholic, and independent vocational skills training centers.

PROGRAM CONTENT

Sabatino (1974) recommended a vocational curriculum that deemphasizes the use of standard textbooks and emphasizes an instructional approach with preprogrammed high-interest, low-vocabulary material. This material would be geared specifically to the reading and interest level of the students and would interface with the students' career-vocational goals and needs. While there has been some attempt at developing this material, the review of the literature reveals significant gaps in its availability (Sachs & Miller, 1980). Extensive use of audiovisual equipment and guest lectures heightens the interest of handicapped youths. Selected materials should accommodate the variety of skills and motivational levels of participating youths. Whether the subject be language, mathematics, or science, the material should reflect the interests of adolescents, such as cars, jobs, personal identity, career directions, and social values.

FIELD SUPERVISION

Schools, like other institutions, sometimes become overly involved in their own efforts to the neglect of other critical components of the educational process. An obvious component of career-vocational education that has been neglected is the development of jobs for students in the field, and the supervision of the students as they seek to cope with the world-at-large. The responsibility of the school is to identify job markets, contact potential placement sites, make the student placement, and ensure that the relationship between the student and the on-site supervisor is appropriate and results in learning. Contemporary texts and work manuals, such as the *Work Experience and Career Exploration Guide* (Board of Vocational Education and Rehabilitation, 1974), have ignored field supervision and its responsibilities though they imply the need for such individuals and recognize the necessity of outside implementation practices. Traditionally, vocational personnel have sought to work with handicapped youths in the institution and/or school, providing career counseling, job stations, and skill training. The need for job supervision is particularly imperative when the youth has a history of social and academic adjustment. Among such youths, the recidivism and societal conflict is high (Sabatino, 1974). While the reasons for the recidivism are multiple, major contributions are poor follow-up once the youth is placed out beyond the school environment and the lack of close cooperation with business, industry, and other agencies in the community.

Cooperative efforts among various community and business agencies are essential for career education programs to succeed (Burt & Lessinger, 1970; Miller, Ewing & Phelps, 1980). Such cooperative efforts (1) produce programs of instruction more effective than those provided solely in training centers, (2) enable both training and business officials to measure instructional and training appropriateness, (3) provide an ongoing quality control process, and (4) ensure relevance of career training for youth. The necessity for cooperation and the integration of training and on-site experiences was cited in a report by Clark and Sloan (1960). The authors reported a general attitude among school officials that training ends with the conclusion of schooling. The interfacing of training and practical experience generally benefits the youth's performance in training and in school. There have been studies which indicated that youth in work programs generally showed gains in school performance. Many of the major difficulties with existing programs have been caused by the lack of linkage between program and work experience in the field. Of the problems, the most frequently cited include the lack of coordination between school and work, the insufficient number of social service agencies involved, and the absence of clear criteria to measure student performance.

An important aspect to practical work experience can be its contribution to an individual's assessment of self as well as the world of work. Work opportunities can be provided either on a full-time or part-time basis. Another view of joint school-work experience states:

- The work experience should be treated as an educational experience, and not as a final answer.

- A variety of work experiences should be provided so the student can become better acquainted with alternative career directions.

- Any experience should be safeguarded against violation of various legal restraints.

- Cooperation of business, industry, community agencies, and other interested groups is essential. It is recommended that the employer provide experiences of the least and most attractive features of the position, offer varieties of experiences during a single day, insure the youth against injury, and designate an experienced, understanding adult to assist the youth.

- School follow-up of the experiences should be made so that the appropriateness and usefulness of the placement can be evaluated.

- Parents should be a part of the placement and assessment process.

ALTERNATIVE PROGRAMS

Many varied alternatives exist for placement of handicapped youths. As has been observed, handicapped students require wide ranges of experiences so they can evaluate themselves against potential career choices. It is imperative that the students recognize the flexibility they have in selecting careers so that they are not limited by their first choice. School personnel and the student must weigh a variety of factors in making placements and establishing alternatives. They are

1. career choice
2. age

3. aptitude skills
4. social skills
5. academic level of achievement
6. reliability
7. physical appearance
8. leadership ability
9. commitment to goals
10. health

Once these factors have been assessed, the supervisor must decide which of the following best matches the youth's needs, interests, and abilities:

1. full-time school;
2. part-time school, part-time work;
3. part-time school, part-time vocational training;
4. full-time vocational training;
5. part-time vocational training, part-time work;
6. full-time work.

Whether the placement be full-time school or full-time work experience, the supervisor can best serve the youth by ensuring that the client's skills are being constantly upgraded. It is the essence of good educational services that levels of competencies are regularly assessed and developmental career goals are revised to meet societal, personal, and economic realities. Without such continual review and program alteration, the youth may tire or become frustrated with career placement.

CAREER PLACEMENT CRITERIA

Numerous considerations require assessment prior to career placement. These considerations range from working conditions to the personal and professional ability of the potential placement station to assist the youth. They are: (1) convenience of location, (2) health and safety conditions, (3) hours that must be worked, (4) adequacy of facilities and equipment, and (5) potential agencies' compliance with applicable laws.

All persons involved in the cooperative career education program must have the skills necessary to instruct youth so that new skills and performance competencies are achieved. Personnel working with the handicapped youth should be trained to (1) manage the youth's general behavior, (2) provide professional technical assistance, (3) exhibit exemplary behavior for the youth to model, (4) organize the work experiences, (5) communicate with the youth, (6) understand the career education program and the youth, and (7) recommend alternatives in the career program for the youth.

Students need to be acquainted with the requirements of the job and the persons they will be working with during a particular placement. If it is a business employer, they must be informed about the nature of the business. The fact is that the business is operating for profit, and that in accepting the position, the student has tacitly accepted responsibility for promoting the business's efforts. If it is a training or school site, the students need to be informed about the school's needs and problems and how they might succeed in such an environment. Should the students refuse to cooperate with the placement site officials, they should be told of the consequences of their activity, which may be interpreted as disruptive. Termination should only follow after the students understand both the positive and negative consequences of their actions and have demonstrated an unwillingness or inability to interact effectively.

DELIVERY OF SERVICES

Any program developed by a public school must establish clear operational procedures for assessment of the students' skills and delineate how a program will be provided and the types of experiences that will be provided. In addition, the personnel who will participate in the vocation program must be identified. Personnel considered to be most effective with handicapped youths are special education teachers, prevocational counselors, a psychometrician or school psychologist, and a work experience and/or job coach. One individual, possibly a vocational coordinator, ought to be given overall program management responsibilities.

The assessment process is the first constructive effort that school personnel take in developing a student educational program. Relevant data are expected to identify:

1. the academic skill level;
2. the intellectual performance potential;
3. the general interests and goals;
4. the attitudes toward such areas as school, career, and community;
5. level of ability in interpersonal relationships;
6. basic career aptitudes;
7. general physical appearance.

The collection of this information is a critical step in the development of a student's Individual Educational Program (IEP), as a mandate of the 94th Congress, which passed The Education for All Handicapped Children Act (PL 94-142). The following section discusses the procedures school personnel must follow prior to the initiation of assessment, during process, and following assessment process.

INDIVIDUAL EDUCATIONAL PROGRAM PROGRESS

The process of providing services to educationally handicapped adolescents requires school personnel to adhere to PL 94-142. The major ingredient of PL 94-142 mandates that all students must receive a free and appropriate education in the least restrictive environment. More specifically, the schools must allow a student to participate in regular education courses and programs, unless assessment information clearly demonstrates that other types of services would be more educationally beneficial (Turnbull & Schultz, 1979).

Figure 1-4 details a recommended procedure for identifying, assessing, and developing appropriate educational services for handicapped youth. This procedural flow is intended to assist the educator in viewing the entire process and ensuring that each of the steps, mandated in the law, is followed.

1.a. The school notifies the public that screening services are available.

1.b. Screening is implemented and a student is either deemed nonhandicapped (exit via box 2) or is referred for further diagnosis (box 3). A student may enter the system directly through the referral box if a parent, or other interested party, suspects that a problem exists.

Before administering any individualized evaluation instruments, the results of which could be used in a special education placement decision, the school must obtain parental or guardian permission for such evaluation (box 4). If the parents object to the evaluation, the school can either retract its request for evaluation or institute due process procedures (box 5). If the parents agree to the evaluation, or are ordered to agree under the due process provisions, it is conducted (box 6).

7. As the diagnosis nears completion, the school must notify the student's parents that a meeting is pending to plan their child's program, and that it is incumbent upon them to attend. Efforts must be made to schedule the meeting so as to be reasonably accessible to the parent (in time as well as locale). An IEP meeting can be conducted without a parent, but, in such cases, the school should be able to provide evidence that it made a good faith effort to convince the parents to attend, but the parents failed to cooperate.

8.a. It is at the IEP meeting that the IEP is formulated. In many cases well-meaning teachers may prepare an IEP prior to the actual meeting and present it to the child's parents for approval at the meeting itself. Most often the parents are grateful for the teacher's efforts and all return home without realizing the perversion of the law that has occurred! Certainly teachers should come to each IEP meeting with some idea of the direction in which they anticipate the student's program should be heading. The teacher should also be prepared to take the lead in the actual writing of the IEP. Nevertheless, the law does state clearly that the IEP is to be developed by the parent as well as the other people—such as the student—at the IEP meeting. Among the decisions made at the IEP meeting should be the child's placement (box 8.b.). Again, parental permission must be obtained before

Figure 1-4 IEP Process

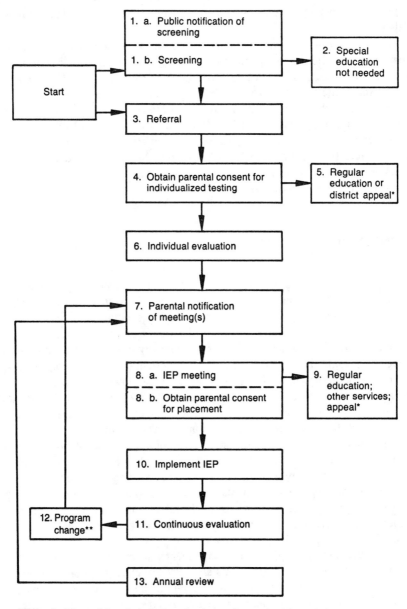

*At the decision points noted, disagreements may be resolved through due process procedures.

**Placement, goal, a short-term objective change.

actual placement can occur. If the student is deemed not eligible for special education services, he or she is assigned to regular education (box 9). If either school or parents object to the placement decision, they can appeal to due process (also box 9).

If parents and school are in agreement regarding a special education placement, that occurs and the IEP is implemented (box 10). While not a required part of the law, it is assumed that good teaching practice will be accompanied by continuous evaluation of the student's progress (box 11). If, at any time, the teacher, parent, or student feels that the program is unrealistic or inappropriate, a new IEP meeting can be called to suggest an internal program change (box 12, back through box 7). In any event, at least once each year each student's IEP must be reevaluated and updated at an IEP meeting (box 13, back through box 7). Once every three years a complete diagnostic evaluation must be conducted on each student and his or her special placement reconsidered.

CONCLUSION

Effective educational services for the handicapped youth require the school systems, universities, and state educational agencies to investigate and adopt a variety of changes in such areas as: assessment procedures; personnel training; program availability and flexibility, and instructional materials; behavior management; and instructional strategies. Unfortunately many of the procedures and concepts employed in serving the preadolescent child are being employed with handicapped adolescents. Inappropriate, watered down, and ineffective approaches in the programs provided students must make way for educational practices validated for individuals on the upper end of the 3 to 21 age continuum.

One major factor associated with poor programs is the fact that only 9 of the 50 states require the secondary educators to have training significantly different from that of the teacher of preadolescent children. The lack of differentiation of training has produced, in many schools, remedial and tutoring programs that closely parallel that provided to the elementary school child. As a result, many educationally handicapped youths become frustrated with the nonproductive, nonrewarding educational experience and drop out of schools to take unstable, low-paying jobs that often do not provide a career path.

To ensure such education and employment patterns are not continued, the schools must reassess their programs and service delivery options. Rather than becoming societal burdens, many individuals in the school-aged handicapped population are capable of obtaining productive jobs in the community. Existing data suggest that the handicapped tend to be reliable and productive members of the work force.

Currently, many handicapped youths perceive existing programs as irrelevant and nonproductive, and the efforts in developing and redeveloping meaningful programs for such youths have not proven to be successful. One reason for the failure is the lack of integration of academic, vocational, and personal needs of each student into the program design. As in nearly all human endeavors, education affects job options, and jobs affect social standing in the community.

For this integration to be achieved, the schools, the courts, and counseling agencies joining with the various state and community agencies, such as the Departments of Employment and Vocational Rehabilitation and the United Way, must cooperate and work in unison to ensure the continuity from class to vocational placement, and from entry level placement to sustained employment and community involvement.

REFERENCES

Ausubel, D. P. *Theory and problems of child development.* New York: Grune & Stratton, 1957.

Bandura, A. *Principles of behavior modification.* New York: Holt, Rinehart & Winston, 1969.

Board of Vocational Education and Rehabilitation, Division of Vocational and Technical Education. *Work experience and career exploration guide.* Springfield, Ill., 1974.

Brolin, D. E., & D'Alonzo, B. J. Critical issues in career education for the handicapped student. *Exceptional Children,* 1979, *45,* 246-253.

Bruner, J. S. *Toward a theory of instruction.* Cambridge, Mass.: Belknap Press of Harvard University, 1966.

Burt, S. M., & Lessinger, L. M. *Volunteer industry involvement in public education.* Lexington, Mass.: Heath Lexington Books, 1970.

Cegelka, P. T. Sex role stereotyping in special education—A look at secondary work study programs. *Exceptional Children,* 1976, *42,* 323-328.

Clarizio, H. F., & McCoy, G. F. *Behavior disorders in school-aged children.* Scranton, Pa.: Chandler Publishing Co., 1976.

Clark, H. F., & Sloan, H. S. *Classrooms in the factories.* Rutherford, N.J.: Fairleigh Dickinson University, 1960.

Deno, E., Henye, R., Krantz, G., & Barklind, K. *Retarded youth—Their school rehabilitation needs—Final report.* Minneapolis, Minn.: Minneapolis Public Schools, 1965. (ERIC Document Reproduction Service No. ED 010 926)

Erikson, E. H. *Identity: Youth and crisis.* New York: Norton, 1968.

Evans, E. D., & Potter, T. H. Identity crisis: A brief perspective. In E. D. Evans (Ed.), *Adolescents—Readings in behavior and development.* Hinsdale, Ill.: The Dryden Press, 1970.

Flavell, J. H. *The developmental psychology of Jean Piaget.* New York: Van Nostrand Reinhold Co., 1963.

Gadlin, W. (Ed.). *Directory of sheltered workshops serving the emotionally disturbed.* Altro, N.Y.: Altro Health and Rehabilitation Services, 1966. (ERIC Document Reproduction Service No. ED 011 164)

Gillespie, P. H., & Fink, A. H. The influence of sexism on the education of handicapped children. *Exceptional Children*, 1974, *41*, 155-162.

Gorelick, M. C. *An assessment of vocational realism of high school and post-high school educable mentally retarded adolescents*. Los Angeles, Calif.: Exceptional Children's Foundation, 1966. (ERIC Document Reproduction Service No. ED 011 163)

Handbook for career guidance counselors. Urbana, Ill.: University of Illinois, 1975.

Heggen, J. R., & Irvine, F. *A study of the factors that may influence the implementation of a vocational education curriculum at the Utah State Industrial School*. Logan, Utah: Utah State University, 1967. (ERIC Document Reproduction Service No. ED 016 786)

Herr, E. L. *Review and synthesis of foundations for career education*. Washington, D.C.: U.S. Department of Health, Education and Welfare, Office of Education, 1972.

Hewett, F. M. *The emotionally disturbed child in the classroom*. Boston: Allyn & Bacon, 1968.

James, P. R. *The relationship of vocational outlook and special educational programs for adolescent educable mentally handicapped*. Urbana, Ill.: University of Illinois, 1966. (ERIC Document Reproduction Service No. ED 018 883)

Kunzelman, H. P. *Precision teaching: An initial learning sequence*. Seattle, Wash.: Special Child Publications, 1970.

Lazarus, A. A. *Behavior therapy and beyond*. New York: McGraw-Hill, 1971.

McCandless, B. R. *Adolescents—Behavior and development*. Hinsdale, Ill.: The Dryden Press, 1970.

Miller, S. R. Career and vocational education. In D. A. Sabatino & A. J. Mauser (Eds.), *Educating norm-violating and chronic disruptive secondary school-aged youth* (Vol. 2). Boston: Allyn & Bacon, 1978.

Miller, S. R. (Ed.). *Illinois secondary handicapped consortium report on career/vocational education: Personnel needs for secondary-handicapped clientele in Illinois*. Carbondale, Ill.: Southern Illinois University, 1980.

Miller, S. R., Ewing, N. Y., & Phelps, L. A. Career and vocational education for the handicapped: A historical perspective. In L. A. Mann and D. A. Sabatino (Eds.), *The fourth review of special education*. New York: Grune & Stratton, 1980.

Miller, S. R., Lotsof, A. B., & Miller, T. *Survey of secondary program needs and directions*. Unpublished report, 1976.

Miller, S. R., Sabatino, D. A., & Larsen, R. Issues in the professional preparation of secondary school special educators. *Exceptional Children*, 1980, *45*(5), 344-350.

Parnicky, J. J., & Kahn, H. (Eds.). *Evaluating and developing vocational potential of institutionalized retarded adolescents*. Bordentown, N.J.: Edward R. Johnstone Training and Research Center, 1963. (ERIC Document Reproduction Service No. 022268)

Peter, L. J. *Prescriptive teaching*. New York: McGraw-Hill, 1965.

Phelps, A. L., & Lutz, R. J. *Career exploration and preparation for the special needs learner*. Boston: Allyn & Bacon, 1977.

Piaget, J. In G. N. Sedgrim (Ed. and trans.), *The mechanisms of perception*. New York: Basic Books, 1969.

Rice, F. P. *The adolescent—Development, relationships, and culture*. Boston: Allyn & Bacon, 1975.

Sabatino, D. A. *Neglect and delinquent children*. EDC Report, Wilkes-Barre, Pa.: Wilkes College, 1974.

Sabatino, D. A. A review of diagnostic and classification antecedents in special education. In D. A. Sabatino & T. L. Miller (Eds.), *Describing learner characteristics of handicapped children and youth*. New York: Grune & Stratton, 1979.

Sabatino, D. A., & Schloss, P. Adolescent social-personal development: Theory and application. In D. A. Sabatino, C. Schmidt, & T. L. Miller (Eds.), *Learning disabilities: Systemizing teaching and service delivery.* Rockville, Md.: Aspen Systems, 1981.

Sachs, J. J., & Miller, S. R. Personnel needs in career/vocational education for the handicapped: Are we prepared? *ICEC Quarterly,* Fall 1980, *29*(4).

Scurlock, V. C., West, J. A., Keith, D. L., & Viaille, H. *Vocational rehabilitation in juvenile delinquency: A planning grant to determine the role of vocational rehabilitation in juvenile delinquency—Final report.* Stillwater, Okla.: Oklahoma State Board for Vocational Education, 1964. (ERIC Document Reproduction Service No. 052334)

Shaw, C. R., & McKay, H. D. *Juvenile delinquency and urban areas.* Chicago: The University of Chicago Press, 1972.

Skinner, B. F. *The technology of teaching.* New York: Appleton-Century-Crofts, 1968.

Sloan, C. A. Curriculum integration and its implications for chronic disruptive youth. In E. Sloan, S. Miller, & D. A. Sabatino (Eds.), *Integrated career/education handbook.* Springfield, Ill.: State of Illinois Department of Corrections, 1975.

Smith, G. The mentally retarded: Is the public employment service prepared to serve them? *Mental Retardation,* 1970, *8,* 26-29.

Subcommittee on Elementary, Secondary and Vocational Education of the Committee on Education and Labor, House of Representatives. Study report. Washington, D.C.: U.S. Government Printing Office, 1977.

Turnbull, A. P., & Schultz, J. B. *Mainstreaming handicapped students: A guide for the classroom teacher.* Boston: Allyn & Bacon, 1979.

U.S. Department of Labor. *Supplement to the dictionary of occupational titles.* Washington, D.C.: U.S. Government Printing Office, 1968.

U.S. Department of Labor. *Supplement of the occupational outlook handbook 1974-75.* Washington, D.C.: U.S. Government Printing Office, 1974.

Chapter 2

Adolescent Handicapped Populations

Educational systems have long advocated the utility of grouping students with similar characteristics. Movement from the one-room schoolhouse to graded classrooms was popularized in part because of the increased efficiency with which the instructor could deliver educational experiences to students of similar maturational levels. Even within a classroom of students of a similar age, however, substantial differences among students were found to exist. Thus, teaching systems, in which students were grouped on the basis of general and specific achievement scores within an age level, became prominent. Despite the precision of the particular grouping system, a small number of students exhibited handicapping conditions which set them apart from any particular track or group. It was apparent that these students displayed characteristics that significantly reduced their ability to benefit from the general program.

A wide range of educational programs was established to develop the full potential of handicapped youth. These programs have relied on homogeneous grouping to provide the best match of services to specific handicapping conditions. Groups of handicapped individuals have been established on the basis of specific behavioral deviations that interfere with the individual's development. Students are classified as having a specific handicapping condition when their intellectual, social/emotional, physical, communication, and sensory abilities are markedly different from the general population. The major handicapping conditions include:

- auditory handicaps
- visual handicaps
- physical and health disorders
- speech and/or language impairment
- specific learning disability

31

- mental retardation

- behavior disorders

The following section of this chapter identifies and defines each of the major handicapping conditions. The reader is cautioned to remember that gross classification schemes can only provide the educator with a rough sketch of how handicapped students differ from the normal population. A subsequent chapter will present an approach that goes beyond a gross categorical label into the study of differences between and within individuals.

AUDITORY HANDICAPPED

Definition and Classification

The major effect of an auditory handicap is that the individual has difficulty in acquiring functional communication skills. Auditory handicaps, including a range of hearing loss in one or both ears, may substantially reduce an individual's ability to benefit from typical classroom activities. Social, educational, and career development may be adversely affected by the inability to communicate efficiently with others. The extent to which an auditory handicap impairs the individual's development is associated with two major variables: (1) the age at which the hearing loss occurs, and (2) the severity of the hearing loss. These variables are specified in Connor, Hoover, Horton, Sands, Sternfeld, and Wolinsky's (1975) definition of deafness and hearing impairment:

> the deaf are defined as those individuals whose hearing loss is so severe at birth or during the prelingual period that it precludes the normal acquisition of language comprehension and expression. The partially hearing are persons whose hearing loss, although significant in degree, was acquired either after the critical period of language acquisition, thus enabling the individual to develop some communicative skills, or does not totally impair oral language development. (p. 242)

The age of onset and severity dimensions are further emphasized by the classification scheme of the Committee on Nomenclature: Conference of Executives of American Schools for the Deaf (1938). Its classification includes two populations with auditory impairments:

1. The deaf: those in whom the sense of hearing is nonfunctional for the ordinary purposes of life. This general group is made up of two distinct classes based entirely on the time the loss of hearing occurred. These include:

   The congenitally deaf—those who were born deaf.

   The adventitiously deaf—those who were born with normal hearing but in whom the sense of hearing becomes nonfunctional later through illness or accident.

2. The hard of hearing: Those in whom the sense of hearing, although defective, is functional with or without a hearing aid. (p. 2)

Assessment

The diagnosis of a hearing loss results from an assessment of the auditory system. The use of a pure-tone and special audiometer allows the audiologist to determine the degree of hearing loss and the person's ability to comprehend speech sounds. Based on this and other specialized auditory tests, etiological factors, and prognosis for medical restoration, educational strategies and vocational goals may be identified. The assessment may also reveal the anatomical anomaly to which the hearing loss may be attributed. There are three nonexclusive types of hearing impairment: a conductive hearing loss in which there is an obstruction of sound transmission resulting from a lesion to the external or middle ear mechanisms; a sensory-neural hearing loss resulting from damage to the nerve endings of the inner ear (cochlea) or the auditory nerve; and a central auditory hearing loss in which a lesion exists in the central auditory nervous system and the auditory area of the cortex.

Prevalence

The prevalence of hearing deficits is generally not agreed upon in the professional literature. It appears that the wide discrepancy in reported rates is influenced by the assessment procedure, the classification scheme used by the investigator, and the geographic location of the sample studied. A review of literature reported by the Illinois Commission on Children (1968) revealed that from one to three percent of the school-aged population exhibit hearing losses of sufficient severity to warrant medical or special educational attention. The commission reported that only one (1) in one thousand (1,000) children exhibit hearing losses sufficiently severe to be classified as being deaf. In contrast, the U.S. Department of Health, Education and Welfare (USDHEW; 1979) reports that .17 percent of all school-aged children have an educationally limited hearing loss.

VISUALLY HANDICAPPED

Definition and Classification

A visual deficit may affect the educational, social, and vocational development of an individual in a number of ways. Traditional educational practices rely heavily on the students' ability to perceive visual images. Colors, forms, sizes, textures, and actions are frequently utilized in instructional presentations. The interpretation of these stimuli may be impossible or highly difficult for students with impaired vision. Acceptable social behaviors are also acquired in part through the use of vision. The visually impaired individual is less able to read and interpret social cues that are necessary to the development of socially skillful behavior. One of the greatest limitations imposed on the visually impaired is that of reduced mobility. The effectiveness with which visually impaired individuals can move in their environment has been demonstrated to be the primary determinant of vocational success (Knowles, 1969).

Visual impairments may be the result of reduced visual acuity, a limited field of vision, defective color vision, or an external muscle imbalance. Visual handicaps have traditionally been classified by two major categories: (1) *partially sighted* in which visual acuity is better than 20/200 but worse than 20/70 in the better eye with correction; and (2) *legally blind* in which visual acuity is 20/200 or less for distance vision in the better eye, with correction; or visual acuity of 20/200 or more if the widest diameter of field of vision subtends an angular distance less than or equal to 20 degrees (National Society for the Prevention of Blindness, 1966). However, the range of vision emphasized by this classification has little utility for educators in the public schools. Students with visual acuity in the legally blind range may be able to read print under special magnification conditions. Bateman (1967) has proposed a functional definition of blindness that has direct implications for special educational provisions. She suggests that the *visually impaired, partially sighted* are those who can use their vision for reading when adaptations are made in the presentation of reading materials and that the blind Braille reader must rely on Braille as a primary reading medium.

Assessment

Visual acuity is usually reported in the form of a fraction derived from the use of a Snellen chart. Visual acuity of 20/200 indicates that the eye is able to see at a distance of 20 feet what the normal eye is able to see at 200 feet. The greater the disparity between the numerator and the denominator, the greater the impairment in vision. A visual acuity of 20/20 indicates normal vision of sight of the tested eye when compared with the normal eye. The field of vision is assessed with the use of a perimeter that maps out field limitations in various directions on a chart. Color vision is assessed by determining the individual's ability to discriminate hue, saturation, and brightness. While color blindness is generally considered a visual impairment, it generally is not included as a handicapping condition.

Prevalence

The prevalence of visual impairment in school-aged populations was reported by Hatfield (1975) to be one (1) in twenty-five hundred (2,500). Of this group one-third were considered to be without useful vision, one-third had visual acuity less than 20/200 in the better eye, and the remaining one-third tested at 20/200, or the upper Snellen measurement limit for those classified as legally blind. The USDHEW (1979) has reported data estimating that approximately .07 percent of all school-aged students require special education services because of visual impairments.

PHYSICAL AND HEALTH DISORDERS

Definition and Classification

Children and adolescents with physical and health disorders represent a broad and diverse population. Specific handicapping conditions range from cerebral palsy to asthma. Because of the heterogeneity of this group, general statements regarding the cognitive, psychological, or affective characteristics of its population cannot be made. The severity of the handicapping condition, the age at which it was incurred, the nature of the condition, the visibility of the condition, and the support systems available may all contribute to the influence of the disability on the student's development. As with other categories of exceptional children and adolescents, specific physical and health disorders do not exert a simple or predictable effect on the development of the student. Rather, the impact of a disability on the characteristics of the individual can only be understood through studying the complex interaction of physical, cognitive, and environmental variables.

The diverse nature of physical and health disorders and the resulting variability in associated psychosocial characteristics have led to broad descriptive definitions. Current definitions make few assumptions of common academic, social, or personal characteristics. Kirk (1972), for example, defines these students as:

> those who are crippled, deformed, or otherwise physically handicapped (exclusive of the visually and auditory handicapped) and those who have health problems which interfere with functioning in a regular classroom . . . comprise heterogeneous groups with varying disabilities,

each a unique problem which limits the effectiveness with which a child can cope with the academic, social, and emotional expectations of the school and community. (p. 349)

Similarly, Sirvis (1978) has suggested that the physically handicapped are "individuals with functional limitations related to physical ability and medical conditions, such as strength and stamina" (p. 361).

In addition to educationally relevant definitions, physicians working through the American Medical Association have devised and refined an extensive system for classifying permanent physical impairments. Individual guidelines target anatomical features that may be affected by physical or health disorders. These include: extremities and back (1958); visual system (1958); cardiovascular system (1960); ear, nose, and throat (1961); central nervous system (1964); respiratory system (1965); the endocrine system (1966); and mental illness (1966). Although these publications focus on the extent and nature of a disability or illness and facilitate medical interventions, they also provide a common conceptual foundation through which educators may understand physical or health disorders.

Assessment

The initial diagnosis of physical and health disorders is the responsibility of a physician. The child or adolescent diagnosed as having a physical or health disorder may then be referred to other agencies for special services. Disabled students coming to the attention of educators in the schools may be evaluated to determine if the condition limits the individual's ability to benefit from the regular classroom environment. Psychometric instruments, including tests of academic achievement, intelligence, interests, and personality characteristics as well as formal and informal observational procedures, anecdotal records, and criterion-referenced academic evaluation procedures, may provide relevant data. Thus, consistent with Kirk's (1972) definition, a bifaceted evaluation occurs. First, a specific health or physical disability is identified. Second, assessment data indicate whether this condition impinges on the student's adaptation to the school setting.

Prevalence

The prevalence of physical and health disorders is considered to be approximately .36 percent of the school-aged population (Dunn, 1973). An equal percentage of these students have physically handicapping conditions and chronic health disorders. The USDHEW (1979) suggests a higher prevalence estimate of .5 percent of the school-aged population having physical and health disorders that result in special educational services.

SPEECH AND/OR LANGUAGE IMPAIRMENT

Definition and Classification

Speech is defined as the ability to utilize oral symbols in a manner that conveys meaningful utterances to others. Speech requires the individual to develop sounds into words and words into sentences. Speech disorders result from deficiencies in oral production regardless of whether the individual is able to encode or formulate verbal messages. Language refers to the ability to express verbal messages (formulation or encoding). Speech is the production of the "sound" that the listener hears, while language involves the convention or code by which oral symbols are organized. Language deficits are included within speech deficits since speech is comprised of both the organization of sounds and the production of sounds.

Bankson (1978) emphasizes the differentiation between speech and language disorders in the following definition:

> The term speech impairment is used in a generic sense to refer to disorders of articulation (speech sound production) and fluency (rhythm). Each of these parameters relates to the mechanics of producing speech. Language impairments, as defined by speech pathologists, usually refer to disorders in comprehending or verbally expressing the symbols and grammatical rules of language. (p. 389)

The speech literature generally divides speech defects into eight major areas: (1) articulation disorders including omissions, distortions, or substitutions; (2) voice defects including improper loudness, pitch, or duration; (3) stuttering; (4) aphasia and related disorders; (5) delayed language; (6) cleft-palate speech; (7) cerebral-palsied speech; and (8) speech disorders resulting from hearing defects. Another popular classification scheme targets specific speech disabilities without consideration of the handicapping conditions associated with the speech defect. Within this scheme, speech disabilities may include articulation defects that impair sound production, phonation defects that impair voice quality, and defects of fluency including stuttering and cluttering.

Assessment

Speech deficiencies interfere with an individual's ability to communicate effectively with others. In the classroom, the speech-disabled individual may attract an excessive amount of unpleasant attention. Such attention may be the result of frustration on the part of others attempting to interact with the individual, or it may result from peer recognition of the inappropriateness of the speech. Speech deficiencies that do not receive appropriate professional attention may result in a number of maladaptive behavioral characteristics. For example, a child with an articulation deficit may withdraw from verbal interactions or grimace and become flushed when speaking to unfamiliar people.

Eisenson (1980) has emphasized the impact that a speech disorder may have on an individual. He argues that even the slightest speech deviation may be serious if the disabled speaker is sufficiently self-conscious or apprehensive so that social, educational, and vocational adjustment is diminished. He offers eight criteria by which defective speech may be identified:

1. It is not readily audible.
2. It is not readily intelligible.
3. It is vocally unpleasant.
4. It is visibly unpleasant.
5. It is labored in production or lacking in conventional rhythm and stress.
6. It is linguistically deficient.
7. It is inappropriate to the individual (content or manner of production) in terms of age, sex, or physical development.
8. The speakers respond to their own speech as if one or more of the above were present.

The identification and remedial planning of speech disorders typically involves a three-stage process. The first stage is a general screening of the general school-aged population to identify students who may exhibit speech defects. The second stage is a more detailed assessment that provides a diagnosis for those identified in the initial screening. The final stage involves the selection of students who can benefit from speech therapy. Students identified in the screening procedure are usually administered a standardized picture test that determines the extent to which a student's speech deviates from the norm. Frequently administered tests include the Templin-Darley Tests of Articulation and the Goldman-Fristoe Test of Articulation (Goldman & Fristoe, 1969). In addition to tests that provide normative data, many speech therapists use unstandardized picture test cards and a simulated conversation format.

The diagnosis of a speech disorder involves a comprehensive assessment of the student's intellectual, speech, and associated or causal defects. Intellectual assessment is conducted to determine if the speech defect is a function of limited intellectual development. In cases where the student is obviously not mentally impaired, intellectual assessment may be deleted. Specific speech defects may be identified through a variety of informal procedures including obtaining speech samples through: picture presentations, structured conversations, observations in the natural environment, and asking the student to repeat nonsense syllables or words. Associated or causal defects are identified by: (1) observing the structure and function of speech-producing mechanisms (e.g., tongue movement, jaw occlusion, palate structure), (2) evaluating the home and educational environments, and (3) assessing the student's aural and cognitive functioning.

Prevalence

The prevalence of speech deficits reported in the literature represents a close approximation at best. Factors that have obscured these data include subjectivity on the part of the evaluator, regional dialectical differences that are confused with speech disorders, and sound omissions or substitutions that result from an individual's failure to understand grammatical rules.

With these limitations in mind, Perkins (1977) has surveyed the literature and reports that 5 percent of the population exhibits speech defects. The National Institute for Neurological Diseases and Stroke (1969) reports data that identify the percentage of school-aged children and adolescents (ages 5 to 21) who have specific speech problems. The data indicate that 3.0 percent of all students have functional articulation problems, .7 percent have fluency defects, .5 percent have impaired hearing with a speech defect, .3 percent have delayed speech development, .2 percent have voice irregularities, .2 percent have cerebral-palsied speech, and .1 percent have cleft-palate speech. The authors report an overall prevalence of 5.0 percent for school-aged children and adolescents. Finally, the USDHEW (1979) has reported data indicating that 2.39 percent of the school-aged population is currently receiving special services for the speech impaired.

SPECIFIC LEARNING DISABILITIES

Definition and Classification

Of all the handicapping conditions identified in this chapter, specific learning disabilities stand out as the most recent category of exceptional children and youths. Prior to the early 1960s, programs for learning-disabled students were virtually nonexistent. Even as late as the early or middle 1970s, many educational systems in the nation did not recognize learning disabilities as a category of exceptionality. At the present time, there is still considerable debate and confusion associated with the field. A review of the literature conducted by Clements (1966) revealed 38 labels that have been used to describe children and adolescents with characteristics subsumed by the label learning disabilities. Frequently cited labels have included minimal brain damage, cerebral dysfunction, specific reading disorder, perceptually handicapped, attention disorder, minimal brain injury, and dyslexia in hyperactive children.

In spite of the controversy surrounding terminology used in the field, there is little question that a group of children and adolescents exists who exhibit marked disabilities in one or more areas of academic achievement while performing within the normal range in others. With regard to the variability of performance, this represents the most heterogeneous group of exceptional children and adolescents addressed in this chapter. This fact may account for the diversity of professional views in the field. Cruickshank and Paul (1980) report literature that highlights deficits in discrimination, memory, sequencing, affect, motor inhibition, impulse control, gross motor functioning, figure-ground discrimination, visual motor functioning, visual perceptual functioning, auditory acuity, sensory integration, conceptual and abstract thinking, language usage, socioemotional functioning, self-concept, and body-image.

Kirk's (1968) definition of learning disabilities emphasizes the broad range of characteristics associated with this group of exceptional individuals: "A learning disability refers to a specific retardation or disorder in one or more of the processes of speech, language, perception, behavior, reading, spelling, writing, or arithmetic" (p. 398).

Kirk's definition characterizes learning disabilities as deficiencies in a specific academic skill or ability in relation to general academic functioning. Kirk also distinguishes learning disabilities from mental retardation in that mental retardation implies a general deficit in all areas of academic functioning, while learning disabilities are denoted by deficits in specific areas. For example, one would expect the mentally retarded adolescent to be several years below grade level in all or most academic areas including reading, mathematics, spelling, language, etc. The learning-disabled individual may be below grade level in but a few of these areas while the remainder are within the normal range. Thus, the mentally retarded individual exhibits a general deficit in academic performance, while the learning-disabled person is deficient in a restricted range of academic skills.

Wepman, Cruickshank, Deutsch, Morency, and Strother (1975) have proposed an alternative approach to the definition of learning disabilities. Their definition proceeds from a psychoeducational orientation that emphasizes the underlying pathology presumed to result in a learning disability. In an expanded version of the Wepman et al. definition, Cruickshank and Paul (1980) define learning disabilities as "resulting from perceptual processing deficits which are in turn the result of a malfunction in some aspect of the central nervous system. Learning disabilities may occur in a child or youth of any age, of any intellectual level, and be of widely diversified etiologies" (p. 503).

Cruickshank and Paul's definition is in sharp contrast to Kirk's in that an emphasis is placed on underlying neurological conditions. According to this position, learning disabilities may coexist with other conditions, including mental retardation. The authors contend that perceptual processing deficits may occur in the mentally retarded, physically handicapped, behaviorally disordered, etc. From this frame of reference, learning disabilities are not restricted to individuals within the normal range of intelligence. Rather, learning disabilities are defined by the presence of a neurological disorder, regardless of general cognitive functioning.

Hallahan and Kauffman (1976) have identified five common themes contained within most of the prevalent definitions of learning disabilities. While subtle deviations may be present in many of the current definitions, these points bring a degree of order to the search for a unified definition. The five major points are

1. Learning-disabled students are academically retarded.
2. Learning-disabled students have an uneven pattern of development.
3. Learning-disabled students may or may not have central nervous system dysfunctioning.
4. Learning-disabled students do not owe their learning problems to environmental disadvantage.
5. Learning-disabled students do not owe their learning problems to mental retardation or emotional disturbance.

Assessment

Kirk (1972) has proposed a five-stage diagnostic process for learning-disabled children and youths. The first stage involves determining whether learning problems are general, specific, or spurious. This assessment process requires that the discrepancy among the student's chronological age, mental age, and specific academic skill be identified. Adolescents with a comparable mental age and chronological age, exhibiting a deficit in mathematics, may be identified as having a learning disability, while students with a deficit mathematical skill level that is consistent with their mental age may be considered to have a general learning deficit. This discrepancy analysis generally involves the use of standardized intelligence and achievement tests.

The second stage involves a more detailed analysis of the specific problem. Through this stage, the diagnostician seeks to delineate the specific response capabilities of the learner. For example, beyond determining that the student reads at a particular grade level, information is obtained that details specific word attack skills, faulty habits, attention deficits, and scanning techniques. Information from the student, interview data from the parents, a physician's examination, as well as various formal and informal performance measures obtained through the normal course of the school day are also considered by the diagnostician.

The third step suggested by Kirk is to identify the physical, environmental, and psychological correlates for the disability. Correlates may include poor diet, auditory defect, excessive family pressure, educational deprivation, traumatic school experiences, etc. These factors may be associated with the child's or adolescent's deficit in a specific academic area and as such may become a focus of the educational prescription. Assessment of these correlates generally involves informal observations of the student's interactions in the home and school environment, as well as the technique of self-report. For example, observations of a student may reveal that he or she is frequently inattentive during group presentations in language class. A systematic analysis of the student's classwork may indicate a substantial difference in performance when comparing work completed following group presentations and work following individual instruction. Further observations of the student may substantiate that during individual instruction the student requires continual verbal prompts and praise from the teacher.

The fourth stage in diagnosing a specific learning disability is to develop a diagnostic hypothesis based on data accumulated in the preceding stages. This step involves organizing data from the previous steps so that hunches regarding the relationship between the correlators and the academic performance deficit can be generated. Criterion and norm-referenced instruments as well as informal assessment approaches are used by diagnosticians for this purpose.

This information is then utilized in the fifth and final stage. In the fifth stage, data generated in stages one through four are used to develop a systematic remedial program. In the previous example, the program may involve providing primary language instruction in a one-to-one fashion while systematically reducing the demand for teacher attention. As students become more independent, they may be gradually integrated into the regular class structure.

Prevalence

While there is little agreement as to the prevalence of learning disabilities among children and adolescents, it does represent the largest exceptional group served in the public schools. Because of the disagreement existing in the field over definition and assessment procedures, prevalence estimates have ranged from 1 to 30 percent of the school-aged population. Data reported by USDHEW (1979) suggest that 1.89 percent of the school-aged population exhibit learning disabilities. Dunn (1973) reports prevalence estimates of 1 to 3 percent of children and adolescents in school.

MENTAL RETARDATION

Definition and Classification

Mental retardation refers to a developmental delay associated with intellectual and adaptive functioning that is substantially deviant from the general population. Because of the varying degrees by which functioning can be impaired across academic, social, personal, and career-vocational skills, mental retardation designates a highly heterogeneous group of individuals. Numerous classification systems have been proposed to establish homogeneous subgroups. The public schools dichotomize retarded students as mildly or educably mentally retarded individuals and as severely or trainably mentally retarded individuals.

Telford and Sawrey (1972) have identified five common characteristics that warrant the use of mild mental retardation as a functional label. First, the subgroups in the mild range are virtually indistinguishable based on socially and educationally relevant variables. Second, they represent an arbitrarily established low end of the normal distribution curve of intelligence. Third, subnormal intellectual functioning is typically the result of an interaction between constitutional and environmental factors. Fourth, while research data indicate that this group is statistically below average in physique and general health, individual members within this group are not perceptibly different from the general population. The majority of individuals within this population can compete successfully in physical endeavors with individuals of normal and above levels of intelligence. Fifth, most mildly mentally retarded individuals are identified only after a thorough and intensive assessment of intellectual and adaptive functioning. Additionally, research has indicated that once the mildly retarded leave school and enter careers, their adjustment to the demands of society is only slightly less adequate than their age and socioeconomic matched peers.

In general, the mildly mentally retarded represent a group of children and adolescents whose general intellectual capabilities limit their ability to benefit from the typical classroom structure. This group frequently includes students who are considered culturally disadvantaged or educationally handicapped.

Unlike the mildly mentally retarded, the severely retarded can often be distinguished from the general population by their physical characteristics. Severe mental retardation is often attributed to (1) chromosomal aberrations such as Down's syndrome, Klinefelter's syndrome, and Turner's syndrome; (2) biochemical anomalies such as phenylketonuria (PKU) and Tay-Sachs disease; (3) endocrine disturbances the most prevalent of which is cretenism; (4) cranial anomalies of genetic origin such as microcephaly; and (5) syndromes resulting from environmental insult, including hydrocephaly, epilepsy, infection of the brain, and cerebral palsy. It is important to note that the preceding conditions do not presuppose the coexistence of mental retardation.

Mental retardation has been classified and defined from a psychological and educational frame of reference. The American Association on Mental Deficiency (AAMD) sixth revision of the *Manual on Terminology and Classification in Mental Retardation* (Grossman, 1973) defines mental retardation as referring to "significantly sub-average general intellectual functioning existing concurrently with deficits in adaptive behavior, and manifested during the developmental period" (p. 5).

Kirk (1972) has proposed an educationally sensitive definition for educably and trainably mentally retarded students. He suggests that the educable mentally retarded individual is one who may achieve: "(1) minimum educability in the academic subjects of the school, (2) social adjustment to such a point that he can get along independently in the community, and (3) minimum occupational adequacy to such a degree that he can later support himself partially or totally at the adult level'' (p. 191). According to Kirk, the trainable mentally retarded child is one who, because of subnormal intelligence, is not capable of learning in classes for the educable mentally retarded but who does have potentialities for learning: ''(1) self-care, (2) adjustment to the home or neighborhood, and (3) economic usefulness in the home, a sheltered workshop, or an institution'' (p. 221).

Assessment

The definitions proposed by the AAMD and by Kirk rely on the assessment of general intellectual functioning and adaptive behavior. Intelligence measures used by psychologists in the diagnosis and classification of mental retardation most often include the Wechsler scales, the Stanford-Binet, and the Cattell. Table 2-1, adapted from the AAMD *Manual on Terminology and Classification in Mental Retardation,* depicts the levels of mental retardation as distinguished by levels of intellectual functioning.

In addition to measures of general intellectual functioning, both Kirk's and the AAMD's definitions refer to some measure of personal independence or social responsibility (i.e., adaptive behavior). A number of adaptive behavior scales have been proposed to assess the social and personal functioning of the mentally retarded. Some of these include the AAMD Adaptive Behavior Scale, the Vineland Social Maturity Scale, and the TMR Performance Profile.

Each of these instruments attempts to sample a range of skills from economic, language, leisure, social, physical development, and vocational and/or mobility domains. The *Manual on Terminology and Classification in Mental Retardation* suggests that data scores from these measures may be scaled from level I to level IV in association with the degree of deviance in adaptive behavior from the general population.

Table 2-1 Levels of Mental Retardation

Level of retardation	IQ range of Stanford-Binet	IQ range to Wechsler scales
Mild	68-52	69-55
Moderate	51-36	54-40
Severe	35-20	39-25
Profound	19	24

Source: American Association on Mental Deficiency. Used by permission.

Prevalence

Prevalence estimates of mental retardation defined and diagnosed through traditional means range from 2 to 3 percent of the school-aged population. USDHEW (1979) estimates that 1.84 percent of the school-aged population is receiving services for the mentally retarded.

BEHAVIOR DISORDERS

Definition and Classification

The behaviorally disordered may well be the most difficult group of adolescents to work with in the general educational setting. Frequent verbally and physically aggressive outbursts, self-abusive behavior, withdrawn behavior, and/or irrational verbalizations are not only a problem for the behaviorally disordered individual but also for other students in the classroom. A behavior disorder differs from a specific or general learning disability in that a learning disability, in and of itself, does not interfere with the learning of others. An aggressive adolescent's disruptive behavior may limit the ability of all students to benefit from the learning environment. Further, disruptive responses may be emotionally provoking for both the teacher and other students. Thus, the behaviorally disordered adolescent becomes a catalyst for disruptive behavior on the part of other students.

Characteristics associated with behavior disorders range from frequent excessive disruptive behavior, including physical aggression, verbal aggression, self-abusive behavior, and noncompliance to withdrawn or depressive-like behavior. Excessive or inappropriate emotional reactions such as anxiety, fear, and hostility are also characteristic of the severely behaviorally disordered adolescent. Current literature emphasizes that behaviorally disordered adolescents do not vary from the general population on the basis of the specific types of behaviors that they exhibit. Rather, differences exist in the strength of specific responses.

The fact that behaviorally disordered adolescents exhibit aggressive behaviors does not, in and of itself, distinguish them from their peers. It is the frequency, magnitude, or duration of the aggressive behaviors that set the adolescent apart from other students. For example, an adolescent that cries in class may not be considered to have an affect disorder unless crying occurs substantially more frequently than would be expected with the average student.

As with the other areas of exceptionality, there is little agreement in the professional literature on precisely how behavior disorders should be defined. Hewett and Forness (1974) have identified nine definitions that have appeared over the past 20 years. The authors emphasize the association of specific definitions with the theoretical orientation of the writer. Examples of each include:

Psychodynamic approach: impairment of emotional growth which results in distrust toward self and others and hostility generated from anxiety. (Moustakas, 1953, 1955)

Psycho-social and psycho-educational approach: socially defective children, children with neurotic conflict, and children with psychotic processes. (Morse, 1967)

Behavioral-educational approach: disorders that consist of inadequate or inappropriate behavior that is learned and can therefore be changed through the application of learning procedures. (Dupont, 1969, p. 59)

Kauffman (1981) has proposed an educational definition that has four features that are important to secondary educators: (1) it recognizes the social context in which behavior occurs; (2) it recognizes students' perceptions of their own behavior; (3) it emphasizes the role of education in altering deviant behavior; and (4) it emphasizes the use of educationally relevant criteria in identifying severity levels of behavior disorders. Kauffman's definition is as follows:

Children (and adolescents) with behavior disorders are those who chronically and markedly respond to their environment in socially unacceptable and/or personally unsatisfying ways but who can be taught more socially acceptable and personally gratifying behavior. Children (and adolescents) with mild and behavior disorders can be taught effectively with their normal peers (if their teachers receive appropriate consultative help) or in special resource or self-contained classes with reasonable hope of quick reintegration with their normal peers. Children (and adolescents) with severe and profound behavior disorders require intensive and prolonged intervention and must be taught at home or in special classes, special schools, or residential institutions. (p. 23)

Current classification schemes in the field of behavior disorders follow two major orientations. The first is an internal deviance or mental illness position; the second is an environmental adaptation or social competence approach. The internal deviance orientation views behavior disorders as being symptoms of a presumed underlying pathology. This position suggests that aberrant behaviors are the visible signs of hypothesized mental illness. To understand the overt behaviors, the therapist or educator must study and diagnose the underlying mental illness. Treatment then focuses on remediating the pathological condition that produces the aberrant behavior. From this point of reference, the overt behaviors are useful only in that they may facilitate the diagnosis of the illness.

Classification schemes that have evolved from this orientation, the most notable of which are the *Diagnostic and Statistical Manual of Mental Disorders* of the American Psychiatric Association (1952, 1968, 1979) and the Group for the

Advancement of Psychiatry (1966), have been criticized in recent literature. Quay (1972) and Werry (1972) have argued that the classification of an adolescent's behavior may vary over time as a function of environmental conditions, the evaluator, and/or the evaluation procedure. Phillips, Draguns, and Bartlett (1975) have reviewed literature that suggests that specific categories tell very little about the treatment or prognosis for an individual. Phillips et al. (1975) summarize current misgivings about medically oriented classification schemes in stating, "Some of these categories are based on a presumed psychodynamic etiology for a disorder; others reflect disapproval of a given behavior; others are listed in simple descriptive terms. Other problems with the present scheme concern the inadequate fit between an individual's behavior and the category to which he is assigned" (p. 30).

Empirical classification schemes, typified by the work of Quay (1972, 1975) have utilized complex statistics to identify problem behaviors that cluster together. Based on Quay and his colleagues' work three stable behavior classes have been identified. These include conduct problems, personality problems, and inadequacy or immaturity. Because of their reliance on observable and measurable behavior, these classifications are substantially more reliable than medically oriented classification schemes (Quay, 1972). As with previous classification schemes, however, they are limited in that psychological or educational treatments cannot be associated with specific behavior patterns. Therefore, they are primarily descriptive and serve only to facilitate professional communication and study in the absence of providing precise intervention tactics.

Assessment

Kauffman (1981) has proposed a three-step process for diagnosing behavior disorders. The first step is to screen the general school-aged population to identify individuals who are likely to exhibit behavior disorders. A number of approaches to screening have been suggested in the literature. The most pragmatic procedure is to solicit teachers' informal comments regarding the students' behavior (Nelson, 1971). A more formal approach may utilize formal rating scales as proposed by Long, Fagen, and Stevens (1971). Another widely used instrument for screening behaviorally disordered youths is the Bower-Lambert Scales for In-School Screening of Emotionally Handicapped Children (Bower & Lambert, 1962).

The Bower-Lambert Scales include three separate rating scales used jointly to evaluate each student. The first scale is a teacher rating scale. With this scale, the teacher evaluates the position of the student in relation to the general population on eight response items. The second scale is a peer rating in which three activities, assigned by grade, identify how the students are perceived by their peers. The final scale, a self-rating, utilizes three activities, also assigned by grade, to identify how the students' self-perceptions differ from their own expectations.

The second step proposed by Kauffman involves selecting students identified through the screening process who actually exhibit behavior disorders. The identification process varies widely from school district to school district. Most of these processes involve a diagnostic assessment conducted by school psychologists, social workers, counselors, psychiatrists, or other clinical personnel. Depending on the orientation of the clinician, assessment data may be generated through behavior rating scales, projective techniques, and/or norm-referenced personality inventories. The third step is intended to translate the preceding data into a diagnostic statement that establishes recommendations for psychological and educational intervention.

Prevalence

The prevalence estimates for students with behavior disorders range from .05 to 15 percent across the nation (Schultz, Hirshoren, Manton, & Henderson, 1971). USDHEW (1979) estimates that .56 percent of the school-aged population exhibits behavior disorders. Based on studies conducted in California, Bower (1969) indicates that 10 percent of the school-aged population requires special education services because of behavior disorders. The research literature suggests that the incidence of behavior disorders is higher among lower class populations (Graubard, 1973) and that boys are more likely than girls to be classified as exhibiting behavior disorders (Schultz, Salvia, & Feinn, 1974).

CONCLUSION

It is apparent from the preceding discussions and summary data presented in Table 2-2 that there is little agreement in the professional literature with regard to major issues in the definition, classification, assessment, and resulting prevalence estimates for each of the major handicapping conditions. The inability of professionals to concur on such crucial issues results from differing theoretical models that address a variety of presumed causes and behavioral dimensions. In addition, assessment techniques used to diagnose specific handicapping conditions have been criticized for their limited reliability and validity. Thus, professionals not only disagree on what to measure, but also on how to measure.

These criticisms are not intended to discourage the search for meaningful definition, classification, and diagnostic schemes. Rather, they should alert the reader to the dangers inherent in an overly zealous acceptance of current labels applied to individual handicapped students. It is expected that the serious reader will, based on information presented in this chapter, have a general understanding of the behavioral characteristics, diagnostic procedures, and prevalence of each of the major handicapping conditions. This information is expected to facilitate

Table 2-2 Summary Data on Handicapped Groups

Handicapping condition	Definition	Assessments	Prevalence
Auditory handicaps	The deaf are defined as those individuals whose hearing loss is so severe at birth or during the prelingual period that it precludes the normal acquisition of language comprehension and expression. The partially hearing are persons whose hearing loss, although significant in degree, was acquired either after the critical period of language acquisition, thus enabling the person to develop some communicative skills, or does not totally impair oral language development. (Connor et al., 1975, p. 242)	Pure-tone and speech audiometer Specialized auditory tests Physical examination	.5 to 3%
Visual handicaps	The visually impaired, partially sighted are those who can use their vision for reading when adaptations are made in the presentation of reading materials and the blind; Braille is a primary reading medium. (Bateman, 1967, p. 258)	Snellen chart Perimeter test Physical examination	.04 to .1%
Physical and health disorders	Individuals with functional limitations related to physical ability and medical conditions, such as strength and stamina. (Sirvis, 1978, p. 361)	Medical examination Educationally relevant assessment data to determine if the physical condition reduces adjustment in the educational setting	.36 to .5%
Speech and/or language impairment	Speech impairment is used in a generic service to refer to disorders of articulation. . . . Language impairments . . . refer to disorders in comprehending or verbally expressing the symbols and grammatical rules of language. (Bankson, 1978, p. 389)	Standardized picture tests (e.g., Templin-Darley Tests of Articulation, Goldman-Fristoe Test of Articulation)	.3 to .5%

Table 2-2 continued

Handicapping condition	Definition	Assessments	Prevalence
		Informal speech sampling procedures Intelligence tests Physical examination of the speech producing mechanisms	
Specific learning disability	A specific retardation or disorder in one or more of the processes of speech, language, perception, behavior, reading, spelling, writing, or arithmetic. (Kirk, 1972, p. 398)	Intelligence tests Academic achievement tests Informal performance measures Specialized tests of perceptual and cognitive abilities	.1 to 30%
Mental retardation	Mental retardation refers to significantly sub-average general intellectual functioning existing concurrently with deficits in adaptive behavior, and manifested during the developmental period. (Grossman, 1973, p. 5)	Intelligence tests Adaptive behavior scales Informal performance measures	.2 to 3%
Behavior disorders	Those who chronically and markedly respond to their environment in socially unacceptable and/or personally unsatisfying ways who can be taught more socially acceptable and personally gratifying behavior. (Kauffman, 1981, p. 23)	Informal observation Behavior rating scales (e.g., Bower-Lambert Scales) Projective techniques Personality inventories	05 to 15%

professional communication in working with handicapped students. However, the reader should also be aware that current definitions and diagnostic procedures used with handicapped students do not produce meaningful information with reference to individual students and their individual educational programs. The educator must go beyond gross classification schemes that attempt to identify differences among groups of adolescents.

In summary, this chapter has been a study of how groups of adolescents differ from one another. The following chapter will be a study of individual differences across specific performance dimensions. This chapter has been intended to: (1) provide the reader with a broad background in current issues and trends relating to the definitions of exceptional characteristics, and (2) provide information to the reader that may facilitate professional interactions regarding exceptional adolescents in general. The following chapter is intended to provide the reader with a tool for identifying differences within the individual that will facilitate functional and effective academic, social, personal, and vocational education.

REFERENCES

American Medical Association. Guides to the evaluation of permanent mental and physical impairments. *Journal of the American Medical Association,* 1958-1966.

American Psychiatric Association. *Diagnostic and statistical manual of mental disorders* (2nd ed., DSM-I). Washington, D.C.: Author, 1952.

American Psychiatric Association. *Diagnostic and statistical manual of mental disorders* (2nd ed., DSM-II). Washington, D.C.: Author, 1968.

American Psychiatric Association. *Diagnostic and statistical manual of mental disorders* (2nd ed., DSM-III). Washington, D.C.: Author, 1979.

Bankson, N. W. The speech and language impaired. In E. L. Meyer (Ed.), *Exceptional children and youth.* Denver: Love Publishing Co., 1978.

Bateman, B. D. Visually handicapped children. In N. G. Haring & R. L. Schiefelbusch (Eds.), *Methods in special education.* New York: McGraw-Hill, 1967.

Bower, E. M. *Early identification of emotionally handicapped children in school* (2nd ed.). Springfield, Ill.: Charles C Thomas, 1969.

Bower, E. M., & Lambert, N. M. *A process for in-school screening of children with emotional handicaps.* Princeton, N.J.: Educational Testing Service, 19 i2.

Clements, S. D. *Minimal brain dysfunction in children: Terminology and identification, phase one of a three-phase project* (NINDS Monograph No. 3, U.S. Public Health Service No. 1415). Washington, D.C.: U.S. Government Printing Office, 1966.

Committee on Nomenclature: Conference of Executives of American Schools for the Deaf, 1938. *American Annals of the Deaf, 83.*

Connor, F. P., Hoover, R., Horton, K., Sands, H., Sternfeld, L., & Wolinsky, G. F. Physical and sensory handicaps. In N. Hobbs (Ed.), *Issues in the classification of children* (Vol. 1). San Francisco: Jossey-Bass, 1975.

Cruickshank, W. M., & Paul, J. L. (Eds.). *Psychology of exceptional children and youth* (4th ed.). Englewood Cliffs, N.J.: Prentice-Hall, 1980.

Dunn, L. M. (Ed.). *Exceptional children in the schools: Special education in transition* (2nd ed.). New York: Holt, Rinehart & Winston, 1973.

Dupont, H. (Ed.). *Educating emotionally disturbed children.* New York: Holt, Rinehart & Winston, 1969.

Eisenson, J. Speech defects: Nature, causes, and psychological concomitants. In W. M. Cruickshank & J. L. Paul (Eds.), *Psychology of exceptional children and youth* (4th ed.). Englewood Cliffs, N.J.: Prentice-Hall, 1980.

Goldman, F., & Fristoe, M. *Test of articulation.* Circle Pines, Minn.: American Guidance Testing Service, 1969.

Graubard, P. S. Children with behavioral disabilities. In L. M. Dunn (Ed.), *Exceptional children in the schools: Special education in transition* (2nd ed.). New York: Holt, Rinehart & Winston, 1973.

Grossman, H. J. *Manual on terminology and classification in mental retardation.* Baltimore: Garamond/Pridemark, 1973.

Group for the Advancement of Psychiatry, Committee on Child Psychiatry. *Psychopathological disorders in childhood: Theoretical consideration and a proposed classification* (Vol. 6), Report No. 62, June 1966.

Hallahan, D. P., & Kauffman, J. M. *Introduction to learning disabilities: A psycho-behavioral approach.* Englewood Cliffs, N.J.: Prentice-Hall, 1976.

Hatfield, E. M. Why are they blind? *Sight-Saving Review,* 1975, *45,* 3-22.

Hewett, F. M., & Forness, S. R. *Education of exceptional learners.* Boston: Allyn & Bacon, 1974.

Illinois Commission on Children. *A comprehensive plan for hearing impaired children in Illinois.* Springfield, Ill.: The Commission, 1968.

Kauffman, J. M. *Characteristics of children's behavior disorders* (2nd ed.). Columbus, Ohio: Charles E. Merrill Publishing Co., 1981.

Kirk, S. A. *The Illinois Test of Psycholinguistic Abilities: Its origin and implications.* In J. Hellmuth (Ed.), *Learning disorders* (Vol. 3). Seattle, Wash.: Special Child Publications, 1968.

Kirk, S. A. *Educating exceptional children* (2nd ed.). Boston: Houghton Mifflin, 1972.

Knowles, L. Successful and unsuccessful rehabilitation of the legally blind. *The New Outlook for the Blind,* 1969, *63,* 129-169.

Long, N. J., Fagen, S., & Stevens, D. *Psychoeducational screening system for identifying resourceful, marginal and vulnerable pupils in the primary grades.* Washington, D.C.: Psychoeducational Resources, 1971.

Morse, W. C. The education of socially maladjusted and emotionally disturbed children. In W. M. Cruickshank & G. O. Johnson (Eds.), *Education of exceptional children and youth* (2nd ed.). Englewood Cliffs, N.J.: Prentice-Hall, 1967.

Moustakas, C. E. *Children in play therapy.* New York: McGraw-Hill, 1953.

Moustakas, C. E. The frequency and intensity of negative attitudes expressed in play therapy. *Journal of Genetic Psychology,* 1955, *86-87,* 309-325.

National Institute for Neurological Diseases and Stroke. *Monograph No. 10.* Bethesda, Md.: U.S. Department of Health, Education and Welfare, National Institutes of Health, 1969.

National Society for the Prevention of Blindness. *NSPB fact book: Estimated statistics on blindness and visual problems.* New York: Author, 1966.

Nelson, C. M. Techniques for screening conduct disturbed children. *Exceptional Children,* 1971, *37,* 501-507.

Perkins, W. H. *Speech pathology* (2nd ed.). St. Louis: C.V. Mosby, 1977.

Phillips, L., Draguns, J. G., & Bartlett, D. P. Classification of behavior disorders. In N. Hobbs (Ed.), *Issues in the classification of children* (Vol. 1). San Francisco: Jossey-Bass, 1975.

Quay, H. C. Patterns of aggression, withdrawal and immaturity. In H. C. Quay & J. S. Werry (Eds.), *Psychopathological disorders of childhood*. New York: John Wiley & Sons, 1972.

Quay, H. C. Classification in the treatment of delinquency and antisocial behavior. In N. Hobbs (Ed.), *Issues in the classification of children* (Vol. 1). San Francisco: Jossey-Bass, 1975.

Schultz, E. W., Hirshoren, A., Manton, A. B., & Henderson, R. A. Special education for the emotionally disturbed. *Exceptional Children,* 1971, *38,* 313-319.

Schultz, E. W., Salvia, J. A., & Feinn, J. Prevalence of behavioral symptoms in rural elementary school children. *Journal of Abnormal Child Psychology,* 1974, *2,* 17-24.

Sirvis, B. The physically disabled. In E. Meyer (Ed.), *Exceptional children and youth: An introduction*. Denver: Love Publishing Co., 1978.

Telford, C. W., & Sawrey, J. M. *The exceptional individual* (2nd ed.). Englewood Cliffs, N.J.: Prentice-Hall, 1972.

U.S. Department of Health, Education and Welfare. *Progress toward a free appropriate public education: A report to Congress on the implementation of Public Law 94-142: The Education of All Handicapped Children Act*. Washington, D.C.: U.S. Government Printing Office, 1979.

Wepman, J. M., Cruickshank, W. M., Deutsch, C. P., Morency, A., & Strother, C. R. Learning disabilities. In N. Hobbs (Ed.), *Issues in the classification of children* (Vol. 1). San Francisco: Jossey-Bass, 1975.

Werry, J. S. Childhood psychosis. In H. C. Quay & J. S. Werry (Eds.), *Psychopathological disorders of childhood*. New York: John Wiley & Sons, 1972.

Chapter 3

Functional Classification of Exceptional Characteristics

The preceding chapter identified and described the major groups of exceptional adolescents. As has been emphasized, it is important that the practitioner be aware of traditional classification approaches for a number of reasons. First, and most crucial, PL 94-142 addresses categories of exceptional children and adolescents in the allocation and evaluation of special services. The Department of Education, Office of Special Education, on a regular basis, collects data pertaining to the number of students served exhibiting a specific handicapping condition as well as the type of program in which special services are provided. Local educational agencies (LEAs) in many states are funded on the basis of the number of students receiving special services that result from classification within an area of exceptionality. Additionally, in many states, special educators are certified on the basis of a sequence of course work and experiences that qualifies them to teach students within a specific exceptional classification.

Second, a knowledge of the categories of exceptional individuals will enhance the practitioner's ability to benefit from the professional literature. Research to date has sought to identify the response capabilities, learning styles, behavioral repertoires, and environmental histories associated with specific handicapping conditions (Gajar, 1976). Researchers have attempted to evaluate the utility of specific intervention approaches and environments when applied to children and adolescents within a specific exceptional classification. Beyond research, many of the issues in special education address current practices with respect to specific exceptional groups. Of the introductory level textbooks available to teacher training in special education, the majority have an organizational format that is congruent with specific exceptional categories (e.g., Kirk, S.A., 1972; Lilly, 1979; Meyen, 1978; Suran & Rizzo, 1979).

Third, exceptional students are frequently placed in special programs on the basis of the categorical label identified in a multidisciplinary staffing. It is assumed that when self-contained or resource placement is appropriate, homogeneous grouping on the basis of exceptional characteristics facilitates instructional presentation and curriculum development. Secondary career-vocational educators must be sensitive to the behavioral characteristics and diagnostic procedures associated with each group so that they may contribute information that will facilitate the placement process. In general, it is important that educators be sensitive to current classification practices so they may communicate more effectively with other professionals about broad issues in the area of secondary career-vocational education for the handicapped. The practitioner's awareness of current issues and trends, research applications, and program placement issues in secondary career-vocational education for the handicapped adolescent has, as its foundation, the understanding of characteristics associated with specific exceptional labels.

INDIVIDUAL VS. GROUP DIFFERENCES

Having emphasized the importance to the practitioner of a knowledge of current classification schemes, this chapter proceeds beyond the study of groups of students and into the study of the individual. The traditional classification schemes have identified common characteristics from which groups of individuals can be identified. For example, mentally retarded adolescents, by definition, exhibit subaverage intellectual functioning and deficits in adaptive behavior. This information tells how the mentally retarded as a group are different from the general population, but it tells very little about the characteristics of the individual student who may be classified as being mentally retarded. (Does he or she belong to a large family? What are his or her vocational interests? Does the student have a successful employment history? Can the student deal with complex ideas or values and operate complex machinery?) Thus, this chapter highlights the study of the individual for the purpose of providing a truly individualized career-vocational education program.

The concept of individual differences among adolescents goes beyond programming for groups of students on the basis of an exceptional label. It implies an educational program tailored to the characteristics of the individual. While two individuals may be identified as being mentally retarded, career-vocational education programs for each may be substantially different. Exhibit 3-1 illustrates how two individuals, classified as being mentally retarded, may exhibit different learning and behavioral characteristics that result in varied educational programs. It can be observed that although both individuals fall within the group label "mentally retarded," individual differences within relevant variables dictate a career-vocational program that addresses unique characteristics of the individuals. Thus, the practitioner goes beyond the recognition of group differences and emphasizes the study of the individual characteristics that are pertinent to a specialized educational program.

Exhibit 3-1 Individual Characteristics

Name: John A.
Age: 17
Exceptional classification: Mentally retarded

Exceptional characteristics:
  (1) IQ of 65
  (2) deficit adaptive behavior
  (3) motivation to work on cars
  (4) reading at third-grade level
  (5) spelling at first-grade level
  (6) mathematics at second-grade level
  (7) deficit social skills
  (8) ability to follow verbal instructions well
  (9) enjoyment of some variation in job assignment each day
 (10) ability to learn a 10-step task in a short period of time

Educational recommendations:
  (1) Develop automotive vocabulary.
  (2) Teach routine skills for service station attendant.
  (3) Develop social skills related to employer-employee and customer-employee relations.
  (4) Emphasize the application of existing mathematics and reading skills to automotive tasks.

Name: Ralph E.
Age: 16
Exceptional classification: Mentally retarded

Exceptional characteristics:
  (1) IQ of 68
  (2) deficit adaptive behavior
  (3) motivation to work in food-related occupations
  (4) reading at first-grade level
  (5) spelling at first-grade level
  (6) mathematics at third-grade level
  (7) high social skills
  (8) ability to follow simple verbal instructions well
  (9) performs best under structured conditions with routine tasks
 (10) has difficulty in learning new tasks

Exhibit 3-1 continued

Educational recommendations:
  (1) Develop skills in using a cash register.
  (2) Develop order-taking and reporting skills.
  (3) Teach other routine food service-related skills.
  (4) Emphasize the application of existing social skills to
      employer-employee and customer-waiter relations.

INTRA-INDIVIDUAL DIFFERENCES

In addition to studying how the individual is different from other individuals across a number of relevant dimensions, the career-vocational educator is also concerned about comparing strengths and weaknesses within the individual. Intra-individual differences refer to the comparison of one or more of the individual's skills and abilities with other personal attributes. This leads to an understanding of discrepancies in performances within the individual. Subsequent program recommendations may be based on an understanding of the student's performance in one area that relates to his or her performance in other areas. For example, upon observing Ralph's characteristics, reported in Exhibit 3-1, it is apparent that there is a discrepancy between his performance in reading and in mathematics. Encouraging Ralph to pursue educational experiences in the food service area resulted in part from the practitioner's recognition of the moderate mathematics requirements and minimum reading requirements of food service-related occupations.

The recognition that an individual is strong in one area as opposed to another also provides data from which specific training experiences can be generated. Ralph, for example, has difficulty learning new tasks but follows simple verbal instructions well. His training program may involve teaching a variety of tasks common to food service through verbal instruction. Similarly, John would enjoy being a service station attendant but exhibits deficit social skills. His educational program would make use of his interest in automotive-related occupations and would develop social skills within that context. Thus, not only does the educational program recognize the skills necessary for John to pursue his interests, but it emphasizes his strengths (i.e., motivation in this area) to develop deficit skills (i.e., social skills).

DEFICIENCIES OF CURRENT EXCEPTIONAL LABELS

It has been emphasized in previous sections that categorical labels provide little information relevant to the development of an individualized career-vocational education program. In addition to this, critical issues have been raised about the psychological and sociological impact of exceptional labels on the learner. A recent study by Gollub and Sloan (1978) suggests that *exceptional labels are frequently assigned on the basis of socioeconomic status as opposed to school performance.* Rivers, Henderson, Jones, Lodner, and Williams (1975) have argued that exceptional labels are often applied to minority children as the result of inappropriate testing practices. The authors stress that inappropriate labeling has had an adverse influence on the social, economic, educational, political, emotional, and cognitive aspects of black youths' development.

Franks (1971) provides further data supporting the influence of race and social class on the exceptional label identified by school personnel. The author reported that in 11 Missouri school districts providing services for both mentally retarded and learning-disabled students, black students composed 34.21 percent of the students in mentally retarded classes, but only 3.22 percent of the students in learning disabilities classes. The data clearly indicated that race and/or socioeconomic status had a biasing effect on the exceptional label assigned to the learner.

Data reported by Schloss and Miller (1982) demonstrate that public school teachers have differing expectations for educational services of adolescents labeled "institutionalized" vs. those labeled "regular school students." Despite the fact that both populations were identified as exhibiting exactly the same behavioral and learning characteristics in the school environment, the educators identified a more restrictive and exclusionary educational placement for the student identified as having been institutionalized. This finding was reported to be consistent with the thesis of MacMillan, Jones, and Aloia (1974) that labels have a significant and potentially adverse influence on the expectations of teachers and that exceptional labels, regardless of how valid, may be a major factor in determining the type, level, and efficacy of special services.

Reynolds and Balow (1972) have suggested that *professionals attribute characteristics to an individual that are overgeneralized from an exceptional label.* The authors contend that these characteristics are often not reflected by an assessment of the individual. Overgeneralization from an exceptional label may set into place a "self-fulfilling prophecy" described and studied by Rosenthal (1966). Rosenthal and Jacobson (1968), though criticized for the methodological limitations of their study, have demonstrated that educators who expect low performance levels from students, based on an exceptional label, will often obtain low performance. On the other hand, teachers expecting superior performance will obtain high performance. Thus a student's exceptional label may encourage teachers to establish expectations that are contrary to best educational practices for the individual.

A related issue is that exceptional labels typically emphasize limitations of the individual without recognizing characteristics that may be within the norm for the general population. A review of definitions presented in the preceding chapter indicates the negative bias of our current classification schemes. Mental retardation is defined by deficits in intellectual functioning and adaptive behavior. Specific learning disabilities result from a specific retardation or disorder in one or more processes of speech, language, perception, reading, writing, or arithmetic, and behaviorally disordered individuals chronically respond to their environment in socially unacceptable ways. Of the definitions presented in Table 2-2, there is a distinct paucity of positive characteristics associated with any handicapped group. When positive characteristics are identified, they are generally viewed as symptoms of underlying pathology rather than as assets. This is typified by the recognition of splinter skills in the diagnosis of autism.

Another limitation of current categorical approaches is the misconception held by many professionals and the general public that exceptional characteristics are static and that once a child or adolescent is diagnosed as being handicapped, he or she will remain handicapped. This issue is exemplified by the concept of pseudomental retardation. This label was applied to individuals originally diagnosed as being learning-disabled who progressed to the degree that their intellectual functioning and/or adaptive behavior fell within the normal range. The assumption made by professionals is that learning disabilities cannot be remediated. Thus, individuals who perform beyond previously anticipated levels are assumed to be misdiagnosed (Bialer, 1966). Beyond definitional issues, Ysseldyke and Foster (1978) have demonstrated that professionals in the field are reluctant to reevaluate and alter an individual's exceptional label as his or her behavior changes. Additionally, the researchers have demonstrated that the exceptional label, independent of the student's behavior, biases teachers' expectancies.

Research conducted by Jones (1970, 1972) emphasizes that exceptional labels and class placement may have an adverse effect on the self-esteem of the adolescent. Two separate investigations demonstrated that the exceptional adolescents (1) avoided disclosing that they were enrolled in the special classes, (2) complained of being ridiculed and made to feel different as a result of their placement, and (3) felt that being enrolled in a special class limited their chances for later job placement. Rivers et al. (1975) suggest that exceptional labels are psychologically harmful in that "the lifelong labeling process militates against the individual's developing and sustaining a healthy conception of self" (p. 217).

CHARACTERISTICS OF A FUNCTIONAL CLASSIFICATION SCHEME

The deficiencies of current classification schemes have been highlighted in the writings of numerous authors. The effect of exceptional labels in removing students from positive learning environments (Bruininks & Rynders, 1971), the limited evidence that special class groupings facilitate performance for slower students (Bartel & Guskin, 1980; Dunn, 1973), the stigmatizing effect that special class placement may have on students (Bloom, Hasting, & Madaus, 1971), the impact of exceptional labels on teacher expectations (Schloss & Miller, 1982), and the limited information that exceptional labels provide with regard to treatment and/or prognosis (Bartel & Guskin, 1980) emphasize the need for alternative strategies to the diagnosis and classification of exceptional characteristics. This chapter presents an alternative for the secondary career-vocational educator.

Behaviors Rather Than Adolescents

The major difference between the proposed classification scheme and the classification approaches presented in the preceding chapters is the emphasis placed on the behavior characteristics of an individual youth as opposed to the procedure of assessing the student's behavior when compared with supposed peers. In effect the characteristic-specific system seeks to describe the strengths and weaknesses of the individual across relevant behavioral dimensions. In this fashion, gross comparisons between individuals on the basis of one or two measures (e.g., IQ and adaptive behavior) are avoided. Rather than establishing a stigmatizing label that isolates students from their peers, the present scheme identifies the students' strengths and weaknesses and provides direct implications for educational intervention.

Complexity of the Individual

Current labeling or classification practices in special education give the practitioner very little useful information about the individual's learning and behavioral characteristics. A major reason for this is that current classification schemes identify and label individuals on the basis of one or two deficit characteristics rather than the total behavioral repertoire. This position is supported in the writings of Telford and Sawrey (1972) who have noted that many exceptional individuals exhibit exceptionality in more than one area. Some students labeled as learning-disabled may exhibit problems associated with visual-perceptual deficits, behavior disorders, and speech impediments. Other more severely handicapped may exhibit sensory deficits, poor motor coordination, and no oral language skills.

The characteristic-specific classification system recognizes that in order for educators to develop an effective educational plan for a student they must be sensitive to both the skills and deficiencies of the individual across a broad range of response requirements. The exceptional individual cannot be programmed for on the basis of one or two relevant pieces of information. Rather, all of the relevant learning and behavioral dimensions must be identified and evaluated prior to developing the educational program.

Development of Positive Characteristics

Gardner (1977) has noted that "if the child does not learn academic skills at a rate or level expected, or if he does not behave emotionally or socially as expected, too frequently it is assumed categorically that the fault lies within the child" (p. 10). Kauppi (1969) recognizes the potential circularity of attributing behavior or learning deficits to presumed causes within the child. He argues that children's learning deficits are frequently attributed to mental retardation, not the educational system that failed to measure and meet their other needs.

Phillips, Draguns, and Bartlett (1975) have argued that current classification schemes employed in psychology and psychiatry are somewhat distant from the person's actual behavior in typical environmental situations. Further, these classification approaches provide little useful information. Similarly, classification schemes used in special education have little to do with actual classroom behavior and tell the teacher very little about the actual characteristics of the individual. The characteristic-specific system delineates educationally relevant characteristics for each adolescent. Rather than identifying the student as behaviorally disordered, the system produces a detailed description of characteristics that influence the student's adjustment in relevant settings. The identification of these characteristics provides a target for specific educational procedures.

The characteristic-specific classification system removes blame for deviant characteristics from the individual while highlighting specific target behaviors. In this way, the identification of specific exceptional characteristics is the foundation for an effective educational program. Factors unrelated to the direct instructional and management process are no longer considered operant. Thus, the circularity of attributing learning and behavior problems to mental retardation, behavioral disorders, learning disabilities, etc., that are subsequently defined by the presence of the same exceptional characteristics is avoided.

Empirical Foundation

Empiricism, or the reliance on objective and reliable data to generate educational decisions, is central to the rationale of the characteristic-specific classification system. The system requires the educator to identify specific exceptional behaviors that may influence the student's adjustment in educational, vocational, living, and recreational settings. The behaviors targeted are a function of directly observable events. Rather than identify a student as being learning-disabled with an auditory discrimination deficit, the educator would identify specific performance problems that could be reliably observed and measured. These behaviors then would become the focal point of the teacher's educational strategies. Because they are observable and measurable, the impact of the educational program can be evaluated by monitoring these behaviors.

Measurement procedures proposed for use with the classification system are the monitoring and evaluating of classified behaviors directly. Direct measurement avoids the presumption of covert processes or internal events. The educator-evaluator is not concerned with a theoretical underlying process that may or may not be valid, but with the overt behavior of the adolescent; that is, with the discrepancy between what the individual does prior to intervention and what is expected following intervention.

Validity of Learning Principles

A popular notion in special education research over the past two decades has been that various groups of individuals learn best through different teaching approaches. For example, mentally retarded adolescents achieve best in programs designed for the mentally retarded, and learning-disabled adolescents achieve best in programs for the learning-disabled. Similarly, auditory learners acquire information most effectively through auditory presentations, and visual learners benefit most from visual presentations. The aptitude treatment interaction (ATI) assumption, as it is referred to in the literature, has been highly criticized in recent publications (Gardner, 1977; Ysseldyke, 1973). The general consensus of the literature is that while future investigation of aptitude by treatment interactions in education may be fruitful, the clear association between curriculum treatments and psychological variables has yet to be demonstrated.

On the other hand, a common set of principles associated with applied behavior analysis or behavior modification has been validated with individuals exhibiting a diverse range of characteristics. The learning theory principles involve viewing behavior along various skill dimensions. Complex behaviors are considered to be comprised of component behaviors that are chained together. Educational programs involve directly teaching and chaining component skills until a terminal objective is met. In utilizing these principles, the teacher systematically arranges the learning environment to produce the desired behavior change. A more detailed discussion of how these principles may be used to teach new behaviors, strengthen existing behaviors, reduce excessive behaviors, and influence the persistence of behaviors will be provided in subsequent chapters.

Identification of Educational Goals

Just as traditional classification systems tell very little about the specific characteristics of the individual, they tell very little about expected outcomes of educational interventions. Knowing that an adolescent is behaviorally disordered tells the teachers very little about the goals or objectives they may establish for the individual. Goals relating to specific behaviors such as the reduction of aggressive outbursts, the increase of positive self-statements, the development of job-seeking skills, etc., are not easily identified from the diagnostic label. The speed at which goals may be achieved and settings in which the new behaviors will be exhibited are even less easily discerned.

The characteristic-specific classification system provides a direct link between classification and performance expectations following the educational intervention. Target behaviors identified in the system may result in more global goal statements. For example, the goal of developing more positive employer interaction skills may be established for an individual with specific behavioral deficits by encouraging the individual to make complimentary statements to others, use appropriate greetings, initiate conversations, etc.

Exceptional Characteristics Not Stable over Time

The general purpose of any educational intervention, regardless of the severity of the learner's handicap, is to improve the extent to which the adolescent adapts to current and future environments. Educational interventions, maturation, or changes in environmental demands often result in the increased adaptability of the individual across specific behavioral dimensions. A classification system must be sufficiently flexible to account for these changes (Cromwell, Blashfield, & Strauss, 1975). Traditional classification systems that require the diagnostician to determine that the adolescent either is or is not mentally retarded, learning-disabled, or behaviorally disordered are limiting in that they do not account for the educator's demonstrated ability to facilitate behavior change across functional skill areas. In addition, research has demonstrated that once individuals are placed in a traditional exceptional category, teachers are reluctant to change the exceptional label as their behavior changes (Ysseldyke & Foster, 1978).

Similarly, it has been argued repeatedly that characteristics that may be designated exceptional are as much a function of the environment and the observer as the identified individual (Bartel & Guskin, 1980; Kauffman, 1981). This view is exemplified in Rhodes' (1967) conceptualization of behavioral disorders. He states that, "The child judged to be the most disturbed is the one who uniformly arouses disturbed reactions in those around him. What is considered deviant, how it is designated, interpreted, and treated is viewed as much a function of the perceiver as the behavior" (p. 449). A functional classification system must account for the differing expectations of individuals in various environments. A student may have a behavioral disorder in the school setting as defined by the teacher, but may be a model worker on the job as viewed by the employer.

The characteristic-specific classification system accounts for these limitations by objectively evaluating specific behaviors in association with relevant environments. A student's profile within the classification system can be periodically evaluated and reevaluated to reflect change associated with the educational objectives and intervention approaches. In short, rather than saying that individuals are behaviorally disordered throughout their high school careers, specific exceptional behaviors are identified. As these behaviors are remediated, they cease to be identified as exceptional. An individual is not viewed as being behaviorally disordered across settings. Rather, specific behaviors he or she exhibits in specific settings are identified as being excessive (occurring too often) or deficit (occurring too seldom) in relation to the expectations of people in those settings.

Contemporary Maintaining Conditions

It is generally understood that a variety of causal agents may produce specific learning disabilities, mental retardation, behavioral disorders, etc. For example, the *Manual on Terminology and Classification in Mental Retardation* of the American Association on Mental Deficiency (Grossman, 1973) identifies infections and intoxications, trauma or physical agents, postnatal gross brain disease, unknown prenatal influence, chromosomal abnormality, gestational disorders, psychiatric disorders, and environmental influences as being potential etiological agents of mental retardation. Similarly, Kauffman (1981) has identified family biological and school factors that may be associated with the development of behavioral disorders. Although potential etiological agents have been enumerated for each exceptional category, recent literature estimates that 80 percent of all educable mentally retarded children have unknown etiologies, and etiological agents are less seldom identified for behaviorally disordered and learning-disabled youths (Hallahan & Kauffman, 1976).

The characteristic-specific classification system avoids assumptions of common etiology and treatment by emphasizing the reliable observation of current conditions that influence the specific target behaviors. It is acknowledged that historic events (e.g., parental neglect, brain injury, trauma, malnutrition) may have produced the adolescent's current behavioral characteristics. However, educational approaches that deal directly with the student's current characteristics and contemporary maintaining conditions offer the most promise for effective intervention and treatment. To emphasize, the characteristic-specific classification system is primarily concerned with the identification of specific exceptional behaviors, and explanations of these behaviors rely on the defining of the influence of contemporary events. For example, we may know that Robert is mentally retarded as the result of a chromosomal abnormality. We also know that we are unable to alter Robert's genetic structure. Thus, we seek to identify events in the current environment that will influence Robert's positive development. In short, knowing that Robert has a skill deficiency in small part assembly that may be remediated through systematic instruction, and that Robert is highly motivated by infrequent praise from a supervisor, is far more important than knowing that he is mentally retarded as a result of the translocation of the 21st chromosome.

THE CHARACTERISTIC-SPECIFIC CLASSIFICATION SYSTEM

As has been emphasized in previous sections, the characteristic-specific classification system facilitates the identification of exceptional characteristics within the individual rather than categorizing an individual as exceptional. The classification system provides for two general classes of behaviors within which are a number of behavior clusters. Additionally, an exemplary set of specific behaviors within each cluster is identified. The classification system branches from two broad classes—academic and social-personal—to more precise clusters including mathematics readiness, mathematical numeration, mathematical symbols, etc., within the academic class; and affective expression, positive social interaction, excessive disruptive interaction, attending skills, etc., within the social-personal class.

Academic and social-personal classes are established because skills within these areas are closely associated with adjustment in career-vocational settings. Basic academic skills are fundamental to job acquisition and performance in many areas including clerical, retail, food service, automobile maintenance, and social service professions. Equally important to performance in these areas are positive social-personal skills. Not only must clerks be able to compute change correctly for the customer, they must also be able to exhibit a pleasant demeanor. Thus, deficit characteristics within these general classes are of paramount concern to the career-vocational educator.

Behavioral clusters identified within the academic and social-personal classes provide a more precise description of intervention areas. Clusters identified in the classification system are somewhat arbitrary and by no means exhaustive. Similarly, specific behaviors identified within each cluster represent only a small sample of the range of behaviors that may compose the specific cluster. For this reason, open spaces follow each set of specific behaviors so that potential educational targets not identified may be included.

Along with the classification of specific behavioral excesses or deficits, the system encourages the identification of a number of variables that are associated with the performance or nonperformance of the specific behaviors. These performance factors add a greater understanding to the nature of the student's behavior. They also may suggest potentially effective educational strategies. The following section discusses each of the performance factors with respect to behaviors identified in the characteristic-specific classification system.

Performance Factors

Three major performance factors are addressed in the system: degree of the exceptional characteristic, nature of the performance factor, and contemporary events that influence the exceptional characteristic. These performance factors are a critical component of the system because information they provide is essential to developing and evaluating an effective career-vocational education program. Simply knowing that a student does not do mathematics assignments tells us about the student's current behavior, but very little about how to change the behavior, and therefore falls short of the criteria of a functional classification established earlier in this chapter.

Information provided through the performance factors indicates the degree of the discrepancy between what students do and what they are expected to do; the relationship between students' behavior and their skill, discrimination, and motivational characteristics; and, finally, events in the learning environment that influence the students' exceptional characteristics. These data, as will be explained in the following sections as well as in subsequent chapters, provide the foundation for understanding how the learners' characteristics interact with potential educational strategies.

Degree of Exceptional Characteristics

The degree of exceptional characteristics indicates the extent to which the adolescent's current behavior deviates from what is expected by others. This is accomplished through a three-step process. First, a reliable measure of the student's current performance is obtained. Procedures for obtaining these data are discussed in Chapters 6 and 7. They may include systematic observations, criterion-referenced tests, norm-referenced tests, or a measure of permanent product. Second, a decision is made regarding what is expected of the student. Ideally, this decision results from a multidisciplinary staff meeting in which all individuals concerned for the student's academic, vocational, and social-personal development contribute. Finally, the discrepancy between the student's current performance and the expected performance is computed. This discrepancy becomes one of the terminal objectives of the educational program.

Exceptional characteristics may be either excessive or deficit. An excessive characteristic occurs more often than expected, and a deficit characteristic occurs too seldom. Physical aggression, for example, may be considered excessive because it occurs more often than is viewed acceptable by significant people in the adolescent's environment. Homework completion, on the other hand, may be considered deficit because the rate of assignments completed is below the expectations of the teacher.

For example, it may be determined through the administration of a criterion-referenced test that an individual correctly multiplies three-digit numbers 60 percent of the time. Because the individual desires to be an appliance sales person and three-digit multiplication is an important skill on the job, the academic teacher, the vocational instructor, the student, and the parents agree that the student should correctly multiply three-digit numbers 100 percent of the time. Therefore, the resulting exceptional characteristic is a deficit of 40 percent of three-digit problems multiplied correctly.

In the social-personal class, a student may be observed to swear on the job from 4 to 20 times an hour. Since the student works as a waiter and excessive swearing may lead to dismissal, a multidisciplinary staffing may agree to an expected level of swearing of zero times an hour while on the job. Thus, the exceptional characteristic is an excess of 4 to 20 swear words uttered an hour while on the job.

Nature of the Performance Factors

The discrepancy between what adolescents do and what they are expected to do results from any or all of three deficits. These include *skill deficits, motivational deficits,* and *discrimination deficits*. The recognition of how these factors influence the student's current behavior is essential to developing an effective educational program. Performance problems that result primarily from skill deficiencies would be most strongly influenced by a skill training approach. Performance problems that result primarily from a motivational deficit would be most strongly influenced by a motivational approach. Finally, performance problems that result primarily from a discrimination deficit would be most responsive to procedures that teach the student specific conditions under which the behavior is expected to be performed.

Skill Deficits

The student does not have the prerequisite behavior in his or her repertoire. Skill deficits are assessed by observing whether or not the student has ever performed the desired behavior. If the student has not, it is reasonable to assume that he or she does not have the skill. For example, a student may fail to call in sick prior to being absent from work. The observer, recognizing that the student has never been observed to use the telephone, may indicate that he or she has a skill deficiency in this area. A similar evaluation strategy would provide strong incentives for using the telephone as desired. If the student fails to use the telephone, even though the motivational conditions are very strong, one would expect that the performance problem results from a skill deficiency.

Motivational Deficits

The student does not wish to perform the behavior, although the prerequisite skills are present in his or her repertoire. Motivational deficits are assessed by determining whether or not the student has ever been observed to perform the behavior. If he or she has, then one may assume that the skill is in the individual's repertoire but that the present motivational conditions are not sufficiently strong. If the student had, on occasion, called in sick, in the previous example, it would be clear that the student possessed the necessary skill, but that he or she was not motivated to call the employer. In the present example, the educator would develop a motivational strategy to increase the likelihood that the individual would call the employer, and in the previous example the educator would teach telephone usage skills.

Discrimination Deficits

The individual does not know under what conditions to exhibit the desired behavior, although the prerequisite skill is present. Discrimination deficits may be assessed by observing if the student consistently performs the desired behavior but under the incorrect stimulus conditions. For example, the student may repeatedly call the employer at all hours of the day. Thus he or she has the skill and would appear to be highly motivated. However, the student is not able to discriminate times at which calling the employer is considered acceptable from times that it is considered a nuisance. In this case, the educator may wish to teach and motivate the individual to telephone the employer only under specific conditions (e.g., prior to being absent from work).

Two points must be emphasized. First, *different exceptional characteristics may result from different performance factors.* For example, students may not do their mathematics homework because they would rather watch television (a motivational deficit), but they may not do their piece work on the job for which they are paid very well because they do not know how (a skill deficit). Second, *the performance factors may influence a specific behavior in isolation or in combination.* A student may behave aggressively toward a peer because it produces compliance from the peer and status from other peers (a motivational deficit). Additionally, a student may behave aggressively because he or she does not have the ability to gain compliance and status through positive social behaviors (a skill deficit). In this case, the educational approach would consider both the motivational factors and skill factors.

Influencing Events

Influencing events data further delineate conditions that may be associated with the exceptional characteristics. In effect the influencing events describe cue and motivational conditions that have been observed to increase or decrease the likelihood that the expected behavior will occur. The influencing events category is broken down into two sections: The first requires a description of antecedent events associated with the occurrence of the expected behavior; the second requires a description of consequent events associated with the occurrence of the target behavior.

Antecedent events are defined as conditions that precede the occurrence of the target behavior and influence (i.e., increase or decrease) the probability of its occurrence. For example, failure on an excessively difficult assignment may be observed to precede truancy and increase the likelihood that the student would be truant. Therefore, difficult assignments may be recorded as an antecedent that increases truancy. Consequent events are defined as conditions that follow a target behavior and influence (i.e., increase or decrease) the probability of its occurrence. For example, it may be observed that once a student is truant, the teacher withdraws the assignment with no unpleasant consequence to the student. As this occurs, the rate of truancy increases. Thus, the removal of the assignments following an absence may be a consequence that increases truancy.

Antecedents and consequences that are recorded may be associated with increasing the strength of deficit exceptional characteristics or decreasing the strength of excessive exceptional characteristics. In either case, identifying the conditions that cue and consequate exceptional behavior characteristics is an important part of understanding the learners and their environment. With this information, the teacher not only knows whether skill training, discrimination training, or motivational procedures are indicated, but also the events that occur in the career-vocational setting that currently influence the behavior.

CONCLUSION

In summary, traditional categorical labels have provided little information for developing an individualized career-vocational education program; have been subject to critical inquiry concerning the psychological and sociological impact of exceptional labels on the learner; and are limited by the misconception, held by professionals and the public, that exceptional characteristics are static.

The characteristic-specific classification system (Tables 3-1 to 3-7) serves four major functions. First, it facilitates the identification of specific behaviors that may be considered as being excessive or deficit. These behaviors become the target of the career/vocational education program. Second, it assists the multidisciplinary team in identifying terminal objectives or the expected level of the identified behavior following successful educational intervention. Third, it encourages the educator to consider the relative impact of skill, motivational, and discrimination factors on the identified behavior. Finally, it emphasizes the assessment of conditions in the environment that cue or consequate the identified behaviors. Each of these elements is critical to establishing an effective career-vocational program for the handicapped adolescent.

REFERENCES

Bartel, N. R., & Guskin, S. L. A handicap as a social phenomenon. In W. M. Cruickshank (Ed.), *Psychology of exceptional children and youth.* Englewood Cliffs, N.J.: Prentice-Hall, 1980, pp. 45-73.

Bialer, I. Conceptualization of success and failure in mentally retarded and normal children. *Journal of Personality,* 1966, *29,* 303-320.

Bloom, B. S., Hasting, J. T., & Madaus, G. F. *Handbook on formative and summative evaluation of student learning.* New York: McGraw-Hill, 1971.

Bruininks, R. H., & Rynders, J. E. Alternatives to special class placement for educable mentally retarded children. *Focus on Exceptional Children,* 1971, *3,* 1-12.

Cromwell, R. L., Blashfield, R. K., & Strauss, S. S. Criteria for classification systems. In N. Hobbs, *Issues in the classification of children* (Vol. 1). San Francisco: Jossey-Bass, 1975.

Dunn, L. M. (Ed.). *Exceptional children in the schools: Special education in transition* (2nd ed.). New York: Holt, Rinehart & Winston, 1973.

Franks, D. J. Ethnic and social status characteristics of children in EMR and LD classes. *Exceptional Children,* 1971, *37,* 537-538.

Gajar, A. Educable mentally retarded, learning disabled, emotionally disturbed: Similarities and differences. *Exceptional Children,* 1976, *6,* 470-472.

Gardner, W. I. *Learning and behavior characteristics of exceptional children and youth: A humanistic behavioral approach.* Boston: Allyn & Bacon, 1977.

Gollub, W. L., & Sloan, E. Teacher expectations, race, and socioeconomic status. *Urban Education,* April 1978, *13*(1), 95-106.

Grossman, H. J. *Manual on terminology and classification in mental retardation.* Baltimore: Garamond/Pridemark, 1973.

Hallahan, D. P., & Kauffman, J. M. *Introduction to learning disabilities: A psycho-behavioral approach.* Englewood Cliffs, N.J.: Prentice-Hall, 1976.

Jones, R. L. *New labels in old bags: Research on labeling blacks culturally disadvantaged, culturally deprived, and mentally retarded.* Paper presented at annual convention of Association of Black Psychologists, Miami Beach, September, 1970.

Jones, R. L. Labels and stigma in special education. *Exceptional Children,* 1972, *38,* 553-564.

Kauffman, J. M. *Characteristics of children's behavior disorders* (2nd ed.). Columbus, Ohio: Charles E. Merrill Publishing Co., 1981.

Kauppi, D. R. The emperor has no clothes: Comments on Christoplos and Renz. *Journal of Special Education,* 1969, *3,* 393-396.

Kirk, R. *Experimental design: Procedures for the behavioral sciences.* Monterey, Calif.: Brooks/Cole Publishing Co., 1968.

Kirk, S. A. *Educating exceptional children* (2nd ed.). Boston: Houghton Mifflin, 1972.

Lilly, S. M. (Ed.). *Children with exceptional needs.* New York: Holt, Rinehart & Winston, 1979.

MacMillan, D. L., Jones, R. L., & Aloia, G. F. The mentally retarded label: A theoretical analysis and review of research. *American Journal of Mental Deficiency,* 1974, *79,* 241-261.

Meyen, E. L. *Exceptional children and youth: An introduction.* Denver: Love Publishing Co., 1978.

Phillips, L., Draguns, J. G., & Bartlett, D. P. Classification of behavior disorders. In N. Hobbs (Ed.), *Issues in the classification of children* (Vol. 1). San Francisco: Jossey-Bass, 1975, pp. 26-55.

Reynolds, M. C., & Balow, B. Categories and variables in special education. *Exceptional Children,* 1972, *38,* 357-366.

Rhodes, W. C. The disturbing child: A problem of ecological management. *Exceptional Children,* 1967, *33,* 449-455.

Rivers, L. W., Henderson, D. M., Jones, R. L., Lodner, J. A., & Williams, R. L. Mosaic of labels for black children. In N. Hobbs (Ed.), *Issues in the classification of children* (Vol. 1). San Francisco: Jossey-Bass, 1975, pp. 213-245.

Rosenthal, R. *Experimenter effects in behavioral research.* New York: Appleton-Century-Crofts, 1966.

Rosenthal, R., & Jacobson, L. *Pygmalion in the classroom: Teacher expectation and pupils' intellectual development.* New York: Holt, Rinehart & Winston, 1968.

Schloss, P. J., & Miller, S. R. The effects of the label "institutionalized" vs. "regular school student" on teacher expectations. *Exceptional Children,* 1982, *48,* 263-264.

Suran, B. G., & Rizzo, V. R. *Special children: An integrative approach.* Glenview, Ill.: Scott, Foresman & Co., 1979.

Telford, C. W., & Sawrey, J. M. *The exceptional individual* (2nd ed). Englewood Cliffs, N.J.: Prentice-Hall, 1972.

Ysseldyke, J. E. Diagnostic-prescriptive teaching: The search for aptitude-treatment interaction. In L. Mann & D. A. Sabatino (Eds.), *The first review of special education.* Philadelphia: Journal of Special Education Press, 1973, pp. 5-33.

Ysseldyke, J. E., & Foster, G. G. Bias in teacher observations of emotionally disabled children. *Exceptional Children,* 1978, *45,* 18-26.

The Characteristic-Specific Classification System (Tables 3-1 to 3-7) is found on pages 74 to 111 and describes exemplary behaviors for the following classes and clusters.

Table 3-1 Characteristic-Specific Classification System—Mathematics*

CLASS: ACADEMIC
CLUSTER: MATHEMATICS

This includes academic behaviors such as numeration (readiness, numerals, place value), basic facts (addition, subtraction, multiplication, division), computational skills (addition, subtraction, multiplication, division), geometry and symbols, word problems, fractions, time, money, measurement, missing elements, numerical reasoning, decimals, percentage, and calculator skills.

---

*Appreciation is expressed to Fred Barns, Billie Buell, Steve Bundren, Lenora Harris, Debbie Hill, Sherry Knight, Linda Larsen, Dan Ramsey, Mary Reed, Ann Sabatino, Sharon Smaldino, Maureen Smith, Jim Stunson, and Steve Tancora for contributing descriptors to the classification system found in Tables 3-1—3-7.

Table 3-2 Characteristic-Specific Classification System—Reading
CLASS: ACADEMIC
CLUSTER: READING
This includes academic behaviors such as readiness, sight vocabulary, phonics, structural analysis, writing skills, comprehension, interpretative, critical, and literal reading, and reference skills.

Table 3-3 Characteristic-Specific Classification System—Survival Skills Cluster
CLASS: ACADEMIC
CLUSTER: SURVIVAL SKILLS

Table 3-4 Characteristic-Specific Classification System—Attending Skills
CLASS: SOCIAL/PERSONAL
CLUSTER: ATTENDING SKILLS
These include appropriate classroom skills (staying on task, attention span), persistence, and concentration. Those skills may be skills prerequisite to effective learning in academic, social, or vocational settings. Readiness or willingness to engage in a learning activity is also included in attending skills.

Table 3-5 Characteristic-Specific Classification System—Self-Control
CLASS: SOCIAL/PERSONAL
CLUSTER: SELF-CONTROL
This includes the individual ability to exhibit positive social behaviors in the absence of apparent external contingencies.

Table 3-6 Characteristic-Specific Classification System—Disruptive Behavior
CLASS: SOCIAL/PERSONAL
CLUSTER: DISRUPTIVE INTERPERSONAL BEHAVIOR
This includes behaviors such as aggression, defiance, negativism, and other behaviors involving direct social interaction of a disruptive nature.

Table 3-7 Characteristic-Specific Classification System—Self-Help/ Self-Care
CLASS: SOCIAL/PERSONAL
CLUSTER: SELF-HELP/SELF-CARE
This includes grooming and personal hygiene in the classroom. These behaviors are important to adult adjustment.

Table 3-1 Characteristic-Specific Classification System—Mathematics

PERFORMANCE FACTORS

Class: Academic
Cluster: Mathematics—Readiness

Exemplary behaviors	Degree		Nature			Influencing events	
	Current level	Expected level	Skill deficit	Motivation deficit	Discrimina- tion deficit	Antecedents	Consequences
1. Identify comparisons of height and length.							
2. Identify comparisons of weight and texture.							
3. Identify and calculate numerical representation of set membership.							
4. Identify the relationship between two equal sets and their one-to-one correspondence.							
5. Identify the relationship between equivalent sets.							
6. Identify the relationship between nonequivalent sets and their "more than," "fewer than" comparisons.							
7. Compare and construct graphs comparing sets.							
8. Identify the relationship when a set increases or decreases by one or more items.							
9. Identify relationships of pairs of opposite terms: off/on, up/down, big/little, left/right, small/large, many/few, under/over, more/less, above/below, tall/short, after/before, and in/out.							
10. Differentiate likenesses and differences in sequenced patterns arranged accordingly.							
11. Identify specific objects given an oral description relating to the object.							
12. Construct duplicate pattern arrangements of one to five objects when given patterns and manipulatives.							

13. Construct duplicate pattern arrangements given manipulatives, a pattern, and the first object of a series.

14. Identify and verbally differentiate different geometric shapes.

15. Identify and construct pictorial representations of shapes —oral directions.

16. Identify through oral directions comparisons between three different objects: long-longer-longest, big-bigger-biggest, short-shorter-shortest, large-larger-largest, and small-smaller-smallest.

Class: Academic
Cluster: Mathematics—Numeration

1. Mark numerals as directed to match the quantities given picture set cues, 1 to 10 objects.

2. Say the number name for pictured sets of 1 to 10 objects.

3. Circle the sets of zero.

4. Match the quantities of 0 to 99 objects and 0 to 99 numerals with pictured sets.

5. Count by 1s, 2s, 3s, 5s, and 10s.

6. Circle numerals 1 to 10.

7. Mark the set associated with the numeral.

8. Say the number names 0 to 10.

9. Put numeral cards in natural order (0-10, 1-100).

10. Write the numerals 0-5, 0-10, 1-50, and 1-100.

Table 3-1 continued

PERFORMANCE FACTORS

Class: Academic
Cluster: Mathematics—Numeration

Exemplary behaviors	Degree		Nature			Influencing events	
	Current level	Expected level	Skill deficit	Motivation deficit	Discrimina-tion deficit	Antecedents	Consequences
11. Write the verbally presented words 0-5, 0-10, 1-50, and 1-100.							
12. Write the numeral that comes before, after, or between the numeral or numeral pair.							
13. Write the numeral that is one more/less than the specified numeral.							
14. Write the numeral that is 10 more than the specified numeral.							
15. Write the numeral that is 100 more than the specified numeral.							
16. Write the numeral that is 1,000 more than the specified numeral.							
17. Write the whole number as directed, written as a word (1 to 999).							
18. Discriminate odd from even numbers.							
19. Mark objects according to their ordinal position 1-10.							
20. Match/write the ordinal name for a given series.							
21. Write the numeral given the number of tens and number of ones.							
22. Identify the place value of each digit of a two-digit numeral —nine digits.							

23. Write numerals given the number of hundreds, tens, and ones.

24. Write numerals given the number of thousands, hundreds, tens, and ones.

25. Write numerals given the number of ones, tens, hundreds, thousands, ten-thousands, and hundred-thousands.

26. State the place value as directed for one nine-digit numerals.

27. Round numerals off to the nearest tenth, hundredth, and thousandth.

Class: Academic
Cluster: Mathematics—Geometry and Symbols

1. Given multiple geometric shapes, identify a circle.

2. Observing a completed design, properly identify two specific parts needed to construct an identical disc figure.

3. Observing a completed design, properly identify three specific parts needed to construct an identical star figure.

4. Comparing a variety of geometric shapes, properly identify the square.

5. Comparing a variety of geometric shapes, properly identify the tallest.

6. Comparing a variety of geometric shapes, properly identify the triangle.

7. Observing a completed design, identify four parts needed to be joined with another to make an identical disc figure.

Table 3-1 continued

PERFORMANCE FACTORS

Class: Academic
Cluster: Mathematics—Geometry and Symbols

Exemplary behaviors	Degree		Nature			Influencing events	
	Current level	Expected level	Skill deficit	Motivation deficit	Discrimination deficit	Antecedents	Consequences
8. From a number sentence presented visually (+), (−), (=), (×), obtain differentiation of symbols related to mathematical functions.							
9. From a presented monetary expression, identify dollar sign.							
10. Identify from a variety of line abbreviations, the one related to foot (feet).							
11. Identify percent sign in a given percent expression.							
12. Identify from a variety of abbreviations for time periods, the abbreviation for hour.							
13. Identify from two abbreviations for weight, the abbreviation for pound.							
14. Identify from the symbols for feet and inches, the symbol for feet.							
15. Identify from a geometric representation of three lines, the parallel relationship between two of them.							
16. Identify from two lines joined at a 90° angle, their perpendicular relationship.							

Class: Academic
Cluster: Mathematics — Addition

1. Match equal/nonequal sets.

2. Identify sets by numeral (union).

3. Write the plus sign for the union of two sets.

4. Mark the sum and the addend as directed.

5. Demonstrate with manipulatives the addition of two sets.

6. Compute basic addition facts 0 + 0 through 9 + 9.

7. Write the sum of two one-digit problems.

8. Write the sum of three one-digit problems.

9. Write the sum of a one-digit and a two-digit number.

10. Write the sum of three two-digit numbers with regrouping required.

11. Write the sum of three numbers with up to four digits requiring regrouping.

12. Write the sum of whole numbers as teacher-directed that demonstrate place value notation.

13. Write the sum of whole numbers in horizontal position.

14. Compute the sum for word problems with the addition of whole numbers.

Table 3-1 continued

PERFORMANCE FACTORS

Class: Academic
Cluster: Mathematics—Subtraction

Exemplary behaviors	Degree		Nature			Influencing events	
	Current level	Expected level	Skill deficit	Motivation deficit	Discrimination deficit	Antecedents	Consequences
1. Remove manipulatives as teacher-directed to demonstrate subtraction of sets.							
2. Identify sets by numeral.							
3. Write the minus sign for the subtraction of two sets.							
4. Compute basic subtraction facts 0 – 0, 9 – 9.							
5. Compute the difference of a one-digit from a two-digit number without borrowing.							
6. Compute the difference of a one-digit from a two-digit number requiring borrowing.							
7. Write the difference of two to four-digit numbers from two to four digits not requiring borrowing.							
8. Write the difference of stated whole numbers and check by inverse operation.							
9. Write the difference of two-digit numbers from two-digit numbers requiring borrowing.							
10. Write the difference of three-digit numbers from three-digit numbers requiring borrowing.							
11. Write the difference of three-digit numbers from two-digit numbers requiring borrowing.							
12. Write the difference of whole numbers in horizontal position.							

13. Write the difference of whole numbers in vertical position.

14. Compute the difference of whole numbers given a word problem.

Class: Academic
Cluster: Mathematics — Multiplication

1. Identify multiplication as an operation of two numbers that yield a third number.

2. Construct repeated addition problems.

3. Differentiate repeated addition problems and multiplication problems.

4. Write the multiples of 2-10.

5. Write the "$\times$" symbol to complete a multiplication sentence.

6. Write the basic multiplication facts (0×0) through (9×9).

7. Solve multiplication problems with 0, 1, 10, 100, and 1,000 as multipliers.

8. Solve multiplication problems with single-digit multipliers.

9. Solve multiplication problems with two-digit multipliers.

10. Solve multiplication problems with three-digit multipliers.

11. Solve multiplication problems with single-digit multipliers requiring carrying.

12. Solve multiplication problems with two-digit multipliers requiring carrying.

13. Solve multiplication problems with three-digit multipliers requiring carrying.

Table 3-1 continued

PERFORMANCE FACTORS

Exemplary behaviors	Degree		Nature			Influencing events	
	Current level	Expected level	Skill deficit	Motivation deficit	Discrimination deficit	Antecedents	Consequences

Class: Academic
Cluster: Mathematics—Multiplication

14. Solve multiplication problems with single/three-digit multipliers with a remainder.
15. Solve word problems requiring multiplication.
16. Solve multiplication problems with multiple-digit numbers by multiple multipliers.

Class: Academic
Cluster: Mathematics—Division

1. Identify division as an operation of two numbers that yield a third number.
2. Construct repeated subtraction problems.
3. Differentiate repeated subtraction problems and division problems.
4. Write the "division" symbol to complete a division problem.
5. Solve division problems with one and zero as a divisor.
6. Identify division words as teacher-instructed.
7. Compute basic division facts of $0 \div 1$ through $81 \div 9$.

8. Solve division problems with a one-digit divisor, no remainder.

9. Solve division problems with a two/four-digit divisor, no remainder.

10. Construct the checking of division by using multiplication.

11. Solve division problems with a one-digit divisor, zero in quotient.

12. Solve division problems with a two/four-digit divisor, zero in quotient.

13. Solve division problems by dividing whole numbers by 10, 100, and 1,000.

14. Solve division problems with a one-digit divisor, with a remainder.

15. Solve division problems with two/four-digit divisor, zero in quotient.

16. Solve division word problems.

17. Solve division word problems with "average" and "mean."

Class: Academic
Cluster: Mathematics—Introduction to Fractions

1. Identify fractional parts from pictorial representation.

2. Identify a fraction as a representation of one or more equal parts of a whole unit.

3. Identify a fraction as a representation of one or more equal parts of a set (subset).

Table 3-1 continued

PERFORMANCE FACTORS

Class: Academic
Cluster: Mathematics—Introduction to Fractions

Exemplary behaviors	Degree — Current level	Degree — Expected level	Nature — Skill deficit	Nature — Motivation deficit	Nature — Discrimination deficit	Influencing events — Antecedents	Influencing events — Consequences
4. Compare ratio situations of whole numbers and fractions, i.e., 3 out of 4 children have books, 3/4 of the children have books.							
5. Identify the fractional bar to express quotients of numbers $2 \div 4 = 2/4$.							
6. Identify prime factors.							
7. Write the greatest common factor.							
8. Write the least common multiple (LCM).							
9. Construct the union of a set of factors.							
10. Construct the intersection of a set of factors.							
11. Identify the numerator as "how many."							
12. Identify the denominator as "the size of the fractional part or name."							
13. Compare $\dfrac{\text{numerator}}{\text{denominator}} = \dfrac{\text{dividend}}{\text{divisor}}$							
14. Construct equivalent fractions.							
15. Differentiate proper and improper fractions.							
16. Simplify an improper fraction.							
17. Write an improper fraction given a mixed number.							

18. Write a mixed number given an improper fraction.

19. Reduce a fraction to lowest terms.

20. Identify fractional-related vocabulary (numerator, denominator, proper, improper, mixed number, reduce, simplify, prime, lowest common denominator, lowest common multiple, greatest common factor).

Class: Academic
Cluster: Mathematics — Addition of Fractions

1. Add fraction with like denominators, given a common denominator (1/5 + 2/5 = 3/5).

2. Identify the common denominator as the product of each denominator.

3. Identify the lowest common denominator (LCD).

4. Add fractions with like denominators, with missing addend (1/5 + ?/5 = 3/5).

5. Add fractions with like denominators, equal to one.

6. Add mixed numbers to mixed numbers, like denominators, no carrying.

7. Add mixed numbers to mixed numbers, like denominators, requiring conversion to a whole number.

8. Add fractions with like denominators, requiring reducing.

9. Add mixed numbers to mixed numbers, requiring reducing.

10. Add mixed numbers to fractions that require carrying.

Table 3-1 continued

Class: Academic
Cluster: Mathematics — Addition of Fractions

PERFORMANCE FACTORS

Exemplary behaviors	Degree — Current level	Degree — Expected level	Nature — Skill deficit	Nature — Motivation deficit	Nature — Discrimination deficit	Influencing events — Antecedents	Influencing events — Consequences
11. Add mixed numbers to fractions that require carrying and reducing.							
12. Identify lowest common denominator given two unlike fractions.							
13. Write the lowest common denominator given two unlike fractions.							
14. Add unlike fractions given the lowest common denominator.							
15. Add unlike fractions with unlike denominators/numerators.							
16. Add mixed numbers and fractions with unlike denominators.							
17. Add mixed numbers to mixed numbers with unlike denominators.							
18. Add mixed numbers to mixed numbers with unlike denominators, requiring carrying.							
19. Add mixed numbers to mixed numbers with unlike denominators, requiring reducing.							
20. Add mixed numbers to mixed numbers with unlike denominators, requiring carrying and reducing.							
21. Solve word problems that require addition of fractions.							
22. Identify vocabulary used for addition of fractions (like, unlike, denominator, common denominator, reduce, LCD).							

Class: Academic
Cluster: Mathematics—Subtraction of Fractions

1. Subtract fractions with like denominators, given a common denominator 2/5 − 1/5 = ?/5.

2. Subtract fractions with like denominators with missing addend 2/5 − ?/5 = 1/5.

3. Subtract proper fractions with like/unlike denominators.

4. Subtract one minus a proper fraction.

5. Subtract whole number minus fraction, regrouping required.

6. Subtract mixed number minus whole number, regrouping required.

7. Subtract mixed number minus mixed number, no regrouping required.

8. Subtract mixed number minus mixed number, regrouping required.

9. Subtract mixed number minus mixed number, like denominators.

10. Subtract mixed number minus mixed number, unlike denominators.

11. Subtract mixed numbers minus mixed numbers, unlike denominators, regrouping required.

12. Subtract mixed numbers, fraction, unlike denominators, regrouping required.

13. Subtract mixed numbers minus mixed numbers, unlike denominators, conversion to whole numbers.

Table 3-1 continued

PERFORMANCE FACTORS

Class: Academic
Cluster: Mathematics—Subtraction of Fractions

Exemplary behaviors	Degree		Nature			Influencing events	
	Current level	Expected level	Skill deficit	Motivation deficit	Discrimination deficit	Antecedents	Consequences
14. Subtract mixed numbers minus fraction, unlike denominators, regrouping required.							
15. Subtract mixed numbers minus mixed numbers, unlike denominators, regrouping required.							
16. Solve word problems that require subtraction of fractions.							
17. Identify vocabulary used for subtraction of fractions (like, unlike, denominator, reduce, mixed fraction, regrouping, borrowing, carrying).							

Class: Academic
Cluster: Mathematics—Multiplication of Fractions

1. Multiply proper fraction, numerator of one.
2. Multiply proper fractions by proper fractions, no reducing.
3. Multiply proper fractions by proper fractions, reducing required.
4. Multiply proper fractions by a whole number, no reducing.
5. Multiply proper fractions by a whole number, reducing required.

6. Identify multiplication of two fractions as division of numerator and denominator.

7. Identify cancellation as a renaming of the product of two fractions.

8. Multiply mixed numbers by fractions, no reducing required.

9. Multiply mixed numbers by fractions, reducing required.

10. Multiply mixed numbers by mixed numbers, reducing required.

11. Multiply mixed numbers by whole numbers, no reducing required.

12. Multiply mixed numbers by whole numbers, reducing required.

13. Solve multiplication of fractions problems demonstrating "one way" cancellation.

14. Solve multiplication of fractions problems demonstrating "two way" cancellation.

15. Solve word problems that require multiplication of fractions.

16. Identify vocabulary words used for multiplication of fractions (like, unlike, reduce, cancellation).

Class: Academic
Cluster: Mathematics — Division of Fractions

1. Divide proper fractions by proper fractions.

2. Divide proper fractions with common denominators.

3. Divide whole numbers by fractions.

Table 3-1 continued

Class: Academic
Cluster: Mathematics—Division of Fractions

PERFORMANCE FACTORS

Exemplary behaviors	Degree		Nature			Influencing events	
	Current level	Expected level	Skill deficit	Motivation deficit	Discrimination deficit	Antecedents	Consequences
4. Divide fractions by fractions.							
5. Identify division of fractions as multiplication by a reciprocal.							
6. Identify multiplicative inverse.							
7. Divide fractions by a whole number.							
8. Divide mixed numbers by a fraction.							
9. Divide a fraction by a mixed number.							
10. Divide mixed numbers by mixed numbers.							
11. Divide fractions using multiplicative inverse, cancellation, multiplication, and reduce.							
12. Solve word problems that require division of fractions.							
13. Identify vocabulary words used for division of fractions (common denominator, invert, reciprocal, multiplicative inverse, multiply, cancellation, reduce).							

Class: Academic
Cluster: Mathematics—Measurement

1. Identify various lengths—inch, foot, and yard.

2. Discriminate various lengths.

3. Use a ruler to measure objects less than 12 inches in length.

4. Use a ruler to measure an object to the nearest half-inch.

5. Use a yardstick to measure objects that exceed 12 inches in length.

6. Convert information given in inches to other forms of measuring units.

7. Recognize a pound as the standard unit of weight.

8. Weigh objects on a scale.

9. Measure own body weight.

10. Identify liquid measurement units—pint, quart, gallon—and how they relate.

11. Convert amount in the measurings units—pints, quarts, gallons—to another unit.

12. Identify a dozen objects.

13. Identify temperatures with the use of a thermometer.

Table 3-1 continued

PERFORMANCE FACTORS

Class: Academic
Cluster: Mathematics—Money

Exemplary behaviors	Degree		Nature			Influencing events	
	Current level	Expected level	Skill deficit	Motivation deficit	Discrimination deficit	Antecedents	Consequences
1. Recognize coins — pennies, nickels, dimes — and their value.							
2. Demonstrate addition of nickels, dimes, and pennies up to sums of $.50, then up to $1.00.							
3. Construct amounts of $.25 using the established coins— penny, dime, and nickel.							
4. Recognize a quarter and its value.							
5. Recognize equivalent money values for a value.							
6. Identify the half-dollar and its value.							
7. Find equivalent money values for half-dollar for each denomination group.							
8. Recognize a dollar bill and its value.							
9. Find equivalent money values for a dollar for each denomination group.							
10. Construct money values for half-dollar and dollar using a mixture of coins.							
11. Identify a five-dollar bill and its value.							
12. Make correct change up to a quarter.							
13. Make correct change up to a dollar.							
14. Write the correct numerical form of cash amounts using dollar sign, decimal point, and cents values.							
15. Relate cents value to the ability to purchase.							

Class: Academic
Cluster: Mathematics—Time

1. Associate time words with their daily schedule (day, night, morning, noon, afternoon, and evening).

2. Recognize the clock and its associated function.

3. Identify how a clock is used to tell time.

4. Compare the relationships between time units (second, minute, hour, and day).

5. Identify correct time to the half-hour.

6. Identify correct time to the quarter-hour.

7. Tell time to five-minute intervals.

8. Tell time correctly to the minute.

9. Tell time correctly to the second.

10. Differentiate between A.M. time and P.M. time.

11. Record time given a set clock as a manipulative.

12. Solve arithmetic problems involving time.

13. Identify the calendar as an instrument for recording time measurement.

14. Differentiate relationships among calendar units as measurements of time (days, weeks, months, and a year).

15. Write correctly each day of the week in order, starting with Sunday.

Table 3-1 continued

PERFORMANCE FACTORS

Class: Academic
Cluster: Mathematics—Time

Exemplary behaviors	Degree		Nature			Influencing events	
	Current level	Expected level	Skill deficit	Motivation deficit	Discrimination deficit	Antecedents	Consequences
16. Write correctly each month of the year in order, starting with January.							
17. Write correctly any random date in month, day, year order.							
18. Solve time-stated word problems.							

Table 3-2 Characteristic-Specific Classification System—Reading

Class: Academic
Cluster: Reading — Readiness

1. Recognize colors and shapes.
2. Recognize colors relating to a visual cue.
3. Recognize colors on verbal cue.
4. Discriminate a predetermined color from more than one (matching).
5. Recognize shapes with visual and verbal cues.
6. Discriminate mixed colors and shapes achieving one-to-one correspondence.
7. Attend to verbal and auditory information.
8. Discriminate environmental sounds (familiar ones).
9. Identify letters of the alphabet in the lower case.
10. Identify letters of the alphabet in the upper case.
11. Write letters of the alphabet (lower and upper case).
12. Identify words that rhyme.
13. Recognize and say words from a teacher-generated list.
14. Recognize words that begin with the same initial consonant.
15. Listen for the final consonant in a word.
16. Identify sight word vocabulary.

Table 3-2 continued

PERFORMANCE FACTORS

Class: Academic
Cluster: Reading—Phonic Analysis

Exemplary behaviors	Current level	Expected level	Skill deficit	Motivation deficit	Discrimination deficit	Antecedents	Consequences
	Degree		**Nature**			**Influencing events**	
1. Identify initial consonants.							
2. Identify medial consonants.							
3. Identify ending consonants.							
4. Identify two sounds of C and G (C/K/S and G/J).							
5. Identify initial consonant blends.							
6. Identify initial consonant diagraphs.							
7. Identify ending consonant blends.							
8. Identify ending consonant diagraphs.							
9. Identify silent consonants.							
10. Identify variant sounds.							
11. Identify vowels (a, e, i, o, u).							
12. Identify short vowels.							
13. Identify long vowels.							
14. Identify Y as a vowel.							
15. Identify vowel diagraphs—irregular.							
16. Identify vowel diagraphs—regular.							
17. Identify R controlled vowels.							
18. Identify vowel diphthongs.							
19. Identify vowel schwa.							
20. Identify vowel patterns (v, c, c, v, etc.).							

Class: Academic
Cluster: Reading—Structural Analysis

1. Fit words to context.
2. Identify multiple meanings.
3. Identify figurative language.
4. Identify words from definitions.
5. Identify context clues.
6. Identify antonyms.
7. Identify synonyms.
8. Identify definitions.
9. Identify prefixes.
10. Identify root words.
11. Identify suffixes.
12. Identify compound words.
13. Identify homonyms.
14. Identify word origins.
15. Identify similes.
16. State word connotations.
17. Identify derivatives.
18. Identify visual and auditory similarities.
19. Identify contractions.
20. State differences between abstract and concrete words.
21. Identify personification.

Table 3-2 continued

PERFORMANCE FACTORS

Exemplary behaviors	Degree		Nature			Influencing events	
	Current level	Expected level	Skill deficit	Motivation deficit	Discrimination deficit	Antecedents	Consequences

Class: Academic
Cluster: Reading—Structural Analysis

22. Identify prepositions.
23. Identify action words.
24. Identify words that describe.
25. Identify poems.
26. Describe scrambled words.
27. Identify syllabication.

Class: Academic
Cluster: Reading — References

1. Use the dictionary.
2. Use the encyclopedia.
3. Use textbooks as references.
4. Identify appropriate reference books.
5. Use the maps in an atlas.
6. Use textbook table of contents.
7. Use textbook index.
8. Use textbook glossary.

9. Use an atlas.

10. Use a map legend.

11. Use bar graphs.

12. Use card catalog.

13. Use the almanac.

14. Use dictionary for the main idea.

15. Identify part of speech in the dictionary.

16. Identify map scales (atlas).

17. Identify latitude and longitude.

18. Identify circle graphs.

19. Identify pictographs.

20. Identify line graphs.

21. Identify tables.

22. Identify time lines.

23. Identify footnotes.

24. Find book in a library.

25. Use map coordinates.

26. Use reference room.

27. Use book of synonyms.

28. Identify bibliography entries (footnotes).

29. Use Dewey Decimal System.

30. Use thesaurus.

Table 3-3 Characteristic-Specific Classification System—Survival Skills Cluster

Class: Academic
Cluster: Survival Skills

PERFORMANCE FACTORS

Exemplary behaviors	Degree		Nature			Influencing events	
	Current level	Expected level	Skill deficit	Motivation deficit	Discrimination deficit	Antecedents	Consequences
1. Follow time schedules.							
2. Answer help wanted ads.							
3. Fill out a job application form.							
4. Buy from a newspaper ad.							
5. Complete application for a learner's permit.							
6. Follow directions on labels.							
7. Read road signs.							
8. Read a passbook.							
9. Apply for credit.							
10. Buy by mail.							
11. Apply for a driver's license.							
12. Apply for a Social Security number.							
13. Read directions of food labels.							
14. Open a savings account.							
15. Deposit money into a savings account.							
16. Withdraw money from a savings account.							
17. Interview for a job.							
18. File an income tax form.							

19. Demonstrate use of telephone directory.
20. Demonstrate use of bus schedule.
21. Read a sales slip.
22. Price by the unit.
23. Identify the net pay.
24. Identify the gross pay.
25. Read a check.
26. Deposit money into checking.
27. Withdraw money from checking.
28. Write a check.
29. Plan a budget.
30. Buy on sale.
31. Read survival skills vocabulary.
32. Read high-frequency sight words.

Identify high-frequency sight words (i.e., newspaper)

1. the, boy, is, happy, one, girl, was, sad, you, and, I, run, they, will, be, closed

2. did, she, run, fast, my, dog, runs, slow, it, went, down, fast, can, we, go, out

3. his, has, one, left, look, what, they, do, I, am, not, little, we, were, under, them, they, go, right, over

Table 3-3 continued

PERFORMANCE FACTORS

Class: Academic
Cluster: Survival Skills

Exemplary behaviors	Degree		Nature			Influencing events	
	Current level	Expected level	Skill deficit	Motivation deficit	Discrimination deficit	Antecedents	Consequences
4. many, can, get, in, our, TV, is, on, her, car, is, big, but, where, is, hers							
5. would, you, like, one, I, have, one, empty, when, can, you, go, big, or, little, okay, who, could, like, it							
6. few, have, left, full, one, is, for, her, why, is, it, out, which, one, said, no, it, is, for, her							
7. one, is, with, him, his, is, by, her, one, is, to, them, one, of, his, left							

Table 3-4 Characteristic-Specific Classification System—Attending Skills

Class: Social/Personal
Cluster: Attending Skills

1. Raise hand to gain teacher's attention.			
2. Use "please" and "thank you" when making requests of others.			
3. Ask for help when confronted with difficult task (not give up).			
4. Ask permission to leave a certain area of the room or room itself.			
5. Finish assignments before asking for privileges.			
6. Keep track of books and lessons.			
7. Keep own area neat.			
8. Greet visitor appropriately.			
9. Assist teacher when asked.			
10. Participate in classroom activities.			
11. Work cooperatively with other students on projects.			
12. Increase attention span.			
13. Use free time constructively.			
14. Use good posture when sitting at desk.			
15. Follow rules for emergencies.			
16. Be courteous toward other people when entering the classroom.			
17. Ask peers for help.			
18. Encourage other peers to join in (table games, projects, etc.).			

Table 3-4 continued

PERFORMANCE FACTORS

Class: Social/Personal
Cluster: Attending Skills

Exemplary behaviors	Degree		Nature			Influencing events	
	Current level	Expected level	Skill deficit	Motivation deficit	Discrimination deficit	Antecedents	Consequences
19. Share materials with peers.							
20. Volunteer answers to questions.							
21. Be attentive during movies.							
22. Be attentive to guest speakers.							
23. Listen to directions.							
24. Use proper tone of voice.							
25. Read aloud in small groups.							
26. Follow rules of the classroom when teacher is absent.							

Table 3-5 Characteristic-Specific Classification System—Self-Control

Class: Social/Personal
Cluster: Self-Control

1. Become angry infrequently.

2. Do not always demand own way.

3. Cope with peer teasing.

4. Talk out a negative situation.

5. Ask permission before leaving an area.

6. Wait for acknowledgement from teacher before speaking out.

7. Ask for help before giving up.

8. Ignore interruptions from others.

9. Accept punishment without becoming upset.

10. Stay seated.

11. Remain pleasant after failure.

12. Does not tease others.

13. Apologize when wrong.

14. Avoid doing something wrong when encouraged by a peer.

Table 3-5 continued

PERFORMANCE FACTORS

Class: Social/Personal
Cluster: Self-Control

Exemplary behaviors	Degree		Nature			Influencing events	
	Current level	Expected level	Skill deficit	Motivation deficit	Discrimina-tion deficit	Antecedents	Consequences
15. Accept different ideas.							
16. React positively to authority figures.							
17. Adapt to changes in routine.							
18. Participate appropriately in larger groups.							

Table 3-6 Characteristic-Specific Classification System—Disruptive Behavior

Class: Social/Personal
Cluster: Disruptive Interpersonal Behavior

1. Hitting peers.	
2. Hitting staff.	
3. Throwing objects.	
4. Hitting objects.	
5. Running from the classroom or designated area.	
6. Cursing.	
7. Teasing to the point that it makes someone mad.	
8. Yelling.	
9. Threatening peers.	
10. Threatening authority figures.	
11. Stealing from others.	
12. Failing to comply with authority requests.	

Table 3-6 continued

Class: Social/Personal
Cluster: Social Interactions/Behavior Directed Toward Others

PERFORMANCE FACTORS

Exemplary behaviors	Degree		Nature			Influencing events	
	Current level	Expected level	Skill deficit	Motivation deficit	Discrimination deficit	Antecedents	Consequences
1. Respond to questions.							
2. Participate in group activities.							
3. Report emergencies as directed.							
4. Display appropriate manners (social amenities) saying:							
A. "Good morning."							
B. "Hello, how are you today?"							
C. "Thank you."							
D. "Would you mind if I...?"							
E. "Goodbye."							
F. "See you later."							
5. Use friendly manners including:							
A. opening doors							
B. giving right-of-way to others in hall, sidewalks, etc.							
C. assisting those with physical incapabilities							

6. Respond to affection.

7. Discuss strong/weak characteristics.

8. State consequences of certain behaviors (teasing, cursing, compliments, etc.).

9. Respond to introductions by shaking hands.

10. Introduce oneself to another.

11. Introduce two people.

12. Gain attention in appropriate ways.

13. Initiate a conversation.

14. Work cooperatively on a task.

15. Talk before a small group.

16. Display appropriate gestures:

   A. smiling

   B. nodding agreement

   C. expressing curiosity

   D. expressing displeasure

Table 3-7 Characteristic-Specific Classification System—Self-Help/Self-Care

Class: Social/Personal
Cluster: Self-help/Self-Care

PERFORMANCE FACTORS

Exemplary behaviors	Degree		Nature			Influencing events	
	Current level	Expected level	Skill deficit	Motivation deficit	Discrimina-tion deficit	Antecedents	Consequences
1. Select clothes appropriate to leisure activities.							
2. Select clothes appropriate to work activities.							
3. Select clothes appropriate to social activities.							
4. Select clothes appropriate to climate.							
5. Dress properly.							
6. Maintain appropriate dress.							
7. Launder clothes as appropriate.							
8. Iron clothes as appropriate.							
9. Fold or hang clothes as appropriate.							
10. Dry clean clothes as appropriate.							
11. Wash hands and face.							
12. Take regular baths or showers.							
13. Maintain cleanliness through the day.							
14. Wash hair.							
15. Brush or comb hair.							
16. Dry hair.							
17. Use cosmetics and personal care products appropriately.							
18. Use deodorant as needed.							

19. Brush teeth.
20. Clean fingernails.
21. Trim fingernails and toenails as needed.
22. Maintain feminine hygiene.

Chapter 4

Career Counseling and Exploration

Traditionally, the career counseling and exploration process has been handled by the school counselor. Unfortunately, weekly (at best) visits to the guidance counselor have done little to impact the dropout rate and employability record of the handicapped youth. This deficiency may be accounted for by several realities. First, the school counselors have been trained primarily to serve nonhandicapped students, and most of their time is consumed by the college-bound youth. Thus, their training and role responsibilities tend to preclude appropriate and effective career counseling with the handicapped youth. Second, limitations in abstract thinking, memory, and language diminish the ability of the handicapped youth to benefit from infrequent verbal interactions carried out in isolated settings.

It is apparent that an alternative approach to career counseling and exploration must be developed for the handicapped youth. To reflect accurately the youth's learning and behavioral characteristics, the approach must: (1) be as concrete as possible, (2) occur in the natural environment, (3) be responsive to immediate personal needs, (4) be flexible and ongoing, and (5) involve the youth in frequent opportunities to express and clarify career choices to significant people.

The career counseling and exploration model proposed in this chapter is designed to address these needs. This is accomplished by the career-vocational educator assuming the role of teacher-counselor. In doing so, the teacher becomes able to guide the youth through the career exploration and decision-making process in response to daily events. Further, the teacher-counselor is in a position to arrange subsequent experiences that encourage the youth to challenge and clarify these decisions. Table 4-1 contrasts the traditional guidance approach with the present model.

Table 4-1 Career Counseling Model

	Event	Process	Outcome
		Traditional Approach	
	Student observes an assembly line worker during an entire work shift	The counselor and youth discuss the experience and explore how the youth might make it part of next semester's program.	The youth leaves the office to reflect on the discussion. Follow-up may occur with the youth's program, and the youth's interests may be conveyed to the instructional staff.
		Teacher-Counselor Approach	
Level I	Student observes an assembly line worker during an entire work shift.	Teacher-counselor, either in a group or during one-on-one, helps the youth assess the merits of the experience and career option.	Youth formulates one or more statements regarding goals, interests, and abilities.
Level II	Youth explores alternative career choices by watching a movie on cabinetry making.	Teacher-counselor encourages the youth to identify cabinetry-making work tasks that are of interest.	Youth contrasts cabinetry making with assembly line work, and further clarifies career direction.
Level III	Youth indicates a desire to have some skills in a more clearly defined career pattern.	Teacher-counselor discusses with youth how this can be integrated into the existing program and the type of experiences that should be planned for the next semester.	Mathematics, reading, social skills, and other appropriate areas are integrated immediately into the youth's program.

This approach can continue until the youth has reached an exit level and is employed in a full-time position in the community.

CAREER PLANNING

Brolin (1974) suggested that the process of assisting youths to identify a career interest is an important first step in effective training. The integrated nature of career education, involving academic preparation, social learning, and vocational preparation, requires a comprehensive counseling and exploration process. Miller (1978) noted that the procedures used to establish a student's career goals will significantly influence a youth's concept of self-identity, educational program, and long-range personal and professional goals.

The emphasis on form and function in the assessment and planning process of career education awareness, exploration, and preparation is an outgrowth of two separate phenomena. The first phenomenon involves preadolescent assessment and planning processes in which the student is both excluded and not consulted in the development of the educational program. The assumption is that the preadolescent student is neither cognitively nor socially competent to participate in the process. As was discussed in the first chapter, the preadolescent model has been generalized and used with handicapped youths as part of the educational system. Unfortunately, it has failed to respond to the challenge of providing handicapped youths with educational opportunities in keeping with their learning interests and potential.

The second phenomenon addresses the competencies and readiness of handicapped youths to participate in the decision-making process in which the handicapped youth assists in relating the school program to career planning, goal setting, and program outcome. Inhelder and Piaget (1958) and Erikson (1969) all indicated that, cognitively and socially, the adolescent has demonstrated sufficient awareness to understand the effects of educational preparation and the consequences associated with inappropriate and appropriate learning experiences. This position is supported by Samler (1958-59); Glanz (1962); and Kroll, Dinklage, Lee, Morley, and Wilson (1970).

The fact that handicapped adolescents have reached the level of awareness and understanding necessary to participate in the development and implementation of their own educational program has been acknowledged in several court decisions and in state and federal statutes. The statutes, rules, and regulations governing the administration of these statutes indicate that when appropriate, handicapped youths shall participate in the development of their own Individual Educational Program (IEP). While acknowledging the appropriateness of the student's participation in the IEP process, the various federal, state, and local government laws and rules and regulations have not sought to delineate the process through which the handicapped adolescent will participate in the program development phase.

The literature has supported three distinct approaches to involve handicapped youth in the planning process. The approaches include the Group Process (Glanz, 1962; Kemp, 1970; Kroll et al., 1970), Nondirective Guidance (Lyon, 1971;

Rogers, C.R., 1961), and Directive Guidance (Mann, 1972; Perls, Hefferline, & Goodman, 1977). Each of the strategies has the potential to promote handicapped students' awareness, communication, trust, exploration, personal growth, cognitive and social development, and self-dependence when used in conjunction with daily experiences. The following is a discussion of these three approaches.

GROUP PROCESS

Bandura (1969) noted that the social group is a very prominent influence on individuals in our society. Kemp (1970) defines a social group as a collection of individuals having similar interests, needs, and/or goals. For career exploration purposes, the social group is defined as peers, employers, and professionals working together to establish vocational skills and interests with handicapped individuals who interact in a manner that promotes change among the individuals in the group and change within the group itself. Thus, the members of a social group respond individually to other individual members of the group and to the group at-large. Without such interaction, the individuals would be a collection of persons with similar interest needs and/or goals, but they would not constitute a social group. Among the purposes of a social group are (1) to provide a structured learning environment to achieve a task, and (2) to promote social change among the participants (Rabichow, 1980).

The specific purpose of the social group process for handicapped youths is personal and career growth. The handicapped youth has observable and measurable growth lags in such areas as academic achievement, sensory-motor skills, social awareness, interpersonal relations, self-motivation and direction, and career goal-setting (Miller, 1978). A climate in which productive interaction and exchanges occur among handicapped students and school personnel must be established. The exchanges may address issues of school program appropriateness, school frustration, parent neglect or over-concern, personal apprehension, societal ills, and/or job opportunities and personal values. Those issues cited are not totally inclusive, and such issues as drugs, sex, and racial and ethnic differences could be appropriate issues for exploration and resolution.

The literature has addressed a number of variables that influence the effectiveness of the group process. These will be considered separately.

Structure

Individuals, whether functioning independently or in a group, require structure. The structure can result from a variety of factors including mutual rules developed by a group, rules established by a leader, the environment in which the individual or group is functioning, and/or the mutual values possessed by individuals or the group. The size of the group may vary from 2 students to as many as 18, but an optimum number is between 8 and 10 persons.

Teacher-Counselor's Role

Gibb (1960) indicated that students tend to perform best in a group, designed to promote growth, when the activities are supported by a professional trained in group process. The educator can assume this role by fulfilling the following responsibilities:

1. assist handicapped students to define the purpose of the group
2. provide handicapped students with support and guidance in developing rules for conducting the business of the group
3. recommend themes for discussion and exploration
4. assist the group to select and define career themes
5. ensure that once a career theme has been established, the group does not wander from the topic of discussion in an unproductive manner
6. enable all the participants, when appropriate, to express their independent points of view
7. assist the group, when appropriate, to synthesize the points of view discussed in the group and the consequence of various types of behaviors resulting from these points of view.

The teacher-counselor is not expected to assume an authority-oriented role in the group process in any of the above areas. The teacher-counselor's responsibility is to encourage the students to explore issues of concern to them. This strategy is expected to result in growth through group definition and exploration (Bandura, 1969; Inhelder & Piaget, 1958).

The period of adolescence is when personal, social, and community rules are questioned, evaluated, and altered by the student. The questioning, evaluating, and altering processes generally occur during the student's interaction with the peer group. The same groups tend to assert the greatest social and personal influence on the handicapped student's behavior. Glanz (1962) observed that the adult leader, whether a teacher, counselor, or administrator, is often initially uncomfortable with the new nonauthoritarian role.

The uneasiness of the adult leader may be the result of several factors, including the fact that it is the students who establish the group's agenda. This is an unfamiliar phenomenon for the adult, who is accustomed to determining the issues students will explore and ultimate conclusions they will reach. The adult teacher-counselors may also feel under attack since some of the issues directly challenge their previous modus operandi and compel them to reassess their social techniques and overall leadership demeanor. These concerns can be surmounted through participation in other group activities in which the teacher-counselor does not assume a leadership role.

Planning

Participants may be annoyed by a group process in which they are told they are incorrect or do not understand the issues. Glanz (1962) noted that hostility often precludes learning among leaders and participants of a group. One factor critical to the success of the group process is planning. Planning includes determining the number of participants, the generic group rules, and the career issues that will be the focus of the process. Such planning may seem a contradiction to earlier statements that handicapped youths should be responsible for establishing the group's agenda and procedural rules. Group leaders frequently discover group planning and group management processes established by the participants are ambiguous and leave handicapped students uncomfortable. This ambiguity gives the teacher-counselor the opportunity to recommend and guide the structure of the group's activities.

Process

Davis (1970) observed that reasons for group failures are numerous, but basically fall into three separate areas: (1) authority, (2) power, and (3) decision development and implementation. Problems in any of these three areas may contribute to group failure when adults and students do not consider these areas in the collective process.

A common phenomenon negatively affecting group efforts is the teacher-counselor granting authority, power, and decision development and implementation privileges to handicapped students and then withdrawing the covenant when stressful situations arise. Such unilateral decisions seriously disrupt any basis of trust and cooperation, and deny handicapped students the experience of failure or success of career decisions reached within the reestablished guidelines of the group.

Mann (1972) noted that the failure associated with human endeavor is closely linked with poor planning and poor group efforts. Poor planning breeds a lack of congruity, trust, resolution, and experimentation. When the guidelines are well established and the validity of the process is tested, individual student and group growth frequently occurs. As part of the organizational effort, the following factors should be considered:

1. Time: Both the day chosen and the time of day can affect the efficacy of the group. School personnel have found that holding a group activity just prior to a recess, lunch break, or the conclusion of the school day provides the youth with an escape valve following the group effort. Frustrations can then be

expressed in athletic or verbal channels. To ask handicapped youth to deal with frightening and/or contradictory issues and then move into an equally demanding English, mathematics, or science course may prompt disruptive classroom behavior.

2. Personnel: The persons chosen as teacher-counselors must be individuals who believe in the group process and who have confidence in their own interpersonal and leadership skills to facilitate career development. Persons uncertain of their own leadership skills and who are distrustful of the group process may overtly and/or covertly impair the group effort.

3. Integration: Career goals and needs must combine with the school curriculum and social structure. The handicapped student needs to recognize the continuity of education, career-vocational training, and job opportunities.

4. Characteristics-Assessment: The interests, needs, goals, and background of the group must be understood by the teacher-counselor to function effectively with the group and to guide the group into productive areas of career inquiry and discussion.

5. Test Records: The teacher-counselor, and, when appropriate, the handicapped student, should be aware of such test data as academic achievement and aptitude performance. The information will enable handicapped students and teacher-counselors to determine individual student needs, interests, and goals, and to relate these variables to career development.

6. Outside Involvement: When both the teacher-counselor and the handicapped students agree that an outside person or group should be temporarily included in group deliberations, and the ground rules for including outsiders are established, then others may be included. However, the outsiders must respond to the group's needs and must not be allowed to transgress the guidelines.

7. Duration: The length of time the group will operate should be established at the beginning. The group should not be allowed to outlive its usefulness. Establishment and maintenance of these timelines help focus group efforts on the goals and objectives of the group.

8. Group Range and Diversity: The number of handicapped students and their academic and career interests and goals are among the variables that must be considered in developing a group: Another factor is whether the group will represent both sexes or whether the group will be more productive when limited to either all young men or women (Schuerger, 1977).

L.A. Rogers (1965) indicated that with some variability participants pass through a number of phases during the group process. These include:

- a release of inhibitions about personal needs and interests and sharing with other participants

- an exploration of one's own attitudes and the attitudes of other individuals in the group

- an increasing familiarity with acknowledgment of denied needs and interests and with frustrations

- an altered view of one's environment and establishment of new reference points for further discussion and exploration

- an altered view of one's self and those one is associated with, both within and outside the group

- the development of revised behavior and responses to existing and emerging ecological, social, and economic realities

- an increase in amicable, social, and interpersonal relations, combined with increased career direction, clarity, and training needs.

Input

L.A. Rogers (1965), Glanz (1962), and Mann (1972) cited the following variables that must be considered in conducting a group: (1) the level of compatibility among group members, (2) the level of acceptance individuals and the group have for career differences among members, (3) the willingness and ability of members to listen to and monitor the behavior of others, (4) the type and level of problem-solving skills the group and individuals develop, and (5) the ability of the group and individuals to evaluate the direction and efficacy of the group.

The above procedures address the group process and are intended to promote increased self-directive behavior among handicapped youths with learning and behavioral deficits. The entry to adolescence promotes interest and concern about one's personal, social, and career options. Frequently, the handicapped youths' experiences with adults have tended to be negative. For example, teachers who continually insist that the youths learn something they have repeatedly failed; principals who discipline the handicapped youths for inappropriate behavior; and school nurses or social workers who contact the handicapped youths' families to report problems in school.

As a result, the level of trust between many handicapped youths and adults is low. Conversely, handicapped students tend to invest a much higher level of trust in the peer groups. As Bandura (1969) noted, peer group pressure exerts a great deal of influence on youths. The group process attempts to harness the influence of the peer group within a structured milieu to produce an increased flow of information and exchange of ideas between group members and to influence positively general and specific behaviors of individuals within the group.

SPECIFIC GUIDANCE PROCESS

The literature is filled with discussions on specific strategies and tactics of working with individuals and groups. The two most frequently discussed procedures are the "Nondirective" and the "Directive" guidance approaches (Osipow, 1980; Shertzer, 1980). The majority of the basic principles described under the "Group Process" section also apply to the "Nondirective" and "Directive" approaches. Yet, specific tactics may vary between the two. The selection of the tactics is an outgrowth of the teacher-counselor's temperament, the environment in which the process is being conducted, the needs of the handicapped students, and the goals of the group or individual being served. A description of nondirective and directive guidance procedures is presented in the following sections.

NONDIRECTIVE GUIDANCE

The basic assumption for working with youths and adults, according to L.A. Rogers' (1965) nondirective guidance procedure, is that human beings have the capacity to strive for health and relevancy. C.R. Rogers (1961) and Ellis (1973) both note that it is often difficult for professionals to demonstrate confidence in human worth and the national pursuit of health and relevancy. L.A. Rogers (1965) notes that many persons say they believe in human worth and are open to new and varied values, but must continually inquire whether they believe in the capacity of the individual to make appropriate decisions and whether they believe in their ability to be accepting of an individual's value systems. Since the basis of the nondirective guidance approach is that the teacher-counselor and handicapped student become empathetic partners in exploring personal and career options and in establishing training priorities, the teacher-counselor must believe in the handicapped youth's capacity for self-awareness and personal growth. To select the nondirective approach, school personnel must continually question whether they are actually carrying out such an approach. As in the group process, the teacher-counselor has a tendency to advise about, rather than explore, human problems and their varied solutions. C.R. Rogers (1961) notes that counselors must continually question and evaluate their own behavior to prevent their adopting already well-established values and techniques of guiding the student. In the following sections, a description of the structure role of the counselor and student input in the nondirective guidance approach will be fully explored.

Structure

C.R. Rogers (1961) and Ellis (1973) note that a counselor must also be consistent about procedures while maintaining faith in the individual's pursuit of self-awareness and personal growth. Failure to maintain such consistency will impair the interaction of teacher-counselor and handicapped student and thus impair the student's pursuit of self-interests, needs, and development.

The potential for the counselor to stray from the expressed guidance values and procedures, given school and community pressures, is great. Schools generally have established procedures for dealing with handicapped youths and directing them into specific educational program patterns. These patterns frequently reflect the values and standards of the school personnel and the community. Peer and community pressure can also affect the level of openness between the counselor and student.

Thus, the process of personal evaluation must be continuous. The teacher-counselors must continually ask themselves such questions as: Am I doing what I think I am doing? Am I operationally carrying it out?

Whenever possible, the setting in which the counselor interacts with handicapped students should be consistent. If the environment is to be changed, the handicapped student should be given advance notification. The structure of the guidance session needs to be clearly delineated by the teacher-counselor and handicapped student(s) so that the purpose of the interaction is clear to all individuals. Additionally, the interaction should stay within the parameters of a specified theme or focus.

The teacher-counselor's role is to clarify career issues, restate themes or issues, and only when necessary synthesize ideas and goals of the handicapped youth. This role is described more specifically in the following section.

Teacher-Counselor's Role

The role of the teacher-counselor consists of active involvement with the handicapped student, while taking a nonactive role in the actual formation of student values, judgments, and decisions. L.A. Rogers (1965) suggests that a counselor should not be a passive participant, lest the client believe that the counselor is not interested. Thus, the teacher-counselor must be aware of and demonstrate empathy for the handicapped student's career problems, interests, and needs, and guide the youth in the decision-making process. This process must be maintained as the handicapped student moves from lesser to *more inclusive perceptual awareness fields*. Judgment of previous and existing awareness levels is to be shunned since the judgments are frequently self-projections of the counselor. The ultimate goal of the teacher-counselor and the handicapped student is to enable students to learn to alter their behavior through self-guidance. Fiedler (1950) found those counselors employing this methodology were able to establish a closer relationship with the individual receiving counseling. Additionally, Fiedler (1950) found the counselor was able to establish more rapport while at the same time maintaining emotional objectivity. The handicapped students, in this process, should believe that they are responsible for their own behavior and career choices. This concept of responsibility should not be encouraged at the beginning. Often the handicapped student's behavioral denials of specific perceptual fields and awareness are the result of responsibility rejection. Only as the student moves forward toward clarification of values and increasing his or her perceptual field should the process of responsibility assumption be encouraged. During nondirective guidance, students should have the opportunity to: (1) explore attitudes, (2) uncover denied attitudes, (3) reorganize self, (4) experience and become aware of self-progress, (5) become aware that closure is occurring in determining career goals, and (6) recognize that they are ready for initial training in a career area.

Many individuals who participate in either an individual or group process designed to facilitate increased self-awareness and objective evaluation are unprepared to deal with issues such as poor school performance, lack of friends and financial resources, uncertainty about career goals and job availability, curiosity concerning their own sexuality, and anxiety that develops with the approach of a school holiday. In addition, students are frequently concerned with such issues as earning power, establishment of a family, home structure, self-doubt, and academic and social status within their class and school.

The counseling process here is not viewed as intensive therapy; it should encourage comments and information that enable the handicapped student, the teacher-counselor, and peers to gain increased insight into the factors inhibiting academic growth, career exploration and preparation, and social awareness and adjustment. Such shared information will enable the student, teacher-counselor, and peers to investigate factors inhibiting growth and to assist the handicapped student to develop alternative behavior goals designed to promote increased awareness of: (1) ecological factors either positively or negatively affecting self and community awareness; (2) interest factors influencing attitudes and responses to specific school contingencies; (3) school performance and its interface with career preparation; (4) career preparation and its interface with economic earning potential; (5) dress behavior and its influence on peers, potential employers, and/or the opposite sex's perceptions; (6) speaking patterns and responses and how they affect others' perceptions and attitudes; (7) punctuality and its implications for the future employer or acquaintances; and (8) overall attitude toward work and how such attitudes can influence hiring and discharge practices.

As the process proceeds, it is anticipated that the student will find increasing acceptance and have less need for defenses. Hobbs (1975) believes that the nondirective process will promote confidence within individuals in making decisions critical to their personal potential and interests. The teacher-counselor role is one of a facilitator and participant, rather than active establisher of priorities and determiner of student needs and direction. In the nondirective approach, the teacher-counselor does not actively seek to draw out the handicapped student, but enables the participant to establish priorities and allows the youth to bring up cogent issues or problems related to the session's focus.

Planning

In an individual counseling process, the handicapped student and teacher-counselor must establish parameters each will follow and respect. The parameters include:

- when the handicapped students and teacher-counselor will meet,
- where the counseling process will be held,
- what the goals of the counseling procedures are,
- how long the process is expected to take, and
- what the program direction will be at the conclusion of the counseling.

Unlike other approaches, the expectation is that the teacher-counselor and handicapped student will jointly chart the course for the career counseling program. The goal, as previously noted, is for the counselor to encourage students to assume increased responsibilities for making decisions. At the same time, the students must recognize that any decision must conform to the rules established by the school, the community, and their peers.

Process

As noted in the first chapter, decisions on career direction are based on too few factors (Erickson & Wentling, 1976; Sawin, 1969). The counseling process is not intended as a therapeutic period, but as an information collection and guidance process during which the teacher-counselor and handicapped student can learn more about each other and share insights concerning personal needs, goals, and potential training and career opportunities.

A number of professionals have recommended procedures to gather pertinent information in a friendly atmosphere without making handicapped students feel they need to defend themselves. Among the recommendations are:

- General information questions should be asked at the beginning so that the handicapped student is put at ease.
- The questions asked should be within the handicapped student's experience and knowledge.
- The vocabulary should be easily understood by the handicapped student.

- The discussion should follow a logical pattern that makes sense to the handicapped student.

- The teacher-counselor's statements should be clear and definitive.

- Any questions should be phrased so that the student feels comfortable with the direction and intent of the discussion.

Input

As has already been noted in the nondirective approach, handicapped student input is essential to the process. The approach is developed to ensure participant input and guidance and to avoid overbearing counselors who tend to project their own values and needs, or the values and needs of the community. In a sense, if the handicapped students have input into the decision making, and the program reflects their input, then the students are hard pressed later to object to the program's career goals, objectives, and activities. More specifically, student input indicates the handicapped youth has bought into the nondirective guidance process.

DIRECTIVE GUIDANCE

While many of the basic principles discussed in the sections dealing with group process and nondirective counseling are applicable to the directive process, the directive process possesses its own overriding focus and approach. As an example, the directive process assumes that the handicapped students must learn to make decisions about their career life independent of others and then operate on that decision. This posture does not preclude others' input into the decision making, nor the incorporation of other points of view. What it does mean is that the final decision is the individual student's, and that he or she must be responsible for the decision. The further assumption of the directive process is that once students learn to make decisions and to accept the consequences of such decisions, they will be able to assume the initiative upon leaving the counseling process and the school environment. The directive teacher-counselor believes that too frequently a supportive process that encourages mutual dependence does not ready the handicapped student for the outside world. Instead, the directive approach promotes mutual independence among individuals. In short, the handicapped student may make decisions and set career goals that deviate from school or group values and norms. The handicapped student is then responsible for the decision, but is free to explore the consequence with others and discuss ways of coping with its positive and negative aspects. The components of the directive group approach are presented in the following sections.

Structure

The sharing concept advocated in the nondirective procedure is de-emphasized in the directive approach. The directive teacher-counselors seek to establish that they are in control of the process, and that they are going to participate firmly without making the decisions for the handicapped student. This approach does not abrogate the right of the handicapped youth to have a say about the direction of the program. It does mean unreasonable decisions on the handicapped youth's part will be addressed, and consequences will be discussed. The teacher-counselor will also clarify the procedures under which the counseling process will be conducted, including the time and place of the meeting and the focus of the discussion. This assertive behavior can be exercised whether the teacher-counselor is working with an individual or a group of individuals. Within this framework, the students are free to address their career needs and interests and to challenge ideas voiced by others in the group.

Teacher-Counselor's Role

The directive approach emphasizes the role of the teacher-counselor as not only a facilitator but as a director—an interactive agent for the handicapped youth's expressed values, goals, needs, and general behavior. While the handicapped student must agree to participate in the activity and voluntarily become involved in a specific task, it becomes the responsibility of the teacher-counselor to identify observable behavioral patterns that appear to be inhibiting personal and career development. The identified characteristics can be such basic behaviors as voice utilization, body posture, passive and/or aggressive responses, one's physical stance, or continuous complaints.

As opposed to the nondirective teacher-counselor, the directive teacher-counselor actively seeks to structure the environment and to provide objective feedback to the handicapped student, without necessarily judging the behavior. The feedback process involves identifying when the handicapped student's responses may be weak and plaintive rather than strong and assured, and when the handicapped student addresses his peers in a manner that appears to represent a lack of firmness and stability. Perls et al. (1977) and Shepard (1975) have noted that individuals are frequently unaware of how their body language or their quality of voice will betray ideas they are seeking to convey. In the same way, the teacher-counselor can point out how the handicapped student appears to have adopted a value that may not represent the student's explicit or implicit attitudes. As an example, some handicapped students will express an interest in continuing their education at a college or university when neither their school performance nor career goals support such a college orientation. It is not, however, the teacher-counselor's responsibility or role to tell the handicapped student what path should be pursued, but simply to provide the student with facts and behavioral information. This information enables the students to sort out the issues and relevant variables involved and then to make some preliminary decisions regarding their career directions.

Neither the nondirective or directive approach of counseling should pursue the "why" of the behavior or answer the "whys" if perchance they are identified. The basic goal of these procedures is to assist the handicapped student to identify personal goals, needs, interests, and values. Once this has been achieved, the handicapped student is expected to make personal career choices.

Perls et al. (1977) found that an effective technique for having persons deal with issues of values, interests, and needs was to require them to deal with the here-and-now rather than to deal in abstract and nondirective ways with past experiences or projected needs. Using this approach, the teacher-counselor seeks to encourage the handicapped youth to address present interests, personal and vocational goals and needs, and values. Then the teacher-counselor encourages the youth to assess the current realities of school performance, community values, and personal values, and to develop a preparation program that reflects the findings.

Planning

The planning process requires that the teacher-counselor establish procedures for operation. In the directive counseling process, the teacher-counselors must establish limits on the number of handicapped students that can participate in an individual or group process. The teacher-counselor is also responsible for establishing the generic career themes and ensuring that the discussion follows the pattern established by the teacher-counselor.

To ensure that the teacher-counselor has control over the group process and an adequate knowledge of the handicapped students participating in the group, the teacher-counselor must know: (1) time of meetings, (2) assessment data on each of the handicapped students who may participate, (3) the duration of the meetings, and (4) the counseling process.

Additionally, the directive teacher-counselor must establish the goals, objectives, and activities that will occur in each of the counseling sessions. The effective teacher-counselor will frequently inform the group or individual of these goals, objectives, and activities so that they can work toward mutual ends. While the directive teacher-counselor is expected to assume the responsibility for decisions made during the process, this does not preclude student involvement in the rule and decision-making process. It is only when the students' rules and decisions violate good and reasonable principles that their input should be questioned.

Input

While the directive teacher-counselor assumes a more forceful role, handicapped student input is essential to any program design. Handicapped students' interests and values must be solicited and clarified. Erikson (1969) and McCandless (1970) have indicated that without the input of the youth the level of student cooperation would be minimal. Obviously, the appropriateness and efficacy of any career program is subject to the handicapped student's expressed interests and cooperation. Without input, handicapped students are unlikely to support the program and work towards its goals and objectives.

INFORMATION UTILIZATION

The information obtained from the individual or group interaction can be used to assist the school. During the individual and group process, counselors should be employing techniques that enable them to reach objective decisions about a student's responses and behavioral demeanor. During the counseling process, the counselor can be measuring such factors as attention, frequency of appropriate or inappropriate responses to questions or statements, and perceived levels of interest or attitudes as related to such themes as work, family, and wages. The observation and measurement of such behavior can be achieved through frequency, duration, and intensity procedures as described in Chapter 7. The objectives of the guidance process can also be monitored through behavior change in applied settings. Data reporting vocational, social-personal, and/or academic performance can be reviewed in each guidance session, and progress toward the goal can become a focal point of the counseling process. This approach encourages students to evaluate expressed values against their actual performance.

CONTENT OF COUNSELING PROCESS

The ultimate purpose of the counseling process is to elicit information from a handicapped youth that leads to the development of a sequential process resulting in the preparation of an adolescent to be a productive member of the community. To prepare the handicapped youth effectively, several agendas need to be addressed in the counseling process. They include: (1) defining of individual career interests, (2) discussion of each handicapped student's school and community experiences, (3) identification of career options, (4) exploration of the community's job market, (5) examination of the consequences of career choices, (6) exploration of alternative career choices, and (7) selection of preliminary career directions.

Within each of these areas there are issues that require elaboration. Without such information, effective career counseling and appropriate handicapped student adjustment can be impaired (Miller, 1978). Other investigators (Brolin, 1974; Phelps & Lutz, 1977), have supported the importance of the process and the critical value of resulting information in developing effective programs.

This counseling process can be expected to ascertain substantive instruction issues such as the student's reading level, mathematics level, conceptual skills, social skills, and community awareness. The elicitation of information about such areas will enable the counselor to assess the accuracy of the student's self and environmental perceptions. This knowledge will help shape the student's eventual instructional program, work experience, and future counseling needs.

Included in any discussion of career development are such issues as: (1) how the academic program fits into the overall program, (2) what social skills need to be explored in preparing the student, (3) what dress codes and personal care issues would benefit the student in preparing for a career, (4) what the responsibilities of the student are to the community and state, (5) what science and hygiene knowledge and skills are required to function successfully in the community, and (6) what personal-social skills are required to obtain and maintain a one-on-one job.

The following information details more specifically the themes that may be explored in the counseling process and in the student's career development program. The fundamental themes that are explored in the career planning process are important to career development and maintenance. The literature (Miller, 1978; Phelps & Lutz, 1977) clearly demonstrates that the student's abilities to cooperate with others, arrive at work on time, dress appropriately, and manage personal finances are as important to work retention as are the essential academic and job skills. Exhibit 4-1 details some of the themes.

Beyond these content areas the teacher-counselor needs to possess and work toward closure in the following areas.

Career Interests

During adolescence the individual's interests and goals are fluid. Yet the handicapped student must and frequently does identify areas of career interest. His or her interest results from parental guidance, peer attitudes, school program availability, and identification with glamorous role models (Maiers, 1969). Many handicapped youth, at this age, have limited views of career interests and no comprehension of the range of academic, cognitive, psychomotor, and social skills required for careers requiring minimal competencies. As a result, the teacher-counselor needs to identify handicapped student interests and help the student recognize career prerequisites in the areas of academic performance, social maturity, and manual competencies. Additionally, handicapped students need to be familiar with the anticipated training requirements of a career as specified by

Exhibit 4-1 Career Development Program

I. Personal Development

1. Exploration of personal finances

   The student may explore:

   1.1 prudent vs. imprudent expenditures
   1.2 use of bank facilities for
       1.2.1 money exchange
       1.2.2 bank accounting
       1.2.3 savings accounts
       1.2.4 safety deposits
       1.2.5 credit/loans
   1.3 maintenance of financial records
   1.4 calculation and payment of taxes
   1.5 social security payments and other forms of retirement benefits
   1.6 purpose and function of insurance programs
   1.7 purpose and function of workmen's compensation

2. Selection, purchase, management, and maintenance of residence

   The student may explore:

   2.1 selection of adequate housing
   2.2 purchase of a home with consideration of interest rates and bonus points paid to the lending agency
   2.3 physical and aesthetic maintenance of a home
   2.4 purchase and maintenance of home furnishings and appliances

3. Personal dress and hygiene

   The student may explore:

   3.1 selection of appropriate dress for
       3.1.1 work experiences
       3.1.2 school experiences
       3.1.3 social situations
       3.1.4 recreational activities
   3.2 proper grooming
   3.3 hygiene principles
   3.4 physical fitness and its relationship to health
   3.5 good nutrition in
       3.5.1 meal planning
       3.5.2 food purchases
       3.5.3 food preparation

Exhibit 4-1 continued

    3.6   table manners
    3.7   food preservation
    3.8   sanitation
    3.9   personal grooming
    3.10 health care services

4. Family life

    The student may explore:

    4.1   dating
    4.2   courting
    4.3   sexual relationships
    4.4   financial and personal responsibilities involved in marriage
    4.5   responsibilities in child care, including
        4.5.1 nutrition
        4.5.2 personal grooming
        4.5.3 psychological development
        4.5.4 intellectual development
        4.5.5 social development
    4.6   family safety procedures and practice
    4.7   family planning

5. Civic activities

    The student may explore:

    5.1   local government procedures and regulations
    5.2   American government procedures and regulations
    5.3   personal rights and responsibilities as a citizen
        5.3.1 due process
        5.3.2 right to bear arms
        5.3.3 free speech
        5.3.4 freedom of worship
    5.4   Selective service system
    5.5   voting rights

6. Recreation and leisure time

    The student may explore:

    6.1   individual and group leisure time activities
    6.2   available resources
    6.3   the value of recreation
    6.4   planned recreation and vacations

Exhibit 4-1 continued

7. Mobility and transportation

The student may explore:

7.1 knowledge of traffic rules and safety practices as related to
  7.1.1 pedestrians
  7.1.2 vehicle operator of

   7.1.2.1 motorcycle
   7.1.2.2 bicycle
   7.1.2.3 automobile
   7.1.2.4 school bus
   7.1.2.5 train

7.2 responsibilities involved in automotive ownership

  7.2.1 automotive purchases
  7.2.2 automotive ownership
  7.2.3 automotive insurance—liabilities
  7.2.4 legal aspects
  7.2.5 work and leisure

7.3 Various means of transportation

II. Personal-Social Development

Appropriate personal-social skills enable individuals to interact with peers, authority figures, parents, and others in an effective, rewarding manner. This social-personal development should be emphasized carefully by all school personnel and must be explored during the career planning process.
The following are some themes that could be explored:

1. Attain sufficient self-understanding

The student may:

1.1 identify interests
1.2 identify abilities
1.3 identify reactions to a variety of events
1.4 identify personal needs and social goals
1.5 understand physical self including

  1.5.1 physiological development
  1.5.2 biological development

Exhibit 4-1 continued

2. Establish positive self-confidence, self-concept

   The student may explore:

   2.1 feelings of self-worth
   2.2 how others perceive him or her
   2.3 criticism by others

3. Desire and achieve social responsibility

   The student may explore:

   3.1 respect for the rights and properties of others
   3.2 ability to recognize and follow instructions, rules, etc.
   3.3 personal roles in changing environments
   3.4 multicultural values

4. Find, choose, develop, and maintain interpersonal bonds

   The student may explore:

   4.1 listening and responding to others
   4.2 making and maintaining friendships
   4.3 establishing heterosexual relationships
   4.4 establishing close interpersonal bonds

5. Achieve independence

   The student may explore:

   5.1 the impact of one person's behavior on others
   5.2 the need for self-organization
   5.3 goal-seeking behavior
   5.4 self-actualization

6. Make good decisions and solve problems

   The student may:

   6.1 differentiate bipolar concepts
   6.2 understand the need for goals
   6.3 consider alternatives
   6.4 anticipate consequences
   6.5 seek counsel

Exhibit 4-1 continued

7. Communicate appropriately with others

The student may explore:

7.1   recognition of emergency situations
7.2   understanding of the need for effective reading
7.3   understanding of the need for effective communication in
     7.3.1 writing
     7.3.2 oral speech
7.4   understanding of the subtleties of mass and/or personal communication

III. Academic Development

The academic portion of the integrated career education program can be both (1) supportive and (2) developmental.

Academic program components

1. Language arts

   1.1 reading
   1.2 writing and spelling
   1.3 oral speech
   1.4 listening
   1.5 studying effectively

2. Mathematics

   2.1 computation
   2.2 reasoning
   2.3 concepts

3. Social studies

   3.1 residential centers
   3.2 job centers
   3.3 community structures
   3.4 state organizations
   3.5 citizenship rights
   3.6 American history

Exhibit 4-1 continued

4. Science and health

    4.1 living organisms
    4.2 celestial bodies
    4.3 magnets
    4.4 animals
    4.5 minerals
    4.6 vegetables
    4.7 the human organism

5. Visual art, music, physical education, recreation

6. Driver's education

relevant agencies or society. Often students select careers without such information and experience failure, frustration, and/or disillusionment. As noted earlier, handicapped students have a long history of such failure. By continuing such experiences, students will not develop the positive attitudes necessary to make a contribution to the community. When possible, the teacher-counselor should assist the handicapped students to channel their broad interests into areas where achievement and mastery are possible. This process does not preclude the handicapped student from ultimately seeking the stated goal within the interest area. It does mean the school is attempting to structure the process into more manageable incremental steps. The expression of a career interest should be encouraged and supported by the teacher-counselor, and should be ultimately harnessed so as to direct learning, training, and lifelong planning.

Individual Test Performance

As observed in the assessment chapter, the collection of data on the handicapped youth is an essential component of the counseling process and must be available during the process. Such information will enable the counselor to evaluate the interface between expressed career interests and demonstrated school and community performance. The discrepancy between handicapped students' goals and potentials is frequently wide. For example, if a handicapped student who does poorly in mathematics indicates an interest in becoming a carpenter, discussions about the importance of mathematics in the building trade area could be used by the teacher-counselor to motivate the student to focus on mathematics achievement or to channel the student into alternative career choices. Handicapped students frequently do not recognize the prerequisite school-related competencies necessary to perform in specified career interest clusters.

Additionally, possessing the data on the handicapped student's performance level will enable the teacher-counselor to evaluate their accuracy. Sabatino (1980) noted that discrepancies in handicapped student performance may occur as a result of peer pressure or instructional appropriateness within the school. Some handicapped students do poorly on tests but perform well in the classroom, or they may do poorly in class but well on the test. It is important that teacher-counselors note whether expected social or cognitive behaviors are compatible with observed performance. The recognition of situational disorders can enable the teacher-counselor to assist the handicapped student to recognize the situational variances and to develop adaptive responses to varying settings. This situational variance will also have an influence on the type of career counseling the student can and should receive.

Evaluation of School and Community Performance

As noted in the previous section, there exists among some handicapped students a discrepancy between classroom and test performance and between classroom and home behavior. A variety of factors could be attributed to the discrepancy, such as family conflict and expectations, peer pressure, school expectations, and/or teacher attitudes. Gifted educators enjoy describing the minimal teacher expectations concerning such luminaries as Albert Einstein, Eleanor Roosevelt, and Andy Warhol, and their actual performance in the fields of physics, politics, and the visual arts. George Steinbrenner, the noted baseball entrepreneur, was reputedly a renegade in school, but has proven to be innovative, creative, and successful in business and sports. Too frequently the primary tool used to evaluate an individual's performance is formal test scores, and, less frequently, school performance. Seldom does the school look to the behavior of the student at home or in the community to establish the reliability of its observations and expectations. As a result, many of the school's educational decisions reflect a biased ecological sampling upon which educational and career decisions are made. The teacher-counselor working with the handicapped youth can explore the possibility of such discrepancies. Should differences in behavior be identified, the appropriate re-evaluation and programming can occur. The teacher, school principal, and other school-related persons can provide information about school performance. Peers, parents, social workers, school nurses, and other community-oriented agencies can be the source of information on home and community behavior.

Career Options

Given information on school, home, and community performance, and the results of various tests, the process of identifying and evaluating a variety of career options can be effectively initiated. During the beginning stages of the exploration process, the teacher-counselor might investigate career-cluster areas. The cluster areas, such as fast food preparation, can include jobs in building maintenance, food preparation, order taking, bookkeeping, operations management, personnel training, and acting as region franchise liaison.

Obviously, other options exist within the limited focus of the fast food area. Handicapped youths frequently do not recognize the range of skills and career options available as a result of a career choice. It is the responsibility of the teacher-counselor to provide the handicapped youth with these options. Additionally, the teacher-counselor and youths should explore the potential alternative directions the youths could move toward, given the development of specific skills and options.

The exploratory process thus provides the teacher-counselor and handicapped youths the option to explore both the vertical axis (the range of jobs within the fast food area) and the horizontal axis (the range of alternative jobs and settings available given a set of skills and competencies). An example is expressed in Figure 4-1.

Community Job Market

Irrespective of the handicapped student's interests, test scores, school and community performance, and goals for the future, if they do not coincide with the community's needs and interests, the handicapped youth's ability to obtain a position is seriously impaired. For this reason, the teacher-counselor's use of resources such as the state department of employment, social workers, occupational coordinators, the local newspaper, and the questioning of local employers to identify the present and future job market must be an ongoing process. Without these data, handicapped students will be trained for careers that either don't exist within the community, will only become available in one to five years, or that do exist but are being phased-out because of mechanization, industrial movement from the community, or simply because there is no longer a consumer need for the skill. Among the questions that should be raised with various agencies, corporations, and individuals are:

- What are the employment areas for which employers are currently seeking trained and untrained personnel?

- What are the expected employment opportunities in the community in the next five to ten years?

Figure 4-1 Career Opportunities

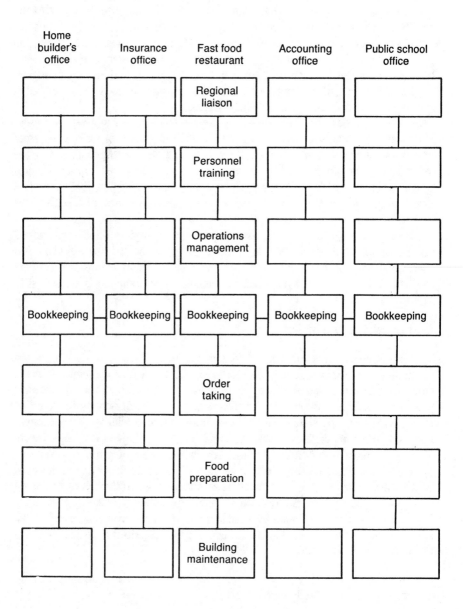

- What are the minimal social skills employers require of prospective employees?
- What types of motor and mechanical skills are required by prospective employers for each of the positions available?
- What levels of verbal and written language and mathematics performance are expected of prospective employees per position?
- What positions expose the employee to continued frustration?

Obviously many other questions can be raised. What is important is that such community contact is initiated and maintained as the schools seek to prepare handicapped youths to assume meaningful positions in the community and to contribute to the general welfare of their friends and neighbors.

Consequences of Career Choice

The selection of a career pattern automatically, at least temporarily, excludes a handicapped youth from other types of training and potential employment opportunities. Handicapped youths, as well as adults, are often uncomfortable when they are required to select a path leading to career development and employment. One factor contributing to the reluctance to select a career pattern is the knowledge that other potential opportunities are denied. While ambivalence can be found among handicapped youths expected to make a choice, the selection of a career is critical to the social maturation process. Perls (1959) noted that individuals are often unprepared to accept the consequences of their behavior, an ability that is required for the individual to grow. In the growing specialized employment market, individuals are increasingly encouraged to make decisions. The important factor that youths should be encouraged to recognize is that most decisions are not irreversible, and that through continuous training, new opportunities that require the utilization of old and new competencies will be called upon.

Alternative Career Choices

As observed in the preceding sections and in the section dealing with career options, the process of exploring alternatives needs to be encouraged. Although training may be directed at preparing the youth for one career pattern, the skills learned are adaptable to other career patterns. Handicapped youths capable of perceiving and operating on alternative strategies are exhibiting career and social flexibility that should assist them as they leave the educational milieu and enter the world of work.

Preliminary Career Directions

Once the variables are identified and reviewed, the decision to select a preliminary career direction must be reached. This testing of the waters enables handicapped youths to evaluate their interests, skill levels, and choices in relationship to an actual academic program reflecting the language, mathematics, science, and social studies skills required. One way of testing the waters without drowning is the establishment of simulated job stations in which the handicapped youth will perform various tasks associated with the career in the outside world. In this way, both school personnel and the youth will be able to determine the appropriateness of the career decisions. As a result, minor or major program changes can be initiated.

A time limit for this investigative process by both the handicapped student and school personnel must be established prior to the actual career preparation process. Often students will become discouraged at the early stages of the process and seek premature changes. The time limit encourages the students to work their way through disappointments and frustrations before making a decision on the career direction's appropriateness and efficacy. The time limit should not be perceived by school officials as something irrevocable. Conditions can be expected to arise that will require early decision making and the establishment of a new career training program.

Career Preparation

Once the career path has been established, the youth and counselor-educator must work cooperatively to establish a diversified program that reflects academic, vocational, and social personal needs. Miller (1978) noted that the communication among school personnel in a career education has been poor, and that this lack of communication has affected the level of services provided to handicapped youths. The preparation process of handicapped youths requires increased communications among school professionals including special educators, regular classroom teachers, vocational educators, school counselors, and other appropriate personnel.

The career education preparation program requires the cooperation and interaction of each of the previously cited professionals to implement the student's program successfully. It is critical that the academic content of the program interface with the needs of the student's career pattern and vocational training. The special educator resource room teacher or the school counselor are the more likely coordinators to ensure that each of the training pieces is in place. Whoever may be the coordinator, it is imperative that the students' mathematics, language, science, health, and/or social studies instruction reflect the priorities of their career pattern and vocational training. Handicapped students with deficiencies will be faced with performance problems when they must carry out a job assignment. Also, educators need to recognize the variety of delivery systems and environments.

Since the training the handicapped student receives is only preliminary and does not constitute his or her entire range of options, the student, the school personnel, and other interested individuals must continuously reevaluate training and environmental appropriateness. If changes need to be initiated, then other alternatives can be explored with the youth.

Transition from School to Work

Often handicapped students are unprepared for the conclusion of their schooling years. They lack knowledge of how to identify a potential job, the dress behavior expected of them as they apply for positions, the verbal responses perceived as appropriate during interviews, and other essential skills. Handicapped youths must be prepared for the transition from school to work. A smooth transition can be facilitated by:

1. teaching them to survey the help wanted section of the newspaper
2. preparing them to complete job applications
3. explaining and discussing the necessity of applying to several employers
4. helping them to evaluate the various job possibilities through the use of the telephone
5. assisting them to recognize the necessity of appropriate dress in applying for jobs
6. providing training in communication skills necessary for interviewing with a potential employer
7. providing training and experience in working with fellow employees on the job
8. acquainting them with the necessity of arriving on time for job interviews and work
9. acquainting them with various methods employers may use to pay their employees, ranging from daily to monthly salaries
10. providing information on the deductions from pay that can be expected including state and federal income tax, Social Security, and any health and retirement benefits
11. instructing them on ways of banking and budgeting one's salary.

This list is not totally inclusive, and the responsibility should not be that of only one professional. Some of the information can be passed on in such classes as consumer education, civics, home economics, mathematics, and senior problems.

CONCLUSION

The process of counseling, involving the receipt and transmission of information, requires the adult figure to be knowledgeable, patient, understanding, firm when necessary, familiar with student needs and characteristics, informed on school programs, and aware of community values and priorities (Whiteley & Fretz, 1980). Unlike the psychometrist who administers tests and receives more objective scores and profiles, the teacher-counselor must deal with information that frequently is subjective. From the information obtained during the counseling process and the impressions produced during various meetings, the guidance process must form conclusions and programmatic orientations.

It is the task of the teacher-counselor to mediate differences of perception and orientation among parties involved. This is an important process since unresolvable disagreements will produce ideas and recommendations that fail to match the student's needs and interests, the school's resources, and school personnel's skills and orientations. Parents can also play decisive roles in the decision making concerning the student's career pattern and the types of experiences to be incorporated into the program. The counselor-educator is an influential individual in a significant process designed to ready the handicapped youth for a career.

It is apparent that the teacher-counselor model is a substantially more intense and direct approach to facilitating career choices. It is ideally suited to the handicapped youth because it relies on direct discussion pertinent to daily activities. Thus, the need for abstract thinking, long-term memory, and complex language is minimized. Finally, rather than assuming that the youth has internalized and clarified his or her career choices, the teacher-counselor provides subsequent experiences that force the youth to affirm or reject his or her decisions. These activities may range from exposure to other occupations that may be more desirable to actual placement on the selected job.

Career-vocational educators are ideally suited to implementing this process as they are the professionals responsible for the development of the individual program. Additionally, they are the professionals most closely associated with educational/vocational activities that force career choices. Unfortunately, just as guidance counselors are untrained or undertrained in working with the handicapped, many career-vocational educators have little exposure to the individual or group counseling process. Aside from presenting a rationale, specific counseling techniques and content will be explored in the following chapters.

REFERENCES

Bandura, A. *Principles of behavior modification*. New York: Holt, Rinehart & Winston, 1969.

Brolin, D. E. *Programming retarded in career education*. Working paper No. 1, University of Missouri—Columbia, September 1974.

Davis, C. S. New developments in the intelligence testing of blind children. In *Proceedings of the Conference on New Approaches to the Education of Blind Persons*. New York: American Foundation for the Blind, 1970.

Ellis, A. *Humanistic psychotherapy*. New York: McGraw-Hill, 1973.

Erikson, E. H. In H. W. Maiers (Ed.), *Three theories of child development: The contributions of Erik H. Erikson, Jean Piaget, and Robert R. Sears, and their applications* (Rev. ed.). New York: Harper & Row, 1969.

Erikson, R. C., & Wentling, T. L. *Measuring student growth*. Boston: Allyn & Bacon, 1976.

Fiedler, F. E. A comparison of therapeutic relationships in psychoanalytic, non-directive Adlerian therapy. *Journal of Consulting Psychology*, 1950, *14*, 436-445.

Gibb, J. R. Sociopsychological processes of group institutions. In National Society for the Study of Education, *The dynamics of instructional groups*, Fifty-ninth yearbook. Chicago: The University of Chicago Press, 1960, pp. 115-135.

Glanz, E. C. *Groups in guidance*. Boston: Allyn & Bacon, 1962.

Hobbs, N. *The futures of children: Categories, labels and their consequences*. San Francisco: Jossey-Bass, 1975.

Inhelder, B., & Piaget, J. *The growth of logical thinking from childhood to adolescence*. New York: Basic Books, 1958.

Kemp, C. G. *Perspectives on the group process* (2nd ed.). Boston: Houghton Mifflin, 1970.

Kroll, A. M., Dinklage, L. B., Lee, J., Morley, E. D., & Wilson, E. H. *Career development: Growth and crisis*. New York: John Wiley & Sons, 1970.

Lyon, H. C. *Learning to feel—Feeling to learn*. Columbus, Ohio: Charles E. Merrill Publishing Co., 1971.

Maiers, H. W. (Ed.). *Three theories of child development: The contributions of Erik H. Erickson, Jean Piaget, and Robert R. Sears, and their applications* (Rev. ed). New York: Harper & Row, 1969.

Mann, J. *Learning to be*. New York: Free Press, MacMillan Publishing Co., 1972.

McCandless, B. R. *Adolescents—Behavior and development*. Hinsdale, Ill.: The Dryden Press, 1970.

Miller, S. R. Career education. In D. A. Sabatino & A. J. Mauser (Eds.), *Educating norm-violating and chronic disruptive secondary school-aged youth* (Vol. 2). Boston: Allyn & Bacon, 1978.

Osipow, S. W. *A story of counseling methods*. Homewood, Ill.: Dorsey Press, 1980.

Perls, F. S. *Gestalt therapy verbatim*. Moab, Utah: Real People Press, 1959.

Perls, F. S., Hefferline, R. F., & Goodman, P. *Gestalt therapy* (2nd ed.). New York: Crown Publishers, 1977.

Phelps, A. L., & Lutz, R. J. *Career exploration and preparation for the special needs learner*. Boston: Allyn & Bacon, 1977.

Rabichow, H. C. *Effective counseling of adolescents*. Chicago: Association Press, 1980.

Rogers, C. R. *On becoming a person*. Boston: Houghton Mifflin, 1961.

Rogers, C. R. *Client-centered therapy*. Boston: Houghton Mifflin, 1965.

Rogers, L. A. A comparison of two kinds of test interview. *Journal of Counseling Psychology*, 1965, *9*, 224-231.

Sabatino, D. A. Secondary special education: A case of benign neglect. In J. B. Jordan, D. A. Sabatino, & R. C. Sarri (Eds.), *Disruptive youth in school*. Reston, Va.: The Council for Exceptional Children, 1980.

Samler, J. *Basic approaches to mental health in the schools*. Washington, D.C.: American Personnel and Guidance Association. (Reprint series of seven articles from the *Personnel and Guidance Journal*, 1958-59.)

Sawin, E. I. *Evaluation and the work of the teacher*. Belmont, Calif.: Wadsworth Publishing Co., 1969.

Schuerger, J. *Using tests and other information in counseling: A decision model for practitioners*. Champaign, Ill.: Institute for Personality and Ability Testing, 1977.

Shepard, M. *Fritz*. New York: E. P. Dutton & Co., 1975.

Shertzer, B. *Fundamentals of counseling*. Boston: Houghton Mifflin, 1980.

Whiteley, J. M., & Fretz, B. R. *The present and future of counseling*. Monterey, Calif.: Brooks/Cole Publishing Co., 1980.

Chapter 5

Learning Strategies and Problems of Adolescents

During the 1970s, a sudden spate of legislation and court decisions required that the education community inform the business sector of the need for providing job opportunities for the handicapped. In addition, educators were required to provide youths and young adults with an education that matched their intellectual, sensory-motor, personal-social, and occupational potential. The primary beneficiary of this legal activity has been the handicapped adolescent.

Legal mandates, however, were but the first step in ensuring the educational rights of the handicapped. Educators who attempted to implement the many federal and state laws and court decisions soon discovered that they themselves were handicapped by a lack of research data and successful program models designed for handicapped adolescents.

Special educators, regular educators, and psychologists had studied the behavioral and developmental characteristics of the 0- to 12-year-old normal and handicapped populations, but equivalent time, creativity, and money had not been expended on the developmental and educational characteristics and interests of persons between the ages of 13 and 21 years. The combination of legislation and the difficulty practitioners faced in implementing court decisions resulted in an examination of programs and research, and the publication of several books dealing with the needs of adolescent individuals with educational handicaps (Brolin, 1976; Mann, Goodman, & Weiderholt, 1978; Phelps & Lutz, 1977; Sabatino & Mauser, 1978). Such books were also accompanied by increased publication of essays addressing the presumed needs of adolescents with educational handicaps (Brolin & D'Alonzo, 1979; Clark, 1976; D'Alonzo & Miller, 1977; Miller, Sabatino, & Miller, 1979).

Despite this flurry of activity, the difficulty now, as in the past, in addressing the needs of the adolescent in special education, is the staggering lack of data to support the development of viable instructional and programmatic alternatives that interface with the adolescent's psychological, sociological, and educational characteristics. Further research is also needed to assess the needs of such students and to implement the preparation of personnel and programs that can be effective.

The data that have been employed to develop services for this population have generally not emanated from research with handicapped youths (Cullinan & Epstein, 1979; Miller, S. R., 1975). The majority of data generated in recent years has typically come from studies conducted by educators and psychologists concerned with normal adolescent populations (Handel, 1975; Yussen & Levy, 1977). These studies have tended to focus on:

1. Achievement motivation: the study of factors that either promote or inhibit learning (Clarizio & McCoy, 1976)
2. Labeling: the study of the effects of a specific word or phrase that was intended to identify or describe a student's learning problem and/or characteristics
3. Memory and information retrieval: the retention and retrieval of information that has been stored and evaluated
4. Moral development: the maturation and emergence of three psychological characteristics: moral judgment, moral feelings, and moral conduct (Clarizio & McCoy, 1976)
5. Cognitive development and integration: the process of an individual's thought development and the application and use of thought in learning (Inhelder & Piaget, 1958)
6. Self-concept: the effects of self-evaluation and perception and their effects on academic performance
7. Sex difference: the effects of sex difference on school performance
8. Juvenile delinquency: the relationship of learning disabilities to social behavior
9. General performance characteristics affecting academic achievement

S.R. Miller (1978) evaluated the programs and research directed at secondary school-aged handicapped populations frequently identified as delinquents, emotionally disturbed, and mentally retarded. Of the programs evaluated, only 10 percent existed in the public schools. The majority were separate special projects operated by either a private group, universities, and other agencies funded by state and federal dollars and/or the state departments of corrections. These programs were primarily intended to establish appropriate psychological attitudes and social adjustment skills with minimal focus on career-vocational development and the supportive skills in language, mathematics, and science. Data from these programs suggest that the majority were well intended, but not measurably successful in either vocational performance (Miller, S.R., Ewing, & Phelps, 1980) or social adjustment (Miller, S.R., 1978). A major deficiency of many of the cited programs was the absence of clear theoretical and research data from handicapped adolescent populations.

Special educators have primarily limited their exploration of issues related to that of the handicapped adolescent to surveys of certifications (Miller, S.R., Sabatino, & Larsen, in press), the use of curriculum materials (Vance, 1977), and the types of programs being developed within the schools (Weiderholt & McNutt, 1977). Therefore, while some special education research can be used, it is primarily the literature of psychology that must be searched to begin the process of establishing a data base. Special educators can use this data base to build a foundation for efficacious identification, assessment, placement, programs, curriculum, teacher preparation, and support services.

There are several basic theories of development in the field of psychology that are applicable to adolescents and employed as guides to problems and needs of the youth. In the following section, these theories are discussed.

THEORIES OF LEARNING

Jean Piaget

Piaget studied the development of the human system, observing the physiological, biological, and ecological phenomena surrounding sensory-motor, intellectual, and social growth between 0 and 16 years. Professional study and discussion have primarily been concerned with Piaget's writings on early human development (0 to 7 years old). It is Piaget's writings of the cognitive developmental phenomena occurring from 11 to 15 years that can provide educators with some clues about the curriculum content, process of instruction, and programmatic goals directed at handicapped adolescent populations.

Piaget found that human development passes through several stages culminating in the formal operations stage at or around 11 to 16 years of age. In the prior stages, the human system interacts with the environment by developing sensory-motor and language skills, labeling objects and persons within the environment, and relating two or more of the sensorial pieces of information into an intuitive whole. Also, the person begins to comprehend the interrelation of processes, the converting of basic units of measurement and values, and the development of rudimentary rational thinking skills.

At approximately 11 years of age, the individual relies less upon sensory information to form ideas, values, and goals, and, instead, utilizes independent thought processes based on previous perceptions, information, concepts, values, and idiosyncratic goals and attitudes. The student, during this period, is expected to replace random, cognitive behavior with a systematic approach to thinking. Piaget found that individuals, during this developmental period, first begin to make qualitative decisions about objects and events, such as evaluating distance, length, and area. Second, they demonstrate the comprehension of abstract concepts through such activities as ascertaining the volume of a cylinder or the distance from a point on the ground to the top of a tree. Third, individuals manifest the ability to see the relationship between concepts, or the relationship between secondary concepts and other secondary or primary concepts. Further, once the student has developed the ability to compare concepts and evaluate their underlying principles, new concepts and principles can be formulated.

These cognitive activities enable the youth to initiate independent behavior such as formulating career goals in relation to existing information about one's self, the community, and the society-at-large. Since the formal operations phase is a time of rapid information processing and organizing, information is used to alter the youth's self-perceptions and goals. Many students, during this period, find the process of evaluating, comparing, and developing new concepts and values stimulating and rewarding. Often reality becomes less important to the 11- to 15-year-old than the possible, such as the pursuit of a career and/or a partner.

The student does not believe that a commitment to the possible must be made, but rather perceives the process as a means to affirm the larger limitless domain of what he or she can achieve. For this reason, youths, during this period, are continuously modifying their goals and directions, and investigating alternative careers and life styles. Once the youth reaches the age of approximately 15 or 16 years old, deductive and inductive thinking skills have developed, and ideas and directions tend to stabilize.

This period of rapid cognitive change and the resulting increase of available information and associations contributes to the student's social, academic, and cultural experimentation. The increased cognitive demands of the school during this general period of development frequently are associated with new or heightened disruptive behavior, accelerated or new academic disabilities, and a fluctuation of self-concepts. For the handicapped student with demonstrated school deficiencies, the advent of adolescence often produces more numerous school-related failures in the realms of language, mathematics, and peer acceptance.

Erik Erikson

While Piaget sought to understand the cognitive process of individuals, Erikson emphasized the psychoanalytical-social (psycho-social) aspects of human development. Erikson was concerned with revealing the interactive effects of biological drives, cultural influences, and the idiosyncratic responses of individuals to personal and societal forces. His developmental theory moves along a linear path from "acquiring a sense of basic trust" for the newborn to "acquiring a sense of integrity" for persons in the twilight of their lives.

Erikson observed that as individuals enter into the adolescent years, they seek to affirm their sense of competency and their ability to cope with societal and family pressures. The individual is continually fending off feelings of inferiority, according to Erikson. The necessity to strive and demonstrate competency is increased by the heightened competitive quality of the environment. As the individual nears puberty and adolescence, the phenomenon of play as a coping mechanism to understand the daily and sometimes traumatic events of life is diminished, and work and other germane coping activities are substituted.

The gradual elimination of play as a coping mechanism occurs as the youths seek to establish more clearly the context in which the competencies they possess and potentially develop can function. Erikson emphasizes that many individuals in late adolescence continue to experience identity diffusion concerning their own potential and their place within the society. He further contends that adolescents strive for a positive image of themselves, but that they prefer a negative identity to a nonidentity. Even a negative identity provides youths with a voice, visibility, and a personality, where previously they lacked all three.

Erikson believes seven critical factors of development occur during adolescence. These factors, which add new and complex dimensions to an individual's behavior, are:

1. *Comprehension of time*. The capability to use and understand time enables a youth to develop a sense of full identity (Maiers, 1969). Youths with poor concepts of time may demand immediate solutions to problems or become completely immobilized in the hope of avoiding stress.
2. *Self-assuredness*. The ability to attend to one's own appearance and demeanor and determine the effect on others, as opposed to being totally indifferent to such factors, contributes to the sense of identity one develops.
3. *Role experimentation*. Experimentation with roles in society enables adolescents to clarify their potential and competency levels. The level and types of success establish a youth's image of self.
4. *Industrious persistence*. Youths must continue the process of working through problems and obstacles that confront them during this formative developmental period. Persistence is a critical quality that is essential to later success, and it must be nourished during this period.
5. *Sexual identity*. During adolescence, youths seek to clarify their sexual identity through role experimentation and patterning.
6. *Values identification*. The development of a pivotal value system begins to emerge during adolescence. The value system enables youths to structure their behavior towards work, learning, family, and community.

According to Erikson, the period of adolescence is a stage of development in which many cognitive and social foundations are established that support the remainder of the individual's psycho-social life. The adolescent entering Erikson's postchildhood period faces several psycho-social processes that will shape his or her young adolescent period. Supporting this view, the exceptional education literature addressing adolescence (McCandless, 1970; Miller, S.R., 1978; Sabatino, 1980) has clearly indicated that one of the major life crisis periods in human development is adolescence. The youth's changing awareness levels and physical needs alter the generally benign personality that has endeared him or her to parents, teachers, and other adult authorities. This benign, malleable individual begins to question adult authority, societal norms, and moral imperatives. An altered state of willingness to follow rules and yield to adult attitudes naturally produces conflict between the adolescent and his or her parents, teachers, and institutions. Until the youth can sort out his or her values, needs, and direction, the conflict between the adolescent and his or her surroundings will persist.

Albert Bandura

Piaget and Erikson appear to agree that the period of adolescence is a time in which individuals are seeking to define who they are and to clarify their personal, professional, and social goals. Albert Bandura extends this view via the construct of modeling or imitation learning. Bandura's research has demonstrated that the milieu in which individuals participate affects their values, identity, and perceptions of personal options. Bandura believes that the people and experiences individuals are familiar with through actual contact or through vicarious opportunities also affect their behavior.

Bandura's theory suggests that individuals learn their social norms and standards of behavior from exemplary persons. During the first 10 to 11 years of life, a young child's model is his or her parents. As the individual enters adolescence, exemplary models become peers, teachers, adults within the community, and other models viewed on television and in motion pictures. Imitation occurs when individuals match their behavior patterns to that of a chosen model. The imitation occurs because the individuals are motivated to pattern their behavior after an exemplary person. The imitation will continue as long as the individuals are motivated to continue this behavior.

The imitative process can be effected by three separate means: first, by observing behavior from a model that is new and that produces positive contingencies; second, by observing behavior from a model that is negative and that produces inhibitory responses; and third, by observing behavior from a model that carries out an act that exists already in the imitator's repertoire but is not employed until prompted by the model's behavior.

Bandura concludes that more imitative persons lack positive self-image and esteem, and have been rewarded for imitative behavior. It also should be noted that Bandura believes imitative learning most frequently occurs in the affective and psychomotor domains.

The writings of Piaget and Erikson suggest that the allegiance of individuals shifts from adults to peers during adolescence. Bandura (1969) also indicates that it is peers and imaginary hero figures that stimulate modeling behaviors. As a result many youths initially develop unrealistic role models and expectations that result in conflicts. This is a phenomenon that frequently affects the handicapped adolescent who comes into contact with students who also represent academic and behavior variance from the norm.

David Ausubel

An important theory of learning that has greater applicability with an adolescent population than with younger audiences is Ausubel's subsumption theory. Piaget suggests that the most effective learning comes from an individual discovery process. Conversely, Ausubel views optional learning as occurring when the material is presented to the learner in its final form. The learner's only responsibility is to assimilate and internalize the material.

This approach is dependent on the learner possessing information that has been organized under various categories such as food, transportation, and living creatures. Under Ausubel's approach, the individual incorporates new information into already existing categories of knowledge. The fact that the learner already possesses a categorical basis enables him or her to use already existing knowledge to gather new information. The existence of these categories is said, by Ausubel, to provide the learner with a stable, clear organizational basis for learning.

The approach is achieved best when the learner understands the function and nature of the categories and their subcomponents. The understanding, or meaningfulness of the categories and their subcategories, enables the individual to incorporate categories representing a less inclusive body of knowledge under a more inclusive category. The placement of lesser categories under more inclusive categories—all of which have meaning—enables the learner to establish appropriate and durable information anchors. Information that is incorporated or subsumed is related to a stable, clear, cognitive organizational structure.

This approach to learning can be used when a teacher, in advance, tells the students the theme of the day's lesson. Then the teacher further explains the various subthemes of the lesson and explains how the subthemes are related to the main theme. The approach tends to work effectively if the student possesses: (1) a basic understanding and facility with language; (2) an ability to use the language to describe and characterize objects, pictures, and events; (3) an aptitude to interrelate ideas, objects, activities, and pictures, either individually or collectively; and (4) an ability to apply this knowledge to new experiences.

Most handicapped adolescent youths do possess the previously cited facilities at various functional levels, and are thus capable of benefiting from the subsumption theory. The critical factor in employing this approach is that the teacher be aware of the student's previous experiences and current level of functioning and develop a lesson that reflects such knowledge. Use of the subsumption theory, Ausubel believes, can accelerate learning by: (1) enabling the student to relate the new material to previously learned material, (2) eliminating the ambiguity of the discovery learning process, and (3) demonstrating the applicability of the new information to emerging activities.

BEHAVIORAL FEATURES OF HANDICAPPED ADOLESCENTS

Several theories of learning have been presented, in the preceding section, that offer the reader plausible explanations of how adolescents learn about themselves, others, and the world around them. Within the general literature there also exists a number of hypotheses that attempt to explicate the behavior exhibited by adolescents. Some of the issues involved include: (1) limited behavioral repertoire, (2) reduced motivation, (3) limited reinforcement, (4) locus of control, and (5) deficiencies in social discrimination. To cope effectively with handicapped youths, educators need to be aware of these issues and to address them when appropriate. The following section presents an overview of these behavioral phenomena as they relate to adolescence.

Limited Behavioral Repertoire

Many handicapped adolescents demonstrate significant behavioral variance existing concurrently with deficits in adaptive behavior (Grossman, 1973). (Adaptive behavior is the degree to which the individual exhibits behaviors that contribute toward social adaptation and personal independence.) These behaviors are identified as being motivational, affective, intellectual, social, motor, and so on.

A more detailed explanation of the function of adaptive behavior is advanced by Leland, Nihira, Foster, Shellhaas, and Kagin (1968). They suggest that adaptive behavior is an indication of an individual's ability to cope with the immediate environment. Three abilities are considered to be subsumed by adaptive behavior:

Independent Functioning

Independent functioning refers to the adolescents' ability to reach successfully closure on a task that is appropriate to their age and expected by the community. Deficits in independent functioning lead to a dependence on more socially competent people in the environment. While a reliance on others may be functional in some instances, a pervasive dependence on others may limit the extent to which all adolescents can benefit from, and contribute to, educational and vocational experiences.

Personal Responsibility

This may be viewed as the adolescents' ability to control their personal behavior and assume the responsibility for its outcome. In addition, personal responsibility refers to the adolescents' willingness to engage in behaviors that they are capable of performing. This area underlies the decision-making process.

Social Responsibility

This facet involves the ability of the individual to conform to standards of the peer group. It also includes social adjustment, emotional maturity, and the acceptance of civic responsibility that ultimately leads to a degree of economic independence.

Numerous studies have demonstrated that handicapped youths do not develop these attributes commensurate with their age group. This is explained in part by the individual's relative inability to interpret and respond to environmental influences in a way that will promote new learning. Limited learning diminishes the number of positive social responses acquired by the individual that may be exhibited when faced with demanding situations. The result may be that the individual behaves inappropriately as the result of not being able to identify and/or utilize adaptive behaviors that others acquire without special learning experiences.

Reduced Motivation

People become socially competent as a result of numerous interactions with their environment. These interactions begin at birth and become more complex through adulthood. People generally become more competent in interacting with, and benefiting from, the environment as they become older. This process of refining individual abilities allows the person to control the environment as he or she reaches social or intellectual maturity (White, 1960).

The motive that underlies this process has been termed "effectance." Effectance can be described as satisfaction gained from the successful completion of a challenging task. Effectance encourages attention to and experimentation in subsequent tasks that require greater skill. The result of this hierarchical process is a continual growth in competence. Effectance motivation is facilitated by the satisfaction gained from a history of successes and failures across many areas. A review of the literature pertaining to effectance motivation by Harter and Zigler (1974) demonstrates that satisfaction is derived from mastery of difficult tasks. Also, the more challenging the task, the greater the sense of personal reward that one gains from its completion. Other reviewers have presented similar findings (Hunt, 1965; Piaget, 1952).

Limited Range of Reinforcing Events

Handicapped youth are often involved in a limited number of reinforcing events (Gardner, 1977). As a result, there are fewer functional incentives that a teacher may offer to promote achievement. Natural reinforcers that elicit the efforts of normal children are typically not effective with the handicapped (Levy, 1974). The limited range of reinforcement is influenced by several factors. The social learning theory of Julian Rotter (1954) advances the premise that people approach objects or events in which they have a high expectancy for success and reinforcement. In contrast, people avoid objects or events in which they have a low expectancy for success and reinforcement. Social behavior may then be predicted by examining one's learning history in relation to goal or threat objects.

Rotter (1975) describes behavior as being a function of four major determinants: expectancy, value of reinforcement, psychological situation, and behavior. The following formula denotes the relationship of the variables expectancy and value of reinforcement: the potential for a behavior to occur is a function of the expectancy of reinforcement following the behavior and the value of reinforcement. A substantial body of research has supported its utility in understanding and predicting the behavior of the mentally retarded (Mercer & Snell, 1977).

Because the handicapped are subjected to an increased frequency of failure experiences, their expectancy for failure in future endeavors is increased (Chandler & Boroskin, 1971). The generalized expectancy for failure and nonreinforcement reduces the likelihood that the individual will approach the event in the future (Keogh, Cahill, & MacMillan, 1972). The reinforcement properties of the event are, as a result, reduced. Thus, events typically viewed as being reinforcing for the average student may not be reinforcing for the retarded because of the generalized expectancy of an aversive or neutral outcome.

Further complicating this effect is the notion that the handicapped individual generally is not exposed to the variety of pleasant activities and events encountered by the average student. This may be due to social deprivation, parental neglect, or institutional upbringing. The lack of exposure to diverse reinforcing conditions inhibits the individual from forming positive associations with those activities or events. The retarded person does not anticipate the reinforcing qualities of an event because of the lack of experiences that would lead to an expectancy of reinforcement.

One would expect that the activities and events typically applied in educational settings as incentives and goals may not be effective with the handicapped. Further, a disproportionate number of events in the educational environment may have acquired aversive properties through the person's learning history. The final result is that the handicapped may actively avoid events that others consider to be intrinsically reinforcing.

External Locus of Control

Locus of control is a construct that has been derived from Rotter's (1954) social learning theory. According to the theory, reinforcement may be viewed as being a consequence of the person's own actions (internal) or as a result of an outside influence (external) such as the influence of others. It is important to recognize that locus of control is viewed as a developmental phenomenon.

Lawrence and Winschel (1975) have posited that the external-internal hierarchy may be described by a five-stage process beginning with an external orientation and culminating in a more internal approach as the individual matures:

1. Stage 1—The student attributes the events of his life, particularly failure, to forces beyond his control.
2. Stage 2—Internality for success begins to emerge while externality for failure, though still evident, begins to fade.
3. Stage 3—The maturing student becomes essentially internal, although this belief is principally evident in self-responsibility for success.
4. Stage 4—The previous stage of development appears to be reversed as a growing awareness of responsibility and a sense of courage in the face of difficulty lead to high internality for failure coupled with a new modesty for one's successes.
5. Stage 5—With the onset of genuine self-reliance, the individual accepts equally the responsibility for his successes and failures. (p. 487)

The authors suggest that many handicapped youths do not progress beyond the first two stages. This is attributed to numerous frustration and failure experiences. Fox (1972) has demonstrated that the handicapped tend to cluster around Stages 2 and 3 and relatively few progress to the upper stages.

Deficiencies in Social Discrimination

Handicapped students often have difficulty in making fine distinctions based on relevant social cues (Gardner, 1977). This is evidenced by the fact that handicapped individuals frequently have adaptive behaviors in their repertoire, but are unable to utilize them at appropriate times. For example, the handicapped student may know how to shake hands but not know the conditions under which it is appropriate to greet a person in this manner. In effect, environmental cues that assist one in identifying appropriate behaviors do not have a strong and reliable influence for the mentally retarded adolescent.

Discrimination deficits have a major influence on typical adolescent behavior. Not only is it important that an appropriate behavior be matched with a given social setting; the intensity, duration, and magnitude of the chosen behavior must be discriminatively selected based on the relevant social cues. For example, moving quickly from one class to the next between periods is generally rewarded, but running to class is punished. Closing one's locker firmly is rewarded, but slamming the locker shut is punished. Playing hard at recess is rewarded, but being aggressive is punished.

Another major discrimination problem is the imitation of inappropriate behavior exhibited by poor models. The functional person is able to discriminate between good models and poor models in a number of settings. The handicapped individual may not have this ability.

The applicability of the foregoing theories of learning and behavior to the handicapped adolescent population has been investigated by comparing nonhandicapped and handicapped on factors contributing to school problems. In the following section, an overview of the research studies in this area is described.

REVIEW OF EMPIRICAL RESEARCH

To assess the accuracy of some of these theories, investigators have conducted studies between nonhandicapped and handicapped adolescents. In many cases, the investigators sought to identify factors that contribute to school problems. The reviews and studies in the area have indicated the concern youths have for peer acceptance, self-identity, personal goals, self-reliance related to academics and work institutional rules, and freedom of choice. More specifically, studies have noted that youths generally use three separate areas to distinguish among members of their peer group. These areas are academic and athletic abilities and physical appearance. Many of the studies have found that physical appearance has the greatest influence on social acceptance among adolescents, but that physical appearance does not alone affect the handicapped students' social acceptance. Another factor that affects social acceptability is peer perception of the adolescent as scared, unhappy, and worried. A parallel finding has demonstrated that handicapped adolescents generally perceive themselves as not intelligent, poor school achievers, and, in particular, as having serious problems with reading.

While the handicapped adolescents often recognize their academic and social deficiencies, the same students frequently seek to inflate their social status within their peer group. By contrast, students not identified as handicapped tend to be more accurate in assessing their social standing. Nonhandicapped youth also have the ability to unduly influence the behavior of their more handicapped peers.

The influence exerted by the nonhandicapped peer can be achieved through friendships or group activities. Also, school personnel may reward appropriate special academic behavior within the handicapped students' repertoire.

The increasing focus on adolescent learning styles and needs has led to some limited research, addressing the types of procedures that have the greatest effect on achievement among adolescent populations. One continual recurring point that much of the research indicates is that adolescents learn best from presentations and experiences that are meaningful to them, and when appropriate, this approach is combined with the use of three-dimensional materials (Miller, S.R., 1978). The use of meaningful formats and three-dimensional materials has generally resulted in more rapid learning and more enduring retention. The studies have emphasized that the meaningful orientation of any instruction should occur prior to the initiation of instruction. This thesis also emphasizes that meaningful instructional orientation can and should also occur during the teaching process. This requires the educator to continue to orient the learner on how such new material is relevant to previously learned material and previously experienced events.

Achievement Motivation

Achievement motivation is an area critical to the educator's search for factors contributing to learning. The area tends to encompass a variety of subthemes such as self-esteem, competition, incentives, birth order, sex stereotypes, and goal setting. In the area of goal setting, Locke (1968) found that the types of goals individuals set were mediated by the incentives associated with the goals' achievement. Research has found that establishing specific goals by the teacher and student improved performance of students regardless of the use or types of incentives.

Appropriate goals coincide with the student's interests and lifelong needs. Sabatino (1978) noted that school programs for adolescent handicapped too frequently neglect these critical and influential educational factors. Prewat (1976) sought to establish whether sex played a role in the goal setting of boys and girls in the beginning stages of adolescence. Using sixth, seventh, and eighth grade students, Prewat found that the personal goals of both males and females declined during grades six and seven, but that females in the eighth grade began to demonstrate increased interest in personal goals and expectations. Based on the research, Prewat concluded that females, during the formative periods of adolescence, were better able to withstand negative school-related peer pressure, while simultaneously formulating personal goals. In other sex-related research conducted by Etaugh and Rose (1975), using neutral stories, it was found that both male and female students in the seventh, ninth, and eleventh grades judged behavior based on stereotypical values and thus tended to devalue the achievement of females. In addressing a similar issue, Horner (1970-72) found that achievement motivation findings appropriate to males were not appropriate to females. In subsequent investigations, Horner's findings were confirmed, noting the sex role stereotyping is primarily responsible for the fear of success, and that the fear of success was largely found in females and handicapped students (Winchell, Fenner, & Shavers, 1974). Other studies have demonstrated that the closer some students come to achieving a poorly defined goal, the more fearful they become of success, and frequently their behaviors seemingly are designed to thwart success (Miller, S.R., 1981).

Johnson and Ahlgren (1976), addressing the sole issue of competition and cooperation, found, in using over 6,000 students in grades one through twelve, that competition is an intrinsic motivator and that competition correlates highly with the desire for the consistent enforcement of the rules. Some of the same studies have indicated that students with historic reputations as low achievers are reluctant to become involved in activities and competitive conditions in the classroom.

In discussing achievement as a factor of birth order, Glass, Nenlinger, and Brim (1974) found that birth order affects achievement motivation only for persons coming from high socioeconomic backgrounds, and that it has little or no effect on the school attitudes of students coming from lower socioeconomic environments. In other studies dealing with peer interaction, Burlingame (1967), Condry and Siman (1974), and Siman (1977) found that both antisocial male and female student behavior was associated with peer group pressure. Many of the antisocial student's peers perceive cooperation and school success as yielding to adult authority. Building upon the peer concept, Carter, DeTine, Spero, and Benson (1975) found that middle school students in the northeast judge individuals on their school performance, rather than on other variables such as race, social class, and physical appearance.

Memory and Information Retrieval

One of the continuing dilemmas facing educators is the definition of memory, its importance to the learning process, and the demonstration that it can be developed. Its existence as a component of the theories of learning of Inhelder and Piaget (1958), Skinner (1969), and Erikson (1963) has been directly noted or tacitly reflected. Its importance to academic achievement has been emphasized by such educators as Harris and Sipay (1975), Myers and Hammill (1976), and Mauser & Sabatino (1978). Holden (1974), in a study of the memory ability of retarded vs. normal groups, found that retarded adolescents have a greater problem in accurate enumeration of stimulus events when their stimuli are presented quickly. Holden further observed that the same adolescents had a greater difficulty when the memory task required the students to use in alternating patterns such senses as visual and auditory perception. Landau and Hagen (1974), in a study comparing handicapped and nonhandicapped preadolescent and adolescent populations, found that preadolescents have difficulty with retention resulting from a mediation deficiency. The adolescents did not exhibit major mediation difficulties, but appeared to be impaired because of deficiencies in the ability to verbalize responses correctly following the presentation of cues.

This and other studies suggest that internalization and verbalization are important mediating tools for students seeking to retain information. Smiley, Oakley, Worthen, Compione, and Brown (1977) studied middle school students, one group with reading problems, and the other group functioning within the normal range. They found that, when the poor reading group was compared to the normal group, the poor reading group had retention difficulties associated with reading comprehension. Further, this comprehension problem was associated with processing deficits. Paralleling the Smiley et al. (1977) study, Tarver, Hallahan, Cohen, and Kauffman (1977) conducted a study using adolescent boys identified as learning-disabled. The study reported that the subjects' learning and retention development was inhibited by selective attention deficits, and that these deficits represented a developmental lag as opposed to a permanent learning deficit.

Brown and Barclay (1976), using retarded students ranging in age from 2 to 7 years and 9 to 13 years sought to determine the ability of the individuals to facilitate their own memory efficiency. The study found that the younger group lacked the ability to develop conscious strategies to retain information and benefited little from training that facilitated the learning. The older group, however, while initially lacking memory skills, was able to learn strategies and techniques that facilitated the retention of information. The investigators also reported that memory problems tended to shape the types of strategies employed by individual subjects. Using preadolescent and adolescent youths, they noted that as an individual cognitively reaches a developmental level—generally around adolescence—the individual is able to develop elaborate memory strategies if the data are the result of personal cognitive activity, not externally imposed events or criteria. The data appear to indicate that information that students find interesting and/or necessary is retained by developing relevant strategies, and that information that fails to meet the criteria of interesting and/or necessary is forgotten.

Morality Interaction

Piaget and Erikson have spoken about the moral development of individuals and have indicated its importance in human development. More recently, Cox (1974) studied the behavior of black 13-year-old students to identify factors that affect the moral development of these adolescents. The findings of the study indicated that prior interactions shape moral judgment feelings and conduct, suggesting that peers and other individuals the adolescents encounter in a continuing and consistent pattern more profoundly affect their behavior than do preconceived values transmitted by the school, parents, and the church. Beech and Schoeppe (1974) found that neither males nor females use religious authority as the focus of moral behavior. They also found that although females tend to use social recognition as their barometer of social behavior, males tend to resist external moral control. Both male and female adolescents tend to measure themselves against measures of achievement, accomplishment, self-respect, and "wisdom." In two separate efforts (Handel, 1975; Turiel, 1977) it was concluded that cognitive behavior more than socioeconomic background tends to regulate attitudinal development. Turiel further echoed Erikson and Piaget in concluding that such behavior evolves through various developmental stages, and cognitive processes of equilibration and disequilibration regulate this attitudinal formation development. In a study addressing the behavior of disruptive and nondisruptive males, Freedman, Donahue, Rosenthal, Schlundt, and McFall (1978) found that the youths: (1) lacked the skills to deal with everyday problems and (2) tended to become increasingly embroiled in illegal behavior as poor moral decision-making skills led to further antisocial interaction. The investigators noted, however, that in seeking to measure various aspects of human behavior, no single variable emerged as a salient predictor. Jurkovic and Prentice (1977) held that neurotic and subculture youths approximate the same level of moral and cognitive development as nondisruptive youths, but their sociocognitive development did not parallel that of the general population.

Research on Cognitive Development and Reading

If moral and social interaction are in part phenomena of cognitive development as suggested earlier, then the questions are: (1) can cognitive behavior be trained in adolescents, and if so, (2) what strategies of training need to be pursued? Whitely and Davis (1974), using randomly selected students from inner-city schools, sought to train various cognitive decision-making abilities. The results indicated training can sometimes significantly affect student decision-making behavior, but the training must be of an intense nature. The study found that certain factors appeared to be more susceptible to training than other variables. Those most susceptible were items dealing with similarities, opposites, word patterns, and functional and quantity relationships. Those variables more resistant to training were instruction in class membership, class naming, and conversion relationships, suggesting that cognitive moral behavior may be less susceptible to formal school training and influence. Barratt (1975) studied the cognitive process and the ability of educators to train further the formal operational cognitive process, in providing instruction to youths 12 to 14 years of age. Barratt found that training for preformal operational age youths was not effective, but the training of 14-year-old adolescents did result in advanced formal operational skills. Additionally, the 14-year-old youths still retained these skills two months after the administration of the training program.

During the 1970s, a series of studies was conducted to assess the problems of the adolescent exhibiting reading difficulties in relation to the information-processing model discussed by Gibson (1969) and Neisser (1970). Otto (1977) observed that approaches to developing reading skills with learning-disabled adolescent readers have paralleled remedial methods validated with younger children. This suggests that educators have traditionally relied on strategies and materials that emphasize primary school-age-level vocabulary and decoding skills. A growing body of literature indicates that this practice may be counterproductive, in that the reading problems of adolescents and young adults seem more closely aligned with poor visual discrimination of graphic symbols within their syntactical structure rather than with problems that young children experience more frequently. Dunn-Rankin (1977) concluded that the major problem for poor readers was the lack of appropriate and efficient focus in the discrimination of words and phrases. The author noted that good readers did not rely solely on the discrimination of the first part of a word or sentence when decoding reading materials, but disabled readers tended to discriminate small units, thus reducing the speed and efficiency of information processing. The author also found that poorer readers frequently did not possess the peripheral processing competencies to process large word and sentence structures. Thus, their reading performances were restricted in discriminant quality, speed, and comprehension.

Other information-processing studies have demonstrated that good readers unconsciously control their discriminant focus and range so that perception is more effectively used. This postulate parallels that of Gibson and Levin (1975) and Neisser (1970), who found that efficient perceptual processes could not be measured and taught without the interaction of semantics and linguistics. Smiley, Pasquali, and Chandler (1976), investigating the factors that differentiate good and poor readers, found that perceptual discrimination with word familiarity was the most important factor relating to reading proficiency. They reported that good readers were more discriminately familiar with a greater number of graphic structures than were disabled readers. Smiley et al. (1976) concluded that disabled readers were not deficient in the basic reading aptitudes, but appeared to suffer from a developmental lag. This position parallels that of Frierson and Barbe (1967), who conjectured that reading problems among handicapped students may result from a slowed maturational development of the central nervous system. This factor has been frequently cited in the learning disabilities literature (Kephart, 1960; Kirk & Weiner, 1963).

Bouma and Legein (1977) concurred with the Dunn-Rankin (1977) findings that graphic discrimination was the primary factor affecting reading. They further observed that disabled readers were able to deal with simple single-unit graphics as well as good readers, but as the graphic presentation became more complex, the difference in reading performance became significantly greater. More specifically, Bouma and Legein (1977) found poor readers less able to deal with increased amounts of graphic presentations, such as longer words and sentences. This position was further substantiated by Kolers' (1975) study of disabled and poor adolescent readers. The investigation demonstrated that reading impairment was not caused primarily by deficits in linguistic or semantic skills, but by inefficient graphemic pattern discrimination and analysis. Silverman (1976) added that the size of the information unit perceived could be associated with an individual's ability to process information. The word is the single smallest integrated information unit, and an individual's ability to discriminate and obtain increasing units of information during a single focus increases the ability to learn and retain data.

Spring and Capps (1974) sought to differentiate the reading skills of normal and disabled readers. They found that disabled readers were slower in decoding symbols, that fewer than half of the poor readers used left-to-right scanning techniques to seek out information, that better than 80 percent of the normal readers used the left-to-right scanning techniques, and that normal readers had better long-term memory than disabled readers. These findings led the investigators to postulate that adolescents learn through an interaction between meaningfulness of constructs and retention of discrete data. This position is supported by the theories of learning of Ausubel (1969), Piaget (1958), and Neisser (1970). Further support is provided by Somerville and Wellman (1979), who found that younger and lower functioning individuals sought to retain information by using rote memory strategies, while older, normally functioning youths would seek to use a strategy of identifying and employing an existing learning system for retaining new material.

Glidden, Bilsky, and Powelski (1977) investigated the effects on differing input structure and their effects on the remediation process of disabled adolescent readers. The investigators found that meaningful context and the pairing of familiar words resulted in improved recall among educationally disabled readers. Emmerich and Ackerman (1978) found that adults tended to learn through the interaction of input, association, and output, while children learned primarily through the simple association of input data with existing data.

Naron (1978), in studying the process of learning among youths and adults, found that conceptual structures were used to decode and recall information, once again affirming that an interaction effect occurs as adolescents and young adults seek to process and learn information presented in a graphemic discriminant format. Maisto and Jerome (1977), studying the scanning and memory scanning techniques, also demonstrated the most efficient retention performance. The study affirmed similar findings of Maisto and Bacharach (1975). Kolers (1975) investigated the encoding skills of good and poor readers, ranging in age from 10.5 to 14.6 on two features of sentences, the semantic and graphemic. The data from the study suggest that older school-aged students with reading problems are not impaired in their reading on a linguistic or semantic basis, but rather on a graphemic pattern-analyzing level. Kolers (1975) noted, however, that the graphemic problem was unrelated to visual acuity, but appeared more closely related to perceptual processing deficits. Curley and Pabis (1978), in dealing with preadolescent students—one group emotionally disturbed, and a second group with normal characteristics—found that the nonemotionally disturbed group was able to form classifications with more stability and in a more "straightforward" way than the emotionally disturbed group. The study further found that those individuals classified as emotionally disturbed made less progress in classification skills than those identified as normal. Lastly, it was reported females had less difficulty in building classification matrices than did males, and thus were less likely to display cognitive emotional disturbance characteristics.

Delinquency and Handicaps

Some investigators have found a relationship between juvenile delinquency and educational handicapping conditions (Sabatino & Mauser, 1978). The findings indicate that many alienated youths exhibit school-related problems in reading, mathematics, and social adaptability. The research since the 1950s has indicated that those youths described as delinquent and those described as educationally handicapped are similar in the following characteristics:

1. The handicapped and juvenile delinquent youths exhibit low self-concept and frustration levels.
2. In both handicapped and juvenile delinquent populations, males outnumber females by a ratio of four to one.
3. Evidence exists that there is a greater occurrence of minimal brain dysfunction in the two populations.
4. Delinquents and students with handicaps tend to have difficulty in school, beginning in the primary grades.
5. Juvenile delinquents and handicapped youths appear to have no single cause and no single cure associated with their problems.
6. Both delinquents and disabled learners lack positive personality characteristics and have poor self-concepts.

Several investigators have found that delinquency may be a reaction against school failure. The studies found that the longer learning-disabled students stayed in school, the more likely they were to become involved with the police. Graubard (1967) found that disturbed delinquents had test profiles similar to students with certain types of learning disabilities. Other studies found delinquent youngsters have suffered from severe language disabilities and reading retardation (Sabatino & Mauser, 1978). The poor verbal performance found among delinquent youths may be a major cause for their poor school performance.

Many educators believe the handicapped and delinquent youths' attitudes need to be reshaped. Sabatino (1978) believes such problems are exasperated by differing expectations of the school and the home, and further notes that the schools are not totally to blame for delinquency. The author argues that national resources must be directed toward our disaffected youths. He recommends beginning programs that would enhance personal improvement of the environment and personal physical fitness. Sabatino also contends that the initiation of a nutrition program, to develop healthy minds and bodies, would be beneficial to these youths.

Community Alienation

Merton (1961) believes troubled youths frequently become alienated from their community. The alienation occurs when youths recognize the discrepancy between their perceived needs and wants, and what the community is equipped to provide and willing to allocate (McCandless, 1970). While, in individual cases, the alienation is often as intense for the nonhandicapped youth, the mildly handicapped youth is more often lost in the gulf between personal needs and wants and the community's ability and commitment to respond (Sabatino, 1978).

This chasm between the individual and the community in such areas as job training, job availability, social acceptance, and the rendering of social services produces frustration. Failure of the community to facilitate the social, moral, and professional development of handicapped youths often results in norm-violating activities including drug use, drug peddling, car thievery, and other rebellious social acts (Landis & Scarpitti, 1965). Upon adjudication by the courts, the youths are labeled delinquent and perceived by the community as a disruptive factor.

McCandless (1970), Sabatino (1978), and Shelton and Hill (1969) have indicated that a significant contributor to the conflict between youth and community is the level of expectation placed on students relative to professional growth, earnings, family involvement, and community conduct. These expectations place a significant pressure on nonhandicapped students from an upper socioeconomic environment, who traditionally are the achievers in our society (Miller, S.R., 1981). It is the nonhandicapped youths from the higher socioeconomic communities who tend to perform well in high school and college, obtain preferred jobs, and establish stable family constellations. For handicapped youths who more predictably come from less affluent homes and communities, the pursuit of the American dream becomes more elusive and thus contains the ingredients that produce community alienation (Scharf, 1978).

Youths and Preparation for Work

S.R. Miller (1978) observed that the handicapped and lower socioeconomic students tend to have a constricted perception of their job options and a distorted expectation of the skills required to perform a specific job. This position was supported by Sabatino (1978) and McCandless (1970). Each investigator reported that handicapped youths are confronted with problems associated with career identification, preparation, and retention as a result of (1) lack of appreciation of job market trends that affect the hiring of persons with new and unique skills and cause the termination of persons with skills in areas no longer in demand; (2) lack of familiarity with the interdependence of skills required for repairing small electrical engines and the wiring of a home; (3) unrealistic expectations of a job's growth potential; (4) unfamiliarity with skills required for job retention that are unrelated to work performance, such as social skills; and (5) inflexibility in addressing evolving work and social situations.

Brolin and Kokaska (1979), Payne (1980), and Alley and Deshler (1979) have addressed the benefits to students the world of jobs provides. Among the benefits articulated by investigators are: (1) developing personal independence, (2) developing personal autonomy, (3) supplementing social skills, (4) developing the ability to cope with routine, (5) identifying career interests, (6) identifying jobs not within the student's skill and/or interest range, and (7) improving self-concept. These authors note that the handicapped do not adapt to work and society as easily as nonhandicapped students. They often become delinquent, rejecting work responsibilities as a result of their inability to cope with social and manual demands of the work environment.

Morse and Weiss (1968) surveyed over 400 persons about their attitude toward work. They found that the majority of persons found work important to their feelings of belonging to society and serving a useful purpose. Morse and Weiss further found that work also served as a therapeutic experience for many persons. The investigators thus concluded that beyond the value of work for monetary and social rewards, work was critical in the U.S. socioeconomic and cultural structure.

Trent and Medsker (1968) report that in a study of 10,000 high school graduates the majority lacked adequate skills to develop career goals, and that many of these individuals eventually became victims of a fluctuating job market. These individuals tended to move from one job to another, without establishing professional skills criteria or employment goals.

Many of the individuals studied by Trent and Medsker (1968), and Morse and Weiss (1968), were youths who had traditionally required specialized services in school. Another significant portion of this handicapped population drops out of school around 16 years of age because of the school's irrelevant approach in addressing their academic, social, and career-vocation preparation needs. S.R. Miller (1978) and Sabatino (1974) reported that many handicapped and disadvantaged youths indicated they did not recognize the importance of reading, writing, and mathematics skills in the work place. As a result of these and other data, Phelps and Lutz (1977), Payne (1980), and Alley and Deshler (1979) recommended career preparation for such students. The preparation should begin in the primary grades and should continue until the conclusion of the formal school experience around the ages of 18 to 21 years old.

Osipow (1968) found that many youths in selecting a career looked to their father's choice in vocations. McCandless (1970) suggested that many youths' selection of the vocation of their parent is related to the concept of the exemplary model, as discussed in an earlier section on Albert Bandura. When the father, a pipe fitter, is the exemplary model, the son frequently chooses pipe-fitting. Such variables as home expectations, the technology of the times, the esteem a career has in the society, and the socioeconomic, racial, and religious background of the youth also contribute to the choices made in career selection. During the past two decades the career directions, choices, and opportunities have changed significantly. Much of the change can be attributed to the technological advances spurred by the rush to reach the moon and explore terrestrial bodies millions of miles from the planet earth (Miller, S.R., 1978).

The momentum, thus, of the technological boom also produced a need to modify job expectations and goals, the type of career counseling and training provided youths in the schools, and the salary levels of the changing job market. In such a volatile job market, the career counselor and student need to demonstrate caution in selecting the training provided the handicapped youth.

McCandless (1970) identified variables that may be considered in establishing counseling direction and training priorities.

1. the types of positions generally available and their technical qualifications
2. the social skills required to be trained and employed in the position
3. the rewards that stimulate the youth and the options available within a spectrum of positions
4. the functional requirements of the positions available in the market
5. the nonfunctional criteria, such as race, religion, and physical characteristics
6. the social forces in operation that can affect the employer's hiring decisions, such as affirmative action and the size of the potential employee pool.

CONCLUSION

Instructional practices in the schools have demonstrated that neither regular nor special educators working with handicapped youths have understood the learning problems, social needs, and appropriate instructional strategies to employ with this population (Brolin, 1974; Miller, S.R., 1978). One of the major impediments to serving the handicapped youth has been instructional personnel's propensity to provide the handicapped learner with inappropriate remedial instruction that contributes to the student's increased school frustration (Sabatino, 1974). Until the 1970s, the standard instructional program for most youths was previously ineffective remedial reading, mathematics, and social-learning programs. Special educators were trained to address the needs of children 5 to 11 years old and focused on the academic areas, in accordance with the general focus of public school programs. The regular educator, and particularly, the secondary educator, had no knowledge of or training on how to serve handicapped students. As a result, the regular educator has found educating the handicapped frustrating, and has contended that having the handicapped in the classroom retards the progress of the entire class.

However, with information concerning how adolescents learn, the types of learning problems handicapped experience, and the awareness of the types of programs that best benefit handicapped students, it can be expected that the adolescent and the school personnel can develop meaningful and appropriate services. Collateral benefits expected from such services include increased learning; heightened social awareness among concerned individuals; and the development of school exit competencies that enable handicapped adolescents to engage in an independent, self-sufficient manner of living.

REFERENCES

Alley, G., & Deshler, D. *Teaching the learning disabled adolescent: Strategies and methods*. Denver: Love Publishing Co., 1979.

Ausubel, D. P. *School learning: An introduction to education psychology*. New York: Holt, Rinehart & Winston, 1969.

Bandura, A. *Principles of behavior modification*. New York: Holt, Rinehart & Winston, 1969.

Barratt, B. B. Training and transfer in combinatorial problem solving: The development of formal reasoning during early adolescence. *Developmental Psychology*, 1975, *11*, 700-704.

Beech, R. P., & Schoeppe, A. Development of value systems in adolescents. *Developmental Psychology*, 1974, *10*, 644-656.

Bouma, H., & Legein, C. P. Foveal and parafoveal recognition of letters and words by dyslexics and by average readers. *Neuropsychologia*, 1977, *15*(1), 69-80.

Brolin, D. E. *Programming retarded in career education*. Working paper No. 1, University of Missouri—Columbia, September 1974.

Brolin, D. E. *Vocational preparation of retarded citizens*. Columbus, Ohio: Charles E. Merrill Publishing Co., 1976.

Brolin, D. E., & D'Alonzo, B. J. Critical issues in career education for the handicapped student. *Exceptional Children*, 1979, *45*, 246-253.

Brolin, D. E, & Kokaska, C. J. *Career education for handicapped children and youths*. Columbus, Ohio: Charles E. Merrill Publishing Co., 1979.

Brown, A. L., & Barclay, C. R. On the metamnemonic efficiency of retarded children. *Child Development*, 1976, *47*, 71-80.

Burlingame, W. V. *An investigation of the correlations of adherence to the adolescent peer culture*. Washington, D.C.: U.S. Department of Health, Education and Welfare, Office of Education, 1967.

Carter, D. E., DeTine, S. L., Spero, J., & Benson, F. W. Peer acceptance and school related variables in an integrated junior high school. *Journal of Educational Psychology,* 1975, *67,* 267-273.

Chandler, A., & Boroskin, A. Relationship of reward value and stated expectance in mentally retarded patients. *American Journal of Mental Deficiency,* 1971, *75,* 761-762.

Clarizio, H. F., & McCoy, G. F. *Behavior disorders in children* (2nd ed.). New York: Thomas Y. Crowell Co., 1976.

Clark, G. M. The state of the art in secondary programs for the handicapped. *Thresholds in Secondary Education,* 1976, *2,* 10-11.

Condry, J., & Siman, M. L. Characteristics of peer and adult oriented children. *Journal of Marriage and the Family,* 1974, *36,* 543-554.

Cox, N. Prior help, ego development, and helping behavior. *Child Development,* 1974, *45,* 594-603.

Cullinan, D., & Epstein, M. *Special education for adolescents: Issues and perspectives.* Columbus, Ohio: Charles E. Merrill Publishing Co., 1979.

Curley, J. F., & Pabis, R. Cognitive deficiencies in emotionally disturbed children. *The Journal of Psychology,* 1978, *98,* 145-158.

D'Alonzo, B. J., & Miller, S. R. A management model for learning disabled adolescents. *Teaching Exceptional Children,* 1977, *9,* 58-60.

Dunn-Rankin, P. Using after images in the analysis of letter and word focalization. *Journal of Reading Behavior,* 1977, *9*(2), 113-122.

Emmerich, H.J., & Ackerman, B. P. Developmental differences in recall: Encoding or retrieval? *Journal of Experimental Child Psychology,* 1978, *25*(3), 514-525.

Erikson, E. H. *Childhood & society* (2nd ed.). New York: W. W. Norton, 1963.

Etaugh, C., & Rose, S. Adolescent sex bias in the evaluation of performance. *Development Psychology,* 1975, *11,* 663-664.

Fox, P. B. Locus of control and self-concept in mildly retarded adolescents (Doctoral dissertation, University of Minnesota, 1972). *Dissertation Abstracts International,* 1972, *33,* 2807B.

Freedman, B. J., Donahue, C. P., Rosenthal, L., Schlundt, D. G., & McFall, R. M. A social-behavioral analysis of skill deficits in delinquent and nondelinquent boys. *Journal of Consulting and Clinical Psychology,* 1978, *46,* 1448-1462.

Frierson, P. C., & Barbe, W. B. (Eds.). *Educating children with learning disabilities: Selected readings.* New York: Appleton-Century-Crofts, 1967.

Gardner, W. I. *Learning and behavior characteristics of exceptional children and youth: A humanistic behavioral approach.* Boston: Allyn & Bacon, 1977.

Gibson, E. J. *Principles of perceptual learning and development.* New York: Appleton-Century-Crofts, 1969.

Gibson, E. J., & Levin, H. *The psychology of reading.* Cambridge, Mass.: Massachusetts Institute of Technology Press, 1975.

Glass, D. C., Nenlinger, J., & Brim, D. G. Birth order, verbal intelligence, and educational aspirations. *Child Development,* 1974, *45,* 807-811.

Glidden, L. M., Bilsky, L. H., & Powelski, C. Sentence mediation and stimulus blocking in free recall. *American Journal of Mental Deficiency,* 1977, *82*(1), 84-90.

Graubard, P. S. Psycholinguistic correlates of reading disabilities in disturbed children. *Journal of Special Education I,* 1967, *4,* 363-368.

Grossman, H. J. *Manual on terminology and classification in mental retardation.* Baltimore: Garamond/Pridemark, 1973.

Handel, A. Attitudinal orientation and cognitive functioning among adolescents. *Developmental Psychology*, 1975, *11*, 667-675.

Harris, A. J., & Sipay, E. R. *How to increase reading ability* (6th ed.). New York: David McKay, 1975.

Harter, S., & Zigler, E. The assessment of effectance motivation in normal and retarded children. *Developmental Psychology*, 1974, *10*, 169-180.

Holden, E. A. Enumeration versus tracking during unimodel and multimodel sequential information processing in normals and retardates. *Developmental Psychology*, 1974, *10*, 667-671.

Horner, M. S. Femininity and successful achievement: A basic inconsistency. In J. Bardwick, E. M. Douvan, M. S. Horner, & D. Gutsmann (Eds.), *Feminine personality and conflict*. Belmont, Calif.: Brooks/Cole Publishing Co., 1970-72.

Hunt, J. Intrinsic motivation and its role in psychological development. In D. Levine (Ed.), *Nebraska Symposium on Motivation*. Lincoln: University of Nebraska Press, 1965.

Inhelder, B., & Piaget, J. *The growth of logical thinking from childhood to adolescence*. New York: Basic Books, 1958.

Johnson, D. W., & Ahlgren, A. Relationship between student attitudes and cooperation and competition and attitudes toward schooling. *Journal of Educational Psychology*, 1976, *68*, 92-102.

Jurkovic, G., & Prentice, N. M. Relation of moral and cognitive development of dimensions of juvenile delinquency. *Journal of Abnormal Psychology*, 1977, *86*, 414-420.

Keogh, B. K., Cahill, C. W., & MacMillan, D. L. Perception of interruption by educationally handicapped children. *American Journal of Mental Deficiency*, 1972, *77*, 107-108.

Kephart, N. C. *The slow burner in the classroom*. Columbus, Ohio: Charles E. Merrill Publishing Co., 1960.

Kirk, S. A., & Weiner, B. B.(Eds). *Behavioral research on exceptional children*. Washington, D.C.: The Council for Exceptional Children, National Education Association, 1963.

Kolers, P. A. Pattern-analyzing disability in poor readers. *Developmental Psychology*, 1975, *11*, 282-290.

Landau, B. L., & Hagen, J. W. Acquisition and retention in normal and educable retarded children. *Child Development*, 1974, *45*, 643-650.

Landis, J. R., & Scarpitti, F. R. Perceptions regarding value orientations and legitimate opportunity: Delinquents and non-delinquents. *Social Forces*, 1965, *44*, 83-91.

Lawrence, E. A., & Winschel, J. F. Locus of control: Implications for special education. *Exceptional Children*, 1975, *41*, 483-490.

Leland, H., Nihira, K., Foster, R., Shellhaas, M., & Kagin, E. *Conference on measurement of adaptive behaviors, III*. Parsons, Kans.: Parsons State Hospital and Training Center, 1968.

Levy, J. Social reinforcement and knowledge of results as determinants of motor performance among EMR children. *American Journal of Mental Deficiency*, 1974, *78*, 752-758.

Locke, E. A. Toward a theory of task motivation and in centuries. *Organizational Behavior and Human Performance*, 1968, *3*, 159-189.

Maiers, H. W. (Ed.). *Three theories of child development: The contributions of Erik H. Erikson, Jean Piaget, and Robert R. Sears, and their applications* (Rev. ed.). New York: Harper & Row, 1969.

Maisto, A. A., & Bacharach, V. E. Utilization of position cues by retarded children in serial learning. *American Journal of Mental Deficiency*, 1975, *79*(4), 391-396.

Maisto, A. A., & Jerome, M. A. Encoding and high-speed memory scanning of retarded and nonretarded adolescents. *American Journal of Mental Deficiency*, 1977, *82*(3), 282-286.

Mann, L., Goodman, L., & Weiderholt, J. *Teaching the learning disabled adolescent.* Boston: Houghton Mifflin, 1978.

Mauser, A. J., & Sabatino, D. A. Reading theory and research with problem adolescents and chronically disruptive youth, 1978, *4*, 137-179.

McCandless, B. R. *Adolescents—Behavior and development.* Hinsdale, Ill.: The Dryden Press, 1970.

Mercer, D. C., & Snell, M. E. *Learning theory research in mental retardation.* Columbus, Ohio: Charles E. Merrill Publishing Co., 1977.

Merton, R. K. *Social theory and social structure.* New York: Free Press of Glencoe, 1961.

Miller, S. R. *Secondary assessment and programming.* Unpublished paper, Carbondale, Ill., 1975.

Miller, S. R. Career education. In D. A. Sabatino & A. J. Mauser (Eds.), *Educating norm-violating and chronic disruptive secondary school-aged youth* (Vol. 2). Boston: Allyn & Bacon, 1978.

Miller, S. R. A crisis in appropriate education: The dearth of data for secondary adolescents programs. *Journal of Special Education*, 1981, *15*, 351-360.

Miller, S. R., Ewing, N., & Phelps, A. Vocational education for the handicapped: A historical perspective. In D. A. Sabatino and L. A. Mann (Eds.), *The fourth review of special education.* New York: Grune & Stratton, 1980.

Miller, S. R., Sabatino, D. A., & Larsen, R. Agreement between university and local educational agency administration of special education on selected issues in the professional preparation of secondary special education. *Exceptional Children*, in press.

Miller, T. L., Sabatino, D. A., & Miller, S. R. Violent behaviors in the secondary school: Problems and preventions. *School Social Work Quarterly*, 1979, *1*, 149-152.

Morse, N. C., & Weiss, R. S. The function and meaning of work and the job. In D. G. Zytoweski (Ed.), *Vocational behavior.* New York: Holt, Rinehart & Winston, 1968, pp. 7-16.

Myers, P. J., & Hammill, D. D. *Methods for learning disorders* (2nd ed.). New York: John Wiley & Sons, 1976.

Naron, N. K. Developmental changes in world attribute utilization for organization and retrieval in free recall. *Journal of Experimental Child Psychology*, 1978, *25*(2), 279-297.

Neisser, U. Visual imagery as process and as experience. In J. S. Antrobus (Ed.), *Cognition and affect.* Boston: Little, Brown & Co., 1970.

Osipow, S. H. *Theories of career development.* New York: Appleton-Century-Crofts, 1968.

Otto, J. Reading cue utilization by low achieving college freshmen. *Journal of Reading Behavior*, 1977, *9*(1), 71-84.

Payne, J. S. *Teaching exceptional adolescents.* Columbus, Ohio: Charles E. Merrill Publishing Co., 1980.

Phelps, A. L., & Lutz, R. J. *Career exploration and preparation for the special needs learner.* Boston: Allyn & Bacon, 1977.

Piaget, J. *Play, dreams, and imitation in childhood.* New York: Norton, 1958.

Prewat, R. S. Mapping the affective domain in young adolescents. *Journal of Educational Psychology*, 1976, *68*, 566-572.

Rotter, J. B. *Social learning and clinical psychology.* Englewood Cliffs, N.J.: Prentice-Hall, 1954.

Rotter, J. B. Some problems and misconceptions related to the construct of internal versus external reinforcement. *Journal of Consulting and Clinical Psychology*, 1975, *43*, 56-57.

Sabatino, D. A. *Neglect and delinquent children.* EDC Report, Wilkes-Barre, Pa.: Wilkes College, 1974.

Sabatino, D. A. Norm-violating secondary school youth: Demographic findings. In D. A. Sabatino & A. J. Mauser (Eds.), *Specialized education in today's secondary schools* (Vol. 1). Boston: Allyn & Bacon, 1978.

Sabatino, D. A. Secondary special education: A case of benign neglect. In J. B. Jordan, D. A. Sabatino, & L. C. Sam (Eds.), *Disruptive youth in school*. Reston, Va.: The Council for Exceptional Children, 1980.

Sabatino, D. A., & Mauser, A. J. *Intervention strategies for specialized secondary education*. Boston: Allyn & Bacon, 1978.

Scharf, P. *Moral education*. Davis, Calif.: Responsible Action, 1978.

Shelton, J., & Hill, J. P. The effects on cheating of achievement anxiety and knowledge of peer performance. *Developmental Psychology*, 1969, *1*, 449-455.

Silverman, W. P. Can words be processed as integrated units? *Perception Psychophysics*, 1976, *20*, 143-152.

Siman, M. L. Application of a new model of peer group influence to natural existing adolescent friendship groups. *Child Development*, 1977, *48*, 270-274.

Skinner, B. F. *Contingencies of reinforcement*. New York: Appleton-Century-Crofts, 1969.

Smiley, S. S., Oakley, D. D., Worthen, D., Compione, J. C., & Brown, R. L. Recall of thematically relevant material by adolescent good and poor readers as a function of written versus oral presentation. *Journal of Educational Psychology*, 1977, *64*, 381-387.

Smiley, S. S., Pasquali, F. L., & Chandler, C. L. The pronunciation of familiar, unfamiliar, and synthetic words by good and poor adolescent readers. *Journal of Reading Behavior*, 1976, *8*, 289-297.

Somerville, S. C., & Wellman, H. M. The development of understanding as an indirect memory strategy. *Journal of Experimental Child Psychology*, 1979, *27*(1), 71-86.

Spring, C., & Capps, C. Encoding speed, rehearsal, and probed recall of dyslexic boys. *Journal of Educational Psychology*, 1974, *66*(5), 780-786.

Tarver, S. G., Hallahan, D. P., Cohen, S. B., & Kauffman, S. M. Visual selective attention and verbal rehearsal in learning disabled boys. *Journal of Learning Disabilities*, 1977, *10*, 26-34.

Trent, J. W., & Medsker, L. L. *Beyond high school: A psychosociological study of 10,000 high school graduates*. San Francisco: Jossey-Bass, 1968.

Turiel, E. Conflict and transition in adolescent moral development, II: The resolution of disequilibrium through structural reorganization. *Child Development*, 1977, *48*, 634-637.

Vance, H. B. Trends in secondary curriculum development. *Academic Therapy*, 1977, *13*(1), 29-35.

Weiderholt, J. L., & McNutt, G. Evaluating materials for handicapped adolescents. *Journal of Learning Disabilities*, 1977, *10*(3), 132-140.

White, R. W. Competence and psychosexual stages of development. In M. R. Jones (Ed.), *Nebraska Symposium on Motivation*. Lincoln: University of Nebraska Press, 1960.

Whitely, S. E., & Davis, R. V. Effects of cognitive intervention on latest ability measured from analogy items. *Journal of Educational Psychology*, 1974, *66*, 710-717.

Winchell, R., Fenner, D. J., & Shavers, P. Impact of co-education on fear of success imagery expressed by male and female high school students. *Journal of Educational Psychology*, 1974, *66*, 726-780.

Yussen, S. R., & Levy, V. M. Developmental changes in knowledge about different retrieval problems. *Developmental Psychology*, 1977, *13*, 114-118.

Chapter 6

Assessment of
Adolescent Handicapped

The process of providing services to educationally handicapped adolescents requires school personnel to adhere to litigation and legislation. The major ingredient of the litigation and legislation mandates that all students must receive a free and appropriate education in the least restrictive environment. More specifically, the schools must allow a student to participate in regular education courses and programs, unless assessment information clearly demonstrates that the types of services would be more educationally beneficial (Turnbull & Schulz, 1979).

In providing services for handicapped youths, the first contributory step is the individualized evaluation or assessment process.

The development of an assessment process for the secondary-aged handicapped youth requires new visions among educators. The vision must transcend the traditional academic curriculum and the achievement test. The emerging demands of legislation and litigation insist that the professional educator build programs and services for the handicapped adolescent that reflect the student's life interests and career potential.

ASSESSMENT

The enactment of federal and state legislation addressing the public school's responsibilities for the handicapped has made mandatory an appropriate and useful assessment process. The purpose of the process is the collection, analysis, and utilization of data in the development of an appropriate educational program. As noted earlier, the information sought for adolescents must significantly deviate from the data collected on preadolescent populations. Yet, the basic purpose of the assessment process remains the same.

Assessment is the collection of data that will enable school personnel, parents, advocates, and whenever appropriate, students, to develop an educational program that fulfills the mandate of federal PL 94-142, The Education for All Handicapped Children Act—a free and appropriate education. The information collected has traditionally included data from parents, physicians, social workers, and school personnel.

Information gathered by the school has included such demographic information as age, sex, birthdate, number of siblings, and previous medical history. Other information includes previous school history, previous test scores, and observations by teachers, psychologists, school bus drivers, and other individuals interacting with the student. Essentially, the information is intended to enable those participating in the Individual Educational Program (IEP) meeting to learn about factors that may be contributing to the student's learning problems, and to reflect this learning history in the development of the educational program. Historical data as well as data on the student's current performance level are expected to provide school personnel the essential information needed to establish clear and concise program goals, objectives, and activities. Additionally, these data enable school personnel to make decisions about educational placement, the types of personnel needed to serve the youth, and ancillary services that may be required. The information is further intended to aid school personnel in evaluating a student's progress in the prescribed program.

SUMMATIVE AND FORMATIVE PROCEDURES

The tendency in the late 1950s and 1960s, which continued into the 1970s, was to prepare the secondary school population for higher education. This narrow view, until recently, impeded the public educator's involvement in career-oriented programs that did not focus entirely on university preparation. The rigidity of educational personnel and the institutions they represent is only one side of the equation. The other side is that the advocates of integrated career education have failed to define clearly their focus and articulate their educational goals. Educators of secondary-aged youths have varied their definitions, scope, and purpose and have usually advocated a mixture of activities and practices. Assessment and programming for the handicapped adolescent prepare students for various career areas through the acquisition of basic academic and/or vocational skills and competency as they are related to specified interests in either industry, the crafts, the arts, or professions. The process of lifelong career preparation is multifaceted, inclusive of academic achievement, work attitudes, vocational aptitudes, and work experience (Jones, Blaney, & Sabatino, 1975). It is thus necessary to operationalize the education program for handicapped youths and to assess the students in many of the following areas, using formative and summative assessment instruments:

1. psychomotor skills (both gross and fine motor)
2. language skills (including reading and verbal fluency)
3. numerical skills (mathematics)
4. self-image
5. attitude toward others, school, and work
6. career interests
7. work experience
8. physiological factors, including general appearance and physical development

This requires implementation of an assessment process that measures such generic factors as intellectual potential, social-personal skills, cultural awareness and adaptation, achievement levels, psychological interest and awareness, and general appearance and capacity.

In the past, educators have relied heavily on standardized assessment instruments that have sought to summarize the student's performance capability through a single number, or series of numbers (e.g., 100 IQ), without identifying particular aspects of an individual's intellect that may demonstrate strengths or weaknesses. The courts and numerous legislators are beginning to conclude that such information is inadequate for program development and services. The position of the courts and the legislators is that: (1) summarizing tests (summative information) fail to provide an adequate amount of information to develop appropriate programs and services; (2) the summative test often is standardized on a population that does not adequately represent the handicapped youth's culture and experience; (3) such information frequently is unavailable to the teacher as a result of school policy; and (4) the data resulting from such tests are frequently uninterpretable by school personnel.

To remedy the limitation of summative test data, educators of handicapped youths are now seeking to balance the assessment process between appropriate summative assessment measures and standardized and nonstandardized formative measures. The formative test is an instrument or series of instruments in which a series of items or test scores can assist the teacher to pinpoint a student's level of performance in a specific variety area of performance and/or attitude. Using such information, instructional personnel can initiate services that are sensitive to the student's ability to perform. The use of summative scores, such as 100 IQ or 4.3 reading performance, frequently provides insufficient information for a teacher to select reading material and instructional strategies, while a formative test identifying word recognition errors provides a baseline for word recognition training.

ASSESSMENT PATTERN

The initiation of the assessment process can best begin with counseling followed by informal testing, more formal testing, and finally assessment conducted on site at experience-based job and work stations. The culmination of this procedure is the creation of a timed sequential path that leads to appropriate placement and educational opportunities. This approach differs significantly from the procedures used in the schools to assess the performance level of elementary level children. In assessing such children, schools have traditionally employed standardized tests that measure only academic achievement. The test administrator and school instructional personnel have not sought to balance the student's progress with school goals and student needs. Decisions on programs, instructional approach, and material have traditionally reflected teacher or school interests and biases.

The following is a semester-long, step-by-step assessment pattern that will produce useful information in educating the handicapped adolescent.

First Day: Consultations

The school coordinator of services for handicapped adolescents meets with the student. The initial contact determines the compatibility of the adult and student. It also establishes the student's general career interests, interpersonal attitudes, and physical appearance.

First Week: Informal Assessment

Assessment is conducted to determine the student's academic competencies, personal characteristics, vocational aptitudes and interests, and other traits deemed to be valuable in the assessment process. The assessment can be conducted and handled using both teacher-made and commercial tests.

Second Week: Consultation and Staffing

Student and teacher discuss interests and identified academic competencies, career goals, and personality variables. The student and teacher establish the types of academic program and simulation stations that reflect the student's interests, needs, and capabilities. This is the point where the goals, objectives, and placement decisions are made.

Third, Fourth, and Fifth Weeks: Simulation Station Assessment

The academic program and simulation station teachers informally pretest and posttest the student's aptitude, interests, and competencies in each of the simulated areas. The data from the tests will be used to guide the decision concerning practical placement and concurrent academic experiences.

Sixth Week to the End of School Semester: Simulation Station Placement and Assessment

The student's ability to function appropriately at the career-vocational station and in the classroom is continuously monitored to determine whether academic, social-personal, and vocational competencies are progressing toward the terminal objectives. Subsequent objectives will address additional experiences required to fuse the student's interests and needs.

Last Week of Semester: Evaluation and Consultation

The student and teacher discuss the student's experiences, acquired skills, and future educational and career plans. It is during this period that the student's academic and career goals for the coming semester are reviewed, modified when appropriate, and finally established. As time permits, this evaluation process should be continued during the entire semester so that the teacher and student are continually aware of the student's rate of progress.

Through the continuous process of assessment, the student must believe that his or her needs, interests, and skills are the critical variables in reaching programmatic and service decisions. As had been noted earlier, the period of adolescence is one of heightened personal and social awareness. Rebellion against authority is a frequent factor in school management, and this factor of rebellion has frequently become acute among educational handicapped youths who have experienced several years of continuing school failure and neglect. Repeatedly they have believed that they lack input into the system and, as a result, have resisted the educational prescriptions composed without their input (Froehlich & Hoyt, 1959; Miller, 1979). The first step in working with youths is fact-finding, accomplished through a consultative process in which the student and educator acknowledge the importance of developing adult independent living skills. These skills will enable the youths to become self-confident and self-sustaining contributors to the community. To achieve this outcome, the educator must: (1) determine the type of data that are needed for an effective career-vocational program, (2) establish interpersonal interactions that will enable the educator to obtain the information in an informal manner, (3) organize the collected data so that they can be used effectively in outlining alternatives, (4) reach general and/or specific conclusions regarding the educational and experiential base, (5) encourage the youths to participate in the process of data collection and decision making, and (6) establish a procedure that will enable all the participants involved in the decision to evaluate its efficacy.

ASSESSMENT PROCEDURES

Among the data parameters required of any assessment process are observable and measurable student characteristics. The data can be obtained through the use of standardized instruments, teacher-made checklists, criterion-referenced tests, or other informal formative instruments yielding data that enable the school to develop relevant and efficient programs. Though a list of assessment targets could be extensive, below are 11 major factors that the educator would be expected to consider:

1. Physical appearance: The student's physical appearance tacitly expresses the importance he or she places on the experience. Appearance is often a major factor to an individual meeting a person for the first time, since the appearance provides information from which to make a judgment about employment compatibility.
2. Punctuality: The student's early or late arrival to a meeting or worksite may reflect his or her attitude toward, and the importance he or she places on, an experience.
3. Oral communication: The ability that an individual possesses in communicating effectively with others is an essential component in human interaction. Those handicapped by poor fluency, inappropriate vocabulary, and improper syntax may experience difficulty in working with others and maintaining open channels of communication.
4. Following directions: The individual who can listen and follow work instructions will generally outperform the student who cannot or will not.
5. Reliability: The individual who assumes responsibility for completing tasks in the agreed manner and who can thus be trusted by an employer is not only more employable, but also more likely to retain the work position.
6. Cooperation: In working with an individual, it is important that the youth not only understand how to work with others, but how to interact in a mutually productive manner.
7. Initiative: The individual able to identify work requirements and independently assume initiative is often prized by employers. Those able to assume initiative are self-starters, who not only make a contribution to themselves but also to the organization.
8. Leadership: The leader is someone who can determine long- and short-term needs and initiate action that leads to the realization of these needs. The ability to lead without offending or threatening the employer often leads to professional advancement.
9. Innovation: The individual possessing the competency to view alternative strategies and select modes different from those presently being practiced may be rewarded by the employer.

10. Flexibility: The individual who is unable to adapt old behavior or adopt new behaviors to meet and resolve new problems frequently comes into conflict with those committed to solving the problem.
11. Social perceptions: The youth's perception of his or her community and the values practiced by the individuals who live and work in it will influence the youth's response to specific work and behavioral expectations. Those youths with inaccurate perceptions will face equivalent difficulties in work stations as the individual with rejecting values.

Awareness and determination of the student's behavior relative to the above factors will assist the educator to determine informally the level of the major job-related behaviors. This information, combined with data from formal assessment and informal consultation, will aid in identifying appropriate training and career goals with the student. In the next section, informal consultative procedures are described.

Interview Data from the Consultative Process

Frequently, decisions on career direction are based on too few factors. Erikson and Wentling (1976) and Sawin (1969) noted the need to use a variety of measures and procedures to assess youths effectively. Many authors also emphasize that the informal consultation process is not intended as a therapeutic period, but as an information collection-sharing time. During this time, the educator and student can learn more about each other and share insights concerning career opportunities and potential training opportunities.

A number of approaches can be adopted to gather pertinent information in a supportive atmosphere. Suggested guidelines include:

- General information questions should be asked at the beginning so that the student is put at ease, and does not perceive the questioning as threatening and improper.

- The questions asked should be within the student's experience and knowledge.

- The vocabulary should be easily understood by the student and should not place the individual in an uncomfortable position. The framing of the questions should not be viewed as demeaning.

- The discussion must follow a logical pattern that makes sense to the student and does not require radical shifts in thought or responses.

- The educator's statements should be clear and definitive.

- The questions should be phrased so that the student feels comfortable with the direction and intent of the discussion.

- The questions should not be phrased in a way that expresses the educator's biases and values.

The information obtained from the student-teacher interaction can be used to assist the educator in determining assessment procedures that need to be pursued along with some general conclusions concerning the types of social environments that would be most receptive to the youth. The consultative procedure is part of the formative assessment process. During this process, the educator should be employing techniques that enable him or her to reach objective decisions about a student's responses and behavioral demeanor. During the interview process, the educator can be measuring such factors as attention, frequency of appropriate or inappropriate responses to questions or statements, and levels of interest or attitudes as related to work, family, and wages. The observation and measurement of such behavior can be achieved through frequency, duration, and intensity procedures described in Chapter 7.

This observation procedure can measure the duration of the student's attention, the frequency of appropriate or inappropriate responses, and the level of interest the student exhibits during the consultative process. The observations can be made during the educator-student exchange, and can be recorded immediately after the meeting, thus enabling the educator to use objective data in reaching decisions about the student's expressed attitudes and interests.

Informal Formative Procedures

The consultative model is part of the formative assessment process, in which the educator seeks to obtain as much relevant data as possible in making programmatic decisions. Among other informal formative procedures available to school personnel are the following.

Criterion Reference Tests

These instruments seek to measure the student's performance level with a specific instructional material or activity. The test has a series of questions or activities that the student must answer or perform. Based on the pretest results, the educator can determine the student's readiness for the material or preactivity, and the instructional proficiency level. Following the completion of the material or activity, the test is readministered and the educator can then judge the student's new level of performance. This information provides the educator and student with objective information of the student's achievement level relative to specific objectives, and enables both to then establish the next logical step in the instructional-experiential path.

Checklists

Checklists are sampling procedures for assessing a series of behaviors that is appropriate to program development or evaluation. The checklist can be used to elicit the student's or teacher's perceptions of his or her school performance; it can be used by potential employers as they identify desired work behavior, or it can be employed by students as they assess their own school or work-related behavior. Although the checklist can be expected to yield some subjective data, it does enable the teacher and student to assess his or her perception of his or her performance against others in critical decision-making positions.

Observations

As noted earlier, observational techniques can be effective measures of the precise strength of the behavior. Observations can be made by either a third party (e.g., teacher's aide), the teacher, or the student. Under any of the above parameters, the observer identifies specific behavior or a series of behaviors that may impede or contribute to the learning process. With the behavior identified and procedure for measurement established, the observer commences the observation process. As an example, an educator may choose to observe a youth's on-task behavior during mathematics class. What the educator is seeking to determine is: (1) duration of time that the youth attends to the task before being distracted, (2) duration of time spent on the distraction, and (3) types of distractions negatively affecting on-task behavior. Once the educator has such information, he or she can map out an instructional strategy designed to increase on-task behavior and reduce off-task behavior. Observations may continue to support the efficacy of the strategy.

FORMAL INTEREST TESTS

Besides the use of the informal formative assessment procedures just discussed, the educator may also make use of formal standardized instruments that have demonstrated usefulness to the education process. For example, Brolin (1976), Goodman and Mann (1976), and Sawin (1969) each noted that assessment should focus on a variety of variables—something formal tests can accomplish well. Further, Erikson and Wentling (1976) noted that a variety of methodologies can be combined to assess the student's skills and readiness for specific experiences. Formal tests, with their varied formats and approaches, accomplish this with comparative efficiency. Despite this, Jones, Blaney, and Sabatino (1975) have warned that there are no magic formal standardized test instruments. Tests generally only help to substantiate or reject the conclusions of the educator, student, parent, and psychologist drawn from other procedures previously cited.

Intelligence Tests

The first area to be explored is the assessment of individual intelligence. Since the 1930s, the developers of tests have sought to develop instruments that provide professional personnel usable data that enable them to plan programs for students more effectively. Of the individual intelligence tests developed since the 1930s, the *Wechsler Intelligence Scale for Children* and the *Wechsler Adult Intelligence Scale* are two of the most frequently used and cited measures. As you will note from the descriptions, both tests have verbal and performance scores, plus individual scores. These scores provide educators with differentiated data from which parts of programs can be initiated.

WISC-R

The *Wechsler Intelligence Scale for Children*—Revised *(WISC-R)* (Wechsler, 1974) covers ages 5 to 16 years. The test addresses such verbal areas as information, comprehension, arithmetic, similarities, vocabulary, and digit span as well as such performance areas as picture completion, picture arrangement, block design, object assembly, coding, and mazes. The test yields scores for each of the specific areas cited above, the general areas of verbal and performance, and an overall score. The standardization of the test includes proportional samples of minority groups, and urban and rural dwellers. The reliability of the test and the subtests is high. Scores on the *WISC-R* tend to be lower than scores on the older *WISC* version. The value of the test is that it yields information about an individual's performance profile, using a variety of different subtest scores as well as an overall score. Such information is potentially more useful to an educator seeking to develop a program for a student.

WAIS

The *Wechsler Adult Intelligence Scale (WAIS)* (Wechsler, 1955) begins at age 16 and extends into adulthood. The test addresses such verbal areas as information, comprehension, arithmetic, similarities, digit span, and vocabulary, and such performance areas as digit symbol, picture completion, block design, picture arrangement, and object assembly. The test yields scores for each of the specific areas cited above, the general areas of verbal and performance, and an overall score. The test has good reliability, but lacks data on predictive validity. Like the *WISC-R*, the *WAIS* yields scores that enable educational personnel to develop individual profiles that reflect an individual's intelligence in relation to the total spectrum of human ability.

Formal Aptitude Tests

For the early childhood and primary level teacher, aptitude is the assessment of basic sensory-motor and perceptual (auditory and visual) functions. For the education of handicapped adolescents, aptitude assessment includes perception and sensory-motor skills, but these skills are integrated into a composite, multifactor, mental ability test. As Froehlich and Hoyt (1959) note, the simple scholastic aptitude test that yields a single summative score has definite limitations if it is to be used to assess a student's readiness for specific career preparation. The work of Thurstone (1938) enabled the designers of tests to identify seven basic factors related to mental ability. They are: verbal meaning, space, reasoning, number, word fluency, memory, and perception. It was not Thurstone's contention that these factors were the only ones related to mental ability, and subsequent researchers have sought to further delineate mental ability and achievement-related factors (Bloom, Engelhart, Furst, Hill, & Krathwohl, 1956; Guilford, 1967; Guilford, Kettner, & Christensen, 1956). Many test designs still rely upon Thurstone's findings and postulates.

The collection of sufficient data to reflect the student's academic, social, and interest competencies, and to meet new federal guidelines that now require the schools to obtain information from more than one test, mandates the aptitude assessment battery. This includes instruments from the areas of reading, mathematics, and general career-vocational education.

Reading Tests

The tests that can be utilized are individual reading tests that are designed to yield information about a student's word attack skills, oral reading fluency, silent and oral reading comprehension, and listening skills. These tests are administered to the student by the educator, generally on a one-on-one basis. The advantage of such tests is that they enable a school to obtain information about the student's achievement level and, equally as important, his or her style of learning. Such information is critical in the development of instructional strategies and programs for the educationally handicapped learner.

The following are some individual reading tests that could be used as effective measures of the secondary-aged handicapped youth's reading level.

The Gates-McKillop Reading Diagnostic Tests

This set of tests (Gates & McKillop, 1962) has been called the most comprehensive diagnostic reading battery. It provides 28 scores: omissions, additions, repetitions, mispronunciations (reversals, partial reversals, total reversals, wrong beginnings, wrong middle, wrong ending, wrong in several parts, total), oral reading total, wordsflash presentation, recognizing and blending common word parts, giving letter sounds, naming capital letters, naming lower-case letters, recognizing the visual forms of sounds (nonsense words, initial letters, final letters, vowels), auditory blending, spelling, oral vocabulary, syllabication, and auditory discrimination. Administration of the entire battery requires considerable time and expertise. It is designed for use with second through sixth graders, but has been used with low-reading-level adolescents because of its plethora of information. The test uses four expectancy criteria (mental age, oral reading status, grade level, and oral vocabulary). While the test has some norming problems, its manual is developed and useful to the teacher seeking to use the information for diagnostic purposes.

The Woodcock Reading Mastery Tests (WRMT)

WRMT (Woodcock, 1973) is used with kindergarten through twelfth graders. Six areas are assessed for a total score: letter naming, word identification, nonsense, word attack, word comprehension, and passage comprehension. For each, several scores may be derived: grade equivalent, percentile rank, age scores, and four levels of criterion scores (easy reading level, reading grade level, failure reading level, and relative mastery of grade level). The battery requires about 30 minutes to administer and is presented in two parallel forms.

The test was prepared so that both professionals and paraprofessionals can use the instrument. The developers have developed a well-normed instrument that provides separate norms for sex and socioeconomic status populations. It can be useful to personnel working with special populations.

Mathematics Tests

Mathematics is another critical area of assessment concern. Indigenous to any academic and career-vocational program is the use of numbers, whether for computing the radius of a circle or balancing a ledger. The following are two individual mathematics tests.

The Comprehensive Tests of Basic Skills: Arithmetic (1970)

This battery of tests is divided into four levels covering grades 2.5 to 12. Three areas are covered by the test: computation, concepts, and applications, with scores given for each area, plus total scores. Test administration requires approximately 70 minutes. Scoring can be either manual or by computer. The test on computation is geared toward low-performing students, though these same students may experience difficulty with the subcomponents on concepts and applications. The test has been refined and the norms reflect a slight overrepresentation of minority populations. Norms can also be obtained for large cities. A variety of norm-referenced scores is provided including percentile ranks, grade-equivalents, stanines, and scale scores. Reviews of the test indicate construct validity studies needed to be conducted on this instrument.

The Peabody Individual Achievement Test

The mathematics section of *the Peabody Individual Achievement Test* (Dunn & Markwordt, 1976), commonly referred to as the *PIAT*, covers the following content areas: number recognition; basic computation; mathematics concept; and mathematics reasoning. The test is designed to be administered by a single individual to one student. All student responses are verbal, as opposed to written. *PIAT* is designed for use with ages kindergarten through adult. The test takes about 30 to 40 minutes to administer, although it is not timed. For each of the five areas tapped, there are grade equivalents, age equivalents, percentile ranks, and standard scores that can be derived. The test is well normed, with emphasis on minority and handicapped populations. Overemphasis of minorities and handicapped is one major criticism of this test.

Aptitude Tests

Tests measuring general career-vocational aptitudes frequently contain several factors, including reading, mathematics, sensory-motor skills, and other general informational skills. Aptitude tests are directed to assessing identified individually appropriate career-vocation tasks and jobs. For this purpose, general aptitude tests cover a variety of factors associated with various other more specific tests.

The General Aptitude Test Battery (GATB)

This test, published by the Bureau of Employment Security, U.S. Department of Labor (1946-1970), for ages 16 and over, is useful in determining career directions that youths and adults should pursue. It produces measures in 10 areas: intelligence, verbal, numerical, spatial, form perception, clerical perception, aiming, motor speed, finger dexterity, and manual dexterity. The B-1001 edition of this battery includes eight pen-and-paper tests plus four performance tests: Book I (1966) contains three tests—tool matching, name comparison, and computation. Book II (1966) includes four tests—three-dimensional space, arithmetic reasoning, vocabulary, and form matching. Part K (1965) contains a mark-making test. A fourth component (pegboard) comprises two tests, Place and Turn; and the final section (Finger Dexterity Board) is composed of two tests, Assemble and Disassemble. The manual states that the battery is designed to measure capacities to learn various jobs, but its developers have failed to provide evidence indicating that those who score high on a specific test learn to perform a job more competently than those with low scores. It is maintained that the *GATB* subtests should be viewed as indices of current learning status, not projected potential. Data reported from a *GATB* longitudinal follow-up study support this view.

The Differential Aptitude Tests (DAT)

This battery (Bennett, Seashore, & Wesman, 1947-69) is published by the Psychological Corporation for ages 13 and over. It measures six areas: verbal reasoning, numerical reasoning, space relation, mechanical reasoning, clerical speed and accuracy, and language usage. The tests are easily administered, scored, and interpreted. An extensive sample of 50,512 U.S. public school children in grades 8 through 12 in 43 states composed the norm population. However, the test is considerably overrepresented and, in addition, information concerning the ethnic and socioeconomic characteristics of the sample is lacking. Separate norms for males and females are provided. The manual provides extensive evidence of the test's validity. Quereshi (1972) noted that correlations of *DAT* scores with high school educational and vocational careers are high. According to the author, DAT performance can adequately differentiate various occupational groups.

The Non-reading Aptitude Test Battery

This test (1969) is published by the United States Training and Employment Services for ages 14 to adults. This measures nine areas: intelligence, verbal, numerical, spatial, form perception, clerical perception, motor coordination, finger dexterity, and manual dexterity. The *Non-reading Aptitude Test Battery* is a nonreading version of the *General Aptitude Test Battery (GATB)*. It is composed of ten pen-and-paper tests and four performance tests. Book I (1969) includes two tests, Picture-Word Matching and Oral Vocabulary; Book II (1969) contains a Coin Matching exercise; Book III (1969) includes a Matrices test; Book IV (1969) is the Tool Matching exam; Book V (1969) is the Form Matching test; Book VI (1969) is Coin Series; and Book VII (1969) contains the Name Comparison test. The battery also includes Part VIII of the *General Aptitude Test Battery (GATB)*, Mark Making (1965); the two tests of the Pegboard section of the *GATB*, Place and Turn; and the two tests of the *GATB* Finger Dexterity Board-Assemble and Disassemble.

The educator should be aware that aptitude tests are more valuable as a measure of what aptitudes a student does not possess. Froehlich and Benson (1948) noted that an individual must possess certain minimum aptitudes to succeed in any specified area. Lack of the aptitude or aptitudes will frequently argue for alternative vocational training, but possession of the aptitudes will not conversely argue that the individual will succeed in specific vocations, since success is based also on interest, social and personal motivation, family expectations, peer pressures, and numerous other factors. The following interests tests may yield data that will enable the educator and student to achieve clear career goals and programmatic direction.

Interest Inventory

The Kuder Occupational Interest Survey (KOIS)

This survey (Kuder, 1956-70) is published by Science Research Associates, Inc., for ages 11 through adulthood. It provides the educator and student with general data on the student's occupational interests. The *KOIS* is a 100-triad inventory in which the respondent indicates his most and least preferred activity from three choices. An individual's score represents the correlation between his or her responses and those of individuals involved in 37 occupations and 19 college majors (normed on female populations), and 20 additional occupations and 8 college major scales (normed on males). The highest *KOIS* scores in each occupation and college major are reported separately for each sex. Walsh (1972) noted that only concurrent validity information is provided in the test manual. These data indicate that the *KOIS* adequately discriminates between various existing occupational groups, but no information on predictive validity is provided. With regard to reliability, Walsh (1972) reported that test-retest coefficients, for a two-week interval, were quite adequate for 25 twelfth graders and 25 college students. A three-year test-retest study involving three groups of college students majoring in engineering (n=93) produced a median group reliability coefficient of 0.89. Walsh found these results encouraging, but called for studies utilizing larger populations.

Dolliver (1972) outlined the following advantages of the *KOIS* over the *Strong Vocational Interest Blank:*

1. Scoring of college major interests
2. The covering of a broader range of occupations (specifically more technical and trade-level occupations)
3. Use of the same form for males and females
4. Provision of scores for female examinees on certain male occupations and college major scales
5. Recently tested norm groups

The *Vocational Agriculture Interest Inventory*, published by Interstate Printers and Publishers, Inc., is for males age eight. This inventory is composed of 75 items dealing with agricultural concepts. The examinee rates each item on a five-point scale ranging from "strongly like" to "strongly dislike." According to Campbell (1972), scoring weights were developed by comparing a criterion group of "Successful Vocational-Agriculture Students" to a group of eighth grade boys from 20 schools. The normative data provided in the manual are generally inadequate, and no data on validity or reliability are cited. Campbell (1972) criticized the test for its poor psychometric foundations, but did point to its development by three professional agriculture educators as a strong point in its favor.

The California Occupational Preference Survey (COPS)

This survey (Knapp, Grant & Demos, 1966-70) is published by Educational and Industrial Testing Service for ages 14 to adulthood. The test measures preference for: science professional, science skilled, technical professional, technical skilled, outdoor, business professional, business skilled, clerical, linguistic professional, linguistic skilled, aesthetic professional, aesthetic skilled, service professional, and service skilled. The *COPS* utilizes a free response format to identify individual occupational preferences. Interests are divided into 14 occupational clusters, six of which are further divided into professional vs. skilled classification. Bauernfeind (1972) maintains that this procedure is useful in determining whether a student's vocational interests warrant postsecondary education. French (1972) praised the construction of the survey's scales, its consideration of both professions and skills, and the instructive nature of the test and manual. The *COPS* free-response format has been both applauded and criticized. Bodden (1972) maintained that this procedure may be more comfortable and less restricting for the respondents. The psychometric properties of this instrument are such that French (1972) reported that the instrument's construct validity appears to be quite high, but criticized the lack of data on predictive validity. With regard to reliability, Bodden considered coefficients obtained with high school groups satisfactory, but questioned the absence of reliability data on college populations. Long-term reliability figures are less adequate. The median (test-retest) coefficient for one year is 0.66, and for two years equals 0.63. A final point advanced by Bodden involved the homogeneous keying of the test, and the possibility that high scores may, therefore, not always match the interest of persons actually engaged in the expected occupation.

CONSULTATIVE PROGRAMMING

Following the completion of all phases of formal and informal testing on areas of achievement, personality, interest, and aptitudes, the educator and the student need to discuss the results to determine available training direction and placement alternatives. It should be evident that the flow of information based on the testing will be most advantageously used when controlled by the educator. The educator can most effectively guide the student by explaining the results and noting that aptitude and interest measures by design have scoring peaks and valleys. The programming phase should focus on several variables.

Student Academic and Aptitudinal Strengths and Weaknesses

This discussion will enable the student to determine his or her readiness for specific vocational opportunities. Failure to do this may leave the student believing that the school and the educator are unwilling to offer opportunities he or she is qualified to pursue.

Discrepancy of Belief and Measurement

This discussion focuses on the agreement or discrepancy between the student's stated interests and what the interest inventory measured. Collectively, the student and educator must resolve any discrepancies and agree on what the information indicates.

Matching Student Traits with School Capability and Community Vocational Opportunities

The need to discuss realistically the interface of the student's background with training and vocational opportunities must proceed on four fronts. First, many educationally handicapped and academically retarded youths must become familiar with their career opportunities and the related jobs that are available in industry, commerce, and government. Without this information, youths tend to perceive narrow employment opportunities (i.e., pipe fitter and plumber) and are unable to relate their skills in other career fields (i.e., tool and die making, air conditioning installation, and metal working). Second, consideration must be given to the changing configuration of the United States' economy and the resulting employment opportunities. Third, youths, once out of formal training, are often unaware of the employment agencies and training centers that can better prepare them or upgrade their skills so that they can obtain and retain employment. Efforts must be made to create an awareness of these helping agencies. Fourth, in career planning, youths must become acquainted with the many union and guild restrictions on membership and employment.

Student Needs

The student needs to be made aware that further training must be pursued if he or she is to achieve his or her vocational goals.

Program Development

The program that fails to integrate the essential personal, educational, and social variables will not enable the youth to better prepare for the future. Therefore, the program must, of necessity, address: (1) academic goals, (2) vocational goals, (3) performance objectives, and (4) the strategies that will be used.

Organizing the Formal Background Data

Once the information from the counseling, tests, and other sources is collected, the data evaluation procedures must be formulated so that educational personnel can extract information that will enable them to understand the youth's overall skills, interests, needs, attitudes, and behavior. Tables 6-1, 6-2, and 6-3 present suggested formats.

Brolin (1976) suggested the work sample as a criterion-based procedure for assessing the student's performance as it relates to the specific process or product associated with the selected career-vocational experience. Alpern and Sabatino (1975) further recommended that the youth be assessed on his or her ability to interact with peers and colleagues at the career-vocational experience station. However, unlike the student's interests and aptitudes, the student's performance at the experience station can be best assessed informally. The informal procedures can involve using commercial or self-made instruments and checklists assessing behaviors demonstrated to be essential to job performance.

One of the best procedures is the job and work samples. These samples enable the student to perform and the educator to assess in a condition that approximates reality. This avoids placing the youth in an actual work situation for which he or she may be unprepared. The sampling process also enables the youth and the educator to assess the appropriateness of job and work and the student's attitudes associated with the experiences. The station should be viewed by the student as a preview rather than a test. Many field-based educators contend that employers prefer to see the results of work completed and job samples rather than test results. A step-by-step approach to developing work samples is presented below:

Step 1: Using local departments of employment, a newspaper's classified employment advertisements, and contacting major employers, determine: (1) what jobs are most suitable, (2) what jobs are likely to develop within the next 5 to 10 years, and (3) what personal and professional competencies the potential employers are evaluating when they hire an individual and when they decide whether the person will be retained. The data collected can be categorized into various job cluster groupings (industrial, business, marketing, applied biological, and agricultural occupations) to make identification of sampling packages easier and more generalizable.

Step 2: Once these data are collected, determine whether: (1) the student's interests in a particular area are sustained; (2) the job is one the student can perform; (3) the job is one the student can be trained to perform; (4) the job opportunities are short- or long-term; and (5) the job lends itself to the sampling procedures.

Step 3: When specific samples are identified as appropriate to the school's needs, task analysis is undertaken to determine the specific steps a job requires and the independent and overlapping skills that are necessary. This step is critical in the design and development of the sample package, since failure to identify critical steps and skills can lead to poor sampling and student failure. The most effective way of analyzing a job is through onsite observation and the questioning of those who perform the job. Dependency by the school personnel on recollections and job descriptions in books frequently results in poor job work samples.

Table 6-1 General Aptitude Test Battery

Aptitude

	(High)																				(Low)
	20	19	18	17	16	15	14	13	12	11	10	9	8	7	6	5	4	3	2	1	
A Intelligence																					
B Verbal																					
C Numerical																					
D Form Perception																					
E Clerical Perception																					
F Aiming																					
G Motor Speed																					
H Finger Dexterity																					
I Manual Dexterity																					

Reading Mastery Test

	(High)																				(Low)
	20	19	18	17	16	15	14	13	12	11	10	9	8	7	6	5	4	3	2	1	
A Passage Comprehension																					
B Word Comprehension																					

Comprehensive Tests of Basic Skills—Arithmetic

	(High)																				(Low)
	20	19	18	17	16	15	14	13	12	11	10	9	8	7	6	5	4	3	2	1	
A Concepts																					
B Computation																					
C Application																					

Table 6-2 Interest and Personality Tests

California Occupational Preference Survey

	(High)																			(Low)
	20	19	18	17	16	15	14	13	12	11	10	9	8	7	6	5	4	3	2	1

A Science Professional
B Technical Skilled
C Outdoor
D Business Professional
E Business Skilled
F Service Professional
G Service Skilled

California Test of Personality

	(High)																			(Low)
	20	19	18	17	16	15	14	13	12	11	10	9	8	7	6	5	4	3	2	1

A Self-reliance
B Personal Worth
C Personal Freedom
D Feeling of Belonging
E Withdrawn Tendencies
F Nervous Symptoms

Observation Classroom and Interview Data

	(High)																			(Low)
	20	19	18	17	16	15	14	13	12	11	10	9	8	7	6	5	4	3	2	1

A Physical Appearance
B Punctuality
C Oral Communications
D Follow Directions
E Reliability
F Cooperation
G Initiative
H Leadership
I Innovative
J Flexibility
K Social Perception

Table 6-3 Career Programming Format

Perceptual-Motor skills strengths weaknesses	Goals and objectives responsible personnel: outcome:
Social skills, interests, and attitudes strengths weaknesses	Goals and objectives responsible personnel: outcome:
Conceptual level strengths weaknesses	Goals and objectives responsible personnel: outcome:
Language skills strengths weaknesses	Goals and objectives responsible personnel: outcome:
Mathematics skills strengths weaknesses	Goals and objectives responsible personnel: outcome:

Placement:
Expected duration of services:
Other agencies cooperating:
Job status:
Work status:

Step 4: Before the sample is constructed, the school must determine whether any specialized equipment is necessary, and if so, whether it either has or can gain access to the equipment. Berelson (1954) has noted that the content analysis needs to be analyzed sequentially and this recommendation must be applied to the development of the content material. Among the other factors that must be considered in the development of the sample are:

- steps required to perform the task,

- time required to complete the task,

- visual format of material presentation,

- procedures to be employed in assessing the student's readiness and performance of the sample,

- prerequisite and overlapping skills that are required to perform satisfactorily on the sample,

- temperament variables associated with success work on the job,

- procedures to be employed in presenting the material to the youth.

Among the variables to be considered in presentation are:

- a review of job samples,

- sampling procedures,

- expected time the sample will require,

- procedures to follow when difficulties are encountered, and

- the educator's role in the process.

Step 5: Once the prototype sample is complete, the school personnel must administer it to students to assess its utility. It is essential that all factors associated with the design of the package are met and that the students demonstrate an interest in the process and can achieve success with the sample. It is not uncommon for a task or test to be imperfect and require modification after the final package is complete.

Work Station Assessment

The experience station placement is typically located on an actual work site under supervision of employees and education staff. It generally has a twofold purpose. First, it gives the student an opportunity to discover and assess the factors associated with the specific experience (Alpern & Sabatino, 1975). Second, it moves the school personnel into the field where they are called upon to evaluate the student, his or her preparation efforts, and the conceptual framework of the school's educational model (Miller, 1975).

The evaluation of the student should reflect the input of the three primary parties, the student, the employer, and the on-site educator. Again, it is important that the youth be provided data on how others evaluate his or her performance. Evaluation tools must reflect the student's positive behaviors and be a guide for the behaviors that require more training and/or attitudinal changes. Among the variables that require assessment are the following.

Job Aptitude: Does the student possess the cognitive and manipulative skills that are required by the job? If a skill deficiency exists, is the acquisition of the skill a reasonable objective, or can the task be modified to accommodate the youth's skill deficiency?

Work Judgment: Does the student possess the knowledge to determine when specific operations are to be undertaken and when they are to be delayed? The student should also be assessed on his or her ability to make judgments concerning the appropriate use of equipment and materials associated with the work.

Initiative: The quality and quantity of job performance is often influenced by the individual initiative demonstrated in the work situation. The student who will obtain clarification on work schedule and job responsibilities, or begin new activities, is more likely to succeed than the individual who is unwilling to question and inquire, and to try something new.

Adaptability: Can the student alter or change his or her behavior, task direction, or job responsibilities without disrupting others or becoming disorganized by a change in routine? The individual capable of adaptive behavior will be able to cope in a job situation better than one who is resistant to change.

Social-Personal Characteristics: As noted earlier, appearance, social skills, voice quality, and mannerisms can influence the prospective employer's decision in hiring as well as the attitude of coworkers. Often the social-personal characteristics are more influential in an employer's decision than the task-related skill level.

Temperament and Interests: The student's ability to cope with the frustrations, disappointments, patience, and/or impatience required by the work situation often affects a student's performance. The student's technical competence to perform a job may fail because either his or her temperament is inappropriate or he or she lacks the interest to learn more about the people and the job.

Attitude: The student's attitude toward work and those individuals he or she will work with is a significant variable in the determination of job appropriateness. This attitude will influence virtually every other aspect of his or her job performance.

General: Besides the variables above, the employer, student, and educator must become aware of general factors such as communication skills, acceptance by others, and personal reliability. Awareness of these general factors will assist all parties to assess the student's progress and others' reactions.

CONCLUSION

Only in the past five years have educators turned to the assessment of the handicapped adolescent. Initially, the assessment process involved the use of instruments that had been employed to diagnose preadolescent populations. This approach produced assessment data that were irrelevant and/or unusable by the school personnel. During the decade of the 1970s, the process evolved to the level discussed in this chapter. As presently practiced, all relevant aspects of the student's characteristics of aptitudes, attitudes, mastery areas, physical appearance, etc., are scrutinized so that programs appropriately interface with the youth's career-vocational competency and social awareness levels.

The assessment process for handicapped youths is still developing, and what educators need most are validated and reliable instruments. Instruments available for use with handicapped adolescent populations largely remain of questionable use because of their limited validity and reliability. For this reason, this chapter has emphasized the necessity of pairing formal standardized test data with observational and informal test information. This assessment procedure accomplishes:

1. the collection of data that affect the student's demonstrated skills within an educational milieu
2. the use of data that enable school personnel to project the student's capacity to perform skilled and semiskilled tasks
3. the analysis of the data producing a program, discriminating between desire and ability
4. the development of functional programs that can be continually evaluated and altered as the student's progress is charted

---

REFERENCES

Alpern, S., & Sabatino, D.A. *Establishing a meaningful career education plan (Manual on integrated career education)*. Springfield, Ill.: Department of Corrections, 1975.

Bauernfeind, R. H. Review of the California Occupational Test Survey. In O. K. Buros (Ed.), *The seventh mental measurements yearbook* (Vol. 2). Highland Park, N.J.: The Gryphon Press, 1972.

Bennett, G. K., Seashore, H. G., & Wesman, A. G. *Differential Aptitude Tests*. New York: Psychological Corporation, 1947-69.

Berelson, B. Content analysis. In G. Lindzey (Ed.), *Handbook of social psychology, I: Theory and method*. Reading, Mass.: Addison-Wesley Publishing Co., 1954.

Bloom, B. S., Engelhart, M. D., Furst, E. J., Hill, W. H. & Krathwohl, D. R. *Taxonomy of educational objectives, Handbook I: Cognitive domain*. New York: David McKay, 1956.

Bodden, J. L. Review of the California Occupational Preference Survey. In O. K. Buros (Ed.), *The seventh mental measurements yearbook* (Vol. 2). Highland Park, N.J.: The Gryphon Press, 1972.

Brolin, D. E. *Vocational preparation of retarded citizens*. Columbus, Ohio: Charles E. Merrill Publishing Co., 1976.

Campbell, D. P. Review of the Vocational Agriculture Interest Inventory. In O. K. Buros (Ed.), *The seventh mental measurements yearbook* (Vol. 2). Highland Park, N.J.: The Gryphon Press, 1972.

Comprehensive Tests of Basic Skills. Monterey, Calif.: CTB/McGraw-Hill, 1970.

Dolliver, R. H. Review of the Kuder Occupational Interest Survey. In O. K. Buros (Ed.), *The seventh mental measurements yearbook* (Vol. 2). Highland Park, N.J.: The Gryphon Press, 1972.

Dunn, L., & Markwordt, F. *Peabody Individual Achievement Test*. Circle Pines, Minn.: American Guidance Testing Service, 1976.

Erikson, E. H. In M. J. E. Senn & B. Inhelder (Eds.), *Discussions on child development*. New York: International Universities Press, Vol. III, 1958.

Erikson, R. C. & Wentling, T. L. *Measuring student growth*. Boston: Allyn & Bacon, 1976.

French, J. W. Review of the California Occupational Preference Survey. In O. K. Buros (Ed.), *The seventh mental measurements yearbook* (Vol. 2). Highland Park, N.J.: The Gryphon Press, 1972.

Froehlich, C. P. & Benson, A. L. *Guidance testing*. Chicago: Science Research Associates, 1948.

Froehlich, C. P., & Hoyt, K. B. *Guidance testing*. Chicago: Science Research Associates, 1959.

Gates, A. I., & McKillop, A. S. *Gates-McKillop Reading Diagnostic Tests*. New York: Teachers College Press, 1962.

General Aptitude Test Battery (GATB). Bureau of Employment Security. U.S. Department of Labor, 1946-70.

Goodman, L. & Mann, L. *Learning disabilities in the secondary schools*. New York: Grune & Stratton, 1976.

Guilford, J. P. *The nature of human intelligence*. New York: McGraw-Hill, 1967.

Guilford, J. P., Kettner, M. W., & Christensen, P. R. *A factor analytic study across the domains of reasoning, creativity and evaluation: II. Administration of tests and analyses of results* (Report No. 16. Psychological Laboratory, University of Southern California, 1956).

Jones, R. W., Blaney, R. L., & Sabatino, D. A. *Ascertaining vocationally retarded behaviors (Manual on integrated career education)*. Springfield, Ill.: Department of Corrections, 1975.

Knapp, R. R., Grant, B., & Demos, G. D. *California Occupational Preference Survey (COPS)*. Educational and Industrial Testing Service, 1966-70.

Kuder, G. *Kuder Occupational Interest Survey* (KOIS). Chicago: Science Research Associates, 1956-70.

Miller, S. R. *Secondary assessment and programming*. Unpublished paper, Carbondale, Ill., 1975.

Miller, S. R. Career education: Life-long planning for the handicapped. In D. A. Sabatino & T. L. Miller (Eds.), *Describing learner characteristics of handicapped children and youth*. New York: Grune & Stratton, 1979.

Non-reading Aptitude Test Battery. United States Training and Employment Services. Washington, D. C.: U.S. Government Printing Office, 1969.

Quereshi, M. Y. Review of the Differential Aptitude Tests. In O. K. Buros (Ed.), *The seventh mental measurements yearbook* (Vol. 2). Highland Park, N.J.: The Gryphon Press, 1972.

Sawin, E. I. *Evaluation and the work of the teacher*. Belmont, Calif.: Wadsworth Publishing Co., 1969.

Thurstone, L. L. *Primary mental abilities*. Chicago: The University of Chicago Press, 1938.

Turnbull, A. P., & Schulz, J. B. *Mainstreaming handicapped students: A guide for the classroom teacher*. Boston: Allyn & Bacon, 1979.

Walsh, T. P. *Blueprint for the possible: A citizen's program for better schools*. Washington, D.C.: Chamber of Commerce of the United States, 1972.

Wechsler, D. *Manual for the Wechsler Adult Intelligence Scale*. New York: Psychological Corporation, 1955.

Wechsler, D. *Manual for the Wechsler Intelligence Scale for Children—Revised*. New York: Psychological Corporation, 1974.

Woodcock, R. W. *Woodcock Reading Mastery Tests*. Circle Pines, Minn.: American Guidance Testing Service, 1973.

Chapter 7

Behavior Management: Program Analysis

The preceding chapters have emphasized repeatedly that the career-vocational educator is concerned with the development of a wide range of skills beyond simple or complex academic tasks. Task-related occupational skills, appropriate work habits, and a variety of social skills within an occupational context are also critical to the adaptation of the handicapped youth to the work environment.

The student who has difficulty reading printed materials or remembering academically related concepts may also have difficulty in understanding employer-employee relations, employer expectations, occupational responsibilities, and a general work ethic. It is critical that the career-vocational educator be prepared to develop social-personal behaviors necessary for the student's adjustment in the work setting.

A review of prevalent definitions for handicapping conditions emphasizes the variety of exceptional characteristics attributed to handicapped adolescents (refer to Chapter 2). Each of the major handicapping conditions can be associated with performance problems that limit the adolescent's ability to succeed in a vocational setting. For example, mental retardation is defined in part by the individual's ability to adjust to his or her environment (Grossman, 1973), and behavior disorders are defined by persistent unacceptable responses to environmental demands (Kauffman, 1981). Several authors have argued that the various areas of exceptionality may place an individual at risk for the development of social-personal adjustment difficulties (Bryan & Bryan, 1977; Menolascino, 1977; Sanders, 1980).

Research reported by Bryan (1976); Bryan, Wheeler, Felcan, and Hanek (1976); and Bryan and Bryan (1977) has presented data that highlight the association between learning disabilities and social-personal deficits. Their research has demonstrated that: (1) learning-disabled students are more likely to be rejected by their peers and teachers, (2) learning-disabled students do not benefit from others' social cues well, and (3) learning-disabled students' responses in social interactions reflect an insensitivity to the feelings of others. Similarly, numerous authors have addressed the relationship between social-personal deficits and mental retardation (Heber, 1964; Rutter, 1971; Sternlicht, 1977). Menolascino (1977) has argued that the sensory, cognitive, and environmental limitations often associated with the mentally retarded diminish their ability to develop positive social and emotional characteristics. Other authors have discussed the relationship between auditory defects (Malkin, Freeman, & Hastings, 1976; Schlesinger & Meadow, 1971), visual impairment (Miller, 1970; Nagera & Colonna, 1965), and physical handicaps (Lewandowski & Cruickshank, 1980; McMichael, 1971) and social-personal adjustment difficulties.

The importance of activities that promote social-personal development in career vocational settings cannot be understated. As Lerner (1971) has emphasized, "a lack of sensitivity to people and poor perceptions of social situations . . . affects every area of the child's (or adolescent's) life. This is probably the most debilitating learning problem the child (or youth) can have" (p. 247). It is the purpose of this chapter to present an approach to analyzing social-personal deficits from the content of the setting in which behavioral excesses or deficits occur. Chapter 8 will then translate this information into ecologically based strategies for teaching and motivating social competency behaviors.

Prior to embarking on a discussion of procedures used in analyzing social-personal problems, a review of the learning theory orientation that underlies these chapters will be presented.

SOCIAL LEARNING THEORY APPROACH TO SOCIAL-PERSONAL DEVELOPMENT

The basic premise upon which the social learning theory approach is based is that both acceptable and deviant behaviors are learned through individuals' interactions with present and past environments. Environments that provide adolescents with a number of pleasant and appropriate social models, and which consistently consequate appropriate behavior with desirable events and/or the reduction of aversive events, will strengthen social competence. Environments that include few positive social models and do not reward appropriate behavior are not effective in developing social competence.

Many handicapped children and adolescents do not process information as effectively as the general population. Sensory or cognitive deficits that interfere with the acquisition of academic skills also impact on the acquisition of social and emotional behaviors (Bijou, 1972). Thus, environments that generally produce positive social and emotional characteristics may not be effective with handicapped youths. Rather than providing special environments that foster social and emotional growth, teachers, parents, and peers often establish aversive consequences for social deficiencies. Punishing a student for a lack of social competence has been shown to be a highly inefficient method for developing social competency behaviors (Gardner, 1977).

At best, punishment used excessively or in isolation only motivates the student to refrain from exhibiting the undesirable behavior in subsequent situations. If a desirable behavior is present in the student's repertoire, he or she may respond appropriately on subsequent occasions. A child or adolescent with learning deficits, however, may not have the ability to engage in the expected behavior and therefore may exhibit another unacceptable behavior in following situations. As more and more attempts to gain satisfaction and avoid failure are punished, the student may become helpless and cease to attempt to work through the situation (Seligman, 1975). The high rate of failure in social endeavors reduces the handicapped adolescent's expectation for success and reward in future social encounters, thereby reducing the likelihood that he or she will approach such situations (Cromwell, 1963).

The student may learn through frequent experiences that disruptive behavior may function to produce satisfaction in the absence of reward for positive social behavior. Adolescents who are unable to gain peer approval for good grades or friendly interactions often learn that social disruptions have a high probability of producing peer support and adult interest. This learning process is strengthened as disruptive behavior frequently excludes the individual from environments in which positive social learning may occur, and as the student, his or her peers, and professionals establish expectancies for future disruptive behavior.

UNDERLYING PRINCIPLES

The following is a series of general social learning theory principles that provide a conceptual and methodological foundation for the behavior management program analysis and development chapters.

Behavior is influenced by the environment. A student's social behavior at any given time results from the cumulative learning that has occurred through present and past environments. Behavior that repeatedly produces positive consequences or leads to the avoidance of unpleasant consequences will reoccur. Behavior that consistently produces unpleasant consequences for the student will diminish.

An individual's internal or biological characteristics contribute to his or her current behavioral repertoire. Sensory or cognitive deficits may limit the student's ability to benefit from the environment. Over time, these limitations may reduce any individual's ability to adapt to new environments. Thus, a student's behavior is the result of a biologically unique individual interacting repeatedly with a unique environment.

Functional explanations of behavior are based on empirical relationships. By reliably and objectively studying the student's behavior in the context of the environment, the educator can make confident statements about conditions that strengthen or maintain the behavior. Assumptions regarding the internal state of an individual or presumed pathology are useful only in that they bear on the individual's observable and measurable behavior.

Similar social-personal repertoires of different individuals may or may not be caused or maintained by the same events. Although it is often useful to group students with similar learning or behavioral characteristics together, it is improper to assume that their social-personal repertoires have developed and are maintained through the same factors. It is critical from a learning theory standpoint that the experiential and biological uniqueness of each student be considered in the analysis of social-personal deficiencies.

An adolescent's behavioral characteristics can change in a predictable and desirable manner through the systematic manipulation of the learning environment. Numerous research reports have demonstrated that educators can systematically change an adolescent's behavior by altering the learning environment. Truancy (Schloss, Kane, & Miller, 1981), academic performance (Schumaker, Hovell, & Sherman, 1977), social skills (Elder, Edelstein, & Warick, 1979), self-care behaviors (Snyder & White, 1979), and disruptive classroom behaviors (Marlowe, Madsen, Bowen, Reardon, & Logue, 1978) have been targets of recent investigations. In each case, intervention involved the analysis and manipulation of environmental conditions that were hypothesized to be associated with performance problems. The social learning theory position evaluated in these studies emphasizes that since the behavior developed or failed to develop through a faulty learning environment, effective intervention occurs by altering the environment.

Because social-personal deficiencies result from numerous interactions with a faulty learning environment, successful intervention may require numerous interactions with an altered environment. The development of positive social behaviors may require consistent and sustained attention to the environment in which deficits occur. It is not sufficient to spend one hour a day working on a positive social behavior and then return the youth to an environment that fails to reinforce the desirable behaviors at an effective rate.

Continuous data are useful in designing, monitoring, and evaluating social development programs. Data reporting the strength of the student's behavior in relation to specific environmental events facilitate the identification of those events that contribute to the social-personal deficiency. Data reporting the strength of the student's behavior after the presumed maintaining events are changed can be compared to the previous data (baseline) to determine the program's effectiveness. If the baseline and intervention data are not substantially different, then other potential maintaining variables may be considered.

PROGRAM PLANNING

An overview of the procedures followed in developing a behavior management program will be presented prior to discussing individual program analysis and development strategies. The sequence of activities from the determination that a problem exists to follow-up of the intervention program is intended as a general guide in planning a behavior management program.

It must be emphasized that these chapters represent a process model that is applicable to the social-personal needs of the handicapped student in a career-voca-tional education program. Specific intervention strategies, data collection proce-dures, target behaviors, etc., must all be identified on the basis of the educator's understanding of handicapped youths and their environments. Important con-siderations and recommendations in making these decisions are presented here, but the formal program must reflect the students' unique behavioral features and the resources available to the educator. Specific procedures to be followed in designing, implementing, and monitoring a behavior management program include:

- Determine that a problem exists.
  1. Identify expectations of significant people in the adolescent's environ-ment.
  2. Observe the student to obtain a general idea of the current strength of the behavior.
  3. Decide whether there is a sufficiently large discrepancy between the current strength of the student's behavior and the expectations of others to warrant intervention.

- Prioritize target behaviors.
  1. Specify potential targets of the intervention program.
  2. Rank the behavioral targets from least to most important to the student's adjustment in important settings.
  3. Identify high-priority behavioral targets that can be programmed for without placing excessive demands on the student.

- Define target behaviors.
  1. Describe each target behavior in clear terms that permit objective meas-urement.
  2. Describe each target behavior completely so that all information that may be relevant to the observation is included.

- When behavioral targets include excessive disruptive behaviors that are to be reduced, specify alternate prosocial behaviors that can be developed or strengthened to replace the disruptive behavior.

1. In general terms, determine the function of the disruptive behavior (e.g., aggressive behavior allows the student to gain satisfaction from conflict situations).
2. Identify a prosocial competency behavior that may serve the same function (e.g., assertive behaviors, if strengthened, may produce an equal amount of satisfaction).

- Identify scope of the intervention program.
  1. Identify the setting in which the behavior change is expected to occur.
  2. Identify important conditions under which the behavior is expected to occur.
  3. Identify professionals, paraprofessionals, peers, relatives, etc., that are expected to participate in the intervention program.

- Establish a criterion for acceptable performance across short-term and terminal objectives.
  1. Determine the acceptable level of performance expected following the intervention program.
  2. Delineate a set of short-term expectations that collectively compose the anticipated outcome of the intervention program.

- Continuously record the student's behavior to determine program target areas.
  1. Identify conditions in the natural environment that often precede the target behavior and may influence the probability of its occurrence (antecedent conditions).
  2. Identify conditions in the natural environment that often follow the target behavior and may influence the probability of its occurrence (consequent conditions).

- Identify individual characteristics that may be associated with the target behavior.

- Assess the student's reinforcement hierarchy.
  1. Generate a list of items or events that are considered to be pleasant to the student.
  2. Rank the items or events from least to most enjoyable for the student.
  3. Designate items and events that are natural to the school setting.

- Select a measure of behavior strength.
  1. Determine the resources available for collecting data.
  2. Determine the behavior to be measured (completed in procedure 2).
  3. Identify the measure of behavior strength that is best suited to the characteristics of the behavior and the resources available to the teacher.

- Collect baseline data.
  1. Initiate data collection under natural program conditions.
  2. Monitor data until the strength of the behavior is stable.

- Formalize and initiate the intervention program.
  1. Synthesize information from the preceding procedures into an intervention program that maximizes student involvement, maximizes peer involvement, and maximizes parent involvement.
  2. Prepare a written description of program procedures so that all individuals participating in the social development program are aware of their responsibilities.

- Fade the intervention program so that appropriate behavior is supported and maintained by natural events.

DETERMINE THAT A PROBLEM EXISTS

The initial step in designing and implementing a behavior management program involves a decision on the part of the adolescent and significant people in his or her environment that a problem of sufficient magnitude exists to warrant intensive intervention. This decision can be reached by: (1) identifying the expectations of the student and significant people in the environment; (2) determining the current strength of the student's behavior; (3) and determining the discrepancy between the student's present behavior and expectations of self and others for future behavior.

The behavior management program may serve a number of functions including: (1) increasing the consistency with which the adolescent performs existing skills such as washing hands regularly before returning to work, (2) developing new skills such as learning for the first time to call an employer when ill, (3) refining existing skills such as improving voice tone when responding to an employer's criticism, and (4) reducing excessive disruptive responses such as eliminating the use of swear words when talking to customers. The precise targets of the intervention program must be considered prior to the development of the intervention program.

Assessment data from a variety of sources may be used to aid in the identification of behavior management objectives. Other teachers, parents, siblings, peers, employment supervisors, and school personnel may all contribute information that will assist in determining the program's focus. Interdisciplinary staffings and career guidance sessions discussed in Chapters 1 and 5 are ideal times to discuss intervention priorities for the individual. During the staffing, representative individuals should be present to consider the total service plan.

Assessment data that support the identification of program targets are discussed in Chapter 6. In addition to criterion- and norm-referenced tests, anecdotal reports of direct observations, situational performance tests, and permanent products may be used in considering the focus of the behavior management program. Collectively, these data should provide a general idea of the frequency or intensity of potential intervention targets across relevant settings. Vague descriptions such as inhibited, lazy, unhappy, flighty, and uncooperative are of little use in deciding the program focus.

Specific behavioral descriptions such as "refuses to wash dishes when asked by his supervisor," or "fails to wash his hair over the weekend," describe the behavioral deficiency within the context of the relevant environment.

Beyond obtaining information regarding the current strength of social-personal behaviors across settings, it is important to know what significant people in those environments view as being the optimal level of functioning for the student. Parents, peers, and supervisors are among the individuals who should provide information that allows the designer of the program to determine the expected level of the target behavior following intervention. This level will become the terminal objective of the intervention program. For the purpose of program development, a handicapped adolescent's exceptionality will be defined by the discrepancy between what others expect and what he or she does across a number of important settings. This view is consistent with the principles outlined in the functional classification chapter. Having identified a number of behaviors that are excessive or deficit in relation to the expectations of others, the teacher must identify specific targets of the intervention program. This is accomplished by prioritizing potential target behaviors.

PRIORITIZE TARGET BEHAVIORS

Exceptional characteristics identified through the preceding procedures must be prioritized from least to most important to the adolescent's adjustment following high school. Priority behaviors that can be programmed for without placing excessive demands on the student may be selected as the target of intervention.

The number of behaviors targeted by the behavior management program should be limited by the degree to which the adolescent may be expected to respond favorably. It is generally understood that excessive demands result in frustration and failure for handicapped youths. Programs that induce high rates of failure violate the basic assumptions of a social learning theory view by confirming the student's expectancy for failure and punishment in social situations (Gardner, 1966). The goal of behavior management programs is to promote a positive association between prosocial behavior and pleasant social outcomes. Therefore, an intervention program should focus only on the range of high priority behaviors that can be developed or reduced without establishing excessively frustrating conditions for the student. Behaviors that are excluded from the initial intervention program may be identified as the targets of future programs.

As a general rule, programs designed to reduce the likelihood that an adolescent will exhibit a certain behavior should have a very narrow focus. At most one or two behaviors should be associated with the punishing consequence. Targeting one or two well-defined behaviors will maximize the effectiveness of the punishment procedure while minimizing emotional side effects resulting from potential unpleasant consequences (Johnston, 1972). Programs that seek to increase the occurrence of positive consequences may have a broader focus. Reinforcement programs may associate up to five behaviors with potentially pleasant consequences. The program should be designed so that the student is continually striving for positive consequences by exhibiting prosocial behavior. A fortunate side effect of a well-designed, well-prescribed program may be that while a select number of behaviors are targeted for intervention, a number of related behaviors may change (Twardosz & Sajwaj, 1972).

For example, Schloss, Sachs, and Miller (in press) recently reported a study that involved the reduction of stereotypic behaviors and increase in positive social behaviors of an adolescent female in a workshop setting. While production rate was not directly addressed by the intervention procedure, an increase from 20 percent of the production norms to 80 percent of the production norms was reported to be a collateral benefit of the behavior management program.

DEFINE TARGET BEHAVIORS

The clear and complete definition of target behaviors helps to maintain the objectivity of behavioral observations. The objectivity of the observer is a critical part of ensuring the consistency with which contingencies are enforced. Additionally, objective data are required to make valid conclusions regarding the influence of the program on the adolescent's behavior.

General descriptions of a student's characteristics such as insensitive, unfriendly, lazy, and uncooperative will invariably produce unreliable assessment data. Such data are of little use in implementing, monitoring, or evaluating intervention programs. Laziness, for example, may refer to deficits in academic performance, refusal to participate in physical education exercises, excessive sleeping during the day, excessive television watching after school, and/or frequent daydreaming at work. Any one or all of the specific behaviors may be characteristics of the individual. The general description ''lazy'' does not specify precise behavioral excesses or deficits. Also, lazy does not describe important conditions that may be relevant to measurement. For example, is the individual not working up to capacity as established by prior observations all of the time, only at school, or only in mathematics class?

The adequacy of response definitions is traditionally evaluated by determining the extent to which two independent observers agree on the occurrence or non-occurrence of the behavior. This test of a response definition is called inter-rater reliability. The actual procedure for determining the reliability of a response definition will be presented later in this chapter.

Examples of clear, objective, and complete response definitions include:

Work productivity—the number of work assemblies completed during a work period (e.g., bolts packaged per four-hour day).

Punctuality—the difference in minutes between the time the student is expected to report to work and the time he or she actually reports to work.

Ignoring the teacher—the adolescent does not attend to, or change, his or her behavior when addressed by the teacher.

Swearing—the adolescent emits such words sufficiently loud to be heard by another individual.

Screaming at others—the adolescent directs voice sounds toward another individual with sufficient intensity to be heard at a distance of 80 feet. Any voice sound that does not include words is also recorded as screaming at others regardless of the intensity.

IDENTIFY SCOPE OF THE INTERVENTION PROGRAM

It is important that intervention take place in the setting in which the behavior change is expected to occur. A number of studies have demonstrated that behavior changes do not automatically transfer from one setting to another (Bates, 1980; Koegel & Rincover, 1974). Recent literature emphasizes the importance of teaching exceptional students in the setting in which the target behaviors are expected to be exhibited (Kazdin, 1980). For example, social skill training would best be implemented during activities in which social greetings are appropriate including school parties, sports events, free time in class, walking down the school halls, or entering a new room. Each of these areas would best be included within the scope of a social skill development program. A highly ineffective approach would be to limit social greeting training to the classroom or a counseling setting and expect that social greeting skills would generalize.

Important conditions within each setting should also be identified. If a program is to focus on improving the production rate of an adolescent in workshop, it is important to know the conditions under which the student is expected to work. The program may focus on teaching and motivating the student to work quickly when sitting at an isolated work station or when stationed in a large group. A program designed to reduce verbal aggression should specify important conditions under which the student will not be verbally aggressive—for example, when confronted by a coworker, when criticized by a teacher, or when frustrated by a difficult assignment. As with setting specifications, the most effective way to influence the student's behavior is to teach and motivate with reference to specific conditions (Risley & Wolf, 1967).

Finally, implementors of the behavior management program should be identified prior to the formalization of the program—professionals, paraprofessionals, work supervisors, relatives, peers, and others who will be responsible for implementing parts of the program. The teacher must ensure that all program participants are aware of their responsibilities as detailed in the intervention plan. If the objective of a program is to develop positive self-statements while the student is at school and work, the student's teachers, coworkers, and supervisors may be asked frequently to label the student's positive social and academic behavior and encourage him or her to do the same. In this example, the success of the intervention plan will depend on the teacher communicating the program approach to a variety of other people.

ESTABLISH A CRITERION FOR ACCEPTABLE PERFORMANCE ACROSS SHORT-TERM AND TERMINAL OBJECTIVES

Research over the past two decades has emphasized the importance of success experiences in the development of positive motivational characteristics with the handicapped (Cromwell, 1963; White, 1960; Zigler, 1973). Intervention programs that include drastic changes in educational programs or environments may result in excessive frustration and failure for the handicapped student. Such programs may not afford the student frequent opportunities to succeed. Short-term objectives are small, easily attainable behavior changes that progress in a logical sequence toward the long-term or major objective of the social development program. Identification of short-term objectives results from the teacher's understanding of the individual student's learning and behavioral characteristics. The student's entry skills, learning rate, and competing behavioral characteristics must be considered prior to establishing and sequencing short-term objectives.

Each short-term objective should identify the criterion level considered to represent acceptable performance. Once the student performs at criterion level consistently, the intervention may be redirected to a subsequent objective. Once mastery is achieved on all of the sequential short-term objectives, the terminal objective will be completed. Figure 7-1 illustrates the flow of sequential short-term objectives that compose a terminal objective.

The process described above is illustrated in a program designed to develop positive employer-employee interactions:

Terminal Objective: Paul will be able to respond appropriately when addressed by his employer while at work.

Figure 7-1 Sequence of Short-Term Objectives

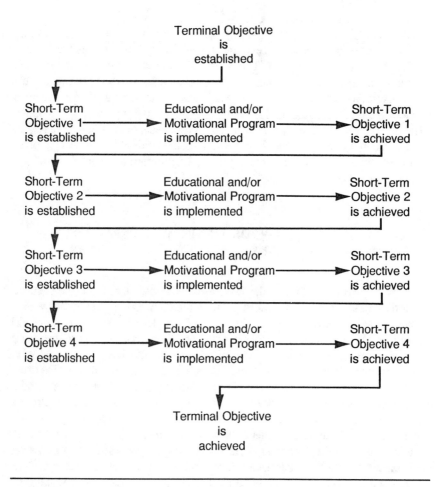

Four sequential short-term objectives were identified that composed the terminal objective:

Short-Term Objective 1: Paul will be able to respond with an appropriate statement of appreciation following a compliment from his employer.

Short-Term Objective 2: Paul will be able to respond with an appropriate statement indicating compliance following a request by the employer.

Short-Term Objective 3: Paul will be able verbally to acknowledge error and indicate future corrective action when criticized by his employer.

Short-Term Objective 4: Paul will be able to exchange an appropriate amenity when greeted by his employer.

It must be emphasized that the scope of each short-term objective reflects the learning characteristics of the adolescent. Using the previous example, a student with more severe learning and behavioral deficits may work toward responding with appropriate statements of appreciation as a terminal objective. Short-term objectives may then be sequenced as follows:

Short-Term Objective 1: Sue will be able to say "thank you" following an employer's compliment on quality of work.

Short-Term Objective 2: Sue will be able to say "thank you" and make a general statement as to how her work is satisfying.

Short-Term Objective 3: Sue will be able to say "thank you," make a general statement about pleasant aspects of her job, and identify a specific part of her work activity that is particularly satisfying.

Identifying Influencing Events

Observations of the adolescent in relevant environments are conducted to identify events that may be associated with problem behavior. These target events may be identified as being *antecedent conditions* that influence the likelihood that a behavior will occur, and as *consequent* conditions that either reinforce or punish the target response. The environmental target areas and related behavioral characteristics, which will be addressed in the next section, may become the focus of an intervention program. Antecedents and consequents that are believed to maintain or strengthen disruptive behaviors will be identified and removed, while antecedents and consequents that support positive social behaviors will be intensified.

Antecedent Conditions

Antecedent conditions can either cue a desirable response, cue an undesirable response, fail to cue a desirable response, or fail to cue an undesirable response. Once it is known that a specific event cues disruptive behavior, the cue can be altered, thereby reducing the frequency of disruptive behaviors. For example, being critized by an employer may be an antecedent to a verbal outburst.

Intervention in this case may focus on antecedents by reducing employer criticism. Once the student learns to respond appropriately to mild criticism, the employer may gradually increase the rate of criticism. Similarly, if it is observed that a naturally occurring event that should cue a positive social behavior does not serve this function, the event can be developed as a cue, thereby increasing the strength of the positive social behavior. For example, observing the student may reveal that an adolescent, working as a grocery checker, seldom says "thank you" as a customer pays for his or her purchase. Intervention may develop the receipt of money as an antecedent for saying "thank you."

Consequent Conditions

Consequents can either increase, decrease, or maintain the strength of the target behavior. Observing the student may help to generate hunches as to the function of specific consequents. If it is known that a specific consequent increases the likelihood that an undesirable behavior will occur, the reinforcing consequent may be removed. If it is known that there are few positive consequents associated with a desired social behavior, favorable consequents may be established.

Consequents can be described as being positively reinforcing, negatively reinforcing, or punishing. *Positive reinforcement* is an event that follows a behavior and increases the probability that the behavior will recur. Positive reinforcers are generally pleasant to the individual; however, sometimes consequents perceived by the teacher to be unpleasant may be positive reinforcers. For example, if it is observed that the frequency of aggressive outbursts increases when consequated by one-day suspensions, it may be concluded that the suspensions positively reinforce aggression. *Negative reinforcement* involves the removal of an unpleasant event following a behavior, thereby increasing the probability of the behavior's occurrence. For example, a teacher's observations may reveal that being late for work often results in the adolescent not having to stock shelves. If tardiness continues, it can be said that the avoidance of shelf-stocking has negatively reinforced tardiness. On the other hand, *punishment* is defined as a reduction in the strength of a behavior resulting from the presentation of an unpleasant consequent. For example, if incorrectly completing a work assignment is consequated by a dockage in pay, and subsequently the number of incorrectly completed assignments decreases, one may say that incorrect work completion was punished.

The contingency relationships previously described occur over time as a part of the adolescent's natural learning history. The sum total of an individual's experiences determine, to a large extent, the individual's current performance in specific situations. One would expect that behaviors that have been positively reinforced consistently and frequently would be a strong part of the adolescent's response repertoire. On the other hand, behaviors that are consistently punished become weakened and eventually drop from the individual's stable performance pattern.

Continuous recording is utilized to identify contemporary events that reinforce or punish target behaviors in a specific setting. These data are then translated directly into an environmentally based intervention program.

Table 7-1 illustrates a form that may be used when conducting continuous observations. The student's name, the time when observations were conducted, the observer's name, and setting in which observations were made are reported at the top of the form. Specific target behaviors are identified in the middle column. Antecedents and consequents are described in relationship to the target behaviors.

Table 7-1 Continuous Observation Recording Form

Student's name _____

Time of observation _____

Observer's name _____

Setting _____

Antecedent	Behavior	Consequent

IDENTIFY INDIVIDUAL CHARACTERISTICS THAT MAY BE ASSOCIATED WITH THE TARGET BEHAVIOR

In addition to antecedents and consequents, associated characteristics may become the target of an intervention program. Associated characteristics include inferred or observed features of the handicapped adolescent that are hypothesized to mediate between antecedent or cue conditions and target response. Figure 7-2 illustrates the relationship between antecedents, associated characteristics, the target behavior, and consequents.

A characteristic that may be associated with depressive-like behavior, for example, may be mediational responses that promote feelings of helplessness (Beck, 1972). While an intervention program may focus on the antecedents and consequents of depressive-like episodes, it may also be important to develop mediational statements that help the student to assert his or her control over the environment. For example, an antecedent to withdrawal may be the receipt of a poor work evaluation. A mediational response that the student may develop could be, "I didn't do well on this evaluation, but if I work harder, I'll do well on the next one." It is expected that the development of this and other verbal mediational responses would decrease the probability that the student would withdraw following subsequent experiences of a similar nature.

Similarly, special social skills could be identified as associated characteristics that, if developed, would reduce aggressive outbursts for the handicapped adolescent. For example, in a case where continuous recording demonstrates that verbal confrontations by peers are antecedents to aggressive behavior, informal observations may suggest that the individual lacks assertiveness skills. It may be speculated that the student is not able to exhibit assertive behavior that would allow him or her to gain satisfaction from others without being disruptive. In this example, assertiveness may be developed as an associated characteristic that is expected to reduce the likelihood that the individual will become aggressive.

Figure 7-2 Relationship between Antecedents, Associated Characteristics, the Target Behavior, and Consequents

Antecedent →	Associated characteristics →	Target behavior →	Consequents
Conditions that precede the target behavior and influence the probability of its occurrence.	Observable and inferred characteristics of the individual that influence the target behavior.	Behavior that the intervention program is intended to strengthen or weaken.	Conditions that follow the target behavior and influence the probability of its occurrence.

ASSESS THE STUDENT'S REINFORCEMENT HIERARCHY

Continuous recording often reveals that consequents that normally occur in school or vocational settings are not effective in motivating performance for some students. For example, the average student is generally considered to be a good worker because of personal pride in the product and salary increases and/or promotions that are considered to be the consequents of diligent work. Because of cognitive deficits, a deficient learning history, excessive failure experiences, etc., the same events may not motivate the handicapped adolescent (Schloss & Sedlak, in press). While a prevalent position may be to label the student "lazy," "disinterested," or "immature," it is the responsibility of the career-vocational educator to alter the motivational characteristics of the adolescent.

The motivational analysis guide presented in Table 7-2 is designed to assist the career-vocational educator in identifying factors that may influence a student's motivational development. Central to the analysis of motivational deficits is the instructor's knowledge of events that occur as consequents of work performance that are satisfying or aversive to the adolescent. Two general recommendations can be made when a motivational deficit is attributed to the inability of consequent conditions to maintain consistent performance. First, natural consequents should be presented more frequently or immediately. Second, alternate consequents that may be expected to motivate the student should be structured into the work environment. In either case, the teacher must be skilled in identifying viable reinforcers, prioritizing potential alternate reinforcers, and assessing the reinforcement hierarchy of the adolescent.

CLASSES OF REINFORCERS

Consequents have been described as being either primary or secondary reinforcing events. *Primary reinforcers* are those events that satisfy basic biological needs and are important to sustain life. These events do not depend on previous learning or conditioning for the development of their reinforcing properties. Primary reinforcers including food, warmth, and drink are used more frequently with primary-aged children and the severely developmentally disabled. *Secondary reinforcers,* on the other hand, are used more frequently in intervention programs for the mildly and moderately handicapped adolescent. Secondary reinforcers include events that have acquired reinforcement status through frequent association with a primary reinforcer. For example, money acquires its power as a reinforcer through its association with the acquisition of food, water, shelter, and other primary reinforcers. Secondary reinforcers frequently available in the school setting include grades, praise, approval, privileges, activities, and other factors associated with school success and acceptance. Secondary reinforcers associated with career-vocational settings include money, work, evaluation reports, production data, special privileges based on rank, etc.

Table 7-2 Motivational Analysis Guide

Continuous recording reveals:	Recommendation	Examples
Antecedents for the desired behavior are highly variable.	Teach the student to respond appropriately to the range of antecedents that should cue the desired behavior.	Rehearse appropriate response in a number of work situations (e.g., say "thank you" when praised by the boss, paid by a customer, complimented by a coworker, etc.).
The student's performance is frequently substandard and frequent failure often produces unpleasant consequences.	Teach appropriate work behavior. Establish a criterion for success that is easily attainable.	Instruct and provide practice time for specific work tasks. Establish a criterion for performance based on current skill level.
The natural consequences of the behavior are not satisfying to the adolescent.	Identify satisfying outcomes that may be incorporated into the work situation.	Schedule "coffee breaks" contingent on a specific performance rate.
The student is not aware of the relationship between performance and positive consequences.	Provide graphic feedback depicting the relationship between performance and outcomes.	Instruct the adolescent to record the number of assemblies completed on a comparative graph each work period.
Reinforcing consequents do not occur if sufficiently frequent to motivate performance.	Increase the frequency with which positive consequences are delivered.	Pay the student each day as opposed to once every two weeks. Compliment the adolescent on his or her performance more frequently.

The natural consequents of the behavior are aversive to the adolescent.	Teach the student to avoid aversive aspects of the work. Also, minimize aversive consequents associated with the working.	Encourage the student to wear heavy clothes on a cold day. Teach the student to avoid disruptive coworkers.
The student has a negative response toward the work.	Encourage the student to state frequently the relationship between performance and positive outcomes.	Frequently discuss how much money the student is earning, what he or she did to earn the money, and what he or she may do with the money.
The student is not aware of the expectations of his or her supervisor.	Set precise performance goals each day, week, and/or month.	Establish a daily criterion for work rate and quality. Monitor and provide feedback with respect to meeting or failing to meet the criteria.

PRIORITIZING REINFORCERS

Primary and secondary reinforcers can be prioritized from least to most effective in motivating a behavior and least to most likely to occur naturally in the educational or vocational environment. Prioritization on the basis of reinforcer strength is critical to establishing incentives that are sufficiently powerful to motivate the student to engage in the target behavior. Once a range of reinforcers is identified that is likely to be effective, potential reinforcers that are natural to the setting can be selected. For example, a teacher may have a hunch that candy, money, and free time will reinforce schoolwork completion. Food items and money are seldom natural incentives in the school setting, while free time is a natural and logical result of early completion of work. Free time would be an appropriate incentive for work completion because it is hypothesized to be sufficiently powerful and it is a natural and logical consequence of work completion. Career-vocational education programs should emphasize the use of reinforcing events available in traditional work settings. Exhibit 7-1 presents a list of potential reinforcers that are natural to many vocational placements and may be built into a career-vocational education program.

SELECT A MEASURE OF BEHAVIOR STRENGTH

Several procedures may be used to assess the strength of potential reinforcers for an adolescent. The most pragmatic is simply to ask the individual what he or she enjoys. In addition to an informal discussion, self-report data can be developed through a number of interesting and enjoyable vocationally related activities. Small group activities can be structured that focus on identifying and clarifying pleasant events in the vocational environment. One approach may be for the instructor to ask the students to write, independently, 20 things that they really enjoy about their jobs. Next, the teacher may ask the pupils to rank the items from most to least enjoyable. Each class member may then discuss his or her top five selections and write them on the board. Finally, the class may be asked to reach consensus on the rank order of items placed on the board. When self-report data are used, information provided by students should be substantiated through other assessment approaches. It is generally understood that an individual's verbal behavior (what a person says he or she will do) is not always the same as the person's overt behavior (what he or she actually does).

An approach that may augment self-report data is to observe what the adolescent does during free time or unstructured activities. One would expect the student to engage in preferred activities when free to do so. If a student frequently plays basketball during an unstructured recreation or recess period, it could be assumed that basketball was an enjoyable and potentially reinforcing activity. Another

Exhibit 7-1 Potential Reinforcers Natural to Vocational Placements

Tangible

1. Special work station
2. Telephone
3. Favorable evaluation in personnel file
4. Merit raise
5. Bonus check
6. Tips
7. Commission
8. Piece-rate bonus
9. Profit sharing
10. Special equipment
11. Small gifts
12. Letter of recognition
13. Achievement award
14. Trips
15. Vacation
16. Banquet
17. Lunch with the employer
18. Tickets to sporting events
19. Parking place
20. Uniform

Social

1. Praise from boss
2. Praise from coworkers
3. Job title
4. Picture in paper
5. Presentation of ideas to others
6. Eye contact and smile
7. Handshake
8. Pat on back
9. Having work put on display
10. Name in company paper or on a complimentary memo

Activity

1. Free time
2. Coffee break
3. Special job-related trip
4. Work with friend
5. Special assignment
6. High-preference job
7. Supervisor responsibility
8. Day off
9. Extra training
10. Parties

method of identifying potential reinforcers is to observe what students do with their spending money. If a student often purchases record albums, it is likely that listening to records is a rewarding activity, and that "stereo time" and record albums are potential reinforcers. Parents may be valuable resources in identifying potential reinforcers. They are often in a position to observe what a student does during free time as well as how the student spends money.

Reinforcer sampling is another effective approach to identifying and developing incentives. Reinforcer sampling involves exposing the student to a potentially enjoyable activity. Once the student has been exposed to the activity, the teacher may make the activity contingent on a desirable behavior. For example, a teacher may initiate a special break period in which all of the students are encouraged to participate in board games. After several sessions, the teacher may say that students will be allowed to play only if they have completed their homework. This procedure is particularly useful when exposing students to unfamiliar or novel incentives. Students may not have worked for break time initially. However, once they have a chance to experience the new card sessions, its reinforcement value may increase.

MEASURING BEHAVIOR

It has been stated repeatedly through the past section that an event is hypothesized to be reinforcing only until it is demonstrated that the behavior is more likely to occur when consequated by the event. One may speculate that money is a reinforcer for work production, but its actual status as a reinforcer is not known until it is presented, contingent on work output. If work rate increases, then it is likely that money does reinforce the positive affect. If the work rate remains low, the strength of money as a reinforcer may be questioned. Similarly, one may hypothesize that yelling at a student for talking out is a punishing event. However, until yelling is made contingent on talking out and the number of talking out episodes decreases, the influence of yelling as a punishing event is not known. Fundamental to any intervention program is the confidence that the teacher has that the prescribed consequents will motivate the desired behavior. The data-keeping system utilized by the teacher provides a level of confidence in the efficacy of the behavior management program. Having measured the strength of the target behavior prior to and during intervention, the teacher can be relatively certain that the program is or is not influencing the student's behavior.

Event Recording

Of all measures of behavior strength, event recording is probably the most useful and least time consuming. A frequency measure is obtained by counting each episode of the behavior through a specified period of time. This procedure is appropriate when: (1) the start and stop time of the event is distinct, such as words spoken, units broken, or breaks taken; and (2) the response lasts a relatively constant amount of time (Kazdin, 1980). Event recording should be avoided when measuring behaviors that are not discrete or of constant duration. For example, behavior management may effectively reduce the number of times a student is late for work from eight per month to two per month, but not change the total amount of time the student is tardy. Therefore, the frequency measure would be sensitive to change in the number of tardiness episodes but not in the duration of each occurrence.

To make valid comparisons of frequency data from day to day, or student to student, the amount of time available for observation must be held constant. A student may be in mathematics class for 20 minutes one day, and 30 minutes the next day. Six problems were completed on the first day, eight on the second. It cannot be concluded that mathematics completion behavior was stronger on the second day, because the amount of time observed confounded the data. The frequency of response can be transformed to a rate of response that gives comparable data across observation periods. The rate of response is computed by dividing the number of occurrences (frequency) by the amount of time observed.

$$\text{Rate} = \frac{\text{Frequency}}{\text{Time}} = \frac{6}{20} = .3$$

In the previous example, six problems were completed in 20 minutes yielding a rate of .3 mathematics problems per minute, while eight problems were completed in 30 minutes on the second day, producing a slower rate of mathematics work (i.e., $\frac{8}{30} = .27$).

A number of devices have been used to reduce the amount of staff time involved in event recording. For example, Mahoney (1974) used an abacus watchband, and Lindsey (1968) reliably used a golf counter. These devices are especially useful in classroom or vocational settings because they require only one hand to make a tally, can be carried by the teacher, and can be operated without disrupting ongoing classroom activities. Regardless of the instrument used to tally information throughout the day, a recording sheet that stores data from day to day is essential. Table 7-3 illustrates a commonly used data sheet for observations of varying length.

Table 7-3 Recording Sheet for Rate Data

Student: Behavior:

Teacher/observer: Setting:

Date	Start time	Stop time	Total	Frequency	Daily rate
4/16	8:30	10:00	90	3	
	12:30	3:00	150	5	
Total			240	8	.03
4/17	8:45	10:00	75	8	
	12:10	3:15	185	6	
Total			260	14	.05

MEASUREMENT OF PERSONAL PRODUCT

Measurement of personal product is particularly useful in vocational activities that result in a quantifiable product. The computational procedure for the measurement of personal product is very similar to event recording. The primary difference is that the student's actual behavior is not recorded. Rather, data represent the product of his or her behavior. Table 7-4 represents a data sheet that has been used by the authors to measure the production rate and percentage of correct assemblies completed by handicapped adolescents and young adults.

Interval Recording

Interval recording is appropriate when measuring the strength of behaviors that do not have discrete start or stop times and that vary in length (e.g., laughing, hand waving, talking, attending, sitting). Interval data are collected by dividing a long period of time into shorter time periods. For example, a 20-minute class may be divided into 40, 30-second intervals. The behavior would be scored as occurred or not occurred in each of the intervals. The actual number of occurrences in the interval does not affect the scoring. Often, interval data are time sampled (i.e., taken in random periods of time throughout the day).

Kazdin (1980) describes an interval procedure by which a number of students in a classroom can be observed over the same period of time. The first child was observed in the first interval, the second child in the second interval, and so on, until all children were observed. Then the recorder returned to the initial child until all of the children were observed for a number of intervals. Another variation of the interval recording procedure involves observing the student through an interval and then taking a short period of time to record the response before beginning the second interval. Observation intervals may be 15 seconds in length, while scoring intervals are 5 seconds in length.

Table 7-5 represents a common scoring sheet used with interval recording. The numbers over each square denote the time of the interval. A + or a − are used to indicate the occurrence or nonoccurrence of the behavior. The interval data are transformed to the percentage of intervals in which the behavior occurred by dividing the number of occurrences by the number of intervals.

Duration Recording

Duration recording is useful when the intervention approach is expected to increase or decrease the amount of time an individual engages in an activity. An instructor may seek to increase the amount of time an individual spends working on homework, or decrease the amount of time an adolescent spends in the halls between classes. In these cases, the dependent measure would be duration.

Table 7-4 Production Data Sheet

Worker: _____

Date	Task	Start time	Stop time	Time working (in minutes)	Units completed	# correct	Production rate = $\frac{\text{units completed}}{\text{minutes working}}$	Percent correct = $\frac{\text{\# correct}}{\text{units completed}}$

Table 7-5 Recording Form for Interval Data

Student:

Teacher/Observer:

Behavior:

Setting:

Date	Time Period	15	30	45	1	15	30	45	2	15	30	45	3	15	30	45	4	15	30	45	5	% scored	Daily %
4/16	8:30-8:35	+	–	–	+	–	–	–	–	–	–	–	–	–	–	–	–	–	–	–	–	10	
	10:15-10:20	+	+	+	+	+	–	–	–	–	–	–	–	–	–	–	–	–	–	–	–	25	
	2:00-2:05	–	+	–	+	–	+	–	–	–	+	+	+	+	+	+	+	–	–	–	–	50	28
4/17	8:30-8:35	–	–	–	–	–	–	–	–	–	–	–	–	–	–	–	–	–	–	–	–	0	
	10:15-10:20	+	+	–	–	–	–	–	+	+	+	+	+	–	+	–	–	–	–	+	+	50	
	2:00-2:05	+	+	–	–	–	–	–	–	–	–	–	–	–	–	–	–	+	+	+	+	25	25
4/18	8:30-8:35																						
	10:15-10:20																						
	2:00-2:05																						
4/19	8:30-8:35																						
	10:15-10:20																						
	2:00-2:05																						

4/20	8:30-8:35	10:15-10:20	2:00-2:05		4/23	8:30-8:35	10:15-10:20	2:00-2:05																													

Whitman, Mercurio, and Caponigri (1970) utilized duration data in a program designed to evaluate the effectiveness of a social interaction training procedure. The data collection procedure measured the number of minutes spent in social interaction by program participants. Table 7-6 illustrates a form that is useful in collecting duration data.

Inter-Rater Reliability

The most elaborate behavioral recording system is of little value if the data that it produces are not reliable. The extent to which an observational procedure provides a reliable assessment of the target behavior is termed inter-rater reliability. The degree to which independent observers agree on the occurrence/nonoccurrence, duration, or strength of the target behavior determines the reliability of the observation procedure. Reliability indicates the consistency with which the target behavior is observed and scored (Kazdin, 1980). High reliability is essential so that trends in the data can be attributed confidently to the treatment procedure rather than observer error. Poor inter-observer reliability is often the result of an inadequate response definition or observational procedure. For example, it is unlikely that independent observers would agree on the occurrence of unhappiness using a frequency measure (e.g., number of unhappy episodes). On the other hand, if the response definition were changed to the number of negative self-statements, two observers would probably agree fairly consistently on the occurrence of the statements.

Inter-rater reliability for frequency measures is determined by two individuals observing the student for the same period of time. The lowest frequency of occurrences is then divided by the highest frequency of occurrence to produce the reliability coefficient (i.e., percentage of agreement between two observers). For example, a teacher and aide both record the number of swear words uttered by a student for a two-hour period. The teacher records 10, while the aide records 6. The resulting reliability coefficient would be computed by dividing the smaller number of observations (6) by the larger (10), producing 60 percent of agreement:

$$\frac{\text{smaller frequency}}{\text{larger frequency}} = \frac{6}{10} = .60$$

Reliability in duration recording is computed by dividing the shorter duration by the longer duration recorded by two independent observers:

$$\frac{\text{shorter duration}}{\text{longer duration}} = \frac{40}{50} = .80$$

Table 7-6 Recording Form for Duration Data

Student: _____   Behavior: _____

Teacher/Observer: _____   Setting: _____

Date	Observation time	Start time	Stop time	Incident time	Daily time	Daily rate
4/16	8:30-9:45	8:30	8:35	5		
		8:37	8:38	1		
		8:50	9:01	11		
		9:05	9:15	10		
		9:30	9:32	2	29	29/75 = .39
4/17	8:30-9:50	9:10	9:30	20		
		9:32	9:35	3		
		9:45	9:50	5	28	28/80 = .35

The reliability coefficient in interval recording is determined by dividing the number of intervals in which both observers scored an occurrence by the number of agreements and disagreements. Intervals in which both observers did not score an occurrence are excluded from the computation:

$$\frac{\#\text{agreements}}{\#\text{ agreements \& disagreements}} = \frac{18}{20} = .90$$
$$\text{excluding nonoccurrences}$$

Inter-observer reliability should be evaluated prior to the initiation of formal data collection during baseline, and every week or so through intervention. Reliability should be tested at a level of .80 or better prior to the initiation of formal data collection. Consistently high reliability (e.g., .90) requires fewer checks while low reliability prior to baseline may indicate the inadequacy of the response definition or observation procedure. Once a data collection procedure is established and reliability tested, baseline data can be collected.

COLLECT BASELINE DATA

It has been emphasized earlier that an important feature of any intervention program is the continuous measurement of the target behavior (dependent measure) prior to and during intervention. Baseline data provide a measure of behavior strength under general program conditions, against which the effects of a specialized program may be compared. Valid comparisons can only be made if the baseline is representative of the actual behavior strength under normal program conditions. A valid representation of behavior strength is achieved by collecting reliable baseline data through four or more days, in which there is neither an ascending trend, when a reductive intervention is planned, or descending trend, when an accelerative intervention is planned. There should also be some degree of stability in the data.

An *ascending trend* indicates that the dependent measure is increasing in strength. A *descending trend* indicates that the dependent measure is decreasing in strength. If a teacher initiates intervention while an ascending or descending baseline trend is present in the direction expected following treatment, conclusions regarding the impact of treatment on the target behavior are of questionable validity. The examples on the left side of Figure 7-3 report improper baseline trends. The effects of the intervention procedures on the target behaviors are not clear because there is not an abrupt shift in the strength of the target behavior when intervention is introduced.

An ascending baseline preceding the intervention designed to strengthen a target behavior in a_1 does not present a clear representation of the effect of intervention. A possible solution to this problem, presented in a_2, involves continuing baseline

Figure 7-3 Improper and Proper Baseline Trends

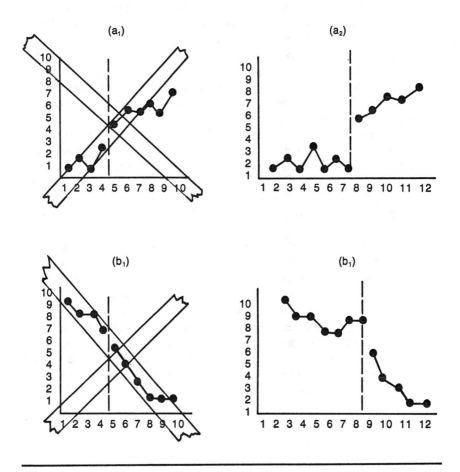

conditions until a plateau is reached. Another solution may be to continue baseline until the behavior reaches acceptable levels through natural program conditions. The descending baseline illustrated in b₁ presents similar problems. Once again, baseline is continued in b₂ until the behavior stabilizes.

A similar baseline pattern involves an ascending baseline preceding a deceleration program, or the inverse, a descending baseline preceding an acceleration program. In this case, the trend in baseline data indicates a deterioration in the behavior that treatment is designed to improve. This pattern presents less of a concern to the teacher than the previous pattern as treatment effects can be ascertained from a shift in the strength of the target behavior.

Group Observation Systems

Up to the present section, this chapter has discussed issues and methods relating to the development of an individualized intervention program. Data collection procedures have been directed toward the expected outcomes of these individualized programs. In addition to individual program data, the use of continuous data to monitor and evaluate general program objectives is equally important. Punctuality, adherence to work rules, compliance with supervisor's instructions, etc., are often common objectives of career-vocational education programs. A data collection system can easily be designed to monitor each of these behavioral targets for all program participants. Exhibit 7-2 and Table 7-7 illustrate such a system.

The objectives presented in Exhibit 7-2 represent important work habits that the vocational program seeks to impact. These include punctuality, maintaining personal possessions in the assigned work area, and compliance with work supervisor's requests. Data collection procedures are provided with each objective. The recording strategies identified were designed to minimize staff time in collecting data. Simple frequency counts, scoring comply ("c") or noncomply ("nc"), and recording times from a punch card provide a substantial amount of useful data while minimizing collection time. Table 7-7 provides a format for recording raw data. This information may be transferred to a graph or summary chart for each student at a convenient time. As will be discussed in the next chapter, students should be involved to the extent possible in the data collection and display activities. In the present case, the individual students may record and/or display their own data. The teacher may then conduct reliability checks with the individual students. This practice may provide a point of departure for career counseling sessions in which the teacher and student jointly evaluate progress and identify future goals and objectives.

DATA DISPLAY

Continuous data presented in raw form are difficult to read and interpret. Subtle trends indicative of improvement are not easily identified when data are presented in tabular form. The relationship between data trends and the initiation of an intervention program is more easily understood when presented in graphic form. The traditional format for charting behavioral data involves major components: (1) a vertical axis that clearly reports the measure of behavior strength, (2) a horizontal axis reporting the day or session number associated with each data point, and (3) broken vertical lines that indicate the initiation of the intervention program or subsequent changes in the program. Figure 7-4 illustrates these components. Notice how a broken line is used to connect two data points that are separated by a missing data point.

Exhibit 7-2 Group Data Collection System:
Objectives and Recording Procedure

Objective

1. The worker will hang up coat/jacket and leave all *nonwork-related pos-
sessions/materials* in his/her locker.
Record "C" or "NC."

2. The worker will *punch time clock on time* (not more than five minutes
earlier or two minutes later than scheduled work time).
Record "C" or "L" or "E" (if L or E is recorded, also *record* the # of
minutes).

3. The worker will *report to work station within two minutes of punching* in
(regardless of the time(s) he punched in).

4. The worker will *remain at work station* during each work period.
Record "+" for each occurrence of leaving work station for each work
period and "−" for nonoccurrence for a given work period.

5. The worker will *go to breaks or lunch on time* (within two minutes of
designated time).
Record "C" or "L" (if L is recorded, also record the # of minutes).

6. The worker will *return to work on time following breaks or lunch* (not before
and no more than two minutes after designated time).

7. The worker will *comply to work supervisor(s)' work day-related requests.*
Record a tally for each "C" or "NC."

8. The worker will *terminate work and punch out within two minutes of
designated work-stop time.*
Record "C" or "L" (if L is recorded, also record the # of minutes).

9. The worker will *leave workshop area within two minutes of punching out*
(regardless of when he/she punches out).

Table 7-7 Group Data Collection Form

Key:
C=comply
NC=noncomply
L=late
E=early

Worker's Name	1. Nonwork related possessions.		2. Punch in (five min. before to two min. after).		3. Report to work station (within two min. of punching in).		4. Remain at work station.	5. Go to break or lunch (within two min. of designated time).			6. Return from break or lunch (within two min. of designated time).			7. Comply with supervisor's requests.	8. Punch out (less than two min. following work-stop time).	9. Leave workshop (within two min. of punching out).
	C/NC		C/L or E & mins.		C/NC		Tally for each time out of seat	C/L & mins.			C/L or E & mins.			Tally each NC	C/L & mins.	C/L & mins.
	A.M.	P.M.	A.M.	P.M.	A.M.	P.M.		Br	Lch	Br₂	Br	Lch	Br₂			

Figure 7-4 Behavioral Data Chart

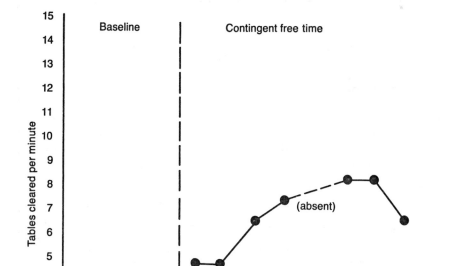

CONCLUSION

The present chapter has addressed the major questions that the career-vocational educator should raise prior to formalizing and implementing a behavioral intervention. Program analysis, as discussed in this chapter, has involved three major activities. First, the teacher raises specific questions that are related to the student's performance problems. Second, the teacher identifies sources of information that may answer these questions, thereby providing a better understanding of the performance problems. Finally, the teacher utilizes the resulting information to develop a behavior management program that reflects the needs of the adolescent, the expectations of significant people in his or her environment, and the resources available to the teacher and student.

Exhibit 7-3 Program Analysis Summary Sheet

Name: _____
Date: _____
Teacher: _____

Target Behavior

1. _____
   definition _____
   _____
   criterion for success _____

2. _____
   definition _____
   _____
   criterion for success _____

3. _____
   definition _____
   _____
   criterion for success _____

Scope

1. setting(s) _____
   _____

2. important conditions _____
   _____

3. change agents _____
   _____

   Potential reinforcers

   tangible _____   social _____
   _____   _____
   _____   _____
   _____   _____
   activity _____   _____
   _____   _____
   _____   _____

Exhibit 7-3 continued

Data collection procedure

_____

_____

_____

Maintaining conditions antecedents _____

_____

_____

Associated characteristics _____

_____

_____

Consequents _____

_____

_____

Exhibit 7-3 presents a program analysis summary form that may facilitate the design, implementation, and evaluation of an intervention program. The questions raised by the program analysis summary sheet are consistent with the methods discussed throughout this chapter. The *Target Behavior* section requires the program engineer to specify the focus of the program, define the target behavior, and establish a criterion for success. The *Scope* section encourages the teacher to identify the setting or settings, important conditions, and change agents that are expected to be associated with the program. The *Potential Reinforcers* section provides a summary of items and events that may be used to motivate the student. The *Data Collection Procedure* section requires the teacher to identify a procedure for measuring, recording, and displaying the strength of the target behavior. Finally, the *Maintaining Conditions* section provides a summary of antecedent and consequent conditions, as well as associated characteristics that may influence the strength of the target behavior.

Having conducted the program analysis, the next stop is to translate the data into a formal behavior management program. The following chapter will present a review of various intervention approaches that are consistent with social learning theory constructs.

REFERENCES

Bates, P. The effectiveness of interpersonal skills training on the social skill acquisition of moderately and mildly retarded adults. *Journal of Applied Behavior Analysis*, 1980, *13*, 237-248.

Beck, A. T. *Depression: Causes and treatment*. Philadelphia: University of Pennsylvania Press, 1972.

Bijou, S. W. Behavior modification in teaching the retarded child. In C. E. Thoresen (Ed.), *Behavior modification in education*. The seventy-second yearbook of the National Society for the Study of Education. Chicago: The University of Chicago Press, 1972, pp. 259-290.

Bryan, T.H. Peer popularity of learning disabled children: A replication. *Journal of Learning Disabilities*, 1976, *9*, 49-53.

Bryan, T. H. & Bryan, J. H. The social-emotional side of learning disabilities. *Behavioral Disorders*, 1977, *2*(3), 141-145.

Bryan, T. H., Wheeler, R., Felcan, J., & Hanek, T. Come on dummy: An observational survey of children's communications. *Journal of Learning Disabilities*, 1976, *9*, 661-669.

Cromwell, R. L. A social learning approach to mental retardation. In N. R. Ellis (Ed.), *Handbook of mental deficiency*. New York: McGraw-Hill, 1963.

Elder, J. P., Edelstein, B. A., & Warick, M. M. Adolescent psychiatric patients: Modifying aggressive behavior with social skills training. *Behavior Modification*, 1979, *3*, 161-178.

Gardner, W. I. Social and emotional adjustment of mildly retarded children and adolescents: Critical review. *Exceptional Children*, 1966, *33*, 97-105.

Gardner, W. I. *Learning and behavior characteristics of exceptional children and youth: A humanistic behavioral approach*. Boston: Allyn & Bacon, 1977.

Grossman, H. J. *Manual on terminology and classification in mental retardation*. Baltimore: Garamond/Pridemark, 1973.

Heber, R. Research on personality disorders and characteristics of the mentally retarded. *Mental Retardation Abstracts*, 1964, *1*, 304-325.

Johnston, J. M. Punishment of human behavior. *American Psychologist*, 1972, *27*, 1033-1054.

Kauffman, J. M. *Characteristics of children's behavior disorders* (2nd ed.). Columbus, Ohio: Charles E. Merrill Publishing Co., 1981.

Kazdin, A. E. *Behavior modification in applied settings*. Homewood, Ill.: Dorsey Press, 1980.

Koegel, R. L., & Rincover, A. Treatment of psychotic children in a classroom environment: Learning in a large group. *Journal of Applied Behavior Analysis*, 1974, *7*, 45-59.

Lerner, J. W. *Children with learning disabilities: Theories, diagnosis, and teaching strategy*. Boston: Houghton Mifflin, 1971.

Lewandowski, L. J., & Cruickshank, W. M. Psychological development of crippled children and youth. In W. M. Cruickshank (Ed.), *Psychology of exceptional children and youth*. Englewood Cliffs, N.J.: Prentice-Hall, 1980.

Lindsey, O. R. Technical note: A reliable wrist counter for recording behavior rates. *Journal of Applied Behavior Analysis*, 1968, *1*, 77-78.

Mahoney, M. J. *Cognitive and behavior modification*. Cambridge, Mass.: Ballinger, 1974.

Malkin, S. F., Freeman, R. D., & Hastings, J. D. Psychosocial problems of deaf children and their families. A comparative study. *Audiology and Hearing Education*, 1976, *2*, 21-29.

Marlowe, R. H., Madsen, C. H., Bowen, C. E., Reardon, R. C., & Logue, P. E. Severe classroom behavior problems: Teachers or counselors. *Journal of Applied Behavior Analysis*, 1978, *11*, 53-66.

McMichael, J. K. *Handicap: A study of physically handicapped children and their families*. London: Staples Press, 1971.

Menolascino, F. J. *Challenges in mental retardation: Progressive ideology and services*. New York: Human Science Press, 1977.

Miller, W. H. Manifest anxiety in visually impaired adolescents. *Education of the Visually Handicapped*, 1970, *2*, 91-95.

Nagera, H., & Colonna, A. E. Aspects of the contribution of sight to ego and drive development: A comparison of the development of some blind and sighted children. In *The psychoanalytic study of the child*. New York: International Universities Press, 1965, *20*, 267-287.

Risley, T. R., & Wolf, M. Establishing functional speech in echolalic children. *Behavior Research and Therapy*, 1967, *5*, 73-88.

Rutter, M. L. Psychiatry. In J. Wortio (Ed.), *Mental retardation: An annual review* (Vol. 3). New York: Grune & Stratton, 1971.

Sanders, D. A. Psychological implications of hearing impairment. In W. M. Cruickshank (Ed.), *Psychology of exceptional children and youth*. Englewood Cliffs, N.J.: Prentice-Hall, 1980.

Schlesinger, H. S., & Meadow, K. P. *Deafness and mental health: A developmental approach*. San Francisco: Langley Porter Neuvo-psychiatric Institute, 1971.

Schloss, P. J., Kane, M. S., & Miller, S. R. Truancy intervention for behaviorally disordered adolescents. *Behavioral Disorders*, 1981, *6*, 175-179.

Schloss, P. J., Sachs, J. J., & Miller, S. R. Increasing work production of a mentally retarded student through the systematic analysis of continuous data. *Journal of Vocational Technical Education*, in press.

Schloss, P. J., & Sedlak, R. Behavioral features of the mentally retarded adolescent: Implications for the mainstream educator. *Psychology in the schools*, in press.

Schumaker, J. B., Hovell, M. F., & Sherman, J. A. An analysis of daily report cards and parent-managed privileges in the improvement of adolescents' classroom performance. *Journal of Applied Behavioral Analysis*, 1977, *10*, 449-464.

Seligman, M. E. P. *Helplessness*. San Francisco: Freeman, 1975.

Snyder, J. J., & White, M. J. The use of cognitive self-instruction in the treatment of behaviorally disturbed adolescents. *Behavior Therapy*, 1979, *10*, 227-235.

Sternlicht, M. Issues in counseling and psychotherapy with mentally retarded individuals. In I. Bialer and M. Sternlicht (Eds.), *The psychology of mental retardation: Issues and approaches*. New York: Psychological Dimensions, Inc., 1977, pp. 453-493.

Twardosz, S., & Sajwaj, T. Multiple effects of a procedure to increase sitting in a hyperactive retarded boy. *Journal of Applied Behavior Analysis*, 1972, *5*, 73-78.

White, R. W. Competence and psychosexual stages of development. In M. R. Jones (Ed.), *Nebraska Symposium on Motivation*. Lincoln: University of Nebraska Press, 1960.

Whitman, T. L., Mercurio, J. R., & Caponigri, V. Development of social responses in two severely retarded children. *Journal of Applied Behavior Analysis*, 1970, *5*, 111-120.

Zigler, E. The retarded child as a whole person. In D. K. Routh (Ed.), *The experimental psychology of mental retardation*. Chicago: Aldine, 1973, pp. 231-322.

Chapter 8

Behavior Management: Program Approaches

The preceding chapter provided a model for analyzing social-personal deficits within the context of the setting in which behavioral excesses and deficits occur. Emphasis has been placed on three factors in the analysis of social-personal deficits: (1) *antecedent conditions,* or events that frequently precede the target behavior and influence the likelihood that it will occur (e.g., Bob sitting next to an open window increases the likelihood that he will be off task); (2) *related personal characteristics,* observable or inferred features of the individual that may be associated with the occurrence of the target behavior (e.g., because Bob lacks assertiveness skills, he is more likely to behave aggressively when confronted by a coworker); and (3) *consequent conditions,* defined as events that follow the target behavior and influence the probability of its occurrence (e.g., Bob's speed in clearing tables at the restaurant increases when the waitresses share their tips with him).

A number of behavior management strategies have been described in the literature that addresses these factors. A cursory review of many texts may suggest to the reader that the actual selection of an intervention approach is done indiscriminately. Contrary to this notion, the underlying theme of a social learning theory orientation is the analysis of specific factors that influence the target behavior. Intervention approaches are selected on the basis of data generated from the careful study of the student's behavioral characteristics in association with influencing factors. The readers who are familiar with the applied behavior analysis procedures presented in the preceding chapter should be able to select from a range of intervention strategies on the basis of their understanding of the learner.

The present chapter describes a number of behavior management tactics that have been demonstrated to be effective in developing positive social behaviors with handicapped adolescents. Strategies presented include educative procedures, designed to teach positive social behaviors that are presently not in the individual's repertoire; decelerative procedures, intended to reduce the strength of excessive disruptive behaviors; accelerative procedures, designed to increase the frequency with which an individual engages in behaviors that he or she has previously learned; and maintenance and generalization procedures, intended to increase the durability of behavior changes over time and across settings. While each procedure is discussed as an isolated program approach, readers will readily see that a number of strategies may be used in combination to produce a more powerful and comprehensive treatment package.

ISSUES IN PLANNING FOR BEHAVIOR CHANGE

Behavior management, as discussed in this chapter and the preceding chapter, involves the systematic application of social learning theory principles. These principles and their treatment implications have been the subject of a plethora of basic and applied research. The upsurge of a number of scientific journals, concerned with advancing behavioral research, evidences this fact (e.g., *Journal of Applied Behavior Analysis, Behavior Therapy, Behavior Research and Therapy, Journal of Behavior Therapy and Experimental Psychiatry, Behaviorism, Behavior Modification, Advances in Behavior Research and Therapy*).

Similarly, behavioral technology has crept into a number of disciplines concerned for the education and treatment of handicapped youths. A review of vocational education journals as well as special education journals reveals a growing percentage of program descriptions, issues articles, and intervention strategies reflecting a behavioral orientation. Along with the influx of new data and technology have come strong negative reactions from many professionals. The weariness of the educational and psychological community from the application of behavioral principles has grown from two major arguments.

First, a behavioral orientation is predicated on the tenet that human actions can be controlled and that control of one's behavior by another individual (e.g., student by teacher) is desirable. This tenet violates a long-standing doctrine highly cherished by Western culture—free will (Skinner, 1971). Free will suggests persons act as the result of inner drives not accounted for through the study of environment or heredity. While there is some security in a belief in control over one's own destiny, the task that continually faces educators is the identification of procedures that exert control over a student's social, personal, vocational, and academic behavior. Whether one adopts a psychoeducational, humanistic, or behavioral orientation, the task still remains to change the student's behavior as he or she progresses through the goals of the educational program. The fact that behavioral technology has been repeatedly demonstrated to be effective in controlling human behavior only emphasizes its utility in the helping professions (Bandura, 1969).

The second argument frequently raised involves the methods by which behaviorally oriented practitioners attempt to change behavior. This argument often results from the mistaken idea that behavioral strategies are limited to token reinforcement, time out, and other contingency-management procedures (Gambrill, 1977). In fact, there is a wide range of behavioral intervention strategies many of which closely parallel procedures employed by decided nonbehavioral practitioners. The present chapter, for example, discusses over a dozen intervention options that may be used independently or as part of a treatment package. As discussed earlier, these tactics are designed not only to punish or reinforce behavior, but also to control the stimulus conditions that cue behavior. Other approaches are designated to teach appropriate responses systematically. The list of intervention tactics in this chapter is limited to procedures most applicable to career-vocational settings and objectives.

A related issue is that misguided treatment approaches often lead to overgeneralized criticisms of behavioral principles. For example, a recent newspaper story discussed the case of a young woman who attempted suicide while placed in seclusion. A lawyer argued that she was engaged in a behavior therapy program (i.e., time out) and because of the dangers of such programs, behavioral interventions should be outlawed. The actual criticism of the approach used in this case may well be justified. However, the criticism is limited to the skills of the psychiatrist and technicians who designed, implemented, and monitored the program. To say that behavior therapy should be outlawed is as fallacious as arguing that psychotherapy should be banned because aggressive individuals engaged in therapy beat their wives.

Behavioral technology has resulted from the empirical study of human behavior. The resulting principles are valid descriptions of relationships that exist in nature (e.g., a behavior that produces satisfying consequences is likely to recur as will behavior that leads to the avoidance of unpleasant conditions). While the principles, as stated, can be ignored, the relationships that they describe will continue. Utilizing behavioral strategies simply allows the practitioner to enhance student change through systematic and well-planned procedures that reflect the practitioner's understanding of learners and their environment.

ETHICAL GUIDELINES

Because of the strong influence that an educator may have in controlling adolescents' behavior, the need to protect their rights is increasingly evident. A number of authors have advanced detailed discussions of ethical issues in the design and application of behavior change programs.

One of the more concise statements of ethical practice is presented in *Law and Behavior* (1976). Exhibit 8-1 presents a summary of the guidelines. Because the IEP process described in Chapter 1 is consistent with many of these principles, an adjoining column demonstrates how the IEP process can be used to facilitate these safeguards.

A final area of concern for those designing and implementing behavior change procedures involves the selection of strategies that are likely to be effective and minimally intrusive. Intrusiveness is defined here as the extent to which the procedure: (1) removes the adolescent from the mainstream of educational activities; (2) is unpleasant to the adolescent; (3) consumes educational resources in the form of staff time, materials, money, etc.; (4) is unusual in the educational or vocational environment; and (5) is potentially dangerous to the adolescent or other individuals in the setting.

It is difficult, if not impossible, to establish an a priori ranking of behavior change strategies on the basis of intrusiveness. The number of ecological and subject variables that enter into each decision quickly invalidate any such ranking. For example, one may suggest that corporal punishment is the most intrusive behavior management procedure. However, for a specific individual corporal punishment administered one time may be highly likely to eliminate a disruptive behavior. On the other hand, a time-out procedure, which removes the adolescent from a number of learning experiences, may require substantially more trials before control is exerted over the behavior. In this case, it could be argued that time out is more intrusive than corporal punishment because it is likely to be a detriment to academic achievement. This example, however, is not designed to argue for or against corporal punishment.

Holding ecological and subject variables constant, a general ranking of intervention approaches can be considered. Procedures that involve the development of new skills that are likely to be supported by the natural environment are undoubtedly least intrusive as judged by the preceding criteria. Procedures that involve the systematic use of natural consequences such as contingent free time and planned ignoring are second. Third are programs that rely on altering the stimulus environment, such as separating antagonistic students and providing cues to prompt performance. Next are procedures that involve unnatural positive contingency arrangements, including token systems and contingent delivery of edible reinforcers. Fifth are procedures that involve unnatural aversive consequences such as time out, overcorrection, and corporal punishment.

Having emphasized that intervention strategy selection is a function of the careful analysis of learners and their environment, and that it is incumbent on the educator to select the least intrusive of available approaches expected to be effective, the following sections present a detailed analysis of behavior change strategies that are relevant to career-vocational education objectives and settings.

Exhibit 8-1 Association between Ethical Standards and the IEP
Process

Ethical standard	*IEP mechanism*
1. A specific description of the adolescent's behavioral characteristics and needs should be prepared prior to the design and implementation of the behavior change program.	1. Psychological and behavioral data are required prior to the formalization of the educational program. Data supporting the need for the behavior change program should be included.
2. Treatment goals should be stated in behavioral terms, short-term objectives should be clearly defined, and a time table for their attainment should be provided.	2. The goal of the behavior change procedure, short-term objectives, and expected date of completion should be included in the IEP.
3. The intervention plan should be described in detail to the client along with the relationship between the program objectives and procedures delineated.	3. The parents and adolescent should be involved in the IEP process to the extent that they are aware of the goals of the educational program as well as the procedures adopted to meet the goals. A more detailed discussion of this process is provided through the consultative model in Chapters 4 and 6.
4. The behavior change plan should describe how people from the adolescent's natural environment are included in the program.	4. The vocational supervisor, teachers, parents, ancillary personnel, and the student, when appropriate, are required to participate in the development and implementation of the IEP.
5. The individuals responsible for conducting the intervention procedure should be identified.	5. The IEP process requires the identification of individual implementors for each goal statement.
6. The intervention program should be renewed and revised monthly.	6. Multidisciplinary staffings for the purpose of development in the full-service program are required yearly. Beyond that, periodic review is necessary whenever a major program change is anticipated.

SOCIAL REINFORCEMENT

Definition

Reinforcers are events that follow a behavior and increase the likelihood that the same behavior will occur in the future. As discussed in the preceding chapter, reinforcers can be positive in that they strengthen behavior through the presentation of satisfying consequences, or they can be negative as they strengthen behavior that produces the removal or avoidance of unpleasant consequences. Social reinforcement involves the use of interpersonal interactions to increase the likelihood that a behavior will occur. Social reinforcement can be positive or negative. A smile that follows a desirable behavior and results in the behavior occurring more frequently would be identified as a social reinforcer. A behavior that occurs more frequently because it is associated with the avoidance of verbal criticism is also considered to be under the control of social reinforcement.

An event cannot be labeled as a social reinforcer until the relationship between the event and the frequency with which the behavior occurs is demonstrated. Praise, in and of itself, cannot be said to be a reinforcing event for adolescents. Only after it has been demonstrated that praise is effective in strengthening a behavior can praise be labeled a reinforcer. Even then praise can only be said to be a social reinforcer for the specific behavior that was shown to be influenced.

Illustration

Stan, a 20-year-old man, considered to exhibit depressive-like characteristics, was employed in a sheltered workshop. Because of long periods of time in which he exhibited extreme negative affect and would bury his head on the worktable, his production rate was very low. Through a five-day baseline period, Stan averaged fewer than one unit per hour on a task that the average worker could complete in several minutes. The workshop staff tested the effectiveness of a number of potential reinforcers in increasing Stan's work output. Contingency arrangements ranging from "sleep time" to records for a minimum rate of performance were evaluated. In each case, the tangible items failed to reinforce Stan's work performance.

Continuous observations revealed that Stan would frequently look up from his worktable when the work supervisor assigned to the neighboring unit walked by. It was hypothesized that interactions with the supervisor might be effective in reinforcing work performance. A program was developed whereby the completion of two units in a one-hour period would result in five minutes alone with the work supervisor. This objective was met in five consecutive days of the following week.

At that time, the criterion was elevated to four units per hour. By the end of several months, Stan was producing in excess of 30 units per hour and interactions with the supervisor (social reinforcers) were faded to five minutes at the end of the day.

Considerations in Using Social Reinforcement

It has been emphasized that social reinforcement is defined by the influence that the interaction has on the specific behavior. If saying "good work" results in no change in performance, then the interaction was not socially reinforcing. Social reinforcement, however, may be an efficient and effective procedure for motivating a range of behaviors with handicapped youths. It is particularly useful in that (1) no special apparatus or commodities are required; (2) it can be administered with very little time and effort; (3) social reinforcement is natural to most all vocational and educational settings; (4) the effects are likely to generalize to other students through vicarious reinforcement; and (5) social reinforcement can easily be combined with other educational procedures.

The following guidelines should be followed when using social reinforcement:

1. Label both process (e.g., "working fast") and product (e.g., "completed a bunch of units") behaviors.
2. Use the individual's name frequently (e.g., "I really like it when you work that fast, John. You sure have completed a lot of assemblies").
3. Tell the individual the behaviors that are likely to result in social reinforcement (e.g., "I like to talk to you when you work fast").
4. Demonstrate that social reinforcement is effective in motivating the desired behavior.
5. Use a more intrusive procedure if social reinforcement is ineffective. Then, always pair the more intrusive procedure with social reinforcement (e.g., "John, you finished all of your work so you can go to the break room. It really makes me happy when you work fast and complete all of your items").
6. Encourage a number of people including parents, peers, other teachers, etc., to reinforce socially the target behaviors. This will increase the likelihood that the behavior change will generalize to other settings.
7. When working with severely handicapped youths, restrict the range of socially reinforcing statements to one or two. More adaptive and verbal adolescents may benefit from a range of statements.
8. Once the target behaviors reach an acceptable level, gradually reduce the number of socially reinforcing interactions. This will increase the likelihood that the behavior change will maintain in the absence of high rates of social reinforcement.

SHAPING

Definition

Shaping is used to develop new behaviors that are not in the adolescent's repertoire. Reinforcement, punishment, and stimulus control procedures cannot develop new skills when used in isolation. These procedures are designed to strengthen behaviors already existing in the adolescent's repertoire. If an individual does not engage in polite greetings because he or she does not have the skill, appropriate behavior will not be emitted and these greetings may not be reinforced. Similarly, punishment for failing to emit polite greetings will only frustrate the adolescent. When the program analysis reveals that the appropriate behavior is not in the adolescent's repertoire, a shaping procedure may be appropriate to teach the behavior.

Shaping involves the reinforcement of a behavior that approximates the desired response. As this approximation occurs at an acceptable rate, reinforcement is withdrawn and redirected to a closer approximation. Through the course of the program, successive approximations are reinforced as the preceding approximations are extinguished. The shaping program is successfully terminated when the desirable behavior is occurring at an acceptable rate under natural reinforcement conditions. Figure 8-1 illustrates the shaping of smiling behavior through the reinforcement of successive approximations.

Illustration

Bob was a moderately mentally retarded adolescent, 18 years of age, employed in a drapery fixture warehouse. His major job responsibility involved operating a pneumatic stapler to seal plastic envelopes containing drapery hooks. Bob's production rate was well within the norms and he seemed to enjoy the packaging task. Unfortunately, the quality of Bob's work was substantially below industry standards. Invariably, the staples on Bob's assembly were from one-fourth to one-half inch away from the required location, which necessitated destroying the envelopes and recycling the production units.

Following a program analysis, as described in Chapter 7, it was reported that Bob did not have the skill to drive the staples in the proper location. Evidence indicating that Bob's performance problem resulted primarily from a skill deficit included the following:

(1) Bob was seldom if ever observed to drive the staples in the correct location.
(2) Attempts to correct the problem through the contingent use of praise (a highly motivated event for Bob) were unsuccessful.

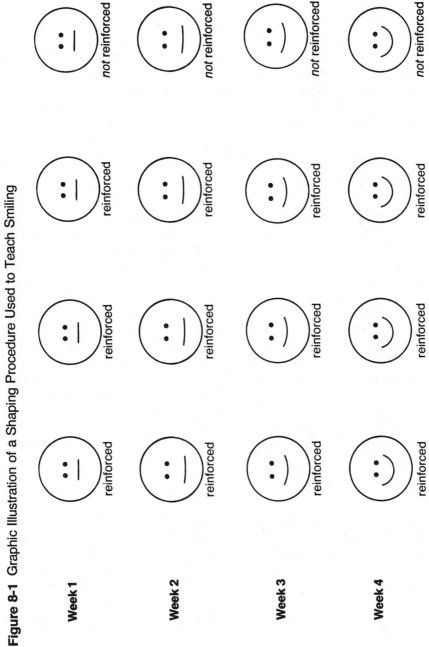

Figure 8-1 Graphic Illustration of a Shaping Procedure Used to Teach Smiling

(3) Bob expressed the desire to do a better job but indicated that it was too difficult.

A program was established whereby Bob was socially reinforced by his supervisor only when the staples were within three-eighths of an inch of the desired location. After approximately two weeks, virtually all of his staples were within this limit, though still not meeting industry standards. The next step was to reinforce Bob socially only for staples within one-fourth of an inch of the desired location. Staples placed outside of this limit would not produce praise as before. Again, Bob's performance met this criterion within a couple of weeks. The next approximation that Bob met was set at one-eighth of an inch, and, finally, Bob was reinforced only for staples driven within the industry standards.

Considerations in Using Shaping

Although the preceding example is intended to illustrate the use of a shaping procedure, it is clear that other behavioral tactics were employed. Social reinforcement played a major role in motivating performance within the established criterion. Also, special cues were arranged to facilitate success. Shaping procedures are highly compatible with other behavioral intervention techniques.

The major value of shaping procedures lies in their utility in ensuring success for the learner. This is particularly critical since a substantial body of literature highlights the impact of failure and punishment on the achievement motivation of handicapped youth (Sabatino & Schloss, 1981). Disinterest in academic pursuits is often the result of educators establishing performance expectations that are beyond the reach of the student. As the student continually strives to meet the teacher's expectations and fails, his or her interest in similar activities diminishes. The shaping process requires the educator to set performance expectations at a level that will maximize success for the learner. Subtle changes in expectations, commensurate with the student's ability to adapt, ensure continued success and reinforcement for the student.

Shaping, with other behavioral tactics, can be done on a formal or informal basis. The following guidelines will increase the effectiveness of the procedure:

1. Define the terminal objective in clear and complete terms.
2. Establish a sequential set of approximations beginning with the student's current behavior and ending with the terminal objective. The "distance" between each approximation should reflect the learning characteristics of the adolescent. The severely handicapped youth generally requires very subtle criterion changes. These steps represent an initial plan. They may be altered to reflect the adolescent's success (or lack of success) in the initial program phases.

3. Identify a positive consequence for successfully meeting each criterion. The consequence should be as natural to the activity and environment as possible and still be likely to motivate performance.
4. Discuss the program with the adolescent. Describe the target objectives, the terminal objective, and the motivational conditions.
5. Initiate the program.

   Reinforce the initial behavior each time it occurs.

   Move to the next approximation only after the first is mastered.

   Do not remain at one level too long or move to another level too quickly.
6. Once the terminal objective is achieved gradually, withdraw unusual reinforcement conditions. This will increase the likelihood that the behavior will maintain over time.
7. Encourage the individual to practice the new behavior in a number of other settings.
8. If the program is not effective:

   Test the strength of the reinforcer.

   Evaluate the size of the criterion changes. Excessively large or small changes in the approximations may result in disinterest.

MODELING

Definition

The effectiveness of modeling in developing positive social behavior and diminishing disruptive behavior has been repeatedly demonstrated in the behavioral literature.

Targets of modeling programs have included pacifier dependence (Schloss & Johann, in press), fear of dogs (Bandura, 1967), aggression (Bandura, 1965), drug use (Warner & Swisher, 1976), and reading-related responses (Haskett & Lenfestey, 1974). Modeling, as described in these investigations, involves the arrangement of instructional conditions so that an individual acquires new response patterns through the observation of another person.

Modeling procedures may be used for three distinct purposes. First, modeling can be effective in teaching new responses not present in the individual's repertoire. For example, an adolescent may learn to change the tires on a car by observing a mechanic at a gas station. Second, modeling may increase the strength or frequency of a previously learned skill. This is exemplified by an individual who begins jogging after observing a friend lose weight through an exercise regimen. Finally, modeling may be used to inhibit a response pattern. An adolescent may discontinue the use of profane language after observing his employer fire a coworker for swearing.

Illustration

Cindy worked at a dry cleaning establishment performing a range of jobs from hanging up clothes to sweeping the floor. Although she was generally able to complete most of her responsibilities, she had a difficult time getting along with her employer. It was apparent that the major source of conflict resulted from her inability to accept criticism. Upon being corrected by the employer she would become agitated and argumentative. Her reactions to criticism became so unpleasant to the employer that he began to avoid her. This led to a reduced amount of guidance that she needed to acquire and maintain acceptable work skills.

The intervention program involved a teacher meeting with her as well as her friend and coworker for the purpose of practicing appropriate employer-employee social skills. A change in the way Cindy interacted was expected to occur through three related program components. First, it was expected that Cindy would learn appropriate ways to interact with her employer by observing her friend in role-playing situations. Second, her social skills were expected to strengthen through practice in the role-playing situations. Finally, since her friend had an equal opportunity to be criticized by her boss, it was expected that Cindy's aversion for being corrected on the job would decline as she observed her friend react cheerfully to criticism.

While the teacher was supervising Cindy and her friend on the job, she made a point to verbally label and socially reinforce appropriate interactions with the boss. Early in the program, the majority of attention was paid to Cindy's friend since Cindy rarely interacted appropriately with the employer. As Cindy observed her friend gain attention and satisfaction from the targeted interactions, she began to imitate her friend's behavior. This led to an increase in praise from the teacher for desirable interactions. Once a reasonably high rate of appropriate responses was achieved, the special sessions were gradually discontinued and social reinforcement for acceptance of criticism was reduced to normal rates.

Considerations in Using Modeling

Modeling may be a very cost-efficient behavior management strategy. In the normal course of a school day an educator may take advantage of numerous opportunities to facilitate behavior change, formally or informally, through modeling. Intervention strategies may run the gamut from highly structured environments in which the opportunities for observational learning are well controlled to brief, unplanned exposures to positive role models. The structure that an educator imparts in a modeling program may be a function of the cost of the program weighed against the severity of the behavior problem.

As with other learning theory principles, modeling can influence the development and persistence of positive as well as negative behavioral and attitudinal characteristics. A student who frequently observes others gain control of situations through the use of violence or physical threats is likely to engage in similar behavior. Conversely, placed in an environment in which the socially skillful behavior of others produces reward, the same student is likely to develop and display positive social behavior. The limited availability of positive peer models in self-contained special education classrooms and residential facilities has been a major factor promoting mainstream education (Bruininks & Ryders, 1971; Csapo, 1972).

A number of researchers have studied factors that influence the likelihood that behaviors may be learned or strengthened through modeling (Bandura, 1971a, 1971b; Kazdin, 1973; Ross, 1970; Stevenson, 1972; Zinzer, 1966). This literature offers five elements that enhance the effectiveness of observational learning: (1) the extent to which the observer has been reinforced for similar behavior under like stimulus conditions; (2) the extent to which the observer views the modeled behavior as common for the situation; (3) the self-esteem of the observer; (4) the degree to which the observer depends on external cues; and (5) the demonstrated competence of the observer in similar situations.

Goldstein, Heller, and Sechrist (1966) and Bandura (1971a) have highlighted characteristics of the model that facilitate observational learning. Strong models have been characterized as being warm, nutritional, powerful, and competent. Also, models of the same sex are likely to exert stronger control over the behavior of the learner. In general, individuals perceived by the learner as having high status are more likely to promote observational learning than low-status models. This is exemplified by the influence that teen-age celebrities have on the behavior, appearance, and attitudes of youths (e.g., consider how the Beatles influenced hair styles of adolescents in the 1960s).

Bandura (1971a) has enumerated activities in the modeling process that enhance the imitation of the model's behavior. These include: (1) reinforcing the model, (2) enhancing the status of the model through his or her behavior, (3) clearly distinguishing situations in which the modeled behavior is appropriate and likely to be reinforced, and (4) ensuring that modeled activities are not excessively difficult for the observer.

In summary, the following principles should be considered when promoting observational learning:

1. Specify behaviors that are expected to be influenced through the modeling process.
2. Arrange situations in which the learner may observe high-status models engaged in the behaviors.
3. Specify and deliver reinforcers contingent on the behaviors (typically social reinforcement).

4. Verbally label the behaviors as they occur, using the person's name (e.g., "you sure have a nice smile today, John").
5. Reinforce the learner for engaging in approximations of the desired behaviors.
6. Vary the models and settings to enhance the generalization of the behavior change.

STIMULUS CHANGE

Definition

A stimulus is an event or object that signals the occurrence or nonoccurrence of a behavior. Reinforcing stimuli increase the probability a behavior will occur, while aversive stimuli are associated with a reduced rate of response. For example, a green light is a reinforcing stimulus because it cues the driver to depress the accelerator on his or her car. The presence of the principal in a classroom may be an aversive stimulus resulting in the suppression of disruptive behavior. Stimulus control occurs when a particular event (e.g., receiving a failing grade on a test) consistently affects the likelihood that a response will occur (e.g., depressive-like behavior). Stimulus change involves the systematic attempt to influence behavior by changing the controlling stimuli.

Educators frequently use stimulus change to establish positive learning environments. Seating arrangements, instructional materials, verbal prompts for quiet, and distinct gestures are among the cues intended to signal a particular response from the students. The failure of the desired response to occur consistently indicates that the particular stimulus does not exert control over the behavior. When this is the case, the educator seeks to develop the strength of the stimuli in controlling the target behavior. Or, in simple terms, the educator seeks to teach the students that when the particular event occurs (e.g., the teacher says, "quiet") they should behave in a specified manner (e.g., stop talking).

Stimulus control can be used in a planned manner to inhibit maladaptive behaviors as well as to promote desirable responses. This may be accomplished in three ways. First, if a naturally occurring event does not cue a desirable response, the educator may develop the discriminative function of the stimulus. For example, a student may be taught to be at her work station when the 8:00 A.M. whistle sounds, or an appropriate social response to an employer's greeting may be developed. Conversely, if a naturally occurring event cues a maladaptive response, the educator may reduce the discriminative function of the event. If the half-hour period prior to breaks cues a reduction in work rate, the educator may teach the student to work at a consistent rate regardless of the time. Finally, events that cue predictable responses may be manipulated to increase or decrease the frequency of the response. For example, the teacher may separate two students who argue frequently when in one another's presence in order to reduce arguing behavior. Promptness to work may be increased by teaching the student to use an alarm clock to cue the individual to get out of bed.

Illustration

David was a 14-year-old adolescent whose behavior had been characterized as hyperactive by his teachers and the school psychologist. During mathematics class, he would frequently look out the window, around the classroom, or up at the ceiling. This off-task behavior severely limited his ability to perform in class, and subsequently his achievement level in mathematics was substantially below that of his classmates. In addition to other remedial tactics, his teacher decided to employ a stimulus control procedure to increase his on-task rate.

Prior to initiating the program, the teacher observed David periodically for two weeks. Each time David went off-task for an extended period of time, she would record the events that preceded the off-task episode. Similarly, when David remained on-task for an extended period of time, she would record the events that occurred through the on-task time. The teacher discovered that the stimuli that were associated with on-task behavior included mathematics work that had a direct vocational application. Stimuli associated with off-task behavior included the immediate presence of his best friend, window shades being open, repetitious problem sets with no direct application, unstructured time, and no stated deadline for work completion.

To establish stimuli that would maximize David's on-task rate, the teacher made the following changes in the class structure:

1. David was seated away from the windows;
2. The window shades were closed far enough to block David's view of the outside;
3. David's friend was seated in the opposite corner of the room;
4. David's mathematics time was structured so that he knew in advance the work that was expected, the time in which it was to be completed, and the consequences for completion; and
5. The teacher discontinued using repetitious worksheets in lieu of work that had an obvious vocational function. As David's on-task rate improved, the instructional conditions were gradually changed to reflect the preprogram conditions (e.g., the window shades were opened, the seating arrangement made more flexible).

Considerations in Using Stimulus Change

The previous example illustrates the importance of observing learners in relation to the stimuli that control their behavior. Stimulus change procedures are based on the careful assessment of events that may be manipulated to produce desirable behavior. Randomly or haphazardly changing classroom or work conditions in hopes of changing a student's behavior will produce mixed results at best. Continuous recording, as described in the preceding chapter, is a critical tool for maximizing the effect of a stimulus change program.

Although a stimulus change program may be highly effective, removing a provoking stimuli may not be in the best interest of the student. Such is the case when a student is indefinitely removed from large group activities because of disruptive behavior. The approach may reduce the likelihood that the student will act out, but it does very little to teach positive ways of behaving under similar stimulus conditions. Thus, while many behaviors may be influenced through stimulus control programs, the educator must consider the importance of developing positive social behaviors in the face of provoking events. As in the previous illustration, an effective strategy may be to limit the provoking stimuli to the extent that the adolescent succeeds. Once the student develops an achievement orientation through success and praise, the provoking stimuli may be gradually reintroduced.

Conversely, a stimulus change procedure may be more pragmatic and less intrusive than teaching a student to conform to stimuli that are idiosyncratic to the school environment. The author was recently asked to design a program to reduce the screaming behavior of an autistic-like adolescent. Continuous recording revealed that the screaming episodes were cued by taunts from other behaviorally disordered youths in the program. Since it is not likely that the student will face similar stimuli in the natural environment, separating the student from the taunting peers was the intervention of choice.

A final consideration in designing and implementing a stimulus change program relates to the presentation of stimuli to cue desirable responses. Stimulus change programs, which involve establishing artificial events to promote adaptive behavior, should utilize cues that are as natural as possible to the setting in which the behavior is to occur. For example, establishing a watch as a cue for following the work schedule is superior to verbal prompts from the teacher. As with other behavior change procedures, unnatural program components may need to be used to establish initial control over the behavior. However, as soon as control is observed under intrusive program conditions, unnatural stimuli should be faded and natural cues established. This procedure will increase the likelihood that the behavior change will maintain once the intervention program is withdrawn. Similarly, fading unnatural stimulus conditions will enhance the generalization of the behavior to other settings.

Procedures to be followed when designing and implementing a stimulus change program include the following:

1. Conduct continuous recording as described in the preceding chapter.
2. Identify stimuli that are associated with the occurrence of adaptive responses.
3. Arrange the environment so that stimuli that support adaptive behavior are increased, and stimuli associated with maladaptive behavior are reduced.
4. Once an acceptable rate of the target behaviors is established, fade unnatural stimuli supporting adaptive behavior and reintroduce stimuli previously associated with maladaptive responses.

BEHAVIOR REHEARSAL

Definition

Behavior rehearsal procedures involve the practicing of low-frequency behaviors under conditions that are naturally associated with the desired behaviors. As such, behavior rehearsal is a teaching strategy that goes beyond simply role-playing or play-acting adaptive responses. The behavior rehearsal strategy assists the adolescent in identifying environmental conditions in which the behavior is expected to occur as well as the natural consequences of the behavior. In general, behavior rehearsal strategies serve three purposes: (1) teaching adaptive responses, (2) identifying or developing natural cues that are expected to prompt the adaptive response, and (3) assisting the adolescent to identify the natural consequences of the adaptive response.

Behavior rehearsal strategies for the handicapped have been used primarily to develop social skills. The major advantage of the tactic is that it minimizes the dependence on abstract thinking required of other social development approaches. Rehearsing positive social behavior in the natural environment or closely simulated environments provides a direct link between the desired behavior and the setting in which it is expected to occur. This may not be the case with social skill training approaches that are removed from the natural setting.

A final factor that recommends the use of behavior rehearsal strategies is that they prompt desirable behaviors that previously occurred so seldom that reinforcement could not occur. The behavior rehearsal strategy provides a structure in which positive social behaviors occur more frequently than are expected under natural conditions. Since the adaptive behavior is prompted to occur at a higher rate, it can be reinforced more often. This process supports the development of social behavior through the use of positive reinforcement while minimizing the use of punishment for maladaptive behavior.

Behavior rehearsal procedures may involve the use of several behavior management strategies at one time. Social reinforcement may be used to consequate the rehearsal behavior. A shaping procedure may be employed to develop approximations of the expected response. Stimulus change may be involved in ensuring the individual's success under less demanding environmental conditions. Finally, modeling may be used to develop and prompt the rehearsed behavior.

Illustration

Judy, an 18-year-old moderately retarded student, frequently coaxed a friend to obtain her lunch from the cafeteria line. It was agreed at her multidisciplinary staff conference that independence in obtaining food from a cafeteria line would be critical to her adjustment to a vocational placement. Thus, it was agreed that this skill should be developed. In studying the problem, Judy's teacher determined that Judy was afraid to go through the line independently because of a previous experience when others laughed at her for dropping her tray. She coaxed a friend to get her lunch served to avoid any future occurrence of the problem.

Judy's teacher designed a behavior rehearsal strategy to teach and reinforce independence in the lunch line. The program involved conducting practice sessions prior to lunch in the cafeteria setting.

Approximately 15 minutes prior to the other students' arriving for lunch, the cafeteria line was set up, tables in place, and the cashier in position. At that time, Judy and her instructor went to the lunchroom so that she could rehearse obtaining lunch independently.

Judy was able to practice going through the lunch line approximately three times in the prelunch period. During these trials, every attempt was made to make the practice session as close to the real event as possible. Upon completion of each trial, her instructor would label the specific behaviors she performed (e.g., "Judy, you did a fine job of picking up your sandwich, drink, and salad. You also paid for the food. You didn't even drop anything"). Also, the instructor helped Judy to identify the consequences of her behavior (e.g., "You went through the line and obtained your food like everyone else. You are acting as an independent student when you do that"). Following three consecutive days with no mishaps, Judy was encouraged to obtain lunch on her own during the regular cafeteria time. Once this was accomplished successfully, the structured rehearsal sequences were discontinued and the instructor simply socially reinforced Judy for being an independent student.

Considerations in Using Behavior Rehearsal

The major consideration in using behavior rehearsal strategies involves structuring a situation as close as possible to the natural events expected to cue and reinforce the rehearsed behavior. In some instances, the actual events can be used. For example, if an individual frequently runs down the hall, structured practice may occur each time the student is to go to another classroom. Exhibit 8-2, for example, describes a format that educators may follow using behavior rehearsals in the natural environment. Sometimes, however, it is preferable to practice the behavior without others present, as was the case in the preceding illustration. In this event, every effort should be made to simulate the actual environmental conditions associated with the behavior.

In designing a simulated environment for behavior rehearsals, special attention should be given to establishing comparable antecedents and consequents of the rehearsed behavior. If behavior rehearsals are to focus on a student's social greetings toward coworkers, then, if possible, coworkers should be involved in the behavior rehearsals. Similarly, if social praise is the natural consequent of a polite greeting, then social praise should occur following the rehearsed greeting.

Exhibit 8-2 Behavior Rehearsal Sequence

1. State the purpose of the behavior rehearsal.
2. Elicit a statement from the adolescent identifying events that may provoke an inappropriate response.
3. Assist the student in evaluating his or her response in reference to the following outcomes: its effectiveness in reducing agitating behavior of others; its influence on personal goals; its influence on the work behavior of others.
4. Assist the student in identifying alternate behaviors that are socially skillful (i.e., facilitate the acquisition of rewards from the environment).
5. Role-play a potentially provoking situation with the student exhibiting socially skillful behavior.
6. Assist the adolescent in evaluating the appropriate response in reference to the following outcomes: its effectiveness in reducing agitating behavior of others; its influence on personal goals; its influence on the work behavior of others.
7. Guide the student in rehearsing the socially skillful behavior under varying conditions. Encourage the individual to verbally label the positive features of the newly acquired behavior. Socially reinforce the student for demonstrating adaptive responses.
8. Elicit a statement from the adolescent that indicates his or her intent to utilize socially skillful behaviors in response to provocations in the school setting.

Finally, the instructor should label the rehearsed behavior, the antecedents to the behavior, and the consequents of the behavior frequently. For example, the instructor may say, "Bob, when the bell went off (antecedent) you got up from your desk quietly (rehearsed behavior), so you can now go to your locker (consequent)." When behaviors are rehearsed in structured situations outside of the natural setting, these verbal labels may provide a channel that increases the likelihood that the behavior will generalize back into the natural setting.

In summary, the following procedures should be used in conducting behavior rehearsals:

1. Specify the behavior that is to be developed.
2. Identify the natural antecedents to the behavior.
3. Identify the natural consequents of the behavior.
4. Determine times in which the desired behavior is to be practiced around the natural antecedents and consequents.
5. Develop and initiate a plan for rehearsing the desired behavior.
6. Frequently label the desired response in relation to the antecedents and consequents of the response.
7. When necessary, combine behavior rehearsal procedures with other behavior management strategies.

CONTINGENCY CONTRACTING

Definition

A contingency contract is a formal agreement between the student and educator that specifies the relationship between specific behavior and consequents. Contingency contracts include concise descriptions of behaviors expected to be performed by the adolescent to gain the designated consequents; a clear statement regarding the positive consequents that will result from performing the behavior to the specified criterion; a clear statement regarding aversive consequents, if any, that will result from failing to perform the behavior to criterion; a delineation of the teacher's responsibilities in facilitating success for the adolescent; and a statement indicating how maintenance of the desired behavior will be consequated.

Contingency contracting is a particularly useful strategy for secondary-level youths. Contingency contracts result from mutual negotiation between the educator and the adolescent. This feature ensures the individual's involvement in the planning, implementation, and evaluation of the behavior change strategy. As such, the adolescent involved in developing the contingency contract becomes a coengineer of his or her educational program.

The contingency contract has many parallels in unsheltered vocational environments. For example, the contract a young adult enters into on employment stipulates the relationship between his or her performance on the job and the consequent of that performance (e.g., a stipulated salary, periodic salary increases, special privileges, a health plan, and retirement benefits). Also, a worker whose performance is not satisfactory will often be presented with an evaluation statement identifying his or her performance deficiencies. The statement may also include the consequents of improving or failing to improve within the deficiency areas.

Illustration

Clifford, a 15-year-old adolescent, was a highly motivated student. Despite a second grade reading and mathematics level, additional effort that Cliff put into his academic course work generally resulted in passing grades. Clifford's major deficiency resulted from his physical size. He was approximately five feet, two inches tall and weighed over 200 pounds. His size severely limited mobility in the school as well as in some vocational settings. Clifford recognized and was concerned with his weight. Early in the semester Cliff approached his resource teacher and asked for assistance in preparing and implementing a weight reduction program. The teacher readily agreed and worked with Clifford, the school dietitian, and Clifford's parents in arranging a diet program. In addition to the diet, it was agreed that positive consequents for maintaining a weight reduction goal would assist in meeting the program objectives. In view of these concerns, a contingency contract was developed as illustrated in Exhibit 8-3.

Considerations in Using Contingency Contracting

Contingency contracts should be stated in terms that are clear and complete to all participants. Behaviors, responsibilities, and consequences addressed by the contract should be clearly delineated so that all individuals involved in the program are aware of the scope and plan of the contract. Attention given to the details of the contract in the planning stage will avoid possible controversies that result from poorly worded or vague agreements.

Equally important to the actual written contract is the process by which the contract is developed. As with most traditional contracts, a contingency contract results from mutual negotiation between two or more parties. This process is critical to maintaining the adolescent's interest in a commitment to the behavior change program. Negotiation sessions are excellent opportunities for verbal interactions between the teacher and student in which: (1) the student's personal goals are clarified, (2) the teacher's expectations of the student are delineated, (3) potential behavior change strategies are explored, and (4) the consequents of

Exhibit 8-3 Contract between Clifford V. and Mrs. W.

I, Clifford V., agree to comply with the following recommendations as of January 2, 1981:

1. negotiate a weekly meal plan with the school dietitian and my parents
2. adhere strictly to the meal plan
3. limit between-meal snacks to fruits, low calorie beverages, or other food items only as approved by the school dietitian
4. report all food consumed to the school dietitian, my parents, and Mrs. W. each week
5. weigh myself weekly in the presence of Mrs. W.

The school dietitian agrees to:

1. spend one hour each Thursday after school with Clifford and his parents preparing a meal plan to be implemented the following week
2. identify snack items that may be eaten by Clifford between meals
3. evaluate and discuss with Clifford food reported to be consumed in the previous week

Clifford's parents agree to:

1. spend one hour each Thursday after school with Clifford and the school dietitian preparing a meal plan to be implemented the following week
2. assist Clifford in preparing the designated meals
3. assist Clifford in accurately reporting food consumption each day
4. provide Clifford with a ticket to a sports event, a movie theatre, or any other recreational activity each week that his weight decreases by one pound.

Mrs. W. agrees to:

1. meet each week with the school's dietitian, Clifford, and his parents for the purpose of preparing a meal plan for the week
2. record Clifford's weight each week and send a copy to each of the program participants
3. provide two hours of free time in the gym each week that Clifford loses a pound
4. provide continual corrective or supportive feedback regarding Clifford's record of food consumption

Exhibit 8-3 continued

Maintenance Bonus: Clifford's parents will provide $5.00 toward the purchase of a ten-speed bicycle for each month his weight remains below 180 pounds.

Date _____   _____
                                  Clifford V.

_____   _____
Rosey V.   Resource Teacher

_____   _____
Robert V.   School Director

current and future behavior patterns are examined. Once the contract is formalized and initiated, every individual involved should make every effort to comply with the stipulated responsibilities.

The final consideration in designing and implementing a contingency contract involves the use of an objective observational and recording system. This system is essential to evaluating the effectiveness of the program. Additionally, the system is useful in providing feedback to individuals involved in the contingency contract. The student may be responsible for recording progress toward the goal, and the teacher or another individual may conduct reliability checks. This is consistent with the underlying theme of putting as much control over the behavior change process in the hands of the student as possible.

The following procedures should be considered in developing and implementing a contingency contract:

1. Specify in clear and complete terms the expectations of the student.
2. Specify in clear and complete terms the responsibilities of others involved in the contract.
3. Identify the positive consequences available to the student through compliance with stipulations of the contract.
4. Specify aversive consequents, if any, that may result from failure to comply with the requirements of the contract.
5. Develop and implement an objective observational and recording system to monitor progress under the contingency contract.
6. Include a maintenance goal in the contingency contract.

Remember:

1. The contract should be developed through mutual negotiation.
2. Behavioral expectations and consequences should be equitable.
3. The contract should be stated in positive terms emphasizing what the students may gain through compliance.
4. The educator, parents, or others should fulfill their responsibilities under the contract.

REDUCTIVE PROCEDURES

Definition

Reductive procedures are behavior management tactics designed to diminish the frequency, duration, or intensity of a behavior or behaviors. Subsumed under the general heading "Reductive Procedures" are a number of more specific intervention approaches. While consequating an undesirable behavior with an unpleasant event is probably the procedure most familiar to the educator, a variety of other approaches has been adopted in educational settings. Alternative reductive strategies include differential reinforcement of progressively lower rates of inappropriate behavior (DRL), differential reinforcement of other behaviors (DRO) expected to replace the disruptive behavior, extinction, response cost, and overcorrection.

As was discussed earlier in this chapter, these and other behavior management tactics range on a continuum from least to most intrusive to the adolescent. The careful analysis and selection of reductive procedures are particularly important because of the potential negative side effects associated with behavior management strategies that are unpleasant to the adolescent. To highlight this concern, each of the preceding strategies is defined and illustrated separately. Special attention is given to the advantages and disadvantages of each procedure.

Differential Reinforcement of Low Rates of Behavior (DRL)

DRL is defined as the reinforcement of responses emitted at successively lower rates. Self-administered reinforcement for eating 2,200 calories a day as opposed to 5,000 a day would exemplify a DRL procedure. The educator who reinforces an adolescent for working at a slower rate on a shop project to increase the quality of the project is using a DRL procedure. This may be contrasted with the aversive approach of criticizing the youth for his or her sloppy work habits. The DRL procedure reinforces slower rates of performance while the aversive approach punishes excessively fast performance.

The DRL procedure has several advantages over aversive strategies that may be equally effective. Foremost, DRL is a positive approach. It promotes behavior change through the adolescent's seeking to acquire positive consequents. This may be contrasted with aversive procedures that promote behavior change through the adolescent's avoidance of unpleasant consequents. The development of a success and reward striving orientation is consistent with the philosophy of secondary career-vocational education espoused by this book. A related advantage of the DRL approach is that it promotes adaptation at a level that is easily attainable by the adolescent. DRL does not require an abolition of the target behavior. Rather, the goal of the procedure is to promote the performance of the target behavior in moderation.

A final advantage of the DRL procedure is that it can easily be applied as a shaping procedure. In doing so, successively lower rates of the excessive behavior are reinforced until the terminal target rate of the behavior is achieved. For example, Dietz and Repp (1973) have demonstrated the effective reduction of misbehavior in a secondary classroom by reinforcing progressively lower rates of disruptive behavior.

There are three major disadvantages of the DRL procedure. First, it requires more time to achieve control over the maladaptive behavior than aversive procedures. The selection of a DRL procedure for reducing aggressive behavior, for example, may be inappropriate as the procedure would reinforce aggressive outbursts that may be detrimental to others in the classroom setting. Second, there are instances when engaging in the disruptive behavior is more rewarding than the positive consequents available. This is especially the case for some handicapped youths who find few events in the school setting reinforcing. Finally, the DRL procedure focuses the educators' attention on undesirable behavior. This may have an undesirable influence on adolescents who observe the educators deliver reinforcement for the inappropriate behavior.

Differential Reinforcement of Other Behaviors (DRO)

As with the DRL procedure, DRO seeks to reduce the strength of excessive behaviors through positive means. DRO is defined as the reinforcement of any behavior other than the maladaptive behavior. The intent of the DRO procedure is to increase the strength of behaviors that will replace the maladaptive behavior. For example, an educator may wish to reduce the frequency with which an adolescent leaves his or her desk. Rather than (or in addition to) punishing the student, the educator may frequently reinforce the youth for any behavior emitted while in the seat.

Aside from being a positive approach, the DRO procedure produces more immediate results than extinction or noncontingent reinforcement approaches (Goetz, Holmberg, & LeBlanc, 1975). Additionally, the DRO procedure increases the strength of behaviors that may replace the maladaptive response. Given that these behaviors are functional, one would expect that once the DRO procedure is withdrawn, the alternate behaviors would be practiced in the place of the deviant behavior. The likelihood of this happening may be increased by specifying the behavior or behaviors to be differentially reinforced. For example, a vocational educator may differentially reinforce positive social interactions between an adolescent and her employer. This may increase the probability that she will engage in positive verbal interactions with her employer and decrease the probability that she will engage in inappropriate conversations. As the adolescent's social skills improve, it may become apparent that prosocial behavior produces more favorable consequents than descriptive verbal behaviors. Thus, the prosocial behavior will be practiced consistently even after the intervention is withdrawn.

The major disadvantage of the DRO procedure is that the alternate behavior may not be as rewarding as the disruptive behavior. This may result from others in the environment reinforcing the disruptive behavior in competition with the DRO procedure. Two obvious solutions to this problem include: (1) identifying competing reinforcing events and removing them (e.g., if a student leaves his or her seat to talk to a friend in the hall, reduce occasions in which the friend is in the hall), and (2) use the DRO procedure in combination with other reductive procedures (e.g., reinforce the student for work done while seated as well as providing a response cost for getting out of the seat).

Extinction

Extinction involves the removal of positive consequents identified as maintaining a behavior. It is expected that if the behavior is no longer functional in producing satisfying consequences, it will reduce in strength. A teacher who ignores a student's complaints about a test is attempting to use an extinction procedure. The complaining behavior is considered to be extinguished if the removal of attention to the student's complaints (nonreinforcement of complaints) results in a reduction of complaining behavior.

Another example of an extinction frequently used in career-vocational settings involves not including products that are below quality control standards on the worker's piece-work rate. In this example, reinforcement in the form of pay, promotion, etc., is withdrawn from poorly completed products. The employer's expectation is that the frequency of substandard units will decrease if the worker's poor performance is not reinforced.

Extinction procedures have been demonstrated to be effective in reducing a wide range of classroom behaviors (Hall, Lund, & Jackson, 1968; Solomon & Wahler, 1973; Wilson & Hopkins, 1973; Zimmerman & Zimmerman, 1962). Several factors have been identified that increase the effectiveness of extinction procedures. First, all sources of reinforcement for the target behaviors must be eliminated (e.g., parents, peers, educators). Simply removing a portion of the reinforcement may have the detrimental effect of developing a more persistent response pattern in the face of a thinner schedule of reinforcement. Second, the exact setting in which the extinction procedure occurs should be continued for a sufficient amount of time to avoid the reinforcement of a higher rate of response that typically occurs in the initial stages of an extinction program. Finally, extinction procedures are recommended to be used in combination with DRO or DRL procedures.

Several disadvantages are associated with extinction procedures. As was discussed previously, there is often an increase in the strength of the target behavior immediately following the removal of reinforcement. If reinforcement inadvertently occurs at a higher rate, a stronger maladaptive response may be developed. For example, a teacher may choose to ignore a student who seeks her attention by waving a hand back and forth. Since this is not reinforced, the student may begin hopping up and down and calling the teacher's name. At some point, if the teacher does not call on the student, the disruptive handwaving will cease. However, if the teacher "gives in" and calls on the student after the behavior has accelerated, she may inadvertently increase the likelihood that the higher rate of the behavior will occur.

An additional disadvantage of the use of extinction involves the inability of the teacher to control events that reinforce the response. It is often difficult to identify all consequences of disruptive behavior, especially if the behavior is maintained by infrequent positive consequences. Even when the consequences are identified, it is often difficult to control them all. As was previously discussed, the failure to remove all of the positive consequences may have the deleterious effect of increasing the persistence of the disruptive behavior. For example, a student's disruptive behavior in class may be motivated by the attention received from others. The teacher may ask the other students to stop attending to this student. If all of the students do not comply all of the time, the continuous schedule of reinforcement that developed the behavior may diminish to a variable schedule of reinforcement. Over time, the behavior may maintain under successively less reinforcement from peers. This is the same process used by the educator in well-planned fashion to develop the persistence of positive behavior.

Because of these limitations, extinction procedures should be used with great caution. Planning that precedes the implementation of the behavior change strategy should consider:

1. Can all the reinforcers that support the behavior be identified?
2. Can they be removed?
3. Is it possible to ignore the behavior for a sufficiently long period of time to produce the desired effect?

If these questions cannot be answered in the affirmative, then an alternate reductive strategy should be considered.

Response Cost

Response cost is defined as the removal of a specified amount of a reinforcer following the occurrence of a behavior. A library fine for failing to return a book is an example of a response cost familiar to most college students (and instructors). The failure to return the book is consequated by removing a specific amount of money. This procedure is intended to reduce the likelihood that books will be returned late. Another familiar example of a response cost procedure is a parking ticket (the withdrawal of money) delivered after one parks in a loading zone.

Response cost procedures are fairly easy to administer in classroom and vocational settings. The suspension of free time, the dockage of pay, and the removal of special privileges are often natural consequents in educational and vocational settings. These procedures have the advantage of being highly effective in reducing inappropriate behavior over a relatively short period of time. Because response cost programs can be designed in career-vocational education settings analogous to response cost procedures in industry, one would expect them to have a lasting effect on vocational performance. For example, if a student learns that tardiness to a supervised work activity results in a dockage of pay, it is likely that punctuality developed through the response cost procedure would transfer to an unsheltered work situation in which a similar contingency relationship existed.

One major disadvantage of the response cost procedure is that it has been demonstrated to result in negative emotional reactions and aggressive behavior (Boren & Colman, 1970; Bucher & Hawkins, 1971; Doty, McInnis, & Paul, 1974). Anyone receiving a parking ticket, library fine, speeding citation, dockage of pay, etc., can attest to these findings. This, in and of itself, may not be bad, as the negative emotionality may do as much to deter future occurrences as the actual loss of reinforcement. However, the educator must be careful not to reinstate the reinforcer as a result of the emotional outburst. Doing so may have the undesirable effect of strengthening maladaptive emotional behaviors (e.g., threats of aggression, somatic complaints, excessive crying, swearing).

Another concern in using a response cost procedure involves balancing the response cost ratio, that is, the amount of the reinforcement to be withdrawn for a given response. Withdrawing too much of the reinforcer may deplete the supply to the point that the reinforcers are no longer available. This is exemplified by the merchant who attempted to sue a destitute vagrant for loitering in his store. Withdrawing too little reinforcement may not be effective in suppressing the excessive behavior. Such is the case when the Internal Revenue Service fines a multimillionaire industrialist several hundred thousand dollars for tax evasion.

One would expect the response cost to have little effect on future tax evasion behavior.

Overcorrection

Overcorrection was originally described and studied by Foxx and Azrin (1972). The overcorrection procedure has two major components. The first involves *restitution,* in which environmental damage resulting from disruptive behavior is corrected. The second is the repeated *positive practice* of a behavior that is more acceptable than the disruptive behavior. An overcorrection procedure applied to a student yelling at another student may involve an apology (restitution) and the repetitious practice of a polite statement that serves the same function as yelling (positive practice). The overcorrection of throwing food in the lunchroom may include a thorough cleaning of the lunchroom (restitution) and the repeated practice of holding and using eating utensils in an appropriate manner (positive practice).

The educative properties of overcorrection make it ideally suited to career-vocational settings. Simply using a response cost or extinction procedure does little to teach alternative prosocial behaviors. The overcorrection procedures, on the other hand, engage the adolescent in a learning experience centered around the events that provoke inappropriate behavior. Because the adolescent is forced to practice prosocial behaviors that may replace the inappropriate behavior, a more rapid and durable behavior change can be expected (Foxx & Azrin, 1973). A related issue is that since the adolescent is practicing appropriate behavior the likelihood of another maladaptive behavior replacing the reduced behavior is diminished.

As with other behavior management strategies, overcorrection should be applied consistently and immediately following the target behavior. Overcorrection applied immediately following the target behavior has the benefit of removing the function of the disruptive behavior. For example, John may shred his worksheet to avoid completing it. The overcorrection procedure effectively replaces the worksheet. Future occurrences of this behavior are diminished as John learns that tearing up a worksheet does not result in its removal. If, however, this is not enforced consistently, the procedure may simply reduce the likelihood that the behavior will be reinforced. Inadvertently thinning the schedule of reinforcement may have the effect of producing a more durable and persistent disruptive behavior.

A final consideration in using overcorrection involves the selection of restitution and positive practice activities. In both cases the activity used should be relevant to the maladaptive behavior. An activity relevant to destructive behavior, for example, is the repair of damage to the environment. Apologies in written or verbal form may be relevant restitution approaches for disruptive verbal interactions. The positive practice procedure should develop a behavior that may function in place of the disruptive or maladaptive behavior. For example, assertiveness skills may be practiced following verbal aggression, and walking in the halls may be practiced following a running incident.

Considerations in Selecting and Applying Reductive Procedures

The advantages and disadvantages of the specific reductive procedures have been discussed throughout this section. Although the use of reductive procedures is often indicated in developing social-personal skills with adolescents, no other set of behavior management strategies has as strong a potential for misuse and subsequent negative side effects. Gardner (1977), in a comprehensive review of the punishment literature, has developed a series of guidelines for the use of reduction procedures. Adherence to these considerations is critical to ensuring the success of reductive programs while minimizing the influence of negative side effects.

Gardner's guidelines include:

1. Use punishment infrequently and only in combination with positive procedures.
2. Prior to punishment, define precisely the inappropriate behavior, the conditions under which it occurs, and its strength.
3. Define precisely the punishment procedure to be used before initiating it.
4. Define explicitly the circumstances in which punishment will be used.
5. Specify alternative behavior which will replace the punished ones along with the reinforcement procedure for strengthening these.
6. Time out or response cost are favored over procedures involving the presentation of aversive events.
7. Inform the child in a clear and precise manner about those behaviors resulting in positive consequences and those producing negative consequences.
8. Implement rules regarding punishment consistently and immediately.
9. Provide alternative behavioral possibilities.
10. Present maximum intensity of the aversive event from the beginning.
11. When using a punishment procedure, exercise care to insure that consequences are in fact unpleasant to the child.
12. Insure that the unpleasantness of aversive consequences is stronger than the positive consequences associated with the undesirable behavior.
13. After the child is informed of the punishment rule, routine use of a threat or warning about further undesirable behavior producing unpleasant consequences is to be discouraged.

14. When reprimand is used as a punishment procedure, present it so that it does not attract the attention of other children.
15. If punishment effects are not evident rather immediately, it is probably best to discontinue the procedure.
16. In using mild punishment to suppress behavior which occurs in numerous settings, it will typically be necessary to implement the punishment contingency in each setting.
17. Punishment procedures should be phased out of an educational program as quickly as possible.
18. To reemphasize, when punishment is used, label the contingencies for the child. (pp. 371-376)

BEHAVIORAL SELF-CONTROL

Mahoney and Thoresen (1974) have proposed a model of self-control that is founded on learning theory principles. The authors emphasize the departure of the behavioral self-control orientation from the traditional construct of "will power." The authors suggest the notion will power is limited by a circularity of logic in which an inner psychic force or trait is explained by the behavior from which it was defined. (Ralph has will power. How do you know? Because he was able to quit smoking. How was he able to give up smoking? Because of his will power.) This logic does little to provide educator's tools for developing will power. Further, traditional will power constructs often propose an all-or-nothing view of behavior control. This is exemplified by the fatalistic attitude of individuals who gorge themselves when eating because they do not have will power.

The behavioral view suggests that control of one's actions results from a knowledge of and control over environmental events that influence behavior. Self-control skills result from the adolescent's ability to manipulate the antecedents and consequents of behavior so that desirable behavior is more likely to occur. For example, the husband who attempts to lose weight by avoiding occasions in which cocktails and hors d'oeuvres are served, removing sweets from the house, and avoiding Girl Scouts cookies in the fall, is practicing self-control by avoiding the antecedents for eating. Similarly, setting a goal for weight loss that is consequated by a special activity (e.g., I'll buy new clothes when my weight reaches 180 pounds) is an example of self-imposed consequents.

Mahoney and Thoresen (1974) have proposed three essential processes that are involved in self-control: (1) the identification of behaviors to be influenced, (2) the identification of antecedents and consequents associated with the target behavior, and (3) the initiation of a plan that alters the antecedents and consequents of the target behavior. These procedures parallel the approach used in the program analysis chapter except that the educator becomes responsible for facilitating the adolescent's own program analysis efforts rather than conducting those activities of one.

Illustration

Susan, a 16-year-old learning-disabled adolescent, was repeatedly late for her 8:00 A.M. job. Recognizing the problem, she approached her high school guidance counselor for assistance in devising a strategy for getting to work on time. The counselor suggested a behavioral self-control approach to the problem. Since Susan had already identified the problem, the remaining procedures involved identifying setting events (antecedents and consequents) associated with tardiness and the development of a formal program. The counselor gave Susan a continuous recording form. He asked that she keep track of all the events that preceded and followed her tardiness episodes for the next several weeks.

The following weeks Susan and her counselor met to discuss the data. They determined that the primary antecedents to tardiness were: (1) oversleeping, which resulted from the failure of her alarm clock or her staying up too late the preceding evening; (2) not allowing enough time to dress, bathe, eat, and groom in the morning; and (3) meeting friends on the way to work and spending too much time in conversation. The consequents, if any, involved a harsh stare from her supervisor as she walked in.

Susan, with the help of her counselor, developed and implemented the following program: Susan purchased and used a new, more reliable alarm clock; she began going to sleep at a more reasonable time on nights before work, reserving late nights out for weekends; she set the alarm to wake her up 15 minutes prior to preprogram wake-up time; she told all of her friends about the program and asked that they not talk to her before work unless it was very important; and, finally, she gave her counselor ten dollars and requested that he send one dollar to his favorite charity for each day she was late.

Susan continued to meet with the counselor every two weeks to discuss her progress. At the end of the semester, the six dollars not used were returned to Susan. Plans for fading the intervention program and new goals for similar intervention strategies were discussed.

Considerations in Using Behavioral Self-Control Tactics

A wide range of tactics that involve the adolescent in the planning and implementation of the behavior change program can be identified by the creative teacher. The major consideration in establishing the self-control program is the extent to which the adolescent can be expected to fulfill the requirements of the program without externally imposed contingencies.

A number of studies have demonstrated a range of self-control procedures beyond the scope of this text—self-recording (McKenzie & Rushall, 1974), self-instruction (Thoresen, 1974), and self-reinforcement (Frederiksen & Frederikson, 1975).

Bornstein and Querillon (1976) demonstrated an approach to self-instruction that greatly enhanced students' ability to manage their own environment. The instructional procedure involved encouraged the students to think to themselves: (1) questions about the teacher's expectations, (2) answers to the questions in the form of cognitive rehearsals, (3) self-instructions that guide through the task, and (4) self-praise.

Two major advantages are evident in self-control procedures. First, they place the control and responsibility of behavior change in the hands of the adolescent. This is especially critical since one of education's major objectives is to provide students with skills that sustain their development into adult life. Self-control procedures can be developed and implemented by young adults without the direct support or supervision of others. Thus, one would expect the adolescents' ability to exhibit self-control skills to enhance their adjustment in adult life. The second advantage of self-control procedures is that they can be highly cost efficient. Since the adolescent is primarily responsible for program analysis and implementation, the educator can assume the role of a consultant. As such, the educator is free to arrange and monitor a larger number of intensive social, vocational, and academic development programs.

Probably the major limitation of the self-control approach is that it relies on the student's motivation to participate in the self-control process. A self-control program may not be a viable option for a youth not willing or able to (1) identify a behavior change goal, (2) complete a valid analysis of antecedent and consequent events, (3) establish a restructured environment, or (4) consistently abide by the requirements of the restructured environment. When one or all of these deficiencies occur, the educator is left to impose program conditions on the adolescent. In any case, to the extent possible, self-control components that will not reduce the effectiveness of the program should be utilized. Once the student succeeds under externally imposed contingencies, it is likely that more self-control components may be added.

In summary, the following procedures should be considered in designing and implementing a self-control program:

1. Assist the adolescent in clarifying and defining the goals of the intervention program.
2. Teach the youth to conduct continuous recording as outlined in the program analysis chapter.

3. Assist the youth in using the continuous recording procedure to identify the antecedents and consequents associated with the target behavior.
4. Work with the adolescent in designing a program that restructures the antecedents and consequents of his or her behavior.
5. Assist the adolescent in developing a continuous monitoring procedure that may be used to determine the effectiveness of the intervention program.
6. Assist the adolescent in implementing and monitoring the program, providing social reinforcement and corrective feedback as required.
7. Suggest strategies to the youth for fading unusual intervention components.

FADING THE BEHAVIOR MANAGEMENT PROGRAM

The social development program can be gradually withdrawn by (1) fading contrived reinforcers in lieu of naturally occurring events that have developed reinforcing properties through the program; (2) reducing the frequency and predictability with which an individual is reinforced following a desirable response; (3) gradually introducing conditions that, prior to intervention, cued disruptive behavior; (4) fading contrived cues; and (5) developing self-control skills.

Once acceptable responses are attained consistently through the social development program, unnatural or intrusive program elements should be accomplished in a gradual and systematic fashion. The haphazard and abrupt removal of a program will most probably result in rapid deterioration of targeted behaviors. This reversal in the behavior may be attributed to (1) the program not being in effect sufficiently long for natural consequents to develop reinforcing properties, (2) the immediate loss of high rates of reinforcement, (3) the immediate return of antecedents that have a long history of cueing unacceptable behavior, (4) the immediate loss of antecedents for acceptable behavior, and (5) the student not acquiring self-control skills. Intervention approaches should include strategies that increase the likelihood that the student will exhibit positive social behavior once the program is withdrawn (Baer, Wolfe, & Risley, 1968).

Program Duration

The first consideration in establishing maintenance is to leave the program in place sufficiently long to develop a positive association between naturally occurring consequents and contrived incentives. As has been stated frequently through these chapters, contrived reinforcers should be paired constantly with natural consequents. It is expected that over time this association will develop the reinforcing properties of the natural event. Once the naturally occurring event has acquired reinforcing properties, the desired response would be expected to be maintained following the withdrawal of the program.

Sequencing of Behaviors

Once students have developed a number of discrete behaviors, they can begin to combine these previously discrete behaviors to promote more complex learning. Until now each of the discrete behaviors had been reinforced individually. Now we are going to promote the performance of a series of activities that produce the achievement of a more complex task, and the reinforcement will occur only at the conclusion of the series of tasks. As an example, the student is reinforced for the performance of discrete activities related to the repair of a tire. Among the discrete activities learned were: use a lugwrench to remove the lugbolts; remove the tire and rim from the hub; remove the tire from the rim; replace the new or repaired tire to the rim and apply a sealant; reset the tire on the hub and reinsert the lugbolts; and tighten the lugbolts.

To promote this sequencing is not difficult. The previously learned activities were previously paired with or directly preceded the reinforcement. The reinforcement of the behavior will tend to maintain the behavior and forge the sequence. Once the sequence has been established to the level desired, the teacher will reinforce the sequenced behavior. Initially the teacher may sequence only to activities and then reinforce the appropriate behavior, as the student masters the process. Other activities can be added and then reinforced.

Thinning the Reinforcement Schedule

A similar consideration involves thinning the reinforcement schedule. Most intensive interventions require continuous reinforcement (e.g., reinforcing each occurrence of the behavior) to establish the desired response. While this is the most powerful approach to developing a new or low probability behavior, behavior maintained by continuous reinforcement is highly susceptible to deterioration following the withdrawal of reinforcement. Therefore, once a behavior is established through a schedule of continuous reinforcement, an intermittent schedule of reinforcement should be introduced. Reinforcement may be thinned through a fixed or variable schedule of reinforcement.

A *fixed schedule* involves reinforcing the student every two, three, four . . . times the behavior occurs. With the fixed schedule the student and teacher are aware of when the reinforcement will be delivered. For example, the student may be reinforced following every four assignments completed, or for every three days of good behavior.

Variable schedules are different in that the student is not aware of when reinforcement will occur. With the variable schedule, the student may be reinforced on the average of every third day. In either case, the student does not know exactly when reinforcement will be delivered.

When possible, reinforcement programs should be faded through the use of variable schedules of reinforcement. It has been demonstrated that fixed schedules produce a highly variable rate of behavior as the student predicts when reinforcement will occur and increases performance prior to delivery. Following reinforcement, the student may be inclined to reduce performance. Variable schedules, on the other hand, produce stable response rates that are highly resistant to deterioration following the withdrawal of reinforcement.

Reintroduction of Natural Antecedents

Another important consideration in promoting maintenance is the gradual reintroduction of the natural antecedents that, prior to the program, cued inappropriate behavior. For example, if failure generally preceded aggression for a learning-disabled student, once aggression control was established under failure-free conditions, reasonable amounts of failure could be reintroduced. This process challenges the students to exhibit control over their behavior under conditions that, prior to intervention, resulted in disruptive behavior. The termination of intervention prior to the reintroduction of provoking cue conditions does not permit the student to practice and be reinforced for positive social behaviors under adverse conditions.

Development of Self-Control

Finally, as emphasized in the preceding section, program components that foster self-control skills should be highlighted throughout intervention. Teaching students to monitor their behavior is first step in placing the tools for change in their hands. Once a program teaches students to monitor their behavior, they may be encouraged to make verbal statements that evaluate the behavior (e.g., "I didn't get upset when Bob called me an idiot. I controlled my temper well"). Finally, a program should encourage students to identify and label natural reinforcers for positive behavior (e.g., "My employer was really happy that I did not stop work to argue with Bob. I am a good worker"). These self-initiated procedures may be expected to continue overtly or covertly following the withdrawal of intervention as they do not rely on the impetus of an external agent. Similar approaches have been demonstrated to be effective strategies for a variety of populations (Mahoney & Thoresen, 1974).

CONCLUSION

The behavior management system, detailed in the program analysis chapter, and the specific intervention strategies discussed in this chapter, offer a comprehensive approach to teaching, motivating, and monitoring positive social behaviors. The system emphasizes the study and modification of antecedents and consequents associated with precise behavioral objectives. Additional emphasis is placed on teaching and reinforcing prosocial competency behaviors that may replace disruptive behaviors. Fundamental to the behavior management system described here is the careful assessment of learner characteristics and ecological influences. Also important is the continuous recording of target behaviors so that program effects can be reliably discerned.

Although this chapter has described a number of isolated intervention approaches, the careful program engineer may select several strategies for use at one time. As discussed previously, the practice of developing a treatment package can often produce a more comprehensive and powerful behavior change program. For example, the differential reinforcement of other behaviors should always accompany reductive strategies. This is to develop and strengthen prosocial behaviors that can function in the absence of disruptive behaviors. Self-control strategies (e.g., individually selected consequents, self-monitoring of the target behavior) may accompany teacher-directed intervention approaches.

In summary, Table 8-1 is offered as a review of intervention approaches described in this chapter.

Table 8-1 Intervention Approaches

Behavior Change Procedure	Definition	Example
Social Reinforcement	The use of interpersonal interactions to increase the likelihood that a behavior will occur	Christine is praised by her teacher for brushing her hair. Subsequently Ellen brushes her hair more frequently.
Shaping	The reinforcement of successive approximations of the desired response	Mr. Green reinforces Steve for sweeping around his work station. Once Steve does this consistently, Mr. Green reinforces Steve for sweeping his work station and the adjoining work station. Then Steve is reinforced for sweeping three work stations. This process continues through the school term until Steve is sweeping the entire shop.
Modeling	The arrangement of instructional conditions so that the individual acquires new response patterns through the observation of another person	Michael is moved into Mr. Robertson's room so that he can sit next to Jim, whom he admires. Through the terms, Michael's social behaviors increase as he observes and emulates Jim's behavior.
Stimulus Change	The influencing of behavior by changing the controlling stimuli	Mrs. Haley moves Anne to the front of the classroom away from the windows. This reduces the frequency with which Anne exhibits off-task behavior.
Behavior Rehearsal	The practicing of a low rate of behavior under conditions naturally associated with the behavior	Having observed that Joel experiences difficulty in interacting with customers, Mr. Jones structures situations in which Joel interacts with peers who act as customers. Mr. Jones helps Joel to identify and practice appropriate interactions. Further, Mr. Jones illustrates the positive consequents of appropriate customer interactions.

Term	Definition	Example
Contingency Contracting	A formal agreement between the youth and his or her supervisor that specifies the relationship between specific behaviors and consequents.	Danny is consistently late for work. His employer develops a written agreement stipulating that he will be docked $1.00 for each day he is late. Further, each week that he is on time for all five work days, Danny will receive a $1.00 bonus. This contract is signed and agreed on by Danny, his parents, the employer, and all other concerned people.
Differential Reinforcement of Low Rates of Behavior (DRL)	The reinforcement of responses emitted at successively lower rates	Mr. Evans reinforces Jean for having only 12 errors in her product assemblies. Then he reinforces her for having only 10 errors, then 8 errors. This process continues until she has less than two errors in her product assemblies.
Differential Reinforcement of Other Behaviors (DRO)	The reinforcement of any behavior other than the excessive behavior	Mr. Smith notices that Randy swears often. To reduce swearing he reinforces Randy for any statements made that do not include swear words.
Extinction	The removal of positive consequents that maintain a behavior	Mrs. Patcher asks her class not to laugh when Ricky acts out.
Response Cost	The removal of a specified amount of reinforcement following a behavior	Mrs. Utterman does not allow Will to go on break when he fails to do the assigned amount of work.
Overcorrection Restitution	The restoring of the environment to its original condition following disruptive behavior	Mr. Dulop asks that Ed replace a table top burned by Ed's cigarette.
Positive Practice	The repeated practice of a behavior more acceptable than the disruptive behavior	Mr. Dulop insists that Ed make ashtrays for the entire shop.
Behavioral Self-Control	The controlling of one's own behavior by manipulating the antecedents and consequents of the behavior	Susan avoids Karen because they often fight with one another.

REFERENCES

Baer, D. M., Wolfe, M. M., & Risley, T. R. Some current dimensions of applied behavior analysis. *Journal of Applied Behavior Analysis*, 1968, *1*, 91-97.

Bandura, A. Influence of model's reinforcement contingencies on the acquisition of imitative responses. *Journal of Personality and Social Psychology*, 1965, *1*, 589-595.

Bandura, A. Behavioral psychotherapy. *Scientific American*, March 1967, pp. 76-86.

Bandura, A. *Principles of behavior modification.* New York: Holt, Rinehart & Winston, 1969.

Bandura, A. Psychotherapy based on modelling principles. In A. E. Beugin and S. L. Garfield (Eds.), *Handbook of psychotherapy and behavior change.* New York: John Wiley & Sons, 1971, pp. 653-708.(a)

Bandura, A. *Social learning theory.* Morristown, N.J.: General Learning Press, 1971.(b)

Boren, J. J., & Colman, A. D. Some experiments on reinforcement principles within a psychiatric ward for delinquent soldiers. *Journal of Applied Behavior Analysis*, 1970, *3*, 222-233.

Bornstein, P. H., & Querillon, R. R. The effects of a self-instructional package on overactive preschool boys. *Journal of Applied Behavior Analysis*, 1976, *9*, 179-188.

Bruininks, R. H., & Ryders, J. E. Alternatives to special class placement for educable mentally retarded children. *Focus on Exceptional Children*, 1971, *3*, 1-12.

Bucher, B., & Hawkins, J. *Comparison of response cost and token reinforcement systems in a class for academic underachievers.* Paper presented at the meeting of the Association for the Advancement of Behavior Therapy, Washington, D.C., September, 1971.

Csapo, M. Peer models reverse the "one bad apple spoils the barrel" theory. *Teaching Exceptional Children*, 1972, *5*, 20-25.

Deitz, S. M., & Repp, A. C. Decreasing classroom misbehavior through the use of DRL schedules of reinforcement. *Journal of Applied Behavior Analysis*, 1973, *6*, 457-463.

Doty, D. W., & McInnis, T., & Paul, G. L. Remediation of negative side effects of an ongoing response-cost system with chronic mental patients. *Journal of Applied Behavior Analysis*, 1974, *7*, 191-198.

Foxx, R. M., & Azrin, N. H. Restitution: A method of eliminating aggressive-disruptive behavior of retarded and brain damaged patients. *Behavior Research and Therapy*, 1972, *10*, 15-27.

Foxx, R. M., & Azrin, N. H. The elimination of autistic self-stimulatory behavior by overcorrection. *Journal of Applied Behavior Analysis*, 1973, *6*, 1-14.

Frederiksen, L. W., & Frederikson, C. B. Teacher-determined and self-determined token reinforcement in a special education classroom. *Behavior Therapy*, 1975, *6*, 310-314.

Gambrill, E. D. *Behavior modification: Handbook of assessment, intervention and evaluation.* San Francisco: Jossey-Bass, 1977.

Gardner, W. I. *Learning and behavior characteristics of exceptional children and youth: A humanistic behavioral approach.* Boston: Allyn & Bacon, 1977.

Goetz, E. M., Holmberg, M. C., & LeBlanc, J. M. Differential reinforcement of other behavior and noncontingent reinforcement as control procedures during the modification of a preschooler's compliance. *Journal of Applied Behavior Analysis*, 1975, *8*, 77-82.

Goldstein, A. P., Heller, K., & Sechrist, L. B. *Psychotherapy and the psychology of behavior change.* New York: John Wiley & Sons, 1966.

Hall, R. V., Lund, D., & Jackson, D. Effects of teacher attention on study behaviors. *Journal of Applied Behavior Analysis*, 1968, *1*, 1-12.

Haskett, G. J., & Lenfestey, W. Reading-related behavior in an open classroom: Effects of novelty and modelling on preschoolers. *Journal of Applied Behavior Analysis,* 1974, *7,* 233-241.

Kazdin, A. E. The effect of vicarious reinforcement of attentive behavior in the classroom. *Journal of Applied Behavior Analysis,* 1973, *6,* 71-78.

Law & Behavior. *Quarterly analysis of legal developments affecting professionals in human services,* 1976, *#1,* 1.

Mahoney, M. J., & Thoresen, C. E. *Self-control: Power to the person.* Belmont, Calif.: Brooks/Cole Publishing Co., 1974.

McKenzie, T. L., & Rushall, B. S. Effects of self-recording on attendance and performance in a competitive swimming training environment. *Journal of Applied Behavior Analysis,* 1974, *7,* 199-206.

Ross, D. M. Effect on learning of psychological attachment to a film model. *American Journal of Mental Deficiency,* 1970, *74,* 701-707.

Sabatino, D. A., & Schloss, P. J. Adolescent social personal development: Theory and application. In D. A. Sabatino, C. Schmidt, & T. Miller (Eds.), *Learning disabilities: Systematizing teaching and service delivery.* Rockville, Md.: Aspen Systems, 1981, pp. 461-509.

Schloss, P. J., & Johann, M. A modelling and contingency management approach to pacifier withdrawal. *Behavior Therapy,* in press.

Skinner, B. F. *Beyond freedom and dignity.* New York: Knopf, 1971.

Solomon, R. W., & Wahler, R. G. Peer reinforcement control of classroom problem behavior. *Journal of Applied Behavior Analysis,* 1973, *6,* 49-56.

Stevenson, H. W. *Children's learning.* New York: Appleton-Century-Crofts, 1972.

Thoresen, C. E. Behavioral means and humanistic ends. In M. J. Mahoney and C. E. Thoresen, *Self-control: Power to the person.* Monterey, Calif.: Brooks/Cole Publishing Co., 1974, pp. 308-322.

Thoresen, C. E., & Mahoney, M. J. *Behavioral self-control.* New York: Holt, Rinehart & Winston, 1974.

Warner, R. W., & Swisher, J. D. Drug-abuse prevention: Reinforcement of alternatives. In J. D. Krumboltz & C. E. Thoresen (Eds.), *Counselling methods.* New York: Holt, Rinehart & Winston, 1976, pp. 510-517.

Wilson, C. W., & Hopkins, B. L. The effects of contingent music on the intensity of noise in junior high home economics classes. *Journal of Applied Behavior Analysis,* 1973, *6,* 269-275.

Zimmerman, E. H., & Zimmerman, J. The alteration of behavior in a classroom situation. *Journal of the Experimental Analysis of Behavior,* 1962, *5,* 59-60.

Zinzer, O. Imitation, modelling and cross-cultural training. Aerospace medical research laboratories, Aerospace Medical Division, Wright-Patterson Air Force Base, Ohio: September, 1966.

Chapter 9

Instructional Methods

The concept of career education includes every possible aspect of a school program, including instruction in the basic academic areas. Without instruction in the academic areas, handicapped youths would be without the essential learning tools needed to pursue a career. It is essential that at the adolescent level of academic instruction an interface with the career-vocational training aspect of the student's program is developed. This interface requires cooperation among all school personnel who either directly instruct or provide ancillary support for youths. During instruction, the general tendency in the secondary school setting has been to focus on the student's academic deficiency, such as reading, mathematics, and language arts (Miller, 1978). Many youths receiving this basic academic instruction have sustained school histories of failure and frustration. These same youths have been exposed to a continuous process of remedial reading instruction, skill building exercises, and tutorial assistance that has often seemed to them to be unrelated to the outside world's expectations and demands. Such an approach for most handicapped adolescents has not been successful, as evidenced by the students' continuance in the special education program. Yet, the school persists in employing a curriculum and methods that reflect school board policy rather than student needs and have not yielded significant achievement and mastery among the handicapped population.

Individuals with a repeated history of school failure sustained over 6 to 12 years are likely to view the educational process with suspicion, frustration, and anger. Often because of their achievement-related problems, they are excluded from opportunities afforded more successful students. Given the documented evidence that the handicapped adolescent is provided instruction through traditional techniques designed generally to serve handicapped primary-aged children (Sabatino, 1974), school personnel are obliged to evaluate their programs and procedures for serving the handicapped adolescent.

One major theme repeated by education as a cause for school failure is inappropriately designed programs (Brolin & Kokaska, 1979; Noar, 1974; Phelps & Lutz, 1977). As observed in previous chapters, adolescence is a period of search for identity, the establishment of basic values, and the clarification of long- and short-term goals. Students with reading and mathematics problems frequently fail to perceive the relevance of purely corrective academic remediation as they search for identity, establish values, and clarify goals.

The assistance the students require does not exclude the basic academic areas, and, in fact, one's values, goals, and identity are often closely associated with school performance in the academic areas. One approach to serving the adolescent is combining the content and academic areas, and providing the youth instruction, values, and goals development through high interest, low vocabulary readers. Publishers of educational materials have begun to focus on the development of new, easier-to-read materials directed toward history, science, and career issues. This chapter is designed to provide content-oriented personnel, who daily serve handicapped youths with academic disabilities in reading, mathematics, written and spoken language, with procedures that could enable them to transmit information and develop skills essential for career development.

INSTRUCTIONAL ISSUES

Practicality of Instruction

Jones (1974) observed that public schools have not oriented their programs to interface the academic deficiencies of handicapped youths with their educational needs. Schloss and Miller (in press) noted that the ecological setting the youth is placed in unduly influences the program students are provided by school personnel, irrespective of the youths' needs and capabilities. Such findings suggest that many youths are not receiving usable, efficacious services that will prepare them to meet the world with meaningful skills and information that are related to their career goals. This phenomenon has contributed to a higher number of educationally handicapped youths dropping out of school (Jones, 1974; Sabatino, 1974). Other investigators have speculated that the high drop-out level is costly to the youths in the educational system. The schools must begin to develop a curriculum that is oriented more toward the career and social-personal goals of the youth and less to the prerequisite liberal arts requirements of colleges and universities. The secondary school's traditional curriculum has not only disenfranchised the handicapped youth, but has neglected life preparation courses and experiences in such craft-oriented careers as auto repair, carpentry, and metal working.

Task Analysis

Hersen and Barlow (1978) and Sulzer-Azaroff and Mayer (1977) have indicated that the process of task analysis is the breaking down of an individual task into a series of incremental steps. The breakdown of the task into more negotiable steps enables the individual, unable to either grasp or perform a complex task, to achieve the goal through a more incremental learning process. This process is critical to the learning of young and old individuals having difficulty in school or on the job. A major difficulty in the secondary schools is that instructional personnel are frequently trained in the content area (e.g., mathematics, home economics, journalism, or history) and have minimal training in the instructional process. As a result, when handicapped youths appear in the secondary classroom and cannot grasp a concept, the teacher is not prepared to task analyze the learning process and assist the student. For example, the student may be having difficulty understanding the complex concept of political boundaries. Among the components of a political boundary are:

Criteria for Agreement

- An agreement that a parcel of land is to be divided is articulated by a written document and/or verbal statements that have been witnessed.

- Those participating in the agreement are generally parties who will reside in or possess the individual land parcels.

- The division may not be based on need of each individual, but on the ability of one or more parties to negotiate an agreement that reflects its best interest.

- The agreement is agreed to by both parties or by some other legally standing body.

Principles of the Boundaries

- Physical characteristics of the land may influence the division of the land, but they are not absolute determinates.

- The political boundaries are defensible in a court of law and are bound by law.

- Political boundaries are established between one state and another, one nation and another, one county and another, and one city and another.

- Political boundaries can be altered or ended by wars, treaties, or arbitration.

- Political boundaries can change every few years, depending on such factors as war, agreements between states or communities, or seizures of land by one or more parties.

Obviously, the issue of political boundaries is a complex one, and each of the nine components could be broken down into additional components. As an example, the third criterion for agreement, addressing the fact that "the division may not be based on need of each individual," could be dissected further. One could look into the issue of negotiability.

First, negotiability is the process of weighing each parties' interests and needs.

Second, it requires an evaluation of the property involved.

Third, it requires the recognition that each party to an agreement must yield in one area to gain in others.

Fourth, what the party gains must have general parity with what was yielded.

As an example, three nations may be negotiating a political boundary. The area is a hilly area with a river running through one portion. One of the nations is interested in irrigation, another is interested in increased pasture land for agriculture, and a third is looking for improved transit of its goods through water navigation. The negotiations will focus on seeking to establish the interests of each without penalizing any one party. The negotiations will hinge on such issues as: (1) the wealth and strength of one nation compared to its neighbors, (2) the urgency of the need to resolve the issue by one or more parties, and (3) the readiness of the parties to yield on one issue to obtain an advantage on another issue.

The evaluation and breakdown of the above themes are comparable to the breaking down and analysis of a youth's career needs and directions. Depending on the youth's disabilities, the school personnel will be required to assess the program and materials and to develop an instructional package whose steps and pace are compatible with the youth's demonstrated capacity to learn. The level and degree of task analysis will determine the instructional steps and pace.

Theoretical Constructs

Maslow (1969) and Ausubel (1969) have indicated that an individual's ability to learn and cope with his or her environment is directly related to the ability to organize and employ ideas and information. This process is related to an individual's ability to think abstractly, such as color, the most abstract term, becoming an advanced organizer for other terms, such as "red," "yellow," and "blue." Each of the later terms (red, yellow, and blue) are types of colors and denote individual properties that reflect and absorb light at varying levels of intensity. Depending on the intensity of reflection and absorption, we can observe a variety of hues. Each of the hues is called a color, and the awareness of the fact that the word "color" represents a variety of hues increases an individual's ability to organize ideas and to communicate this information.

Another example is the word "education." To some, education is the process that occurs in a formal building called a school. Yet, others believe that the process of education extends into the home and community and involves such activities as play, repairing a bicycle, taking a trip, reading a variety of material, and computing and analyzing numerical problems and/or formulas. Each of these experiences can be expected to produce learning and to contribute to the educational process. Education can, at a variety of locations and with a variety of persons, represent differing points of views and experiences and contribute to an individual's educational experiences and personal growth. Knowledge of the term education and familiarity with its many aspects, as well as with the limitations others may place upon it, will also contribute to one's ability to communicate, think, analyze issues, and solve problems.

Handicapped youths need to be taught abstract terms, what they represent, and how they can be used to promote learning and career development. One's ability to think abstractly is directly related to the success or failure many youths experience in taking tests, responding to peers and teachers, and seeking careers. For some youths hearing the phrase "career education" may mean only another class they must attend. To others the concept of career education represents a variety of experiences that can ultimately lead to the development of specific skills and to a position in the community, whether that position be one of physician, carpenter, or fast food preparer.

Students frequently find phrases and terms in textbooks that they either don't understand, or understand only partially. Specific terms that appear to be relevant and important in the student's learning process can be identified. The terms are found in general reading texts, history and geography texts, and career exploration and awareness material (Frostig & Maslow, 1973). Several investigators have sought to explain the thinking process (Fraenkel, 1973; Frostig, 1976; Guilford, 1967). The factors associated with abstract thinking development include: (1) observing factors associated with a series of events or ideas, (2) developing a concept based on the observations, (3) continuously analyzing the concept, (4) testing the concept through an experiment or series of activities, (5) evaluating the results of the activities or experiment with other findings and conclusions, (6) generalizing the finds, and (7) predicting future behavior of events as a result of the findings (Fraenkel, 1973).

Readability Level

Many handicapped youths find the reading material presented to them too difficult. The presentation of the reading material is frequently based on information contained in the book and the need of the students to learn the material. The ability of the handicapped student to read the material, while a consideration, generally has not been determined through a consistent, organized procedure. One of the simplest ways of measuring a book's readability is by (1) determining the average length of a sentence, and (2) the percentage of difficulty that the student is expected to master. Spache (1953) devised the formula and noted the determination of difficult words was based on words that were familiar (easy words) and words that were unfamiliar (difficult words). Familiar words are (1) all letters in the alphabet, (2) regular verbs, (3) plurals and possessives, and (4) first names of persons. Unfamiliar words are (1) irregular words, (2) words with adjectival or adverbial endings ("ly," "er," and "est"), and (3) family names or relations (aunt, uncle). A number of authors have developed procedures for identifying the specific level for which the reading material is prepared (Harris & Sipay, 1975; Smith, Guice, & Cheek, 1972). The use of the readability measure can enable the teacher to avoid negative reading experiences and rejection of the learning process.

Length of Text

Adolescents often find the reading or mathematics text they are expected to handle during a specified time too long. Their poor performance makes the length of standard reading and mathematics material burdensome, and frequently dooms them to failure and frustration. To assist the handicapped adolescent student, school personnel need to recognize that a significant amount of the material is not designed to interface with the student's needs and academic abilities. Several solutions to the problem of material being inappropriately designed are available. They include:

- The length of material could be reduced: Material normally consumed by nonhandicapped students in a day could be broken down into two to three days of assignments for the handicapped youth. Questions could be developed that relate only to the abbreviated material assigned on a specific day.

- Existing material could be rewritten: Texts that are too long, and whose vocabulary is unfamiliar to the student, could be rewritten to reflect the student's performance level. The sentences could be shortened and made less complex, the vocabulary less abstract and more familiar, and the ideas could be summarized to shorten the material.

- Alternative materials could be identified: Alternative material focuses on a theme similar to one contained in traditional texts, less difficult vocabulary, and less complex sentence structure. Several publishers have been developing such material for both handicapped and disadvantaged populations.

- Types of follow-up: Handicapped youths exhibit a variety of handicaps including poor long-term and/or short-term memory and inability to identify critical issues and/or draw inferences. Several publishers have developed specific skill-building material designed to remediate such deficiencies. Some regular textbook publishers have also recognized this need and have structured the follow-up questions to address specific education weaknesses or strengths. The teacher needs to be cognizant of the types of follow-up questions the material uses as instruction decisions are made. Among the variety of follow-ups that can be sought are: (1) recall for detail; (2) recall of inferred behavior; (3) interpretation of events; (4) location of information; (5) organization of the sequence of events; (6) deciphering of maps, charts, and tables; and (7) summary of the story. The follow-up should occur daily so that the student and teacher can measure progress on a regular schedule and so that program changes can be made as it becomes obvious that the material is either too challenging or fails to challenge the youth (Hallahan & Kauffman, 1976). Daily changes of the follow-up types of responses enable the teacher to train a variety of skills while simultaneously providing new and interesting problems for the student to solve.

Regular Testing

One of the deficiencies of instruction is the lack of regular testing and evaluation. As a result, neither the teacher not the student is informed about the youth's overall progress and the areas where growth is greatest and least. The lack of such critical information impairs the ability of personnel to develop an ongoing program that is relevant and successful. The detection of problem areas early can enable personnel to correct the instructional process before it begins to affect the student's progress. In the past, schools have intended to rely on annual district-wide standardized testing. The data yielded by these tests have neither been timely nor helpful. Frequently, the data yielded by the standardized annual tests neither measured the student's progress in specific instruction nor promoted alternative programs and methodology. Criterion-based testing can yield data that measure either daily, weekly, and/or monthly student progress and assist the school personnel to develop alternatives if such alternatives are essential.

Micro-Computers

The relative low cost of micro-computers provides the educators of secondary-aged handicapped students new devices in their attempt to serve these youth in the school environment (Joiner, Sedlak, Silverstein, & Vensel, 1980). The micro-computer is an easily programmed device that can be used to provide instruction in such areas as reading, mathematics, language arts, and career exploration. An advantage to the use of micro-computers is that once the computer has been programmed, the teacher is free to focus his or her attention on another student. Another advantage is that the micro-computer, programmed to notify a student that his or her response is either correct or incorrect, will not become frustrated with the student who is having difficulty with a specific activity. The micro-computer will continue to note incorrect responses until the student has correctly responded to the material.

REMEDIAL AND SUPPORTIVE ACADEMIC STRATEGIES

Some basic principles of remediation and instruction have been formulated that are designed to promote an effective system and efficacious services for handicapped youths. The principles reflect the opinions of educators in the fields of reading, special education, vocational education, and mathematics education. Among the principles are:

- Instruction must be designed to interface with the needs and demonstrated competencies of specific students.

- Instruction should match the student's interests and preparedness to learn.

- Student input is essential to any successful adolescent instructional program.

- The learning process should include monitoring whether the student can receive and can understand the information before the teacher seeks to have the student explain the information.

- The teacher should teach to the frustration level and should avoid overloading students to the point where they are unwilling to resume the learning process.

- The teacher should promote learning without taxing skills or channels that are severely impaired.

- The teacher should control factors such as attention, rate, intensity, and process.

- As the student is readied for a career, the teacher should be certain that both the verbal and motor channels of expression are fully developed.

- The teacher should guide the approach through clearly articulated and attainable sets of goals, objectives, and activities.

- All personnel serving the youth should have a clearly established program that articulates their role in the service delivery process.

These criteria do not support one instructional strategy over another. The supposition is that appropriate materials and procedures will be used, and that only the teacher and the student can determine what constitutes appropriateness during the ongoing instructional process.

To serve the adolescent with academic and vocational performance disabilities appropriately, school personnel must explore new approaches to addressing continuing deficits. Basal readers, phonics instruction, and a second run through in the mathematics text have not and will not be viable instructional approaches to serving the majority of adolescents. The traditional strategy in the past has been to have the youth go through a text a second time in expectation that the mastery not achieved during the first exposure will be achieved in subsequent experiences. The response of adolescents repeating a text is generally not a passive acceptance but an overt rejection and/or questioning. ''I don't want to do this baby stuff again,'' and ''Oh, I don't want to do this, I've done it already. Can't I do something else?''

Thus, new approaches and creative adoption of old approaches need to be considered in educating the handicapped youth. Among some of the less traditional approaches useful in the process of instruction are the following.

Use Alternating Texts

Often in the traditional school environment, the same text is used repeatedly until the student either completes the text or the school year ends. The reading process is controlled by the teacher and the opportunity to employ other instructional material is limited by teacher bias, insufficient funds for the purchase of alternative material, and/or rigid school board curriculum requirements. With handicapped youths, this approach can lead to frustration and failure. As a result, the teacher needs to identify and select four to five texts that can be used in a predictable structure sequence. Each text should address different skills so that the lesson is both remedial and supportive of skill areas considered adequate. These materials will function best if they are developmental and paced at a rate in concert with the student's learning style and programmatic needs. The use of the alternating text is also likely to promote a high level of interest among the youths.

Prepare One's Own Text

Low functioning students will at times reject formal reading material because of their previous failure experiences. When the student either rejects the formal material or performs in it at a very low level, then the development of the student's own personalized dictionary and reading text can be pursued (Frostig & Maslow, 1973). The text and dictionary should be built upon the interests of the youth, and not the interests of the teacher or the school. If the youth's interests revolve around cars and dating, then the words and stories should also reflect those personal focuses. As the dictionary is developed, words from the Dolch List and the Dole-Chall Word List can be integrated into the material. Both lists represent commonly used words found in material for children, adolescents, and adults. The integration of the word lists and words chosen by the student enables the teacher to develop a readability bridge between the student's materials and formal materials that are geared to the same functional level of reading but have a different focus. This methodology requires additional preparation and instructional time on the part of the teacher. Among the responsibilities of the teacher in this approach are identifying student interests, developing a knowledge related to the student's interests, becoming familiar with the Dolch List, working with the student in developing reading material that is both interesting and readable, and then developing follow-up materials that require the youth to demonstrate comprehension of the material just completed.

Use Popular Press

A large number of students are unprepared to read formal classroom materials either because of previous failure experiences, low interest content, and/or because the reading level is too demanding. The reasons just cited are but a few of the reasons why handicapped adolescents reject some formal reading material. The popular press is a viable alternative. Newspapers, sports magazines, and teen magazines are among the most popular reading materials adolescents gravitate toward. These materials generally represent high interest, low vocabulary material. Many major newspapers are written for individuals with fifth and sixth grade reading skills, and they cover such diverse issues as sports, job opportunities, movies, television, and teen-age dating. Magazines tend to be more specialized as they seek to attract special interests readership. The magazines cover such areas as auto mechanics, motorcycle performance, teen-age fashions, food preparation, and family life. Many of these magazines also write and edit their stories so that those with poor reading skills will not be excluded. The difficulty in using the popular press is that frequently youths find them interesting and generally readable, and then become resistant to reading more challenging formal text material. As a result, when possible, the use of the popular press should be used to promote reading, but should not become the sole source of reading.

Rework Material

Rework material so that it is presented at the student's performance level:

1. As an example, the following sentence could be edited to be more easily read: The youth, only 14 years old, had demonstrated a unique and unparalleled capacity to grasp ideas and transform them into operational community projects. Revised, the material could read: The 14-year-old boy was smart. He could learn new ideas and this impressed some older people. The older people were also impressed by his ability to use the idea for a project.
2. When the student cannot understand a noun, match a picture of the object with the noun that describes the object. As an example: a picture of a racing car next to the word "racer."
3. When a student cannot understand a verb, pair the verb with a picture that illustrates the action, such as pairing the word "sprint" with a picture of a person sprinting.

4. Tape the story the student is expected to read. Then let the student follow along in the book while listening to the tape. Upon completion of the taping, ask the student to reread the material into the tape recorder and then monitor the tape to determine the student's level of vocabulary, word attack skills, fluency, comprehension, error rate, and seeming comprehension.
5. Make sure the interest of the material is appropriate to the student's background, age, experience, and interest.
6. Some students will always have difficulty with reading. Some authors have suggested that students who cannot effectively learn to read visually should be treated as though they were functionally blind. This means the school would educate them as though they were blind, using talking books, and/or enlisting a teacher of Braille who can provide the student Braille instruction (Quisenberry, Miller, Johnson, & Sachs, 1981).

READING

Reading is an important learning and social skill. It is needed to obtain a driver's license, complete a job application, discover information, communicate by letter, or read common street signs, a movie marquee, or a restaurant's menu. Poor reading is a prime obstacle to adolescents seeking to surmount the barrier to school and job success. The following are varying approaches to assist youths in overcoming their reading difficulties. The difficulties include:

- poor sound articulation,

- poor visual/auditory association,

- poor visual and/or auditory memory,

- poor word recognition,

- poor comprehension of details,

- poor comprehension of underlying themes,

- poor motivation.

Visual, Auditory, Kinesthetic, Tactile (VAKT) Method: The Grace Fernald and Helen Keller method enables the teacher to offer the student an individual program. One basic supposition of the program is that the handicapped student's initial learning can best be promoted through a sensory-motor approach. The phases of the approach are:

1. Determining the level the student is at in sensory-motor skills and having them select words they would like to learn.
2. Motivating manuscript writing and reading of material developed for the student.
3. Recognizing the printed material that replicates the student's written material, and that the student has demonstrated an ability to read.
4. Learning to recognize new words based on old words the student has already learned.

Phase One

The student selects a word he or she wants to learn. The word is written for the student with chalk on a blackboard, or on a blackboard-sized easel. The student traces the word with his or her eyes closed, using his or her finger, and says each part of the word as it is traced. Once this process has been mastered, he or she repeats the process with eyes open. Following this process, the word is written on rough-textured paper. During this process the following behaviors should be promoted: (1) continuous finger contact, (2) writing the word from memory, (3) writing the word as a unit, and (4) either subvocally or vocally saying each syllable of the word. The pupil is allowed as much time as necessary for the process. The word (or words) is incorporated into a story that the student helps prepare. Then the student traces and reads the story. Next, the story is typed, and the student reads the printed story. The new word (or words) that has been learned is placed into a word-file box. The word box is arranged alphabetically. The use of the word box enables personnel to (1) teach basic study and library skills simultaneously, (2) review words already learned, and (3) allow the student to review the structural and phonic relationship among words.

Phase Two

The student has progressed beyond tracing and has developed to the stage in which words can be learned by looking at them, then saying the words, and, finally, writing the words without visual or auditory aids. The writing and reading process is expected to become easier and the stories can become longer and more challenging. Then the student is encouraged to write and read on subjects that interest him or her. The writing of all words during this phase is expected to result from memory, rather than from tracing activities. The memory can be triggered by visual or auditory signals. All material must be kept at a challenging level without promoting failure and frustration. Students are motivated when reading and writing challenging material, rather than being faced with material that appears inappropriate and unrelated to their interests.

Phase Three

The student looks at the word and is able to reproduce the word without vocalizing, tracing, or copying. In this phase, books are presented. The student is encouraged to read from formal text and is told the words he or she does not know by the teacher. When confronted with words he or she does not know, the teacher repeats the word. The student is then expected to say the word three times and then write it from memory. When the student is through reading a section, the new and difficult words are reviewed and the words are then included in the word-file box. All of the new and difficult words are included in the word box and regularly reviewed to determine the student's level of word mastery.

Phase Four

The fourth stage begins when the student can analyze new words from their resemblance to established words. The student is encouraged to work independently and not seek external assistance from peers, parents, or siblings. The school promotes reading of material that is of career or recreational value (Meyers & Hammill, 1976).

The majority of youths do not require assistance at the phase one and two levels of instruction, yet the principles of involving all primary and secondary sensory-learning systems are necessary for some handicapped students. Individuals without histories of learning disabilities exhibit their sensory-learning system each day. Many individuals, when asked to spell a word, cannot recite the proper spelling, but must resort to writing out the word and then visually judging whether the word is properly spelled. Such individuals have learned from the sensory-motor process of copying and visually confirming the process. Many handicapped youths taught through traditional phonics and "Look and Say" continue to have difficulty until taught through the more time-consuming VAKT methods.

Linguistic Reading

Linguistics is a specific approach toward reading developed by Fry (1972). It employs ingredients of both the phonemic approach—knowing basic sounds relative to consonants, vowels, letter pairing, and the look-say approach—and visually decoding whole words by learning the word's name. The position of the reading strategy is that the phonemic approach is too inconsistent in the various sound patterns ("ou" having various pronunciations—*ou*t, *ou*ght, r*ou*gh) and the whole word approach does not provide the individual tools for analysis and deciphering of words the student is unfamiliar with. The linguistic approach generally uses a developmental word bank, and begins with a consistent sound structure, like "a," "t," and "at." From "at," a variety of consonants can be paired to create words, such as "fat," "cat," "mat," and "rat." As the student develops longer consistent sound structures, more challenging words can be added to his or her reading vocabulary—"sought," "brought," "fought," and "wrought." From the beginning of this reading strategy, the words are formed into stories. The immediate development of stories promotes interest on the part of the student and removes the process of learning to read from the unsalvageable scrap pile of pure drill and frustration with already known words.

MATHEMATICS

Although much of the special and general education literature addresses language-oriented instruction, the learning of mathematics skills is an important career development and personal survival tool. It is a process and skill required in daily living, and youths without such skills are limited in their career choices. Alley and Deshler (1979) have delineated areas that most students must possess competency in to survive in our contemporary society. The areas include:

- the ability to use measuring devices to determine the size or volume of an object or series of objects
- computational skills to determine the size or volume of objects that are not sequential
- the relationship of objects, such as equivalent, parallel, similar, dissimilar, and nonequivalent
- the ability to estimate or approximate size or volume through a systematic mathematical process
- the ability to determine whether sufficient information exists to determine whether a problem can be solved
- the ability to read and analyze graphic representations of basic number facts, such as graphs or maps
- the use of basic logic to analyze and solve problems
- the use of geometric concepts such as square feet and volume to determine, again, size and quantity

The major goal when teaching mathematics skills is to help students develop some consistent methods for solving number-related problems that are encountered in everyday consumer life and in the pursuit of careers. It is essential that when a teacher presents new activities to an academically handicapped student, he or she first starts with three-dimensional objects. For example, when using the basic addition process, use three-dimensional objects first, i.e., sets of colored sticks, basic measuring devices, or other devices, and only then move toward the pictorial representation of the product or process being addressed in the mathematics problem. Following the discussion of the interface between the objects and the illustrations, numerical concepts can be introduced. This procedure suggests that principles applicable to the teaching of reading are also applicable to the teaching of mathematics, and a carefully and tightly sequenced series of steps can be employed that facilitate the process. This process is applicable whether the instruction involves addition, subtraction, multiplication, division, or more analytic processes.

Multiplication and division appear to require an advanced level of rote memory, two processes difficult for handicapped students to master. School personnel must consider the problems of teaching mathematics when integrating the handicapped student into regular mathematics classes and vocational settings if appropriate placement is to be successful. Personnel should attempt to use practical examples in promoting the use of all mathematics processes. Requiring students to verbalize and explain problem-solving operations can enhance the learning process. It is important that students learn rote computational skills and how and when to apply these skills to practical situations. Where students have difficulty with the memorization of basic mathematical equations, teachers can prevent frustration and failure by promoting the use of either the electronic hand calculator or a mathematics chart. The relatively low cost and accessibility of the calculator makes its use both useful and advisable for those with severe learning problems.

New concepts should be presented singularly. The teaching of the concept should continue until the student has reached a predetermined level of mastery, or the teacher determines the continuance in teaching the concept exacerbates the learning experience. When such conditions arise, the teacher can either select a parallel activity that the student views as new and achievable, or the process can be set aside for a more appropriate occasion.

Addition

Arithmetic addition instructions help students develop some consistent methods for solving number-related problems that are encountered in life situations. The following steps are important to providing the youth with an understanding of the process and a recognition of the concepts:

1. Addition—forms the basis for arithmetic operations. First, addition should focus on the three-dimensional (adding one object or one number to another). This manipulative (three-dimensional materials) process can be used during the instruction of any of the other areas whether it be subtraction, multiplication, or division.

2. Once the student has learned the relationship of one object to another, the teacher can move to the pairing of objects to pictorial representations of those objects. This process demonstrates the interface between the actual and pictorial, and prepares the student to comprehend the interface between the pictorial and symbolic (numbers relating to distance, quantity, and time).
3. The pictorial representation is the bridge between the three-dimensional and the symbolic. The pictorial mediation serves the same purpose in mathematics as it does in reading—it helps the student to understand that the symbolic representation is a faster, more economical means of conveying information.
4. Additionally, the student needs to be able to identify the process through the recognition of the symbols that represent the mathematics process such as "+." Other symbols that the student needs to recognize are "−," "÷," "×," "=," "<," ">," "%," and "π."

Among the problems associated with the additive process are poor knowledge, additional sums, improper alignment columns, and the inability to carry numbers from columns right to left. Youths trained to think of numbers in sets of 5s, 10s, and 100s find it difficult to move into such sets of 12, 36, and 16. As a result, they have difficulty adding linear and liquid measures. To rectify this addition problem, school personnel should provide training in addition that prepares them to add, using various numerical sets and subsets.

Subtraction

Subtraction is the reverse process of addition. Just as "plus" (+) is the introductory term for addition, "minus" (−) is the introductory term for subtraction. Initial instruction should start in a three-dimensional manner with a gradual fading to pictorial and then to abstractions. The act of borrowing from one place value column to the next is difficult for academically handicapped students. Another difficulty related to the borrowing process is that many handicapped students fail to understand why the five and two cannot be reversed when subtracting 5 from 20. To bridge this disability, school personnel should demonstrate that by grouping and then regrouping the numbers in question, the lesser number can be revalued and the principles of subtraction can be sustained. Example, 5 from 20: By regrouping 20 into two 10s (20), and then transforming one set of 10s into a 10 1s column, the student will have one 10 set and 10 1s. It is then easy to subtract 5 from 10. This same principle applies to the subtraction of feet and inches, pounds and ounces, and minutes and hours; only the basic sets change.

20	2 tens and 0 ones	1 ten and 10 ones
− 5	− 5	− 5

These and other examples can help the student comprehend both the process and content of subtraction.

Multiplication and Division

Again, the teacher should use three-dimensional (concrete) and practical examples in providing the student with understanding of the multiplication and division processes and how they should be employed in the pursuit of a career. Requiring students to verbalize and explain problem-solving operations enhances the student's understanding of the process. Learning can be promoted by continuous repetition and/or teaching the student how to use a calculator or a multiplication chart. The teacher needs to use the teaching time to explain and clarify what multiplication and division processes are and use examples of how the processes may be applied to shopping, building an object, or computing interest on borrowed money. In all cases, the use of three-dimensional objects and illustrations should be employed regularly in the instructional process.

Multiplication is faster and more efficient than the addition process. For illustrative purposes, it is faster and easier to multiply one number times another (example 5 times 7) than it is to first write five seven times and then add the numbers. There are similarities between multiplication and addition. Carrying from one place to another in multiplication is much the same as in addition. Reversibility is another similarity between multiplication and addition. In the process of addition or multiplication the final answer will be correct whether the student adds or multiplies the numbers left to right, right to left, top to bottom, or bottom to top.

$$3 + 5 = 8 \text{ or } 5 + 3 = 8 \qquad 3 \times 5 = 15 \text{ or } 5 \times 3 = 15$$

Many students' problems are produced by inaccurate alignment of columns and rows, inaccurate addition of columns, and failure to double check their multiplication facts.

Division being the reverse of the multiplication process requires many of the skills and manipulations learned in multiplication. In division, the student is asked to calculate the number of times a number can be contained in another number. An example would be "How many 5s are in 25, or $5\overline{\smash{\big)}25}$, or $25 \div 5$." In each case, the response should be 5 is contained in 25 five (5) times. Beyond this point many youths have difficulty reversing the right to left progression of the general mathematics process, as is found in addition, subtraction, and multiplication. In each of the processes, the student begins at the right of the problem and moves to the left.

Additive process	Subtractive process
45	45
+ 23	− 23

In long division the process is left to right.

$$
\begin{array}{r}
40 \\
25\overline{)1000} \\
100 \\
\hline
00 \\
\underline{00}
\end{array}
$$

Division process

Many students who do not have problems with addition and multiplication have difficulty with subtraction and division. Some investigators have suggested this is psychologically related and is comparable to the reluctance of nonmathematically handicapped persons who do not like subtracting from their checking account as they write checks. This problem will need to be addressed on an individual case basis. The use of good teaching practices and appropriate behavior management can be prime ingredients in this remedial process.

Another problem common to student errors in multiplication and division is the inaccurate use of the decimal point. In multiplication, the simple process of counting the total place value of the decimal in the multiplication and transferring it to the product needs to be reinforced.

$$
\begin{array}{r}
.4 \text{ multiplicand} \\
\underline{.4} \text{ multiplicand} \\
.16 \text{ product}
\end{array}
$$

In the above problem, the two multiplicands have a total of two place values. The student simply counts from right to left and places the decimal after the second number. In division, the process involves the moving of the decimal value from the divisor to the dividend. This process also needs to be reinforced through drill and verbalization of the process. The use of fraction blocks can be used to demonstrate the value of numbers to the right of the decimal point and why, when adding such numbers, the value is altered.

$$
.4.\overline{)25.5.}
$$

Understanding of the basic processes related to addition, subtraction, division, and multiplication will enable students to employ the processes related to percentages, fractions, geometry, and other more abstract mathematical processes. Once the students can demonstrate mastery over the basic process, they are limited only by their ability to handle increasingly abstract terms, formulas, and processes. Lerner (1976) and Goodstein and Kahn (1973) have suggested that mathematics is language, just as are English, Spanish, or Russian. Linville (1969) further suggested that problems in vocabulary and syntax are correlated with problems in mathematics. These findings suggest that the promotion of verbalization and subverbalization of the problems and how they are to be computed will facilitate learning and mastery. For this reason, time and effort need to be expended on story problems (reasoning skills) in working daily with handicapped youths.

Reasoning Skills

Since many handicapped students have language-related problems, word (or reasoning) problems often present severe learning obstacles. In computation, the student is presented with the responsibilities to automatically either add, subtract, multiply, divide, or combine any of the processes. In word problems, the student can perform the computation process only after he or she has comprehended the written story and interpreted its directions. Thus, the problem's complexity is multiplied, and the response required of the student is significantly increased. As an example:

Samuel has $2.00. He used 30 cents to buy milk and 35 cents to buy a cookie. How much money does Samuel have now? While the student may be able to read and understand the words in the problem, the problem does not give obvious directions as to what operation should be performed to arrive at a solution. In this problem, the clue words are "has," "used," and "to buy." "Has" tells the amount Samuel started with. Thus, it is the amount that is to be added to or taken away from. "Used" and "to buy" indicate that money was spent. Therefore, subtraction is the process that should give the solution to the problem.

For many handicapped youths, reading is a difficult and frustrating task. This frustration often shrouds the ability of the student to comprehend problems that he or she might understand when the issue is verbally discussed. For students with severe reading disabilities, it is recommended that the teacher may: (1) read the problem to the student, (2) use a peer to read the problem, or (3) tape-record problems.

Another aid is for the teacher to formulate and ask questions about a given problem, thus encouraging the student to verbalize possible solutions. The student should also be encouraged to ask questions. This approach can assist the youth in learning how to handle the word problems, but it does not free the student from eventually learning to read and interpret word problems. Schools need to continue the process of teaching the basics of verbal and written language, even in the mathematics laboratories and vocational training centers. Repeated training in language and mathematics can promote their combined usage.

WRITTEN EXPRESSION

Handicapped youths have historically had difficulty with the process of written expression. Written expression in our society has lagged behind the other performance areas not only for the handicapped, but also for such populations as normal achieving youths and adults and for college students on the graduate and undergraduate levels. The process requires several skill areas to interface so that ideas can be formulated and written in an understandable manner. Among the skills the individual must possess are:

- the ability to receive and memorize information

- the ability to identify the general category information, along with the ability to shift the information to other appropriate categories or subsumptions

- the ability to relate existing information to newly received information

- the ability to organize all relevant information around a central theme

- the ability to present that information in written form on paper

Many individuals believe they have ideas that they would like to translate into written form but are reluctant to for a variety of reasons including: (1) poor spelling skills, (2) poor idea-organization skills, (3) poor written syntax, and/or (4) critical feedback from the teacher-critic. Teachers often appear to be harsher in critiquing the written composition of students than they may be when critiquing speech, mathematics, and/or reading. Comments about poor spelling, syntax, organization, and comprehension can be found on the papers of students from grade school to high school. The students' sometimes labored written effort is covered with criticism, and little is found that praises the effort or the ideas. As a result, students are reluctant to attempt an endeavor that they view as another negative, personally deflating experience. To promote written expression, the teacher needs to develop a procedure that initially focuses on the students' interests and is structured to promote success. Among some approaches designed to achieve this end are the following.

Language Experience

This process encourages a student or a group to develop a story or description about something that interests them. The teacher can use various types of prompts, such as pictures or objects, to stimulate discussion and recitation among the youths. As the students tell their story, the teacher or another individual writes the story down, using an overhead projector, large sheets of newsprint hung on a board, or the chalkboard itself. The student or students are then asked to copy the story. The students' story reflects their logic and interests. The students can be then judged on efforts that they have had an opportunity to modify and correct prior to the grading process.

Completion Process

This approach requires the teacher to begin initially a set of sentences that the student is expected to finish. The sentences can focus in on a single theme, such as "sensory awareness," "feelings," or "ecology." The teacher would begin the sentences, and the student would complete them as in:

I stood in the park
Seeing   _____
Hearing _____
Smiling _____
Tasting _____ and
Touching _____

The student's response to each of the sensory awarenesses can be one word or a series of words. At the completion of the task, the student has expressed some organized ideas for which he or she can be praised. During the writing process, the teacher needs to be available for assistance in spelling, syntax, vocabulary, and organization.

This approach involves the teacher developing a series of writing activities that promotes increasing independence of writing behavior, until eventually the teacher can offer up a theme and request that the student respond independently.

Another example of the completion process is one directed to a theme such as ecology:

The air used to be cleaner, but then civilization   _____

The forest used to be full of wild life, but then civilization   _____

It used to be that one could go outside and listen to just the birds and the wind, but then civilization   _____

For civilization to preserve the environment, it must   _____

The difference between the two illustrations is significant. The teacher needs to identify the rate and difficulty level of the writing task and to develop this process to match student performance abilities.

Daily School Record Book

Some students are unwilling to express thoughts about current events or their feelings. One approach, in this case, would be to have the student describe portions of his or her school day in a log. During the beginning stages, the student is not expected to develop long, elaborate discussions. For some students, a simple declarative sentence will suffice. As students continue the writing process, the expectations of length and quality of information could be increased. This approach not only promotes writing; it also encourage students to observe and monitor their daily school experiences. The importance of the log can be discussed in terms of the ongoing behavior management, effort, or part of skill development required in some career positions.

HANDWRITING

When an adolescent reaches the secondary school environment, his or her handwriting skills are relatively set. Some changes can be made, but many students have severe problems altering their writing skills at the secondary level. Yet, schools have continually sought to alter the adolescent's handwriting in the secondary school environment. For the youth with severe writing problems, one alternative is to teach him or her to type. Typing does not require the same motor control as handwriting, and the process of spelling, punctuation, and syntax can be integrated into the typing instruction. For some males, living in a more traditional environment, the perception of typing as a female activity could be discussed, and the stereotype could be shown to represent a myth. There are film examples of male journalists, novelists, and politicians typing, and thus, the sexism of the issue could be directly addressed.

SPOKEN LANGUAGE

While many handicapped adolescents are productive in spoken language, their delivery has been cited for its numerous variations from expected behavior (Alley & Deshler, 1979; Smith & Payne, 1980; Wiig & Semel, 1975). Among the behaviors cited as characteristic of inadequate and inappropriate oral production are:

- inability to employ formal and informal language in appropriate settings and under appropriate conditions
- inadequate vocabulary and inappropriate use of words
- failure to complete sentences during oral discussion

- inability to speak logically for more than a few minutes
- inability to shift speech to reflect change in tenor of the discussion
- inability to follow up on the previous speaker's statements and ideas
- poor speech cadence

Despite the fact that spoken language is an important academic and social tool, little research has been conducted in this area (Miller, 1981; Wiig & Semel, 1975). Increasing emphasis on the teaching of the secondary-aged student has compelled the development of instructional strategies to promote improved spoken production among youths. The approaches include the following imperatives:

- The student must have knowledge of the theme being discussed.
- The student should have an opportunity to organize his or her thoughts prior to speaking.
- When the student presents material and has made errors, overt corrections should not be made. Restatements of the material by the teacher and demonstrations of the corrected procedure compose the most viable approach.
- The student should discuss things that he or she has done in a sequential, logical manner.
- The teacher should provide a consistent model of appropriate, spoken language usage.

Appropriate, spoken language is particularly important to the youth in search of a career and the consequent work position. Personnel directors and job supervisors tend to form estimates of students' abilities as a result of their initial interaction with them. This phenomenon increases the importance that school personnel should place on training handicapped youths in oral language. Again, the discussion themes can flow from the reading and writing process. Many of the organizational and articulation skills necessary for good writing are also vital to speaking.

SUBJECT-BASED CONTENT

The discussion concerning the areas of concept development, reading, mathematics, and written expression and spoken language addresses the basic methodology related to the process of learning. Students enrolled in content area courses, such as history, geography, and English, must already possess the reading, mathematics, and language skills essential for survival in our society. Students having difficulty in content courses should be evaluated to determine the learning factors contributing to poor school performance. These factors, as has been noted, can be multiple and can include perception, abstract thinking, reading, and/or written language disabilities.

For school personnel to assist the handicapped youth successfully in the specialized environments of history, journalism, or drafting, they need to adapt existing curricula, materials, and procedures to interface with the handicapped student's learning impairment. To achieve the adaptive process, the content-oriented teachers need to employ procedures for instruction, using a variety of reading, mathematics, and other process area approaches.

The college and university training of content-oriented school personnel has not prepared them to understand the underlying processes related to reading, mathematics, and other academic areas. Most college and university preparation has focused on providing these personnel preparation in the organization and presentation of their content area. As a result, they have been unprepared to teach students with low performance skills effectively in the basic learning processes (Miller, Sachs, Phelps, Batsche, Erekson, Hoernecke, Wagner, Hasbargen, & Greenan, 1980). Despite the lack of training, inservice models employed by the University of Illinois, University of Nebraska, and Southern Illinois University at Carbondale have demonstrated that secondary school personnel can be trained to provide specialized services to norm-violating youths. Content-oriented personnel have demonstrated the instructional flexibility to use taped material, adapted materials, and newly developed materials in servicing the handicapped.

JOB TRAINING

Job training represents the primary activity whereby basic academic skills are integrated into functional life skills. At this level, rote instruction in the academic classroom comes alive, as it provides the tools by which the youth is able to engage in more interesting and rewarding activities. For example, reading skills, painfully acquired in a resource room, suddenly allow the youth to read a parts manual. Mathematics skills become functional in allowing the youth to work as a checkout clerk at a grocery store.

Unfortunately, it cannot be assumed that a youth has the basic academic skills that will allow him or her to compete in even the most basic occupation. Traditional approaches to remediating basic skill deficits in vocational placements have often resulted in returning the youth to the academic setting until prerequisite skills are developed. This practice has often resulted in the adolescent dropping out of school because of the lack of relevant instruction and the limited expectancy that he or she will gain even entry level skills for a vocational placement.

Integrated Basic-Skill Development

An alternative approach to recycling the adolescent in nonfunctional remedial classes is to integrate basic skill development (mathematics, reading, writing, social skills, etc.) with more interesting and functional occupational skill-training tactics. By pairing deficit basic skills with preferred occupational skill development experiences, relevance and functionality are ensured. The two basic processes involved in developing an integrated occupational skills-basic program are the occupational analysis and task analysis.

Occupational Analysis

This involves the identification of all of the basic and academic skills required to succeed on a job. These skills will become the objectives of the integrated program. Occupational analyses are conducted by: (1) determining the youth's career-vocational interests, (2) identifying specific jobs available in the community that match the youth's interests, (3) visiting (with the youth) establishments that include the identified jobs, (4) interviewing managers and employees to determine specific responsibilities associated with the jobs, and (5) constructing a checklist (see Exhibit 9-1) that enumerates the component skills associated with each job.

Once the occupational analysis is completed, the resulting checklist may be used to evaluate the youth's skill level against the identified responsibilities. A simulated work station may be established as described in Chapter 4 for this purpose. The result of this process is a *discrepancy analysis* that contrasts the skills that the youth currently possesses against those required for entry to the job. Based on the discrepancy analysis the youth and educator can determine that the job is inappropriate because of excessive entry-level task demands or can establish a sequence of activities designed to develop identified skill deficiencies. In this case, a criterion for job placement can be established. This criterion represents the minimum skill level the youth must possess before placement on the job may occur. The contingency contract described in Chapter 8 may be used to formalize this agreement. The sequential activities involved in an occupational analysis are as follows:

1. Assess career preferences.
2. Survey the youth's community to identify high preference jobs.
3. Accompany the youth to those jobs.
4. Collect data regarding responsibilities of those associated with the jobs. Construct a checklist of entry-level task demands.
5. Evaluate the youth's current skill level against the task demands.
6. Determine the discrepancy between the student's existing skills and the prerequisite skills.
7. Establish a curriculum of training activities or select an alternate job.

Exhibit 9-1 Occupational Analysis

Cleans, removes, and installs spark plugs.
Adjusts and bleeds brakes.
Replaces wheel cylinders.
Replaces master brake cylinder.
Inspects and flushes radiator.
Tests coolant temperature levels.
Removes the tires from a car.
Repairs tube or tubeless tires.
Installs new tires.
Balances tires.
Rotates tires.
Lubricates vehicles.
Replaces air cleaners.
Cleans or replaces gas filters.
Washes and waxes inside and outside of automobiles.
Sells auto accessories.
Replaces oil filters.
Checks oil, brake fluid, power steering fluid, and automatic transmission fluid.
Washes windshields, replaces windshield wiper blades.
Fills gas tanks, radiators, and window cleaning solvent.
Makes change for cash customers; checks authenticity of customer's
    identification.
Replaces distributor points.
Keeps daily records of sales, inventory changes.
Orders auto parts.
Opens and closes station on time (Mager & Beach, 1967).

Task Analysis

Once a contract is formalized between the youth and instructor, the general sequence of training activities can be delineated into task analyses. Each task analysis involves breaking down the specific job responsibilities into their component parts. The youth is then taught to complete the sequence of smaller steps. The size of the steps in the task analyses is a function of the learning characteristics of the youth. Exhibit 9-2 contrasts large steps designed for a mildly handicapped youth with small steps used with a moderately handicapped individual.

Basic skills in the occupational training sequence are included only when identified in a task analysis sequence. Thus, the relationship between academic objectives and occupational performance becomes direct and concrete. The task analysis of ordering auto parts in Exhibit 9-3 exemplifies the integration of basic academic skills through the task analysis sequence.

Exhibit 9-2 Task Analysis for Tire Changing

Mildly handicapped youth	*Moderately handicapped youth*
1. Apply parking brake.	1. Apply parking brake.
2. Remove hubcaps.	2. Insert tire iron end into crack between hubcap and wheel.
3. Loosen lug nuts.	3. Pry away hubcap.
4. Jack up car.	4. Place box end of tire iron on the first lug nut.
5. Remove lug nuts.	5. Rotate iron until loose.
6. Remove tire.	6. Repeat steps four and five until all lug nuts are loose.
7. Install new tire.	7. Locate placement for jack.
8. Replace lug nuts.	8. Place jack in the identified location.
9. Lower jack.	9. Insert tire iron end into jack lever.
10. Tighten lug nuts.	10. Move tire iron up and down, raising the car until the tire is off the ground.
11. Replace hubcaps.	11. Remove each of the lug nuts by hand.
	12. Remove tire by placing hand on opposite ends of the tire and pulling out.
	13. Insert new tire by aligning lug holes with lugs and pushing in.

Exhibit 9-3 Task Analysis

Task Analysis	*Basic Skill Requirement*
1. Identify understocked or un-stocked items.	Subtraction (number present from number required)
2. Record appropriate part numbers on the order form.	Identification and writing of numbers
3. Locate price from parts catalog and record on appropriate column on the form.	Reading and reference book usage
4. Compute subtotal for the cost of the order.	Addition
5. Determine tax.	Multiplication by a decimal
6. Determine total.	Addition
7. Write address of station on order form.	Writing

CONCLUSION

The instructional process functionally needs to represent the interests and career goals of the handicapped adolescent, and the goals established for the adolescent should reflect the school and student's best estimate of his or her career options. The process of preparing the adolescent requires the overt acknowledgment by all school personnel that the interface between the various personnel is vital to the instruction of a youth and the efficacy of the program. Until recently, regular content instructional personnel have minimized their implied and expressed responsibility toward the handicapped adolescent, and have ignored the efforts of special education personnel. With passage of state and federal legislation, the instructional and program responsibilities of the content-oriented teacher have been enlarged, as has been the role of ancillary support personnel. The barriers erected by various segments of the school personnel are clearly expected to be removed, according to state and federal mandates, and judicial decisions.

Irrespective of the personnel serving the handicapped youth, an important imperative must be accepted: "The youth shall learn at least one new thing each day." Frequently, the handicapped youth has exited the school without being able to claim that he or she had learned anything during his or her school days, whether the areas dealt with the learning process or the content. Programs developed to reflect student interests and instruction designed to facilitate career development are likely to stimulate an increased commitment by the student to explore and adopt portions of the career preparation process.

The academic instruction should not be perceived as separate from the behavior management aspects of the student's Individual Educational Program. A frequent lament of existing school personnel has been their inability to establish contingencies that promote increased instructional attention. Conversely, others have observed that the ability to maintain attention is based on the capacity of the school to provide instruction that is meaningful and is paced to challenge rather than to frustrate or bore the youth. Either perception of the instructional process and/or the problems inherent in the process requires school personnel to employ an integrated strategy involving instruction and management.

REFERENCES

Alley, G., & Deshler, D. *Teaching the learning disabled adolescent: Strategies and methods.* Denver: Love Publishing Co., 1979.

Ausubel, D. P. *School learning: An introduction to education psychology.* New York: Holt, Rinehart & Winston, 1969.

Brolin, D. E., & Kokaska, C. J. *Career education for handicapped children and youths.* Columbus, Ohio: Charles E. Merrill Publishing Co., 1979.

Fraenkel, J. R. *Helping students think and value: Strategies for teaching the social studies.* Englewood Cliffs, N.J.: Prentice-Hall, 1973.

Frostig, M. *Education for dignity.* New York: Grune & Stratton, 1976.

Frostig, M., & Maslow, P. *Learning problems in the classroom.* New York: Grune & Stratton, 1973.

Fry, E. *Reading instruction for classroom and clinic.* New York: McGraw-Hill, 1972.

Goodstein, H. A., & Kahn, H. *A brief inquiry into the pattern of achievement among children with learning disabilities.* Unpublished manuscript, University of Connecticut, Storrs, Conn., 1973.

Guilford, J. P. *The nature of human intelligence.* New York: McGraw-Hill, 1967.

Hallahan, D. P., & Kauffman, J. M. *Teaching children with learning disabilities: Personal perspectives.* Columbus, Ohio: Charles E. Merrill Publishing Co., 1976.

Harris, A. J., & Sipay, E. R. *How to increase reading ability* (6th ed.). New York: David McKay, 1975.

Hersen, N., & Barlow, D. H. Single case experimental designs (Reprinted, 1978). Elmsford, N.Y.: Pergamon Press.

Joiner, L., Sedlak, R., Silverstein, B., & Vensel, G. J. Micro-computers—An available technology for special education. *Journal of Special Education Technology,* 1980, *3*(2), 37-42.

Jones, R. L. The hierarchical structure of attitudes toward the exceptional. *Exceptional Children,* 1974, *40*, 430-435.

Lerner, J. W. *Theories, diagnosis, teaching strategies: Children with learning disabilities.* Boston: Houghton Mifflin, 1976.

Linville, W. J. *The effects of syntax and vocabulary upon the difficulty of verbal arithmetic problems with fourth grade students.* Unpublished doctoral dissertation, Indiana University, Bloomington, Ind., 1969.

Mager, R. F., & Beach, K. M. *Developing vocational instruction.* Belmont, Calif.: Fearon Publishers, 1967.

Maslow, A. H. Toward a humanistic biology. *American Psychologist,* 1969, *24*(8), 724-725.

Meyers, P. J., & Hammill, D. D. *Methods for learning disorders.* New York: John Wiley & Sons, 1976.

Miller, S. R. Career education. In D. A. Sabatino & A. J. Mauser (Eds.), *Educating norm-violating and chronic disruptive secondary school-aged youth* (Vol. 2). Boston: Allyn & Bacon, 1978.

Miller, S. R. Behavioral disorders. *Journal of the Council for Children with Behavioral Disorders,* May 1981, *6*(3), 175-189.

Miller, S. R., Sachs, J. J., Phelps, L. A., Batsche, C., Erekson, T., Hoernecke, P., Wagner, R., Hasbargen, A., & Greenan, J. *Career/vocational education: Personal needs for secondary-aged handicapped clientele in Illinois.* Unpublished manuscript, 1980.

Noar, G. *Individualized instruction for the mentally retarded.* Glen Ridge, N.J.: Exceptional Press, 1974.

Phelps, A. L., & Lutz, R. J. *Career exploration and preparation for the special needs learner.* Boston: Allyn & Bacon, 1977.

Quisenberry, N., Miller, S. R., Johnson, T., & Sachs, J. J. *Classroom instruction and behavior management.* Unpublished manuscript, 1981.

Sabatino, D. A. *Neglect and delinquent children.* EDC Report, Wilkes-Barre, Pa.: Wilkes College, 1974.

Schloss, P. J., & Miller, S. R. The effects of the label "institutionalized" vs. "regular school student" on teacher expectations. *Exceptional Children,* in press.

Smith, E. H., Guice, B. M., & Cheek, M. C. Informal reading inventories for the content areas: Science and mathematics. *Elementary English,* May 1972, *49,* 659-666.

Smith, J. E., & Payne, S. S. *Teaching exceptional adolescents.* Columbus, Ohio: Charles E. Merrill Publishing Co., 1980.

Spache, G. D. A new readability formula for primary-grade reading materials. *Elementary School Journal,* 1953, *53,* 410-413.

Sulzer-Azaroff, B., & Mayer, G. R. *Applying behavior-analysis procedures with children and youth.* New York: Holt, Rinehart & Winston, 1977.

Wiig, E. H., & Semel, E. M. Productive language abilities in learning disabled adolescents. *Journal of Learning Disabilities,* 1975, *8*(9), 578-586.

Chapter 10

A Futures Orientation to Career-Vocational Education for Handicapped Adolescents

Consistent with recent writings (Gardner, 1977; Kauffman, 1977; Miller, 1978; Sabatino & Schloss, 1981), the preceding chapters have emphasized the integration of psychoeducational strategies with more empirically based behavioral approaches. In doing so, the chapters provide an objective and empirical approach to individual program development, implementation, and evaluation. The classification and curriculum-building procedures discussed in Chapter 3 seek to provide an empirical loop from the description of learner characteristics to program development and evaluation. The assessment strategies discussed in Chapter 6 facilitate this process by providing data from which reliable and valid descriptions of learner characteristics and program-related behavior change can be made. Chapter 4, on career planning, and Chapter 7, on behavior management program analysis, provide information from which the goals and focus of the career-vocational program may be derived. Finally, Chapter 8, which discusses behavior management program approaches; Chapter 9, which details instructional methods; and this chapter, which describes service delivery options, provide the tools by which social, personal, academic, and vocational goals may be achieved.

The underlying theme of each of these chapters has been a futures outlook for the students for which career-vocational educational services are being provided. This philosophy demands that the career-vocational teacher look beyond the daily routine of providing didactic instruction to the handicapped youth. To be effective, the educator must project an instructional style that prepares the youth to be a productive member of the competitive work force upon leaving a formal educational setting.

FUTURES ORIENTATION TO CURRICULUM OBJECTIVES

A futures orientation for educators of handicapped adolescents implies that instructional efforts through assessment, classification, program design, program implementation, and program evaluation be directed toward the development of social, personal, academic, and vocational repertoires that prepare the youth to compete in postsecondary school environments. In effect, the educator seeks to predict future environments in which the adolescent is expected to reside. Once these environments are identified, the educator works cooperatively with the adolescent in establishing goals and educational experiences that will prepare the youth to meet the demands in these environments. The model depicted in Figures 10-1 and 10-2 identifies the relationship between future significant environments faced by a secondary level handicapped youth and the educational goals established by the career-vocational educator.

The emphasis in a futures orientation to curriculum design is not on a program sequence based on the needs of the "general handicapped population," but a sequence based on the needs of the individual youth. This view requires careful planning among the adolescent, teacher, parents, and others to identify future environments in which the adolescent will compete. Additionally, the futures orientation requires insight on the part of the teacher as to the precise skills necessary to survive in those settings. Establishing objectives in this manner assures that all relevant performance domains are identified and prioritized on the basis of the learner's needs. The identification and prioritization of objectives on this basis increase the likelihood that the full measure of instructional power is directed toward functional goals.

FUTURES ORIENTATION TO ASSESSMENT

The functional classification and assessment chapters emphasize the dynamic nature of the handicapped youth's learning and behavioral characteristics. The youth is viewed as an active and changing learner whose psychological features are influenced through each significant interaction with his or her environment. The futures orientation to assessment recognizes that data acquired through summative and formative evaluation procedures represent but a sample of behavior emitted at the time of assessment and under the environmental constraints of the assessment setting (Anastasi, 1976; Cronbach, 1970). As such, evaluative data are limited in that they tell us how the youth is currently functioning, not how the youth will function in the future. Numerous studies have demonstrated that psychosocial variables such as intelligence, personality, academic achievement, and overt behavior can be altered through systematic intervention approaches (Barber & Kagey, 1977; Hayden & Haring, 1976; Karnes, 1973; Karnes, Hodgins, & Teska, 1968; Sabatino, Miller, & Schmidt, in press).

Career-vocational educators concerned for the future of their students recognize the assessment is useful in that it determines: (1) the instructional needs of the youth, (2) instructional strategies most appropriate to the youth's learning style, and (3) the extent to which the youth has benefited from an instructional sequence.

Figure 10-1 Futures Orientation Model

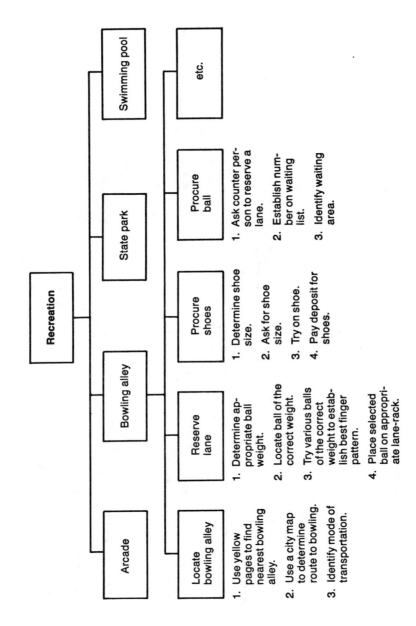

Figure 10-2 Futures Orientation Model-II

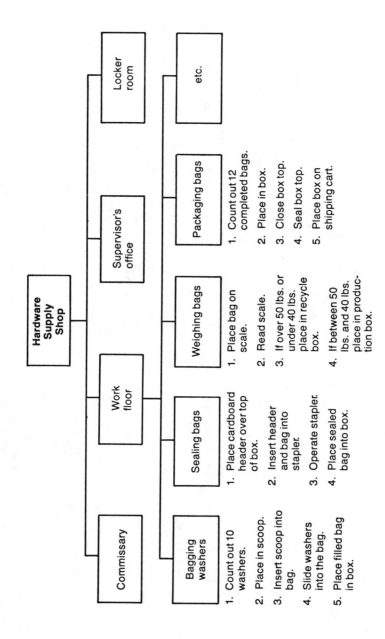

Aside from generating a general estimation of probable future environments, the assessment process should not limit the teacher's or student's expectations for movement into a range of competitive future environments.

Karan (1978) has argued that excluding handicapped individuals from services because of poor performance on standardized vocational and psychological assessment instruments is unwarranted in view of research demonstrating that even the severely handicapped perform well after training and acquire skills generally considered beyond their capabilities (Bellamy & Snyder, 1976; Gold, 1972; Karan, Esner, & Endres, 1974; Wehman, Renzaglia, Schutz, & Karan, 1976). Supporting these data, it has been demonstrated that the severely and nonseverely handicapped are equally likely to succeed once accepted for vocational rehabilitation services (Scheinkman, Andrew, Currie, Dunn, & Menz, 1975).

Though seldom employed (Karan, 1976), the Rehabilitation Act of 1973 makes available a futures orientation assessment option. The approach is referred to in the law as extended evaluation. The regulation provides for an 18-month trial period prior to making an eligibility decision for vocational rehabilitation services. Extended evaluation is described in the act as follows:

> (i) The provisions of vocational rehabilitation services to any individual for a total period not in excess of eighteen months for the purpose of determining whether such individual is a handicapped individual, a handicapped individual for whom a vocational goal is not possible or feasible, or neither such individual; and (ii) an assessment, at least once in every ninety-day period during which such services are provided, of the results of the provision of such services to an individual to ascertain whether any of the determinations described in subclause (i) may be made. (Rehabilitation Act of 1973, p. 5)

FUTURES ORIENTATION TO BEHAVIOR MANAGEMENT

The behavior management program analysis and program approaches chapters highlight the importance of planning and implementing behavior change programs that have a lasting impact on the youth's development. Program design features that influence the futures orientation are: (1) the target behaviors of the program, and (2) the specific methodology involved in the program. Programs with a futures orientation seek to develop social-personal behaviors that will assist the youth to work competitively and to live independently as an adult.

Target behaviors, as well as curriculum objectives, should be relevant to the settings in which the youth is expected to compete after graduation. While maintaining prosocial behavior in the classroom setting is a reasonable first objective, it cannot be the ultimate goal of the futures orientation behavior management program. Research has emphasized the transient and situation-specific nature of many youths' behavior disorders (Kauffman, 1981). Conduct problems evident in one setting may not be evident in other settings. Similarly, social-personal deficits existing at one age may not exist at a later age (Griffiths, 1952; Robins, 1972; Thomas, Chess, & Birch, 1968). Thus, the objectives of intervention programs must be selected only after considering the extent to which program outcomes will have a lasting effect on the youth's social-personal development across relevant leisure, vocational, and residential settings.

Similarly, research has demonstrated that poorly designed intervention approaches may have an immediate and dramatic effect, yet fail to result in a long-lasting and generalized influence on the youth's behavior (Pendergrass, 1972). This is especially evident in programs that involve the isolated use of aversive consequences without differential reinforcement procedures (Gardner, 1977). A futures orientation to behavior management emphasizes the application of social learning principles that have been demonstrated to produce durable and generalizable treatment effects. In general, these are tactics that encourage the youth to approach events that are associated with success and reward as opposed to tactics that result in the avoidance of failure and punishment.

FUTURES ORIENTATION TO INSTRUCTIONAL MATERIALS AND ACTIVITIES

The methods chapter has argued for the restricted use of traditional instructional materials in the career-vocational process for secondary level handicapped youth. As an alternative, the chapter suggests the adoption of functional materials and activities. Functional materials and activities are those that produce naturally satisfying consequences for the adolescent. Nonfunctional materials and activities, by contrast, have little natural incentive value for the youth. Functional reading materials for an adolescent may include a magazine, newspaper, driver education handbook, shop manual, etc. Involvement with each of these materials may be associated with positive events in the youth's environment. Traditional low interest reading series, on the other hand, do little to make reading naturally satisfying to the handicapped youth.

Vocational activities that involve the assembly and disassembly of production units, or routine activities that are performed only for the sake of acquiring or practicing a skill, are equally dysfunctional. Disassembling a production unit is hardly a naturally satisfying consequence of the assembly process, and there are few natural incentives associated with sweeping a floor for the sake of perfecting sweeping skills. As a result, these activities are not likely to be approached with enthusiasm by the handicapped youth. Conversely, assembling a production unit for the sake of marketing it for profit may be a highly satisfying activity. Similarly, sweeping the shop so that ambient dust does not blemish a varnish job is naturally rewarding. The adolescent exposed to the latter activities will be more likely to practice these skills in future experiences because he or she is aware not only of the "how," but also the "why" of performance (Schloss, 1978).

FUTURES ORIENTATION TO INSTRUCTIONAL TECHNOLOGY

Recent research has suggested a variety of instructional procedures that increase the probability that acquired skills will be maintained by handicapped youths over time and generalize across settings (Drew & Espeseth, 1968; Kazdin, 1980; Wehman, Abramson, & Norman, 1977). The adoption of these procedures is highly consistent with the futures orientation to career-vocational education for handicapped youths presented here. In view of research data suggesting that (1) handicapped youths do not maintain and generalize academic and behavioral gains to the same extent that nonhandicapped youths do (Fitzgerald, 1968; Gardner, 1977; Robinson & Robinson, 1976), and that (2) handicapped youths are more likely to have a variety of employment experiences prior to finding a relatively permanent job (Kennedy, 1966; Kidd, 1970), it is critical that career-vocational programs incorporate instructional technology that increases the likelihood that generalization and maintenance of educational gains will occur. Specific instructional suggestions are described in the following sections.

Developing Skills

Varying stimulus conditions is one of the most frequently used methods for programming generalization. It is also one of the most effective and logical of the strategies that can be applied in vocational settings (Wehman et al., 1977). The purpose of this technique is to expand the range of conditions in which the youth is able to apply the skill. This is an important goal since vocational success requires that a person use appropriate behaviors across occupational conditions. For example, a painter must work equally methodically regardless of the color of the paint, texture of the surface, size of the room, day of the week, proximity of the supervisor, etc.

Instructional conditions may be varied by changing the work supervisor, aspects of the task performed, or the working conditions while the basic skill requirement remains constant. Workshop supervisors may alter such conditions as task components, supervisors, proximity of coworkers, and general work conditions. Conditions should be changed in step-wise fashion once the skill is demonstrated under a stable set of conditions. For example, when production rate begins to approach a goal, supervisors may be changed. Following increased progress, a friendly coworker may be stationed next to the client. Finally, the complexity of the task may be changed. Similarly, once youths have demonstrated appropriate skills across conditions in an entry level placement, they may be moved to a dissimilar job. Skills identified in the first setting common to the second would then be monitored to assess generalization. Once the behaviors generalized, a third placement could be considered.

Varying instructional conditions may also be used to facilitate vocational adjustment in job-seeking activities. Adolescents may be taught to complete a specific job application form with reasonable success. However, a problem may be encountered when the client is required to complete a different form, or in an anxiety-producing situation such as the potential employer's office. The youth must be taught that the format of most application forms varies, but the content is generally uniform. Also, the setting in which the form is completed is irrelevant to the information provided on the form. Training tasks should include a wide variety of forms that may be completed in potentially anxiety-producing settings (e.g., in a potential work supervisor's office preceding a transfer from entry level to a second job placement).

Also, the youth must be taught that appropriate responses and social behaviors remain the same regardless of specific factors involved in interview situations. To meet this end, practice interviews should be conducted in a variety of settings with "employers" utilizing different interview styles (e.g., directive, reflective).

Using Natural Reinforcers and Fading Contrived Incentives

The gradual replacement of artificial reinforcers by naturally occurring reinforcers is an essential element in educational programs seeking to produce long-lasting and generalized effects. Career-vocational educators must recognize that, with the exception of pay, incentives in entry-level jobs are generally unpredictable, if present at all. Behaviors maintained solely through systematic reinforcers in educational settings are certain to diminish as the youth enters applied settings in which the delivery of incentives is erratic at best.

The salary one earns for working is probably the most predictable and direct of all naturally occurring consequents. Therefore, vocational trainers may do well to rely on incentives that can be converted to a biweekly paycheck. A primary example is the use of money as a consequence for the performance. Initially, money may be earned on a daily basis. As performance becomes stable, the delivery of money may be gradually delayed until it is earned on a biweekly basis.

Developing Self-Management Skills

Career-vocational programs for handicapped adolescents should enhance the individual's ability to control his or her immediate environment. Self-management programs are consistent with this goal since self-management places the responsibility for monitoring and rewarding behavior in the hands of the youth. Teaching a youth effective self-management procedures will greatly improve the generalization of appropriate work behaviors to competitive employment. Self-management procedures are effective only if the youth is motivated to monitor behavior and apply contingencies diligently. Extrinsic reinforcers have been demonstrated to be effective in motivating individuals for extended periods of time (Bricker, Morgan, & Grobowski, 1972). However, vocational programs should endeavor to promote the internalization of reward systems. Therefore, systematic rewards used to motivate self-management practices must be faded as intrinsic reinforcers are developed. A systematic approach to self-management in the vocational setting is presented in Chapter 8.

Working with Relatives and Peers

Successful career vocational training allows a youth to progress from dependence to independence through most aspects of life. The wage-earning adolescent or adult has the ability to make major decisions about his or her lifestyle not made by those relying on others for housing, food, transportation, etc. This fact is especially critical since rewards for work (e.g., money) give a person the ability to make decisions about his or her own lifestyle. It is clear that success in competitive employment is enhanced by the desire to be independent. This has special significance for the youth living at home. If money is to be a strong natural reinforcer, the youth must have the desire and need to develop independent behavior through its use. This suggests that as the adolescent's earning potential increases, support from significant others should be reduced. Parents should be encouraged to structure the home environment to support a level of independence consistent with the person's potential. The adolescent's work, and the money it provides, will have a stronger influence on his or her life as he or she becomes more independent. This association between work and independence will provide a strong natural incentive for adaptive work behavior in the future.

FUTURES ORIENTATION TO SERVICE DELIVERY SYSTEMS

The demands of the future for handicapped youths can be addressed most directly through the availability of a comprehensive longitudinal service delivery network. The needs and challenges to be addressed by future service delivery systems are summarized in a position statement released by the U.S. Office of Education appearing in the *Federal Register* (September 25, 1978). The statement emphasizes that a comprehensive vocational education suited to individual needs will be made available to every handicapped person. Key components included in a comprehensive vocational education are described as: (1) cooperative relationships between educational and employment sectors to facilitate the transition from school to work, (2) programs and services to develop basic skills and career decision-making skills, (3) appropriate sequential career development instruction, (4) elimination of attitudinal and environmental barriers, and (5) assistance to employers in meeting their affirmative action goals for employment of the handicapped.

A major problem in existing service delivery systems involves the preparation of educators to work with handicapped youths entering career-vocational programs. In a 1977 survey of 113 teacher education programs, Brock (1977) found that 25 schools (22.5 percent) reported existing programs to train vocational-special education personnel. The General Accounting Office (1974) reviewed the inservice training received by vocational educators and found that over 80 percent had received no information and training regarding the handicapped students. While some secondary inservice and preservice training programs have been in existence for several years, many have not realized substantial enrollments until recently (1977-1978). To provide inservice education to the nearly one million educators (teachers, administrators, and counselors) will require substantial time and resources. Efforts to establish and improve teacher-training programs designed for the diverse audiences involved in career programming are needed. The training must focus not only on the delivery of services, academic instruction, assessment, and behavior management, but also on effective strategies for community-based collaboration and cooperation among and within these groups.

CONCLUSION

It should be clear that the futures orientation to career and vocational education for handicapped learners is as much a statement of philosophy as technology. Philosophically, the educational process from admission into the program to successful termination should be replete with activities and experiences that promote adaptation to future adult independent living settings. The educator must project beyond the daily routine of traditional classroom instruction, identifying goals, objectives, and instructional sequences that will serve to prepare the youth to be a productive member of the national work force. Educational objectives based on sequential expectations of nonhandicapped youths must be evaluated against the criteria of adaptability present in the youths' future environments. Those that are unessential to youths' adaptation may be deleted.

From a technological standpoint, a number of academically, vocationally, and socially enhancing instructional strategies have been presented that maximize the extent to which instructional gains will be maintained into adult life. The futures orientation emphasizes the use of procedures that elevate the likelihood that a youth's progress in school will transfer to nonacademic, adult independent living environments. While it is apparent that such strategies require more time, money, and preparation on the part of the teacher and school district, there is little doubt that the benefit a youth derives from the educational program is best measured by behavior changes that have a lasting impact on his or her adult life.

The focus of the future is on improving the quality and availability of vocational service delivery options from prevocational instruction to placement in the work force. The 1960s and 1970s have fostered a clear mandate for access and equality of opportunity. Efforts must be channeled toward evaluating, strengthening, and synchronizing longitudinal vocational services for the handicapped youth. To achieve this end, a number of objectives must be reached. These include:

- improving instructional technology available to handicapped youths

- improving efforts to evaluate programs and disseminate evaluative data

- broadening the awareness and knowledge of educators, parents, and employers regarding the employment capabilities of handicapped youths

- developing channels of communication and accountability through which efficient longitudinal services can be provided

REFERENCES

Anastasi, A. *Psychological testing* (4th ed.). New York: Macmillan, 1976.

Barber, R. M., & Kagey, J. R. Modification of school attendance for an elementary population. *Journal of Applied Behavioral Analysis, 1977, 10,* 41-48.

Bellamy, G. T., & Snyder, S. The trainee performance sample: Toward the prediction of habilitation cost for severely handicapped adults. *The American Association for the Education of the Severely/Profoundly Handicapped Review, 1976, 1,* 17-36.

Bricker, W. A., Morgan, D. C., & Grobowski, J. G. Development and maintenance of a behavior modification repertoire of college attendants through T.V. feedback. *American Journal of Mental Deficiency, 1972, 77,* 128-136.

Brock, R. J. *Preparing vocational and special education personnel to work with special needs students: State of the art,* 1977. Menomonie, Wis.: University of Wisconsin—Stout, 1977.

Cronbach, L. J. *Essentials of psychological testing* (3rd ed.). New York: Harper & Row, 1970.

Drew, C., & Espeseth, U. Transfer of training with the mentally retarded: A review. *Exceptional Children, 1968, 34,* 129-132.

Federal Register, P.L. 94-142, September 25, 1978, *42* (163). Washington, D.C.: Department of Health, Education and Welfare, Office of Education.

Fitzgerald, D. E. A generation follow-up of some former public school mentally handicapped students. *Dissertation Abstracts International,* 1968, *28a*(8), 2892.

Gardner, W. I. *Learning and behavior characteristics of exceptional children and youth: A humanistic behavioral approach.* Boston: Allyn & Bacon, 1977.

General Accounting Office. *What is the role of federal assistance for vocational education?* Washington, D.C.: Comptroller General of the United States, December 1974.

Gold, M. Stimulus factors in skill training of the retarded on a complex assembly task: Acquisition, transfer, and retention. *American Journal of Mental Deficiency*, 1972, *76,* 517-526.

Griffiths, W. *Behavior difficulties of children as perceived and judged by parents, teachers, and children themselves.* Minneapolis: University of Minnesota Press, 1952.

Hayden, A. H., & Haring, N. C. The acceleration and maintenance of developmental gains in Down's syndrome school-aged children. In *Proceedings of the International Association for the Scientific Study of Mental Deficiency Symposium*, August 1976, Washington, D.C. Baltimore: University Park Press, 1976.

Karan, O. C. Contemporary views on vocational evaluation practices with the mentally retarded. *Vocational Evaluation and Work Adjustment Bulletin,* 1976, *9,* 7-13.

Karan, O. C. The use of extended evaluation for mentally retarded clients. In O. C. Karan (Ed.), *Habitation practices with the severely developmentally disabled* (Vol. 2). Madison, Wis.: University of Wisconsin Rehabilitation Research and Training Center in Mental Retardation, 1978.

Karan, R., Esner, M., & Endres, R. Behavior modification in a sheltered workshop for severely retarded students. *American Journal of Mental Deficiency,* 1974, *79,* 338-347.

Karnes, M. B. Evaluation and implications of research with young handicapped and low income children. In J. C. Stanley (Ed.), *Compensatory education, ages 2-8: Recent studies of education intervention.* Baltimore: The Johns Hopkins University Press, 1973.

Karnes, M., Hodgins, A., & Teska, J. An evaluation of two pre-school programs for disadvantaged children: A traditional and a highly structured experimental pre-school program. *Exceptional Children,* 1968, *34,* 667-678.

Kauffman, J. M. *Characteristics of children's behavior disorders.* Columbus, Ohio: Charles E. Merrill Publishing Co., 1977.

Kauffman, J. M. *Characteristics of children's behavior disorders* (2nd ed.). Columbus, Ohio: Charles E. Merrill Publishing Co., 1981.

Kazdin, A. *Behavior modification in applied settings.* Homewood, Ill.: Dorsey Press, 1980.

Kennedy, R. S. A Connecticut community revisited: A study of the sound adjustment of a group of mentally deficient adults in 1948 and 1960. Hartford: Connecticut State Department of Health, Office of Mental Retardation, 1966.

Kidd, J. W. The "adultated" mentally retarded. *Education and Training of the Mentally Retarded,* 1970, *5*(2), 71-72.

Miller, S. R. Career education. In D. A. Sabatino and A. J. Mauser (Eds.), *Educating norm-violating and chronic disruptive secondary school-aged youth* (Vol. 2). Boston: Allyn & Bacon, 1978.

Pendergrass, V. E. Timeout from positive reinforcement following persistent high-rate behavior in retardates. *Journal of Applied Behavior Analysis,* 1972, *5,* 85-91.

Rehabilitation Act of 1973, PL 93-112. Washington, D.C.: U.S. Government Printing Office, 1973.

Robins, L. N. Follow-up studies of behavior disorders in children. In H. C. Quay and J. S. Werry (Eds.), *Psychopathological disorders of childhood.* New York: John Wiley and Sons, 1972.

Robinson, N. M., & Robinson, H. B. *The mentally retarded child.* New York: McGraw-Hill, 1976.

Sabatino, D. A., Miller, P. F., & Schmidt, C. R. Cognitive training: Can intelligence be altered? *Journal of Special Education,* in press.

Sabatino, D.A., & Schloss, P. J. Adolescent social-personal development: Theory and application. In D. A. Sabatino, C. Schmidt, & T. L. Miller (Eds.), *Learning disabilities: Systemizing teaching and service delivery.* Rockville, Md.: Aspen Systems, 1981.

Scheinkman, N., Andrew, J., Currie, L., Dunn, D., & Menz, F. The unsuccessful state vocational rehabilitation client: An analysis (Report Number 6). Menomonie, Wis.: University of Wisconsin—Stout, Research and Training Center, 1975.

Schloss, P. J. Programmatic and ecological influences on adaptive behavior in competitive employment. In O. C. Karan (Ed.). *Habitation practices with the severely developmentally disabled* (Vol. 2). Madison, Wis.: University of Wisconsin Rehabilitation Research and Training Center in Mental Retardation, 1978.

Thomas, A., Chess, S., & Birch, H. G. *Temperament and behavior disorders in children.* New York: New York University Press, 1968.

Wehman, P., Abramson, M., & Norman, C. Transfer of training in behavior modification programs: An evaluative review. *The Journal of Special Education,* 1977, *11,* 11-16.

Wehman, P., Renzaglia, A., Schutz, R., & Karan, O. Stimulating productivity in two profoundly retarded workers through mixed reinforcement contingencies. In O. C. Karan, P. Wehman, A. Renzaglia, & R. Schutz (Eds.), *Habilitation practices with the severely developmentally disabled* (Vol. 1). Madison, Wis.: University of Wisconsin—Madison, Research and Training Center in Mental Retardation, 1976, pp. 60-68.

Glossary

Academics—the learning content areas comprised of reading, language, mathematics, social studies, health studies, and science.

Achievement motivation—the study of factors that either promote or inhibit learning.

Achievement test—the measure of an individual's learning in specified areas of instruction.

Antecedent event—an event that precedes a target behavior and increases or decreases the probability of its occurrence.

Aptitude test—the measure of one or more areas related to an individual's ability to perform a variety of tasks in varying settings.

Associated characteristics—inferred or observed features of an individual that influence the probability of the occurrence of a target behavior.

Aversive event—an unpleasant stimulus that is likely to strengthen behavior that produces its removal or suppress behavior that results in its presentation.

Avoidance behavior—a behavior that increases in rate to postpone or avoid punishment.

Back-up reinforcer—any reinforcing event that may be exchanged for tokens.

Baseline—a measure of the target behavior under natural conditions. Collecting baseline data before and after intervention allows evaluation of the treatment.

Behavior rehearsal—practicing a low rate behavior under conditions naturally associated with the behavior.

Behavioral self-control—controlling one's own behavior by manipulating the antecedents and consequents of the behavior.

Career awareness—familiarization of youths with the career options available to them in various occupational areas.

Career education—a postschool preparation approach in which the students' program is based on their academic skills, vocational skills, and personal interests.

Career exploration—the actual process of determining whether careers youth have identified match up with their skills and interests after the youths have visited sites and experienced the various career environments and activities.

Career preparation—the actual training of a youth for a specified career.

Cognitive development and integration—the process of an individual's thought development and the application and use of thought in learning.

Comprehensive services—the ability of the school to provide all the services required to educate the youth appropriately.

Consequent event—an event that follows a target behavior and increases or decreases the probability of its occurrence.

Contingency contract—a written agreement that specifies consequences for meeting or failing to meet a predetermined performance criterion.

Continuous recording—an observational procedure in which the observer produces a complete description of all behaviors that occur in a specified time period.

Cooperative arrangements—collective efforts by more than one agency or organization to work jointly in providing or ensuring services for the youth.

Delivery of services—the process of placing students in one or more learning environments that conform to their skills and needs.

Differential reinforcement of low rates of behavior (DLR)—the reinforcement of responses emitted at successively lower rates.

Differential reinforcement of other behaviors (DRO)—the reinforcement of any behavior other than the excessive behavior.

Directive guidance—a procedure for individual and group counseling in which the teacher-counselor assumes the role of director of the process, establishing structure, providing feedback, and identifying behavioral deficiencies and strengths.

Duration recording—a measure of behavior strength that reports the amount of time during which a behavior occurred.

Event recording—a measure of behavior strength that reports the number of times a behavior occurred.

Extinction—the removal of positive consequents that maintain a behavior.

Fading antecedent conditions—gradually removing artificial conditions so that positive social behavior will be maintained by natural or internal uses.

Fading consequent conditions—gradually removing artificial consequent conditions so that positive social behavior will be maintained by natural consequences or mediational events.

Formal test—a test that has been statistically standardized on an appropriate population and on which the validity and reliability have been established.

Formative assessment—an assessment instrument that provides scores and/or information concerning a variety of areas, or differentiated information concerning a single area.

Individual Educational Program (IEP)—the mechanism for establishing the goals, objectives, and procedures for providing youths with an appropriate program.

Integrate program—the process through which the students' academic skills are interfaced with their vocational interests, and where both the academic and vocational personnel cooperate in designing and implementing a school program.

Intermittent reinforcement—a schedule of reinforcement in which some of the occurrences of a response are reinforced.

Inter-observer reliability—the extent to which two independent observers agree on the occurrence or nonoccurrence of a target behavior.

Interval recording—a measure of behavior strength that reports the number of intervals in which a behavior occurs.

Juvenile delinquent—the label for adjudicated youths who have demonstrated antisocial behavior.

Labeling—the study of the effects of a specific word or phrase that was intended to identify or describe a student's learning problem and/or characteristics.

Memory and information retrieval—the retention and retrieval of information that has been stored and evaluated.

Modeling—the arrangement of instructional conditions so that the individual acquires new response patterns through the observation of another person.

Moral development—the maturation and emergence of three psychological characteristics: moral judgment, moral feelings, and moral conduct.

Multiple-baseline design—recording several baselines in which teaching variables are introduced in each baseline in succession.

Natural consequents—events occurring in the student's natural learning environment that influence the probability that a target behavior will occur.

Negative reinforcement—a behavior that increases in strength by producing the removal or termination of an aversive stimulus.

Nondirective guidance—a procedure for individual or group counseling in which the teacher-counselor provides minimal instruction and advice to the youth. The expectation is that the youth assumes the guidance role and the teacher-counselor becomes a consultant.

Overcorrection restitution—restoring the environment to its original condition following disruptive behavior.

Positive practice—the repeated practice of a behavior more acceptable than the disruptive behavior.

Positive reinforcement—a behavior that increases in strength by producing pleasant consequents is positively reinforced.

Primary reinforcers—events that have reinforcement properties due to their ability to satisfy biological or physiological needs.

Program content—those subjects and vocational skills that the youth is expected to learn, such as reading, mathematics, electricity, and woodworking.

Punishment—presentation of an aversive event to decrease the strength of a behavior.

Reinforcement hierarchy—the ranking of potential reinforcers on the basis of strength.

Reinforcer sampling—a procedure by which an individual is exposed to a variety of pleasant events prior to the events becoming contingent on the target behavior.

Response cost—the removal of a specified amount of reinforcement following a behavior.

Schedule of reinforcement—the frequency with which reinforcers are delivered.

Secondary reinforcers—events that have acquired their reinforcing properties by being paired with already established reinforcers.

Self-concept—the effectiveness of self-evaluation and perception and their effects on academic performance.

Self-control—the extent to which an individual is able to monitor, evaluate, and consequate his or her own behavior independent of external consequences.

Shaping—reinforcing successive approximations of the desired response.

Social reinforcement—the use of interpersonal interactions to increase the likelihood that a behavior will occur.

Stimulus change—influencing behavior by changing the controlling stimuli.

Subsumption theory—the learning theory that states that learning occurs when the student is first provided the broad concept of that which is to be presented, then the less inclusive concepts.

Summative assessment—summative refers to the type of data yielded by the assessment instrument, such as an IQ of 100. The single score of 100 is a collective measure of the individual's information, vocabulary, sensory-motor skills, social awareness, mathematics, and conceptual development levels, as well as other potential awareness of personal performance.

Supporting services—professional personnel with the education system who, while not working with the youth on an hourly or daily basis, can provide assistance such as counseling, testing, or speech therapy.

Target behavior—the behavior that an intervention program is designed to strengthen or weaken.

Task analysis—breaking down a complex task into simpler, smaller steps.

Teacher-counselor—the instructional personnel—primarily the special education teacher—who provide guidance to the students either individually or in a group.

Terminal objective—the expected result of an intervention program.

Time sampling—recording whether the behavior occurred at specified times.

Token reinforcement—a reinforcement system in which objects of no apparent value (e.g., chips, checks, money, stars) are administered as immediate reinforcers and later exchanged for "back-up" reinforcers (e.g., food, activities, letters to parents).

Vocational center—a facility within a specified geographical area that provides vocational assessment and instruction to handicapped and nonhandicapped youths.

Vocational program—the specific instruction of functional occupation skills that will enable youths to prepare themselves to obtain and maintain a job in the community.

Work sample—an example of the student's work performance in the job or work station.

Index